FIVE HUNDRED YEARS REDISCOVERED
SOUTHERN AFRICAN PRECEDENTS AND PROSPECTS

500 YEAR INITIATIVE
2007 CONFERENCE PROCEEDINGS

FIVE HUNDRED YEARS REDISCOVERED
SOUTHERN AFRICAN PRECEDENTS AND PROSPECTS

500 YEAR INITIATIVE
2007 CONFERENCE PROCEEDINGS

Edited by Natalie Swanepoel, Amanda Esterhuysen and Philip Bonner

WITS UNIVERSITY PRESS

Wits University Press
1 Jan Smuts Avenue
Johannesburg 2001
South Africa

http://witspress.wits.ac.za

ISBN 978-1-86814-474-7

First printed 2008

This publication has kindly been funded by the National Research
Foundation (NRF).

Typesetting and reproduction by Positive Proof
Cover by Hybridesign
Cover photograph by Riaan de Villiers
Printed and bound by Creda Communications

Contents

Preface

The last 500 years represents one of the most formative periods of our past, while being, in many senses, the least known. This was a time when, in a jagged and uneven fashion, some of the key cultural contours and categories of modern identities of the sub-continent came into being. It was also a period of enormous internal economic invention and political experimentation in a context where the expanded mercantile force of Europe started to press upon southern African shores and its hinterlands. This suggests that cultural mixing, interaction and change was more a feature of southern Africa in the last 500 years than the standard view of cultural homogeneity and fixity allows.

While a number of notable archaeological studies have focused on this period of South Africa's past, they have been few and far between, and most archaeological energies have been vested in earlier phases of human activity, historically distant from the immediate identities of the present. At the same time, however, the study of African oral traditions and pre-colonial history in southern Africa has in many areas stalled over the last 25 years. We are thus confronted with the irony of an absence of attention to this critical period in the evolution of southern African societies and identities, at the very moment when the notion of an African Renaissance and its archaeological antecedents is being celebrated.

In 2006 researchers from different disciplines (archaeology, history, social anthropology) and institutions (museums and universities) in southern Africa formed a group and began to take steps to fill in this gap and produce a fine-grained understanding of the last 500 years. Initially, the group called themselves the '500 Year Research Group' (FYRG). This was based on the perception that the form and function of a research group, as defined by university and government institutions, offered the best way to formalise and develop the project. After much consultation, it became apparent that a research group would not allow the broad institutional and international membership that the group deemed necessary. Thus, in order to facilitate broader participation and membership, the name was changed to the '500 Year Initiative' (FYI).

At a workshop in 2006 the FYI formulated the following mission statement.

FYI will foster working relationships across related disciplines in order to re-interrogate and generate a more comprehensive understanding of the last 500 years.

FYI will:

- Provide a framework for cross-disciplinary engagement;
- Carry out an audit of knowledge presently residing in different disciplines in order to, amongst other things:
  1. Identify geographic or theoretical gaps that require urgent redress.
  2. Locate information, especially ethnographic and oral, for translation and dissemination.
  3. Identify archival material under threat and actively facilitate its conservation.
- promote the emergence of new articulations between disciplines, methodologies and sources;
- Foster postgraduate training to encourage a new generation of researchers.

During May 2007 the FYI held its first conference to identify and address key issues pertaining to the last 500 years. Pre-circulated papers were presented at the conference by scholars from tertiary institutions and museums from all over South Africa, Botswana and Zimbabwe; a significant number of which are included in this volume.

After the conference, participants were invited to submit their papers for publication. In line with current peer review processes, each paper was sent to two referees. The referees' comments helped to eliminate and illuminate papers, problems, ideas and issues. Although we cannot thank these individuals by name, we wish to acknowledge and thank them for their valuable insights and suggestions.

As the aim of the conference had been to break new ground and expose possibilities, the papers in this volume represent the first steps in a process which we anticipate being taken further. Already the conference and these papers have helped to kick start the initiative and raise funding to pursue focussed investigations in the following areas:

- The Mpumalanga Koni-Pedi area;
- The Northern Nguni (Ndwandwe/Swazi/Tsonga);
- The Northern Frontier;
- Tswana political centralisation in the Rustenburg and Zeerust area;
- Mission stations;
- Translation of missionary documents and collections of oral traditions.

The results of investigations into these and other research foci will be presented in future volumes of the FYI conference series.

There were many people who helped FYI take these first steps and who merit acknowledgement. We thank the WITS University's Research Office and Trans-Vaal

Archaeological society who generously supported the conference; the Origins Centre, which donated the venue; and the NRF who funded this volume.

Natalie Swanepoel, Amanda Esterhuysen and Philip Bonner

1

Introduction

P.L. Bonner, A.B. Esterhuysen, M.H. Schoeman, N.J. Swanepoel and J.B. Wright

Highlighting the period and the term 500 years may create in the minds of older scholars curious resonances and dissonances. *Five Hundred Years* was the title of a volume published by C.F.J. Muller of the University of South Africa in 1969. There it referred to the length of time claimed for white involvement in South Africa. The book had an entirely white frame of reference, and made next to no reference to an independent history of blacks (who mostly were brought under white domination 180-130 years before and whose past was relegated, in almost an afterthought, to an appendix) (Saunders 1988: 43). In 2006 a group of archaeologists and historians, young and old alike, centred mainly but not exclusively in the Gauteng region, became involved in what they called the *Five Hundred Year Initiative*. Their aim was to invert the old 500 years mindset and to make up for several decades of neglect of certain aspects of our historical and archaeological past. The most profitable route to achieving this goal they saw as interdisciplinary research which generated close collaborations between archaeologists, oral historians, social anthropologists, linguists and others. As their initial manifestos/grant proposals claimed, the last 500 years was a time of immense change, enterprise, and internal invention amongst African societies caught up in an internal African frontier which was subsequently, secondarily but nevertheless vitally impacted upon by a final 'white frontier'. This involves at least partly a clearer awareness of what we have overcome, and upon which we can build, that is to say, the shortcomings, myopias, *and* the strengths of research and writing that has taken place mainly within the constricted confines of individual disciplines over the past decades. Since the principal academic domains which this preliminary volume straddles are archaeology and history, it is with a brief review of the pertinent past of each that this introduction begins.

History

South African precolonial history and archaeology have followed curiously similar paths. Until the 1940s most research on African societies in the precolonial and early contact period was conducted by amateurs, generally government servants involved in native affairs, or missionaries. George Theal, South Africa's first historian to write extensively on precolonial African history and on African societies on the 'other' side of the frontier, worked initially as a teacher at the missionary educational institution of Lovedale and subsequently as a government official. James Stuart, who collected a huge body of oral data on the northern Nguni peoples and published several notable treatises on isiZulu, was an official of Natal's Department of Native Affairs (Webb & Wright 1998; Hamilton 1998). A.T. Bryant, another notable scholar of precolonial Zululand and Natal, was also a missionary, as were Ellenberger, Wangemann, Merensky, Nachtigal, Ayliff, Boyce and others who collected voluminous data on African societies in the interior, some of which was published, though mostly not in English. Their central problem was a 'settlerist' bias, seen most clearly in the later published works of George Theal, which frequently depicted African societies as irrational, despotic and barbaric, but the data they collected, if viewed with a critical eye, remains an invaluable and irreplaceable source to both the precolonial historian and historical archaeologist alike. Indeed, as Saunders notes, Theal gave Africans more coverage than any other historian in a general work on South Africa before the first volume of the Oxford History appeared in 1969 (Saunders 1988: 21).

From the early 20th century little interest was evinced among white amateurs or academics alike in precolonial African history. The central theme in their researches and writings was the relations between and within South Africa's white language groups, Afrikaners and English speakers. In this narrative, Africans were relegated to the background, something which the historian F.J. Potgieter described as 'part of his (white settlers) environment, like the mountains, the grasslands and fever' (cited in Bonner 1983: 70). Such a profoundly unenquiring attitude and such pervasive neglect was only punctuated occasionally by the writings of black converts and intellectuals, men like William Ngidi, Sibusiso Nyembezi, Mazizi Kunene, Samuel Mqhayi, William Gqoba, Magema Fuze, Sol Plaatje, Thomas Mofolo, John Soga and others who wrote between the 1880s and 1930s (for reviews see Saunders 1988; la Hausse 2000; Ndlovu 2001). While many of these voices have yet to be recovered – especially those that expressed themselves in the vernacular language and/or went unpublished – they remained few and far between.

The professional historian's general lack of interest in African societies and a precolonial African past was then partly broken from somewhat unexpected quarters – the University of Pretoria journal *Historiese Studies*, which was published between 1939 and 1949. It remained mostly concerned about understanding what was happening on the black side of the black/white frontier in the interior. While racially skewed in its interpretations, it nevertheless excavated important documentary sources on subjects about which many modern South African historians still remain in ignorance. Where the Pretoria archaeologist

J.F. (Hannes) Eloff stood in relation to this school might prove an interesting excursion in intellectual history. This brief awakening was however brought to an abrupt close (one assumes) by the establishment of apartheid.

The only other body of writers and scholars who took an interest in precolonial history were anthropologists, mostly working in the government service, and sometimes themselves the sons of missionaries, who collected historical data, selections of which were published in the important Department of Native Affairs (DNA) Ethnological series. These studies were distinguished and distorted by their own myopias and bias (S. Hall 2007: 165). Breutz, for example, believed stubbornly, despite the mass of rich oral evidence he collected to the contrary, that the huge 'stonewalled' settlements of the Tswana area belonged to a pre-Bantu-speaking population. Van Warmelo, the head of the ethnological section of the DNA, the unquestioned doyen of them all, whose contribution is still not adequately recognised, was intellectually and politically committed to recovering 'tribes' and frequently distorted his analysis to fit these needs. Their works necessarily had to fit into segregationist/apartheid schemas. Other professional anthropologists like the Kriges and Schapera also made unique and massive contributions to uncovering precolonial African history. Their weakness, all too often, however, was the prevailing structural functionalist paradigm that then dominated social anthropological studies, which tended to view African societies as relatively unchanging and removed politics and power from the analytical frame (substituting culture and custom in its place) (Fields 1985: 58). These scholars nonetheless assembled a massive and extraordinary archive on precolonial African history, most of it still unpublished and which remains to be adequately tapped.

Meanwhile mainstream historians remained resolutely uninterested in and disengaged from precolonial African history and developments on the African side of the frontier. On the one hand, Afrikaner nationalist historians focused on the emergence of the Afrikaner volk and its trials and tribulations at the hands of savage black tribes and of British imperialists. In this kind of history there was virtually no room for precolonial history, though in the 1960s and 1970s some Afrikaner nationalist historians sought to develop ethnically-based histories of black people to fit in with the homelands policy being implemented by the National Party government.

On the other hand, English-speaking popular historians tended to focus, as they had done for well over a century, on the advent of British settlers in the Eastern Cape in the 1820s and in Natal in the 1840s and on their subsequent transportation of 'civilisation' and 'progress' in the spheres of agriculture, mining and business across the subcontinent. Again, there was little room for precolonial history except by way of brief background to the white civilising mission; generally it was cast as having to do mainly with the migrations and wars of savage tribes.

In the Afrikaans-language universities, the great majority of historians were active propagators of Afrikaner nationalist history. In the English-language universities, most historians aligned to a greater or lesser extent with a fading colonial liberalism whose prime concern was with the history of 'race relations' in South Africa since the advent of white settlers in the mid-17th century.

An important shift in emphasis began to occur in English-language universities, mostly following on prior developments in universities in the United Kingdom and the USA, prompted in both instances by the decolonisation of Africa, in the 1960s. As decolonisation approached, a new generation of both black and white postgraduate students began to explore Africa's precolonial past and to search for a useable history of the states which were about to be established. This shift was visible first in West and then in East Africa, and was paralleled by a similar engagement among African archaeologists with Iron Age archaeology. It spilled over into South African studies in the late 1960s. Thompson's (1969) edited volume on *African Societies in Southern Africa* and the African Studies seminar at the School of Oriental and African Studies (where a generation of postgraduate students were inspired by Shula Marks) were landmark developments in this regard. Following on the heels of this process, English-language universities in South Africa began to mirror this trend and created the institutional and intellectual base for a slowly growing number of academic historians to begin researching, writing and teaching topics in the history of South Africa's black societies, including precolonial history. Here the study of the history of black societies provided more progressive white students and academics with a means of intellectually challenging some of the main tenets of apartheid and of white domination more generally.

From the first, precolonial history attracted a cohort of able and energetic researchers. The main theme which they took up was the formation of African states in the late 18th and early 19th centuries – the Zulu, Swazi, Sotho, Pedi, Gaza, Ndebele and others – and their relations with one another and with the Cape, Natal, the Orange Free State and the Transvaal. Other researchers examined the histories of chiefdoms among the Tswana and the Xhosa. A smaller number worked on the history of the Khoekhoen and the Griqua. By the end of the 1970s these researchers had brought about a complete transformation in our academic understanding of the history of southern Africa from the late 18th century to the end of the 19th. In many cases, the PhD theses and published monographs which they produced in the late 1970s and early 1980s are still the prime sources on their respective topics. These works were based on readings of, on the one hand, long-existing colonial documentary sources and, on the other, newly available published sources (such as the James Stuart Archive in the case of Zulu history), and in some cases on the analysis of oral histories recorded in the field by the authors. They were also informed by new concepts – for example, homestead, house, lineage, chiefdom – and understandings of the structures of precolonial African societies acquired from the discipline of anthropology (which was undergoing its own transformation).

From the late 1970s-early 1980s, however, a new silence settled over precolonial African history as a result of three intersecting forces. The first was the Black Consciousness movement which vehemently rejected apartheid's African homelands and which was consequently profoundly suspicious of engaging with the history of precolonial African states in case this lent a spurious legitimacy to homeland regimes. They preferred to emphasise relatively vague and generalised ideas about African achievement. Black intellectuals as a whole continued to hold to the established African nationalist stereotypes about the precolonial past as having been a Golden Age. They might accept new ideas about the importance of the Great Men of the precolonial past, but they strongly resisted arguments that precolonial African societies were not relatively egalitarian and democratic and that African states had been marked by oppression of a class of 'have-nots' by a class of 'haves'.

In addition, in the early and mid-1980s, as political struggles in South Africa become more violent, academic research into the precolonial past largely gave way to what was seen as a more pressing need for research into the political, social and economic history of African societies in the 20th century. Numbers of historians who had been leading figures in the revolution in precolonial historiography moved into more contemporary fields, taking their research students with them. The main arena in which active research into the precolonial past continued was in the history of the early Zulu kingdom and its predecessor states. In this arena, a lively and at times acrimonious debate was sparked off in 1988 by the argument put forward by Rhodes University historian Julian Cobbing to the effect that the widespread upheavals of the 1820s and 1830s had been caused not by the expansion of the Zulu kingdom but by the broadening of the frontiers of slave raiding and trading from the Cape colony in the south and Delagoa Bay in the north. By the mid-1990s many historians had accepted the need to move on from long-dominant Zulu-centric explanations, but few were prepared to accept Cobbing's formulations about the impact of slave raiding without major modification (see Hamilton 1995).

A third factor which initially invigorated but ultimately retarded research into precolonial African history was the influence of French structural Marxist interpretations of African society. These had a different kind of homogenising effect on views of precolonial African society from that produced by the Africanist propagation of the notion of the precolonial past as having been a 'Golden Age'. In their view class divisions cut across and suppressed other lines of division in African society, rendering this kind of analysis often formulaic and drained of meaning to black and white scholars alike.

Over this period, it is probably true to say that Iron Age archaeologists paid more attention to History than historians paid to Archaeology. Shula Marks stands out as a lone voice in the wilderness, carrying on the old SOAS (School of Oriental and African Studies, University of London) Africanist tradition which took archaeology seriously, and sought to comprehend what many other historians found to be arcane archaeological language and techniques. Her chapters in *The Cambridge History of Africa* were exemplary in this regard (Marks & Gray 1975; Marks 1985).

In the early 1990s South African politics was dominated by the manoeuvrings that marked the transition from apartheid to constitutional democracy. Among many historians, the expectation was that the establishment of a black majority government in 1994 would be followed by the active propagation of an African nationalist history, but in fact this did not happen. As is well known, there was instead a general turning away from 'history from on high' throughout South African society. The reasons for this have been widely discussed by historians, and will not be rehearsed here; the important point is that from the mid-1990s there was a sharp drop in the number of students studying history at almost all universities in the country, and in the standing of History as an academic discipline. Research into the precolonial past, already at a low ebb, came to a virtual standstill in History departments, though it continued in Archaeology Departments in universities and museums.

The decline of academic History did not, however, mean the end of a wider public interest in the past, nor of an official concern with it. Contrasting with the fate of History in the universities was the rapid expansion of the Heritage industry, as official bodies and private companies alike invested large sums in developing new heritage sites and establishing new heritage museums. The reasons for the sudden rise of public and private interest in 'heritage' cannot be detailed here; what is significant is that this interest extended to the precolonial past, or at least to particular features of it. In the late 1990s and early 2000s, government bodies and private companies invested considerable amounts of money and energy in setting up heritage sites like the Cradle of Humankind, Mapungubwe and Ncome, in developing rock art centres and in establishing numerous 'cultural villages' of varying quality. Precolonial history, of a kind, was back in vogue in the wider society, if not yet in academia.

A further new development which served to revitalise and perhaps distort precolonial history in non-academic circles was the proliferation of land claims across much of South

Africa. These were often buttressed by oral histories that were either well established and re-salvaged or partially invented. This represents an almost virgin field of research to which the methodologies and practices of archaeology and oral history could be extremely productively applied. Both disciplines as a result need the buttressing of the other; oral history because archaeology can corroborate, date or contradict the claims of oral tradition, archaeology because the discipline risks losing legitimacy in African eyes, if it does not speak directly to African historical issues.

Archaeology

The archaeology of the last 500 years in southern Africa is diverse in its scope, encompassing as it does the archaeology of Cape colonial settlement and contact with the indigenous people at the coast, the internal organisation and changes within farming communities in the interior, and the interaction of those communities with white farmers, traders and missionaries along the expanding colonial frontier. The following discussion will largely focus on the history and trends within the study of African Farming Communities (FC) or Iron Age communities in the interior as the history of the other forms of historical archaeology in southern Africa are examined in Behrens and Swanepoel (this volume).

Much as was the case in early historical work in South Africa, the archaeological study of African Farming Communities (FC) in South Africa grew mainly out of the interest and work of amateurs and academics with no formal training in archaeology. This interest was stimulated particularly in the early part of the 20th century by the work being carried out at Great Zimbabwe, in what was then Southern Rhodesia. The work of MacIver (1906), Dornan (1916), Schofield (1926) and Caton-Thompson (1931) progressively disproved earlier claims of biblical or Phoenician genesis of this site, and established that the ruins were built by people indigenous to the area and probably during medieval times. These ideas elicited much debate and fierce criticism from many quarters in South Africa (see for example Schonken 1933: 23, 53; M. Hall 1996). In the social universe of late 19th and early 20th-century scholarship and public life, many white people were loath to accept that black southern Africans, whom they considered inferior and primitive, had a long history or that they had founded states such as Great Zimbabwe. As a consequence by the 1930s the identity of the ancient gold workers of Rhodesia was still considered a mystery by many (Fouche 1937: 4).

These investigations and debates spilled over into the immediately adjacent parts of South Africa in the 1930s when gold objects were retrieved from graves on Mapungubwe Hill. Van Graan, a student at the University of Pretoria, reported the discovery to his history professor, Leo Fouche. Fouche immediately galvanised support from both Government and the private sector to fund research at Mapungubwe. Long-time political opponents Hertzog and Smuts worked together to ensure that the property was secured and that research was funded. In 1933 Government bought the property and the Department of Interior provided financial support for the excavations.

The initial expedition to Mapungubwe was led by Fouche, a historian, with the support of a zoologist, a geologist, a solicitor and a writer. Van Riet Lowe, who in 1933 had been seconded from the Public Works Department to serve as archaeologist on the project, was too busy to assist at the time. These excavations confirmed the findings of the excavator's 'Rhodesian' counterparts and they thus concluded that Mapungubwe was occupied by people ancestral to the modern Shona and Sotho. Schofield, an architect, and Laidler, a medical doctor, having worked at Great Zimbabwe and Mapungubwe respectively, developed the first ceramic classification systems. Schofield (1937) was heavily influenced by Caton-Thompson's research, and based his challenge to non-indigenous explanations about the founders on an analysis of the ceramics. More problematically he was also influenced by the South African Government ethnologists of the time who operated under the assumption that groups were culturally homogenous, and defined by a common language and custom (Mafeje 1971). Schofield endorsed the view that language permeated and unified every part of the social structure including pottery-making. Potsherds were thus seen to represent groups or tribes (Schofield 1937: 32; M. Hall 1984b: 460). Somewhat contradictorily, while Schofield believed that cultures were distinct he also acknowledged that multi-ethnic political units were the norm: 'Perhaps the most striking of all the Bantu features of these sites is the symbiosis of two distinct peoples in the same social unit. The Venda-Lemba, Makolo-Rozwi, are cases to point and there are many, many more. Indeed we see the perpetuation of the system in our Native Locations.'[1] Here he almost inadvertently grasped the nub of the current debates among archaeologists and historians about precolonial African identities.

Social Darwinism or evolutionist thinking also underpinned many of the new ideas and discoveries. In the absence of dating techniques, much of the thrust behind the classification of archaeological objects or features was directed at developing evolutionary sequences or sequences of cultural development. Schofield thus saw his pottery classes as successive stages in cultural development (M. Hall 1984b: 460). Lawton (1967), building on Schofield's pioneering work, collected, recorded and classified southern African ceramics according to ethnic categories. This laid the foundation of what became 'Iron Age' archaeology. The term Iron Age thus not only implied the appearance of a particular technological innovation, it was also regarded as an evolutionary stage of development bounded by race and culture (M. Hall 1984b). This is explicit in Huffman's statement that 'Iron Age archaeology is Bantu archaeology' (Huffman 1982: 145 in Hall 1984b: 463). It was largely in reaction to this that archaeologists chose to use the term Farming Communities.

The study of stonewalled settlements, corbelled huts and associated material culture also formed part of the early archaeological research. In 1927 Van Riet Lowe reported on the stone huts at Vechtkop; Hoernle (1930) described the stone huts on Tafelkop near Bethal, and Van Hoepen (1939), a professional palaeontologist, described a pre-European Culture in the Lydenburg District. Studies of corbelled huts drew on missionary and ethnographic reports, which demonstrated that they had been built by the Sotho sometime between 1650 and 1810. During the 1950s James Walton described both Sotho cattle-kraals and corbelled stone huts. In the latter he saw an evolutionary sequence. He thought they were first occupied by pastoralists, and later by pastoralists and cultivators. Amongst other things he reported on the use of pestles, mullers and querns from the Orange Free State and Basutoland (1953) and used information from interviews to inform and sequence the archaeological remains. He wrote:

> The Sotho with whom I have discussed this contend that the large central kraal represents the older plan and the idea of smaller individual kraals arose from a greater sense of security and the breakdown of the system of holding stock communally (Walton 1958: 133).

In 1948 the National Party came into power and Iron Age archaeology entered a period of stagnation (Shepherd 2003: 834). In 1962 the Government Archaeological Survey closed and the staff was transferred to Wits University. The focus at the Afrikaans-medium University of Pretoria remained Mapungubwe. After the death of Guy Gardner, who excavated the site between 1935 and 1940, anthropologist P.J. Coertze edited a second Mapungubwe volume which had yet to resolve the racial identity of the human remains from the area. Consequently, the University decided to embark on further research to lay this matter to rest. After failing to entice Roger Summers, the Great Zimbabwe archaeologist, to lead the excavations they encouraged Hannes Eloff, an anthropologist, to retrain as an archaeologist. He succeeded in establishing archaeology as a separate department, which subsequently trained many Afrikaans-speaking archaeologists, with research interests in contact and later historical periods, such as Jan Boeyens (1994 & 2003), Maria van der Ryst (1998 & 2003), and Julius Pistorius (1992).

By the late 1960s archaeology at English-speaking universities began to gather momentum once again, due largely to an economic boom which allowed government to invest more in museums and universities (Shepherd 2003: 835). During this period, universities began to import trained archaeologists, such as Ray Inskeep in 1960 and John Parkington in1966 at UCT, to set up departments and the first generation of locally trained archaeologists began to emerge. Amongst these were Tim Maggs and Revil Mason.

Whereas the English-Afrikaans divide had a marked impact on the discipline of History, it was less visible in the development of southern African archaeology. The archaeology taught at Stellenbosch and Pretoria (UP) was no different from that at English-speaking universities. At Pretoria, archaeologists were surprisingly reluctant to delve into *volkekunde* inspired archaeology. Rather they chose to focus on detailed cultural-history sequences. No doubt Hannes Eloff's discomfort with the work of his anthropological cohort at UP played a major role in this trajectory. Under Eloff's leadership, the department at UP collaborated with Mason, who was then based at the University of the Witwatersrand.

The second half of the 20th century witnessed the systematisation of research on the archaeology of precolonial farming communities in southern Africa. Progress rested on disciplinary advances. Fundamental to this was the development of scientific dating techniques, which allowed archaeologists to start the construction of chronologies, separating the Early from the Late Iron Age. During the 1970s and 1980s, South African archaeologists, influenced by their American counterparts, embraced what was known as 'processual' or 'subsistence-settlement' archaeology. This focused on demography, settlement patterns and subsistence, which at the time were regarded as the 'backbone of the cultural system' (Flannery & Marcus 1996). They produced large-scale studies of settlement patterns in relation to topography and vegetation (see for example Marker & Evers 1976: 153-65; Maggs 1976; Mason 1986). These studies were fairly comprehensive. They provided the first chronological framework for early farming societies and linked these with oral and documented African histories. Indeed, Hall (M. Hall 1990: 74) noted that during the latter part of the 1970s archaeologists and historians still met at conferences and workshops, but collaboration between the two disciplines petered out during the 1980s. This was unfortunate because this period (late 1970s-early 1980s) saw a flourishing in studies of precolonial history. There were key exceptions; for example the work of Jannie Loubser was strongly influenced by Marxist anthropology and history. In line with this, he adopted an approach to oral histories pioneered by Shula Marks and her acolytes (see for example Bonner 1983 and Delius 1983).

Ironically, part of the reason for the growing divergence between the disciplines may lie with the 'cognitive' movement, which was favoured by South African archaeologists during the 1980s. This movement sought to 'revitalise' historical explanation by studying 'cognitive' and 'symbolic' aspects of society, within a positivist framework (Preucel &

Hodder 1996: 308). Thus most cognitive archaeologists continued to use a 'scientific' hypothesis-testing approach and became committed to identifying ahistoric or law-like principles. This allowed them to argue that generalised beliefs and values, or cultural analogues, most often extracted from modern ethnographies, could be applied to the past. By singling out certain aspects of 'mind and meaning' and setting them out as 'universal principals' they avoided the problem of 'contextuality of meaning' (Preucel & Hodder 1996: 308). One dimension of context was contemporary politics. In 1983 when members of the Southern African Association of Archaeologists were called on to denounce apartheid by their African counterparts, they prevaricated because many felt that politics had no place in the pursuit of archaeological knowledge.[2] This apolitical view was challenged by Martin Hall in a series of papers (see Hall 1984a and 1984b) in which he critically examined the historic and social context of southern African Iron Age studies.[3] While historians and anthropologists interrogated the 'tribal' model, along with the role that anthropologists played in the 'invention of traditions' (Hobsbawn & Ranger 1983), Hall's critique did not result in similar introspection by Iron Age archaeologists. As he observed, similarities in the philosophical underpinning between 'cognitive archaeology' and the 'tribal model', or on the 'modelling' of archaeological groups on 'created' tribal groupings received little comment among archaeologists and these ideas continued to be applied.

The cognitive approach was especially influential in the Wits Archaeology and Anthropology departments. It saw every human action as taking place within the context of an ideology or worldview, and claimed that adherence to a particular worldview would produce behavioural regularities that transcended space and time (Huffman 1986: 85). These behavioural regularities then become 'ahistorical' or 'law-like' constants obeying the 'cultural principle' that 'people with the same culture organised themselves according to their unique sets of rules whenever and wherever they live' (Huffman 1986: 92). Like Schofield before, it was maintained that ceramic style was part of 'patterned human behaviour' (1983: 58), and was created, learned and transmitted through language.

Huffman, who took up the position of head of department at Wits in 1977, was nevertheless notable in making major contributions toward archaeological understandings of African farming communities. His work on the Central Cattle Pattern and ceramic sequences laid the basis for subsequent research at a different scale. Huffman and his students, such as Calabrese (2000 & 2005), Murimbika (2006) and Schoeman (2006), also shifted the focus from the capital to commoner and ritual sites at Great Zimbabwe and Mapungubwe.

Much of Huffman's spatial analysis was based on Kuper's (1980) seminal paper on the 'symbolic dimensions of the southern Bantu homestead' which profoundly influenced the way that anthropologists and archaeologists began to look at the use of space and the spatial layout of ancient and modern settlements and households (see for example, Huffman 1982, 2001; Evers 1988; Pistorius 1992; Hammond-Tooke 1993: 56; S. Hall 1998). This structuralist model suited the cognitive mindset in that it reduced spatial and symbolic diversity into binary opposites. A major weakness in this approach, largely skirted around by archaeologists, was the way modern ethnographies were infused by the structural/functionalist paradigm, which saw 20th-century African societies as self-equilibrating and in key respects little changed from the past. The core shortcoming of this static view, as was noted in the historical section of this introduction, is that it abstracted power/force/coercion from the social and historical equation, which analysts of the internal African frontier now see as critically important to understanding Africa's past.

In the 1990s, anthropologists and archaeologists (see for example Davison 1988; Hall 1984c) highlighted the shortcomings of the structuralist model. Kuper, who inspired the structuralist model, moved beyond generalisations and started to engage with historical specificities (see for example Kuper 1993, 1994). Many archaeologists turned to the work of contemporary theorists, for example Pierre Bourdieu and Anthony Giddens. These researchers began to regard space and time as important constituents of action and behaviour (see for example Lane 1994; M. Hall 1992). This approach assumed that artefacts and the space they occupied were part of a social dialogue in which people 'create and recreate' themselves and one another (M. Hall 1992: 376, 396). By factoring in historical context, these studies took cognisance of the fact that people manipulated their 'symbolic framework' to mediate, resist, respond to, or contest power relations (see M. Hall 1992; S. Hall 1998).

This theoretical turn inspired new approaches to Contact Period and Historical Archaeology, shifting the focus to establishing recursive relationships between archaeology, ethnographical accounts and historical sources (see for example Loubser 1991; Schoeman 1997, 1998a, b; S. Hall 1998; Boeyens 2000, 2003; Pikirayi 1993, 2004; Esterhuysen 2006). The 17th, 18th and 19th centuries provide rich ground for projects that can use the interplay between oral traditions, early European travel and missionary accounts, and the archaeological record. The FYI group hopes to build on this trend, re-orienting the study of farming communities in the interior towards a more explicitly 'historical archaeology', that interrogates source materials in a comparative, rather than additive manner, and, furthermore, one that places these communities in a landscape inhabited by diverse populations of differing socio-political character.

The Conference

To overcome some of the disciplinary lacunae and divisions which the study of historical archaeology in southern Africa has inherited, the members of FYI aspire to combine archaeological and historical scales of evidence, together with studies of indigenous knowledge and oral histories in order to understand how and under what influences modern southern African identities have taken shape over the past 500 years. Researchers within focus areas will generate insight into regional political economies, and using the latest mapping, dating and analytical methods available, refine chronologies in order to map out historical trade networks, identify centres of political control, explore how metallurgical and agro-pastoral technologies changed and developed over time and examine the interactions and relations between communities within the context of southern Africa's internal and colonial frontiers.

The conference was entitled 'Identity in Formation: the last 500 years' and, to a greater or lesser degree, all conference participants spoke to this theme. Indeed, we have a collection of papers here that highlight both the material and conceptual bases for the historical expression of corporate identities. In addition, some papers also examine our own disciplinary identities.

Themes

This volume has been divided into three sections that are, more or less, thematically defined. Section One, 'Disciplinary Identities: Methodological Considerations', contains papers that examine the how and why of our historical enterprise, and the way in which we undertake to answer the questions that we pose to ourselves. Behrens and Swanepoel outline some of the issues and surrounding the definition of an 'historical archaeology' in the African context, summarise existing work and point to possible future directions of research. The relationship with history is also discussed, as are the disciplinary/epistemological issues that need to be addressed. They highlight some of the misconceptions that historians and archaeologists have about one another's source materials and methods of study and outline some of the major questions and fields of endeavour in which historical archaeology has proved most useful.

Parsons interrogates the long-standing model of Iron Age migration that archaeologists and historical linguists have developed in their reconstruction of the pre-1500 period. His paper demonstrates the importance for scholars to engage with the 'heuristic models' of their counterparts in other disciplines and underscores the need for the continued questioning of one another's models because those from different fields look at the same dataset from different perspectives. His reinterpretation of the pre-1500 history/movements of people has implications for the questions that we can ask about our 500-year period under study.

The primary contention of the Five Hundred Years Research Group is that it through the making of connections between – and the application of – diverse methodologies we hope to shed more light on the past. One study that demonstrates the fruitful combination of source materials is that of Hall et al, who draw on both oral traditions and archaeology to explore identity, politics and economy amongst Sotho-Tswana groups in the Rustenburg area. More especially, this study addresses issues of differences in scale between different kinds of historical source materials. Chirikure et al also highlight the need for interdisciplinary investigations. Here the point is made that it is highly unlikely that metal production, on the scale necessary to meet the demands of a Later Iron Age population, was possible on the Free State grasslands, and that metal objects found there were thus most likely obtained through trade with metal producers in the surrounding areas. A suite of scientific techniques and interdisciplinary work offers the possibility for tracing the origins of the metal objects recovered from excavations in the grasslands, and Chirikure et al review the extant evidence and outline future research directions.

As can be seen in the paper by Morris, osteological studies are focused on identifying the basics of the individual's identity: their sex, their age at death, their height and weight, but an ascription of cultural identity ultimately relies on being able to identify the cultural context of their graves, through the historical and archaeological records. In the case of deTuin we learn that an historically interesting mission population occupied the site for some years, but it is only through attempting to correlate the historical evidence on the cemetery with evidence from archaeology that we can hope to link the group of burials directly to the 19th-century mission population. In this case the archaeological evidence is scarce and we must rely on the similarities between the skeletal population and historically recorded populations to support the identification.

In the final paper in Section One, Edwin Hanisch tackles the issue of the reliability of oral traditions, with reference to the origins of the Vhavenda, and illustrates how archaeology can be used to point towards alternative histories which do not always feature in predominant historical traditions, and highlights the embeddedness of oral traditions in the social and political context of the present.

The papers in Section Two, 'Material Identities', broach the issue of identity as it pertains to particular sites and classes of material culture. Those by Maggs, and Delius and Schoeman tackle the material culture and identity of the builders of Mpumalanga stonewalled sites. Maggs, in a departure from the traditional CCP-centric analyses of space, proposes that the architecture and settlement patterns speak to agricultural intensification. A new view on the regional past is also found in Delius and Schoeman, who show that interdisciplinary investigations of old data can yield new discoveries. For them the stonewalled ruins materialise the complex dynamics of the area's precolonial past. They accessed the complexities through a dialogue between historical and archaeological sources and perspectives, which linked the stonewalled sites with a dynamic Bokoni past, without reducing the inhabitants to a homogenous and static ethnic group. Rather, the settlement patterns and history of Bokoni, and the identities of its people, were shaped around intensive agro-pastoralist pursuits and control over the coastal-interior trade networks. Settlement choices facilitated intensive agriculture and trade, but resulted in settlements that were neither defensive nor easily defendable. The sites were abandoned when they could not provide refuge in the violence in the 19th century and eventually faded from memory because the area was not worth claiming, as it was impossible to live in.

The remaining papers in this section focus on the role that material culture plays in both shaping and bridging societal boundaries. Wood looks at this question from the perspective of bead consumption. Drawing on examples from a number of sites in the interior, she highlights the way in which this class of material culture can elucidate not only changing trade patterns but also differing preferences on the part of consumers over time. As is fairly well accepted amongst those who study trade in this period, consumers were ultimately the ones who determined what would sell well, and traders had to meet that demand. Esterhuysen lays out the complex social and political processes that define the 19th-century political landscape, and envisages how diacritical markers would have been manipulated and incorporated into this social discourse. She examines the context in which the different kinds of ceramics from Historic Cave, Makapan Valley, are found. Studied in combination with oral and documentary histories this presents the possibility that these ceramics reflect key marriage alliances. Drawing on this data, Esterhuysen highlights the role that these alliances may have played in the late 19th century in general, and more specifically, in the Ndebele's ongoing struggle against colonial domination.

In Section Three, "Troubled Times": Warfare, State Formation and Migration in the Interior,' we bring together papers that deal broadly with the events in the southern African interior, stemming from the upheavals of continual conflict in the 18th and 19th centuries. Wright examines the history of the Ndwandwe who, he feels, have been written out of existing history. In particular, he seeks to move beyond the 'Zulu-centric' version of South Africa's 19th-century history and to broaden our understanding of the other historical players on the landscape and to point to the implications of this for archaeological study. Bonner too, seeks to complicate our understanding of accepted interpretations of history, in his case, of the Swazi Kingdom. Bonner argues that while the Swazi state is often portrayed as being fairly distinctive when compared with neighbouring polities, it may in fact represent trends that were evident over much of the region. He also identifies how an historical archaeology of the Swazi kingdom might be usefully deployed to answer some of the questions that arise from that supposition. Kanduza's paper broadens the analysis of the Mfecane from merely looking at the events of that particular series of conflicts to looking at its far-flung effects. He contrasts the experiences of two groups, the Makololo and the Ngoni, who migrated north, and examines the differential factors that have shaped their individual histories and identities to the present day. The often neglected issue of gender features prominently here, and suggests an important area of future investigation, both here and elsewhere.

*****

The three disciplines most involved in the reconstruction of the social, cultural and political past of Africa's last 500 years are history, archaeology and historical anthropology. While scholars in each of these fields depend to a degree on the productive output of their counterparts in the others, their mutual understanding of and co-operation in one another's scholastic endeavours is by no means assured. This is in large part due to the fact that each field is characterised by its own set of sources, intellectual history, ways of doing, and ways of knowing – its own disciplinary imperative, if you will.

If we are to bridge this gap, it is necessary that we develop a greater understanding not only of one another's work but also of the intellectual context in which that knowledge is produced, including intradisciplinary debates about source material and interpretation. As Behrens and Swanepoel (this volume) explore in greater detail, archaeology in southern Africa is beset by issues revolving around how best to define 'historical archaeology' and the problems that arise from the arbitrary division of sites into stone/iron/colonial-historical based on material culture and the disciplinary identities of the archaeologists who study them. Historians too, are faced with issues of source material – the relationship between the documentary and the oral, and the various debates around orality, oral histories and oral traditions (see for example Cohen 1989).

There is thus a need for structured dialogue, 'conversations', as Beck and Somerville (2005) call them, between the practitioners of diverse disciplines. A dialogue implies not only an exchange of ideas and information but also a parity between the discussants – a mutual respect for each other's epistemologies, and an acknowledgement that our goals are not necessarily the same, indeed do not have to be the same, for us each to make a contribution. The papers contained in this book represent a first, small step in this direction.

Notes

1   MA D/1472 Schofield to C. van Riet Lowe, 25 Feb. 1952.
2   Minutes of the eighth general meeting of the Southern African Association of Archaeologists held on Tuesday 5 July, 1983 at the National Museum of Botswana, Gaborone.
3   This same awareness of the political nature of archaeology in South Africa also led Hall to embark on

a research programme aimed at interrogating South Africa's colonial past, inspired in part by Steve Biko's call that 'whites should develop critiques of white society and culture, rather than write history on behalf of blacks' (Hall in Lucas 2006: 59).

References

Beck, W. & Somerville, M. 2005. Conversations between disciplines: historical archaeology and oral history at Yarrawarra. *World Archaeology* 37(3): 468-483.

Boeyens, J.C.A. 1994. Black ivory: the indenture system and slavery in Zoutpansberg, 1848-1869. In: Eldredge, E. & Morton, F. (eds) *Slavery in South Africa: Captive Labour on the Dutch Frontier.* Boulder: Westview.

Birmingham, D. & Marks, S. 1977. Southern Africa. In: Oliver, R. (ed.) *The Cambridge History of Africa,* Volume 3. Cambridge: Cambridge University Press.

Boeyens, J.C.A. 2000. In search of Kaditshwene. *The South African Archaeological Bulletin* 55, 171: 3-17.

Boeyens, J.C.A. 2003. The Late Iron Age sequence in the Marico and early Tswana history. *The South African Archaeological Bulletin* 58: 63-78.

Bonner, P.L. 1983. *Kings, Commoners and Concessionaires.* Cambridge: Cambridge University Press.

Calabrese, J.A. 2000. Interregional interaction in southern Africa: Zhizo and Leopard's Kopje relations in northern South Africa, south-western Zimbabwe and Eastern Botswana, AD 1000 to 1200. *The African Archaeological Review* 17/4 (2000): 183-210.

Calabrese, J.A. 2005. Ethnicity, class, and polity: the emergence of social and political complexity in the Shashi-Limpopo Valley of southern Africa, AD 900 to 1300. Unpublished PhD thesis. Johannesburg: University of the Witwatersrand.

Caton-Thompson, G. 1931. *The Zimbabwe culture: Ruins and Reactions.* Oxford: Clarendon Press.

Cohen, D. 1989. The undefining of oral tradition. *Ethnohistory* 36(1): 9-18.

Davison, P. 1988. The social use of domestic space in an Mpondo homestead. *The South African Archaeological Bulletin* 43: 100-108.

Delius, P. 1983. *The Land Belongs To Us: The Pedi Polity, The Boers and the British in the Nineteenth Century Transvaal.* Johannesburg: Ravan Press.

Dornan, S.S. 1916. Rhodesian ruins and native traditions. *Journal of the South African Association for the Advancement of Science* 12(11): 502-516.

Esterhuysen, A.B. 2006. Let the ancestors speak: an archaeological excavation and re-evaluation of events prior and pertaining to the 1854 siege of Mugombane, Limpopo Province, South Africa. Unpublished PhD thesis. Johannesburg: University of the Witwatersrand.

Evers, T.M. 1988. The recognition of groups in the Iron Age of southern Africa. Unpublished PhD thesis. Johannesburg: University of the Witwatersrand.

Fields, K. 1985. Revival and Rebellions. In: *Colonial Africa.* Princeton: Princeton University Press.

Fouche, L. 1937. *Mapungubwe. Ancient Bantu Civilization on the Limpopo. Reports on Excavations at Mapungubwe (Northern Transvaal) from February 1933 to June 1935.* Cambridge: Cambridge University Press.

Hall, M. 1983. Tribes, traditions and numbers: the American model in southern African Iron Age ceramic studies. *The South African Archaeological Bulletin* 38: 51-57.

Hall, M. 1984a. Pots and politics: ceramic interpretations in Southern Africa. *World Archaeology* 15(3): 262-273.

Hall, M. 1984b. The burden of tribalism: the social context of southern African Iron Age studies. *American Antiquity* 49(3): 455-467.

Hall, M. 1984c. The myth of the Zulu homestead: archaeology and ethnography. *Africa* 54(1): 65-79.

Hall, M. 1990. 'Hidden history': Iron Age archaeology in southern Africa. In: Robertshaw, P. (ed.) *A History of African Archaeology*: 59-77. London: James Currey.

Hall. M. 1992. Small things and the mobile conflictual fusion of power, fear and desire. In: Yentsch, A.E. & Beaudry, M.C. (eds) *The Art and Mystery of Historical Archaeology Essays in Honor of James Deetz.* Boca Raton: CRC Press.

Hall, M. 1996. *Archaeology Africa*. London: James Currey.

Hall, S. 1998. A consideration of gender relations in the Late Iron Age 'Sotho' sequence of the Western Highveld, South Africa. In: Kent, S. (ed.) *Gender in African Prehistory*: 235-258. London: AltaMira Press.

Hall, S. 2007. Tswana history and the Bankenveld. In: Bonner, P., Esterhuysen, A. & Jenkins, T. (eds) *A Search for Origins*. Johannesburg: Wits University Press.

Hamilton, C.A. 1998. *Terrific Majesty*. Cambridge, MA: Harvard University Press.

Hamilton, C.A. (ed.) 1995. *The Mfecane Aftermath*. Johannesburg: Wits University Press.

Hammond-Tooke, D. 1993. *The Roots of Black South Africa*. Johannesburg: Jonathan Ball Publishers.

Hobsbawn, E. & Ranger, T. 1983. *The Invention of Tradition*. Cambridge: Cambridge University Press.

Hoernle, R.F. 1930. The stone-hut settlements on Tafelkop, near Bethal. *Bantu Studies* 4: 217-233.

Huffman, T.N. 1980. Ceramics, classification and Iron Age entities. *African Studies* 39: 123-174.

Huffman, T.N. 1982. Archaeology and ethnohistory of the African Iron Age. *Annual Review of Anthropology* 11: 133-50.

Huffman, T.N. 1983. Hypothesis evaluation: a reply to Hall. *The South African Archaeological Bulletin* 38: 57-61.

Huffman, T.N. 1986. Cognitive studies of the Iron Age in southern Africa. *World Archaeology* 18(1): 84-95.

Huffman, T.N. 2001. The Central Cattle Pattern and interpreting the past. *Southern African Humanities* 13: 19-35.

Kuper, A. 1980. Symbolic dimensions of the southern Bantu homestead. *Africa* 50 (1): 8-22.

Kuper, A. 1993. The 'house' and Zulu political structure in the nineteenth century. *The Journal of African History* 34(3): 469-487.

Kuper, A. 1994. Culture, identity and the project of a cosmopolitan anthropology. *Man* 29(3): 537-554.

La Hausse, P. 2000. *Restless Identities*. Pietermaritzburg: University of Natal Press.

Lane, P.J. 1994. The temporal structuring of settlement space among the Dogon of Mali: an ethnoarchaeological study. In: Oliver, P. (ed.) *Architecture and Order: Approaches to Social Space*: 196-216. Oxford: Blackwell.

Lawton, A.C. 1967. Bantu pottery of Southern Africa. *Annals of the South African Museum* 49(1): 1-434.

Loubser, J.H.N. 1991. The ethnoarchaeology of Venda-speakers in southern Africa. *Navorsinge van die Nasionale Museum Bloemfontein* 7(8): 145-464.

Loubser, J.H.N. 1994. Ndebele archaeology of the Pietersburg Area. *Navorsinge van die Nasionale Museum Bloemfontein* 10(2): 64-147.

Lucas, G. 2006. Archaeology at the edge: an archaeological dialogue with Martin Hall. *Archaeological Dialogues* 13(1): 55-67.

MacIver, D.R. 1906. *Mediaeval Rhodesia*. London: Macmillan.

Mafeje, A. 1971. The ideology of 'tribalism'. *Journal of Modern Africa Studies* 9 (2): 253-261.

Maggs, T. M.O'C. 1976. *Iron Age Communities of the Southern Highveld*. Pietermaritzburg: Natal Museum.

Marker, M.E. & Evers, T.M. 1976. Iron Age settlement and soil erosion in the eastern Transvaal, South Africa. *The South African Archaeological Bulletin* 31: 153-65.

Marks, S. & Gray, R. 1975. South Africa and Madagascar. In: Gray, R. (ed.). *The Cambridge History of Africa*, volume 4. Cambridge: Cambridge University Press.

Mason, R.J. 1986. Origins of black people of Johannesburg and the southern western central Transvaal AD 350-1880. Johannesburg: University of the Witwatersrand, Archaeological Research Unit.

Murimbika, M. Sacred powers and rituals of transformation : an ethnoarchaeological study of rainmaking rituals and agricultural productivity during the evolution of the Mapungubwe state, AD 1000 to AD 1300. Unpublished PhD thesis. Johannesburg: University of the Witwatersrand.

Ndlovu, S. M. 2001. The changing perceptions of King Dingane in historical literature: a case study in the construction of historical knowledge in 19th and 20th-century South Africa. Unpublished PhD thesis. Johannesburg: University of the Witwatersrand.

Pikirayi, I. 1993. *The Archaeological Identity of the Mutapa State: Towards an Historical Archaeology of Northern Zimbabwe*. Uppsala: Societas Archaeologica Upsaliensis.

Pikirayi, I. 2004. Less implicit historical archaeologies: Oral traditions and later Karanga settlements in south-central Zimbabwe. In: Reid, A.M. & Lane, P.J. (eds). *African Historical Archaeologies*: New York, Boston, Dordrecht, London, Moscow: Kluwer Academic/Plenum Publishers 243-267.

Pistorius, J.C. 1992. *Molokwane: an Iron Age Bakwena Village*. Johannesburg: Perskor Printers.

Preucel, R.W. & Hodder, I. (eds) 1996. *Contemporary Archaeology in Theory: A Reader*. Oxford: Blackwell.

Saunders, C. 1988. *The Making of the South African Past*. Cape Town: David Philip.

Schoeman, M.H. 1997. The Ndzundza archaeology of the Steelpoort. Unpublished MA dissertation. Johannesburg: University of the Witwatersrand.

Schoeman, M.H. 1998a. Excavating Ndzundza Ndebele identity at KwaMaza. *Southern African Field Archaeology* 7(1): 42-52.

Schoeman, M.H. 1998b. Material culture 'under the animal skin': excavations at Esikhunjini, an Mfecane period Ndzundza Ndebele site. *Southern African Field Archaeology* 7(2): 72-81.

Schoeman, M.H. 2006. Clouding Power? Rain-control, space, landscapes and ideology in Shashe-Limpopo state formation. Unpublished PhD thesis. Johannesburg: University of the Witwatersrand.

Schofield, J.F. 1926. Zimbabwe: a critical examination of the building methods employed. *South African Journal of Science* 23: 971-986.

Schofield, J.F. 1935. Natal coastal pottery from the Durban district: a preliminary survey. *South African Journal of Science* 32: 508-527.

Schofield, J.F. 1937. The pottery of the Mapungubwe District. In: Fouche, L. (ed.) *Mapungubwe. Ancient Bantu Civilisation on the Limpopo. Reports on Excavations at Mapungubwe (Northern Transvaal) from February 1933 to June 1935*: 32-62. Cambridge: Cambridge University Press.

Schonken, J.D. 1933. Ofir en verwante beskawings. *Die Huisgenoot* 14: 23-7, 53.

Shepherd, N. 2003. State of the discipline: science, culture and identity in South African Archaeology, 1870-2003. *Journal of Southern African Studies* 29(4): 823-844.

Thompson, L. (ed.) 1969. *African Societies in Southern Africa*. London: Heinemann.

Van der Ryst, M. 1998. *The Waterberg Plateau in the Northern Province, Republic of South Africa, in the Later Stone Age*. British Archaeological Reports, International Series 43. Oxford: Oxford University Press.

Van der Ryst, M. 2003. The so-called *Vaalpense* or *Masele* of the Waterberg: the origins and emergence of a subordinate class of mixed descent. *Anthropology Southern Africa* 26 (1&2): 42-52.

Van Hoepen, E.C.N. 1939. A pre-European Bantu culture in the Lydenburg district. *Argeologiese Navorsing van die Nasionale Museum, Bloemfontein*, D.II.

Walton, J. 1951. Corbelled stone huts in southern Africa. *Man* 51: 45-48.

Walton, J. 1958. Sotho cattle-kraals. *The South African Archaeological Bulletin* 13(52): 133-143.

Webb, C. de B. & Wright, J.B. 1976-2001. *The James Stuart Archive*, volumes 1-5. Pietermaritzburg: University of Natal Press.

.

SECTION 1

Disciplinary Identities: Methodological Considerations

2

Historical archaeologies of southern Africa: precedents and prospects

Joanna Behrens and Natalie Swanepoel

Introduction

The Five Hundred Year Initiative (FYI) has set an important and ambitious agenda: to re-interrogate the last 500 years in order to generate a more comprehensive understanding of modern South Africa(ns) (FYI mission statement 2007). The project has grown, at least in part, from a frustration with the current state of research where a general lack of interdisciplinary vision and co-operation has resulted in the circumscribed use of documentary, oral and material records with an accompanying lack of integration and historical depth. The effort to reconnect these erstwhile disparate sources into a coherent intellectual agenda envisages 'historical archaeology' as a capacitating framework. This is perhaps unsurprising. Archaeology has always been a multidisciplinary subject and such tendencies are well pronounced in the field of historical archaeology where inspiration, analytical methods and intellectual vision straddle the traditional limits of a number of disciplines, most obviously history and archaeology.

The call for a 'new agenda' in the (historical) archaeology of southern Africa's last 500 years mandates a rearticulation of traditionally discrete sub-disciplines within archaeology and the forging of new kinds of partnerships and co-operations with sister disciplines, particularly history and anthropology. Local understandings and practice are poised for change in a collective effort that will recontour the landscape of enquiry. At the outset it is perhaps important to note that such collaborative endeavours do not require the surrender of specific strengths, only a more expansive and contemplative intellectual positioning. Historical archaeological practitioners typically must navigate between and within different kinds of sources, including written and oral accounts and pictorial representations, but we remain ultimately grounded in the materiality of primary source materials that encompass cultural landscapes, the built environment, spatial organisation, artefacts, ecofacts, and the ways in which these change over space and through time (Hicks 2003: 315). Archaeology does not, therefore, play a supplementary role in the larger project of 'history'. Indeed, as Sarah Tarlow (2007) has pointed out, the study of the material world has as much to offer to understandings of the past as a study of texts – a fact admirably demonstrated by generations of architectural and art historians (who, after all, are seldom moved to justify their enquiries). At such a moment then, it seems appropriate to take stock, to look critically at historical archaeology's intellectual derivation, to assess the local status quo, to dwell upon the general importance of the move and to anticipate some of the epistemological and logistical issues inherent in new beginnings.

Precedents

As a field of enquiry historical archaeology is characterised by long-standing definitional debates, by disputes over disciplinary affiliations and by diverse rationales (see contributions in Schuyler 1978; Deetz 1983, 1988, 1989). In multifarious global guises it is aligned more strongly with history in some quarters or with anthropology in others. Commonly it is conflated with 'historical times', a period that begins with the emergence of literacy some 5 000 years ago (Orser 2004). The result in this instance is a definition that rests on methodological criteria, specifically the combined use of written and material sources in order to elucidate aspects of the human past. This sort of 'text-aided' archaeology (see Little 1992) inevitably encompasses thousands of years in some areas, such as Mesopotamia or the Nile Valley, yet barely a few hundred years in other parts of the world that remained technically 'preliterate' until relatively recently. Such a chronological sweep includes, too, a tremendous diversity in culture-history, from Near Eastern and New World civilisations to Egyptology, Classical, Medieval, Post-Medieval, Colonial and Industrial period archaeologies (Funari et al 1999).

The practical and epistemological problems inherent in such a broad definition are obvious – indeed, there is so little overlap, beyond a basic procedural criterion among the different areas, as to make historical archaeology synonymous with a wide range of other, more clearly defined, (or less contested) sub-fields and specialisations. For this reason a number of researchers propose that historical archaeology, while enjoying commonalities with various other types of archaeology, has greater analytical and comparative utility when bounded temporally. For scholars like Kathleen Deagan (1982, 1988) and Charles Orser (1996, 1999, 2000, 2004) it is the 'modern' or post-1500 world, the period that witnessed the emergence of a complex, global system, that constitutes historical archaeology's 'obvious niche' (Deagan 1988: 8). Thus, in some quarters, the sub-discipline is pegged conventionally at 1415, when the Portuguese seized Ceuta on the North African coast, ushering in the imperial and colonial epochs that so profoundly shaped the modern world. By this measure historical archaeology is a global, comparative exercise engaged with key themes: colonialism, capitalism, modernity. Of course there are also problems with this perspective, particularly in the context of African practice where it perpetuates an unsettling Eurocentrism and a problematic sense of historical division. If colonial contact, however broadly defined, delimits historical archaeology then much of Africa's past is left outside of history (prehistory) or rendered non-historical (see Schmidt 2006). Responses to such an untenable position have, perhaps inevitably, fallen back on methodological pronouncements. Thus Lane and Reid (1998: 162) point out that European documents constitute only one of multiple historical sources, which include oral traditions, myths, praise songs, pictograms, paintings and engravings as well as Coptic, Chinese, Islamic and Hieroglyphic texts. Similarly DeCorse (1996) argues that the term historical archaeology should indicate only that non-archaeological sources are used to supplement archaeological interpretations.[1]

Such arguments effectively expand the temporal scale of historical archaeology but, arguably, leave a sense of division intact – 'historical archaeology', however 'stretched', remains set apart in some sense from 'prehistory'. For some scholars such a separation is regarded as intellectually divisive and epistemologically dangerous. Peter Schmidt (1990, 1995, 2006) in particular argues that the prehistoric-historic divide lacks relevance (Schmidt 2006: 7) and that 'history-making' is a process that transcends temporal boundaries. In practice, this means that scholars should 'take account of any moment in which historical representation unfolds' (Schmidt 2006: 7). For Schmidt this has translated into an outspoken and active research agenda which has sought commensurate places for oral traditions and archaeology in understandings of 'Iron Age' culture that stretch from inception to contemporary times. In a similar vein Ann Stahl (1999, 2001), working in Banda, Ghana, has treated the Holocene as a continuum, a 'seamless whole', where the intrusions of globalisation are explored and understood at a local level and as part of much longer historical trajectories. For the purposes of this research group it must be emphasised that, by delimiting for study the societies and events of the last 500 years of southern African history, we do not seek to privilege that period of time most commonly associated with the rise and expansion of European colonialism, but rather to acknowledge that it is the period of time most relevant to an understanding of contemporary society. While the processes of colonialism are an important part of this picture they are not necessarily determinate. We also note that setting a cut-off date at 500 years does not mean that we should not, when necessary, follow the threads of the past further back in time.

Against these wider debates historical archaeology in southern Africa occupies an increasingly ambivalent position. As a discrete and readily identifiable field of study it has flourished relatively recently and in geographically and chronologically limited ways. Nonetheless it is fair to say that historical archaeology has, since the mid-1980s, established itself as a viable sub-discipline with a productive research history throughout much of southern Africa (Lane & Reid 1998; Pikirayi 1999; Pikirayi & Pwiti 1999; Kinahan 2000; Hall 2000). Ironically, this process of self-definition has been accomplished with (or perhaps by) the entrenchment of boundaries that have, in some very real sense, cut off historical archaeology from both parent disciplines. Cooperative endeavours between archaeologists and historians have been rare in southern African contexts (but see Malan & van Heyningen 2001; Delius & Schoeman, this volume) while historical archaeology has, in some ways, remained divorced from a broader southern African archaeological agenda (arguably in favour of more internationally aligned pursuits).[2] Doubtless, this has contributed significantly to the lamentable notion that historical archaeology is about Europeans and colonialism – what is often informally designated as 'Cape Town style' archaeology. This perception is reinforced by the fact that many projects, which, to our mind, are clearly historical, are the efforts of self-inscribed 'Iron Age' or 'Stone Age' archaeologists, or indeed archaeologists who might claim a liminal position, neither historical nor other.

A survey of the *South African Archaeological Bulletin* over the past 20 years highlights this pattern – of 26 published articles that pertain to the last 500 years, 11 (42%) relate to 'Iron Age' or 'Stone Age' sites (Loubser 1985; Sampson et al 1989; van der Merwe et al 1989; Plug & Roodt 1990; Watson & Watson 1990; Behrens 1992; Saitowitz & Sampson 1992; Westbury & Sampson 1993; Maggs 1993; Plug & Sampson 1996; Boeyens 2000).[3] In the pages of *Southern African Field Archaeology* the percentage is lower at 19% but still significant (de Wet-Bronner 1994; Whitelaw 1994; Pistorius & Steyn 1995; Sampson 1995; Voigt et al 1995; Schoeman 1998a, b). It has also become clear in recent years that the rock art of this period is also an important archive, speaking to colonial and other contact relations (see for example Yates et al 1993; Dowson 1995; van Schalkwyk & Smith 2004; Hall & Mazel 2005). Of course, many of the above scholars would not call themselves 'historical' archaeologists – given this, we believe it is important to highlight that even those who do designate themselves as such have not, in practice, defined their field of study as narrowly colonial. This is a perception that operates detrimentally to close off rather than open up debate. Martin Hall (1987) in fact argued, some 20 years ago, that all periods post-dating a 'testimonial threshold', whether documentary, oral or ethnographic in nature, were *ipso facto* part of historical archaeology, an understanding that actively encourages the integration of different lines of enquiry. Understandings of the field as settler-based are the result of circumstantial practice rather than design or intention. Thus we would argue that historical archaeology in southern Africa lends itself to the avowed aims of FYI and is, moreover, consonant with the African-centred agendas advocated by scholars such as Peter Schmidt (1995, 2006).

This publication, and the conference from which it has flowed, are a heartening sign that the borderlands of archaeology and history can be traversed. It is similarly important that a *rapprochement* between historical archaeology and Iron Age and Stone Age archaeologies be navigated. The privileging of chronology (the last 500 years) over discipline (archaeology/history) and sub-discipline (Stone Age/Iron Age/historical archaeology) offers a useful starting place for the delineation of fresh, shared approaches to a common past.

Prospects

In contemplating the shape and outcomes of FYI, it is important to recognise that the disciplines of history and archaeology, as well as discrete intradisciplinary groupings, carry attendant expectations, interests and modes of knowledge production with particular track records of accomplishment for the period of the last 500 years. Thus, in refashioning the archaeology of this time as a joint historical-archaeological enterprise we have set ourselves a series of challenges (not a series of insurmountable obstacles!) that will need to be met in interesting and innovative ways if we are to succeed in our endeavour.

These challenges are both methodological and conceptual in nature. We isolate four here, two somewhat more practical (scale, and how best to make use of different kinds of sources) and two slightly more conceptual (the questions asked, and how to overcome the barriers of existing categorisations). All, however, are a mixture of both aspects.

Pre-existing categories of sites

From an archaeological perspective, the largest obstacle that we have placed in our own path is, undoubtedly, the way that we tend to define various sites by their material inventory. As Reid and Lane (2004) have pointed out, many later agro-pastoralist sites are studied as examples of the Late Iron Age while many Later Stone Age sites were contemporaneous with Dutch settlement at the Cape. While we do not deny that specialist skills are necessary to analyse the material from these sites, the existing boundaries hinder a comparative study of groups who shared the landscape, both spatially and temporally.

A common problem in this regard has been the tendency to seek an entry point through imported material markers (see Hall 1993). We should instead think more innovatively about material culture from rock shelters and stonewalled settlements that date to the last 500 years but which contain no European imports. If the analyses of such assemblages are networked into the wider historical and conceptual agenda proposed here, it is possible that interactions across, or cohabitation of, the same landscape by diverse communities will be thrown into new relief. By placing different kinds of sites – Iron Age, Stone Age, Colonial – within the same framework of inquiry we force ourselves to conceive of different groups of people inhabiting the same landscape at the same time. This is not to say that they were interacting frequently and/or directly but it is nonsensical to think that they did not affect one another in some way.

It is important then that we also start to develop the conceptual apparatus for envisioning how sites and materials can be broached. A number of such frameworks are already in use in archaeology. These include the concept of the 'social field' (Welsch & Terrell 1998: 51), the network (Orser 2005) or regional analyses that facilitate the study of heterogenous inhabitants of the same landscape or regional unit (Kowalewski 1997). All of these framing principles encompass the idea of interaction, cohabitation and heterogeneity. Welsch and Terrell (1998: 52) argue that when social fields are bounded they might be regarded as having the status of a 'social formation' (villages, cultures, tribes, ethnolinguistic groups) but when they are conceived of as open-ended, they might be regarded as social networks: 'web[s] of social, economic and political relations.' Many different kinds of people might operate in these networks, and should be seen as occupying the same social field. Social fields in the Pacific context, as described by Terrell (1998), are occupied by communities that are linguistically diverse yet maintain cultural similarities through the exchange of both trade goods and culture, including ritual knowledge. Taking a wider, global view, scholars such as Orser (2005: 78) advocate the use of the network as an analytical tool for examining interactions and connections at a global scale, arguing that in the 'modern era' even communities that purposefully chose to isolate themselves, such as the maroon slave community of Palmares, Brazil, were integrated into larger regional and global systems of trade and economic and cultural exchange (Orser 1996: 41-53).

Questions

The issue of what questions are asked is complicated by the aforementioned divisions within archaeology and between history and archaeology. Certainly scholars of Iron Age and Stone Age periods are sometimes inclined to carry with them older research traditions that constrain the kinds of questions that are asked and the issues that are brought under the microscope (for important exceptions see Parkington 1984; Smith 1992). The survey of 'non-European' historical archaeology, for example, reveals that certain types of issues and sites (as well as sections within sites) have commanded sustained attention, specifically, Tswana towns, military capitals, sites associated with the Mfecane, and European material culture items (particularly beads and buttons), which are usually subsumed within macro-scale trade analyses. The more traditional agendas of historical archaeology (such as vernacular building traditions, class and gender differentiations, food patterns, quotidian objects and day-to-day lives) (Hall 1993) have thus, in general, received short-shrift (we note that important exceptions to this pattern are represented by the work of Simon Hall (1997) and Garth Sampson (1995; and Sampson et al 1989, 1994) – although neither scholar would perhaps choose the label 'historical archaeologist'). The moment is, therefore, ripe for archaeologists of varied ilk to come together, to pose and answer new types of questions, the general nature of which have long been outlined by 'traditional' historical archaeology.

Historians too, are often concerned with questions that are not easily answered by archaeology and while this is not inherently problematic, it is not always conducive to the development of relevant archaeological projects. One example in this regard is the study of the Mfecane. Historians have spilt a great deal of ink emphasising questions of causality and the events of this period, focusing on what happened when and to whom (see, for example Cobbing 1988; Omer-Cooper 1993; Peires 1993; and the papers contained in Hamilton 1995), but at the same time, there is very little social history about the impact of these various conflicts – whether regarded as part of the same interlinked phenomenon or not – that specifically addressses the changes that must have occurred in the everyday lives of ordinary people (for an exception see Kinsman 1995). Meanwhile the archaeology that has been done on Mfecane-era sites, while hinting at interesting possibilities (Huffman 1986; Dowson 1995; Hall 1995; Perry 1999; Boeyens 2003; Lane 2004), is so piecemeal that it is difficult to draw any substantive conclusions or any linkages between what was happening across various parts of the historical landscape. Essentially it is difficult to link the historical literature with that of the archaeology. The confluence of interest though, is important and again suggests that the time to develop common agendas is upon us.[4]

Combining sources

A major methodological issue in historical archaeology is the concomitant use of material, documentary and oral archives (Little 1992; Feinman 1997; Kepecs 1997). In some measure this is the defining characteristic of the sub-discipline, and a high level of archival and research skills are required to effectively frame and anchor the questions that we ask of these diverse sources. This does not imply that there is a single, correct way of dealing with a non-material complement, and, in practice, historical archaeologists use the multifarious sources at their disposal in a number of ways. Ann Stahl (2001) has emphasised the importance of the direct historical approach and the need for 'source-side' criticism while others (Hall 1999) have focused on the search for *consonance* and *dissonance* between the different sources. Alison Wylie (1999: 26) has argued for the need to tack between the 'concrete particularities' of case studies and 'the encompassing processes and structural conditions' of larger systems. Barbara Little (1992: 4) delineated five basic strategies, which view the data sources as complementary, contradictory, or contextual (mutually informative), as sources for the generation of hypotheses or as yardsticks for the comparative benchmarking of information. Although some archaeologists have chosen to stress the similarities between objects and texts (see discussion in Courtney 2007) it is also important to recognise and negotiate the differences between sources, to recognise what Wylie (1999: 29) terms the evidential 'independence of archaeological ... and historical lines of evidence', while avoiding any undue privileging. Certainly all sources are not equal all of the time, but relative credibility must be determined contextually rather than generically. Different scholars may be inclined to different starting points – Gary Feinman (1997), for example, argues that archaeologists tend to overvalue documents, while Paul Courtney (2007) laments the unfortunate idea, widespread among field archaeologists, that documents are intrinsically biased whilst the material record is not! Of course, all sources contain biases and are open to interpretation and reinterpretation. Doubtless historical archaeologists have much to learn from colleagues in history departments and vice versa, a process that will work to counter predilections for under-theorised and methodologically fraught engagements with multiple sources of information (see Johnson 1999). We suggest that the FYI forum presents an ideal opportunity for this mutual apprisement to flourish. If, as Courtney (2007: 40) suggests, historians are generally unwilling to read technical reports filled with archaeological jargon and lacking in synthesis, or that archaeologists find the narrative preferences of historians to be methodologically unsettling, then the moment to learn and teach has arrived. Fortunately, we all seek the same basic outcome, an understanding of the past, even if the strictures of disciplinary vision and training have resulted in rather different approaches (Courtney 2007). By defining common agendas and working towards the same ultimate goals we can aspire to avoid the pitfalls of both disciplines to a common advantage.

Scale

Among historical archaeologists issues of scale carry particular import, not least for the role they play in definitional debates. While we might disagree with Vansina's (1999: 370) suggestion that archaeological and historical reconstructions are 'mutually incompatible' because of the different sources used (as he puts it, the '*mute*' artefacts of archaeology as opposed to the 'written or oral *messages*' of history (our emphasis)) he does, quite correctly, point out that archaeology is better at documenting situations, or processes, while the sources that historians use generally aid the reconstruction of events (Vansina 1999: 370).

We think that most archaeologists would agree that it is difficult to identify 'events' in the archaeological record unless they are fairly traumatic and led to the abandonment of the site. In general then the record consists of the gradual accumulation of material related to the numerous events of day-to-day life. The great strength of archaeology is that these palimpsests of individual and collective actions build, and build upon, a wider social context and a long-term history (Little & Shackel 1989; Lucas 2006). While prehistorians are most adept at dealing with the latter half of this sliding scale, historical archaeologists enjoy a unique ability to explore both micro (local) and macro (non-local/global) scales of evidence (Gilchrist 2005). There is an obvious resonance here with the Annales' multi-scalar approach to history, a point explored in some detail by Little and Shackel (1989) and, more recently, commented upon by Lucas (2006). Inevitably, as Lucas (2006: 38-39) points out, the problems of top-down analyses persist and the tendency among historical archaeologists becomes to position everyday material culture in relation to bigger structuring processes (capitalism, colonialism, consumerism).

At issue then are conceptions of historical process and the entanglements of material culture (Lucas 2006: 38). In practice archaeologists can become mired in the specifics of sites and assemblages (perhaps resulting in the lack of synthesis historians are wont to perceive). The goal, of course, is to place any particular site within its larger geographic context and in relation to other sites, although, arguably, it is historians who find it easier to move about the landscape in their discussions as the movements of groups and/or individuals in documents and oral traditions direct. In some cases, historical archaeologists interested in the global nature of life in recent centuries accomplish the same thing by following people or processes across continents. As Hicks (2005: 317) points out, this occasionally results in comparisons between places linked by the movements of the fieldworker rather than the subjects under study.

The way forward

Accomplishing this shift in the historical archaeology of southern Africa, begins with the questions we ask of the archaeological record and, ultimately, of the past. At the same time it would be a mistake to think that there is a 'one size fits all' solution to how we navigate our way through the oft-times murky waters of inter- and intradisciplinary co-operation. There are certain methodological and theoretical issues arising in the study of specific historical contexts that can only be worked out in practice and through a collaborative process between research partners. There must thus be a joint recognition that there can be no 'business as usual' approaches from either side. Further, such interactions should be marked by an appreciation of the unique vantage points that practitioners bring to the table. First, archaeology should acknowledge its emphasis on material culture and thus a concern with the material conditions of everyday life. Second, archaeology encompasses the entire span of history, and can offer a longer-term perspective on the events and processes of the last 500 years. Third, archaeologists actually walk the landscape inhabited by the people about whom we write and are often more attuned to the proxemics of historical sites and situations.

Historians are better able to characterise for themselves what they bring to the table, but from an archaeological perspective we can at least note that they pay far more attention to source-side analysis and generally far outstrip archaeologists in making the past accessible to a general readership. It should also be noted that historians are generally, we think, becoming more open to engaging with archaeologists and archaeological theory. A few examples that leap to mind (not counting the contributors to this volume) include: Laura Mitchell (2002), who combines archaeological data on 'Stone Age' sites with documentary evidence of colonial incursions into the Cedarberg to facilitate a discussion on competition for resources; Alan Kirkaldy (2003), who examines how Venda landscapes were experienced and represented by German missionaries by drawing upon landscape work undertaken by archaeologists such as Barbara Bender; Dan Wylie (2006), who uses archaeological data and an evocative discussion of material culture to set the scene in *Myth of Iron*; and Fred Morton (2003), who has explored the links between the degree of political development and the organisation and size of settlements, with direct reference to archaeological models.

What is needed now, is a joint effort to develop specific questions that might be answered collaboratively by scholars from a variety of disciplines. In considering how this might be accomplished, Beck and Somerville (2005) draw on the concept of 'conversation' as a way of characterising the ideal relationship between disciplines when working on questions held in common. More importantly, drawing on Cruikshank (2001: 377), they point out the problematic tendency of scholars to read work from other disciplines as a way of obtaining 'data or evidence' rather than as offering equally valid, albeit different, approaches or insights to the questions at hand.

Obviously there is a wide array of possible questions in southern Africa that historical archaeology is well suited to answer. There are a number of specific foci, however, which, internationally, have captured the interest of historical archaeologists:

1. The role of material culture in shaping and signalling identity.
2. An exploration of class, gender, ethnic, racial and status differences and how these shaped societies.
3. The form and nature of culture contact between frontier populations.

4. The provision of alternative views of those who are poorly represented or absent in other sources.

5. The impact and long-term effects of capitalism, industrialisation, conflict and land dispossession.

6. Changing internal relationships within communities in response to external forces, modes of resistance and incorporation.

7. Environmental reconstructions and the study of the impact of the introduction of new cultigens and domestic animals into local environments.

8. The undermining and questioning of grand historical narratives.

These questions are, of course, very general and should in no way be regarded as setting limitations on what can be asked or answered using a combination of historical and archaeological techniques. Most importantly, the point must be reiterated that, in no way is colonialism intended as the framing mechanism. Issues of inequality, rank and gender pertain to the societies of the southern African interior outside the framework of the process of colonialism as well as within it. Further, we note that in a global comparison, Africanist historical archaeologists are often far ahead of their American and Pacific counterparts when it comes to using a diversity of sources and in looking at the role and status of indigenous societies (see Mason 2000; Lightfoot 2006; Lydon 2006).

Looking ahead to what else our group might achieve, we feel that it is also important to think about what a conceptual shift might mean for the public profile of history and archaeology. Why should communities, at either the local or national level, actually care about what we do? What are the relevant questions or issues in producing these new versions of our past? What is our history beyond apartheid? We think that one of the greatest contributions we can make is to question how we represent and reconstruct the past and to interrogate, most particularly, how different kinds of people in the past interacted. The past was often far more messy and convoluted and much less inevitable than popular conceptions of history portray.

Hicks (2004: 937; 2005: 314-315) has argued for the need to question the increasingly homogenising view of what historical archaeology should be. He argues that an over-emphasis on so-called global processes, such as capitalism, modernity or globalisation, in fact masks the 'diversity and polyvocality' of the period under study, and argues for an increasing focus on the complexitites of the era. Since this group has taken a timeframe, rather than a specific issue, as its focus, we are well placed to meet this challenge. The studies presented in these proceedings, while partially addressing 'larger' issues such as colonialism and globalisation, also encompass: issues of state formation and socio-political organisation (Bonner, Hall et al, Wright); the nature and degree of trade relations (Chirikure); agricultural innovation (Maggs); and the formation and expression of local identities (Delius & Schoeman; Esterhuysen, Hanisch, Kanduza, Morris, Wood) – all with reference to the implications of such new understandings for our comprehension of the long-term history of southern Africa (Parsons). As we begin to engage in broader disciplinary conversations, interactions and partnerships, these will no doubt expand exponentially. The conversation has begun, let us see where it takes us.

Acknowledgements

We thank conference participants at the first FYI conference held at the University of the Witwatersrand in May 2007 and Yvonne Brink for discussion and comments, which have done much to improve our paper. All errors remain our own.

Notes

1   These debates are hardly exclusive to the African context and echo those around the definition of historical archaeology, or aspects thereof, in other parts of the world. There is, for example, still 'no consensus' over what the archaeology of 18th and 19th century Britain should be called and thus what time-frame is encompassed by the term 'post-medieval archaeology' (Tarlow 2007: 2), while in North America much of what Africanist archaeologists might regard as the historical archaeology of Native Americans is still under the purview of self-designated prehistorians (Lightfoot 1995: 203; Gilchrist 2005: 330).

2   An important exception to this pattern is represented by the long-standing and on-going co-operation between the Historical Archaeology Research Group based at the University of Cape Town and historians of the Dutch era in that university's Department of History (see Worden 2007). In many ways this latter relationship is facilitated by the materiality of the Cape colonial archive, where the VOC records in particular were oriented towards the recording of events (Brink 2004), and the itemisation of personal possessions and financial resources, in the form of documents such as official diaries, probate inventories, land grant records, legal disputes and sumptuary laws (see Malan 1990; Hall 2000). This archive has lent itself to comparative analyses with the archaeological record (see, for example, Hall et al 1990b; Hall 2000), both to demonstrate what the most well-documented in Cape society chose not to record, and to illuminate the lives of those under-represented or absent from the documents such as slaves, the working class and women (Hall et al 1990a; Markell 1993; Sealy et al 1993). Further, archaeological/material culture studies of Cape colonial society have addressed the issue of how the power, and other social relations of that society were expressed materially (see Brink 1990; Hall 2000). As Hall and Markell (1993: 4) noted, however, when historical archaeologists turn their attention to contexts outside of this colony, there is a somewhat unequal distribution of information when we come to study the interactions of colonial agents with indigenous people at the coast or in the interior, where records are sketchy, observations tainted by intercultural misunderstandings and power differentials (see, for example, Smith 1993; Brink 2004) and oral traditions disrupted. Nonetheless, the work at the Cape offers a good example of the kinds of collaborative endeavours that need to be nurtured in the interior where the nature of the historical archive (oral and documentary) requires unique approaches in order to facilitate its use by archaeologists (see, for example, Hall et al, this volume).

3   Also see Kinahan (2000: 9-10), for an additional analysis of papers and content in the *South African Archaeological Bulletin* and *Goodwin series* relating to the historical period.

4   For example, Ackson Kanduza's contribution to this volume, which deals with migrations caused by the Mfecane, and the subsequent creation of new social (and material) identities, offers up interesting historical questions that might be approached through the archaeological record.

References

Beck, W. & Somerville, M. 2005. Conversations between disciplines: historical archaeology and oral history at Yarrawarra. *World Archaeology* 37(3): 468-483.

Behrens, J. 1992. European artefacts from Rose Cottage Cave. *South African Archaeological Bulletin* 49: 13-15.

Boeyens, J.C.A. 2000. In search of Kaditshwene. *South African Archaeological Bulletin* 55: 3-17.

Boeyens, J.C.A. 2003. The Late Iron Age sequence in the Marico and early Tswana history. *The South African Archaeological Bulletin* 58: 63-78.

Brink, Y. 1990. The *voorhuis* as a central element in early Cape houses. *Social Dynamics* 16: 38-54.

Brink, Y. 2004. The transformation of indigenous societies in the south-western Cape during the rule of the Dutch East India Company, 1652-1795. In: Murray, T. (ed.) *The Archaeology of Contact in Settler Societies*: 91-108. Cambridge: Cambridge University Press.

Cobbing, J. 1988. The Mfecane as alibi: thoughts on Dithakong and Mbolompo. *Journal of African History* 29: 487-519.

Courtney, P. 2007. Historians and archaeologists: an English perspective. *Historical Archaeology* 41(2): 34-45.

Cruikshank, J. 2001. Glaciers and climate change: perspectives from oral tradition. *Arctic* 54(4): 377-393.

Deagan, K. 1982. Avenues of inquiry in historical archaeology. *Advances in Archaeological Method and Theory*, volume 5: 151-177. Orlando: Academic Press.

Deagan, K. 1988. Neither history nor prehistory: the questions that count in historical archaeology. *Historical Archaeology* 22(1): 7-12.

DeCorse, C.R. 1996. Documents, oral history, and the material record: historical archaeology in West Africa. *World Archaeological Bulletin* 7: 40-50.

Deetz, J.F. 1983. Scientific humanism and humanistic science: a plea for paradigmatic pluralism in historical archaeology. *Geoscience and Man* 23: 27-34.

Deetz, J.F. 1988. History and archaeological theory: Walter Taylor revisited. *American Antiquity* 53(1): 13-22.

Deetz, J.F. 1989. Archaeography, archaeology, or archeology? *American Journal of Archaeology* 93: 429-435.

de Wet-Bronner, E. 1994. The faunal remains from four Late Iron Age sites in the Soutpansberg region. *Southern African Field Archaeology* 3(1): 33-42.

Dowson, T. 1995. Hunter-gatherers, traders and slavers: the 'Mfecane' impact on Bushmen, their ritual and their art. In: Hamilton, C. (ed.) *The Mfecane Aftermath: Reconstructive Debates in Southern African History*: 51-70. Johannesburg: Witwatersrand University Press.

Feinman, G. M. 1997. Thoughts on new approaches to combining the archaeological and historical records. *Journal of Archaeological Method and Theory* 4(3/4): 367-377.

Funari, P.P.A., Jones, S. & Hall, M. 1999. Introduction: archaeology in history. In: Funari, P.P.A., Jones, S. & Hall, M. (eds) *Historical Archaeology: Back from the Edge*: 1-20. London & New York: Routledge.

Gilchrist, R. 2005. Introduction: scales and voices in world historical archaeology. *World Archaeology* 37(3): 329-336.

Hall, M. 1987. Historical archaeology and colonial expansion. Western Cape Institute for Historical Research Symposium, 13 October 1987. Unpublished paper.

Hall, M. 1993. The archaeology of colonial settlement in southern Africa. *Annual Review of Anthropology* 22: 177-200.

Hall, M. 1999. Subaltern voices? Finding the spaces between things and words. In: Funari, P.P.A., Jones, S. & Hall, M. (eds) *Historical Archaeology: Back from the Edge*: 192-203. London & New York: Routledge.

Hall, M. 2000. *Archaeology and the Modern World: Colonial Transcripts in South Africa and the Chesapeake*. London & New York: Routledge.

Hall, M., Halkett, D., Huigen van Beek, P. & Klose, J. 1990a. 'A stonewall out of the earth that thundering cannon cannot destroy'? Bastion and moat at the Castle, Cape Town. *Social Dynamics* 16(1): 22-37.

Hall, M., Halkett, D., Klose, J. & Ritchie, G. 1990b. The Barrack Street well: images of a Cape Town household in the nineteenth century. *South African Archaeological Bulletin* 47: 73-92.

Hall, M. & Markell, A. 1993. Introduction: historical archaeology in the western Cape. *South African Archaeological Society Goodwin Series* 7: 3-7.

Hall, S. 1995. Archaeological indicators for stress in the western Transvaal region between the seventeenth and nineteenth centuries. In: Hamilton, C. (ed.) *The Mfecane Aftermath: Reconstructive Debates in Southern African History*: 307-321. Johannesburg: Witwatersrand University Press.

Hall, S. 1997. Material culture and gender correlations: the view from Mabotse in the late nineteenth century. In: Wadley, L. (ed.) *Our Gendered Past: Archaeological Studies of Gender in Southern Africa*: 209-219. Johannesburg: Witwatersrand University Press.

Hall, S. & Mazel, A. 2005. The private performance of events: colonial period rock art from the Swartruggens. *Kronos* 31: 124-151.

Hamilton, C. (ed.) 1995. *The Mfecane Aftermath: Reconstructive Debates in Southern African History*. Johannesburg: Witwatersrand University Press.

Hicks, D. 2003. Archaeology unfolding: diversity and the loss of isolation. *Oxford Journal of Archaeology* 22(3): 315-329.

Hicks, D. 2004. From 'questions that count' to stories that 'matter' in historical archaeology. *Antiquity* 78: 934-9.

Hicks, D. 2005. 'Places for thinking' from Annapolis to Bristol: situations and symmetries in 'World Historical Archaeologies.' *World Archaeology* 37(3): 227-336.

Huffman, T. 1986. Archaeological evidence and conventional explanations of southern Bantu settlements. *Africa* 56(3): 280-298.

Johnson, M. 1999. *Archaeological Theory*. Oxford: Blackwell Publishing.

Kepecs, S. 1997. Introduction to new approaches to combining the archaeological and historical records. *Journal of Archaeological Method and Theory* 4(3/4): 193-198.

Kinahan, J. 2000. Cattle for beads. The archaeology of historical contact and trade on the Namib Coast. *Studies in African Archaeology 17*. University of Uppsala, Sweden.

Kinsman, M. 1995. 'Hungry wolves': the impact of violence on Rolong life, 1823-1836. In: Hamilton, C. (ed.) *The Mfecane Aftermath: Reconstructive Debates in Southern African History*: 363-293. Johannesburg: Witwatersrand Press.

Kirkaldy, A. 2003. The darkness within the light: Berlin missionaries and the landscape of Vendaland c. 1870-1900. *Historia* 48(1): 169-202.

Kowalewski, S. 1997. A spatial method for integrating data of different types. *Journal of Archaeological Method and Theory* 4(3/4): 287-306.

Lane, P. & Reid, A. 1998. Historical archaeology. In: Lane, P., Reid, A. & Segobye, A. (eds) *Ditswa Mmung: The Archaeology of Botswana*: 161-176. Gaborone: Pula Press and the Botswana Society.

Lane, P. 2004. Re-constructing Tswana townscapes: toward a critical historical archaeology. In: Reid, A. & Lane, P. (eds) *African Historical Archaeologies*: 269-299. New York: Plenum Press.

Lightfoot, K.G. 1995. Culture contact studies: redefining the relationship between prehistoric and historical archaeology. *American Antiquity* 60(2): 199-217.

Lightfoot, K. 2006. Missions, furs, gold and manifest destiny: rethinking an archaeology of colonialism for western North America. In: Hall, M. & Silliman, S. (eds) *Historical Archaeology*: 272-292. Oxford: Blackwell Publishing.

Little, B.J. 1992. Text-aided archaeology. In: Little, B.J. (ed.) *Text-aided Archaeology*: 1-6. Boca Raton: CRC Press.

Little, B.J. & Shackel, P.A. 1989. Scales of historical anthropology: an archaeology of colonial Anglo-America. *Antiquity* 63: 495-509.

Loubser, J.H.N. 1985. Buffelshoek: an ethnoarchaeological consideration of a Late Iron Age settlement in the southern Transvaal. *South African Archaeological Bulletin* 42: 81-87.

Lucas, G. 2006. Historical archaeology and time. In: Hicks, D. & Beaudry, M.C. (eds) *The Cambridge Companion to Historical Archaeology*: 34-47. Cambridge: Cambridge University Press.

Lydon, J. 2006. Pacific encounters, or beyond the islands of history. In: Hall, M. & Silliman, S. (eds) *Historical Archaeology*: 293-312. Oxford: Blackwell Publishing.

Maggs, T. 1993. Sliding doors at Mokgatle's, a nineteenth-century Tswana town in the central Transvaal. *South African Archaeological Bulletin* 50: 32-36.

Malan, A. 1990. The archaeology of probate inventories. *Social Dynamics* 16(1): 1-10.

Malan, A. & van Heyningen, E. 2001. Twice removed: Horstley Street in Cape Town's District Six, 1865-1982. In: Mayne, A. & Murray, T. (eds) *The Archaeology of Urban Landscapes & Explorations in Slumland*: 39-56. Cambridge: Cambridge University Press.

Markell, A. 1993. Building on the past: the architecture and archaeology of Vergelegen. *South African Archaeological Society Goodwin Series* 7: 71-83.

Mason, R. 2000. Archaeology and native North American oral traditions. *American Antiquity* 65(2): 239-266.

Mitchell, L. 2002. Traces in the landscape: hunters, herders and farmers on the Cedarberg Frontier, South Africa, 1725-95. *Journal of African History* 43: 431-450.

Morton, F. 2003. Perpetual motion: resettlement patterns in the Western Transvaal and South-eastern Botswana since 1750. *Historia* 48(1): 265-282.

Omer-Cooper, J. 1993. Has the Mfecane a future? A response to the Cobbing critique. *Journal of Southern African Studies* 19(2): 273-294.

Orser, C.E. 1996. *A Historical Archaeology of the Modern World*. New York: Plenum Press.

Orser, C.E. 1999. Negotiating our 'familiar' pasts. In: Tarlow, S. & West, S. (eds) *The Familiar Past? Archaeologies of Later Historical Britain*: 273-285. London: Routledge.

Orser, C.E. 2000. Taking the pulse of emerging modernity. *International Journal of Historical Archaeology* 4(3): 275-280.

Orser, C.E. 2004. *Historical Archaeology*. New York: Harper Collins.

Orser, C.E. 2005. Network theory and the archaeology of modern history. In: Funari, P., Zarankin, A. & Stovel, E. (eds) *Global Archaeological Theory: Contextual Voices and Contemporary Thoughts*: 77-95. New York: Kluwer Academic.

Parkington, J. 1984. Soaqua and Bushmen: hunters and robbers. In: Schrire, C. (ed.) *Past and Present in Hunter-Gatherer Studies*: 151-174. New York: Academic Press.

Peires, J. 1993. Paradigm deleted: the materialist interpretation of the Mfecane. *Journal of Southern African Studies* 19(2): 295-313.

Perry, W. 1999. *Landscape Transformations and the Archaeology of Impact: Social Disruption and State Formation in Southern Africa*. New York: Kluwer Academic.

Pikirayi, I. 1999. Research trends in the historical archaeology of Zimbabwe. In: Funari, P., Hall, M. & Jones, S. (eds) *Historical Archaeology: Back from the Edge*: 67-84. London: Routledge.

Pikirayi, I. & Pwiti, G. 1999. States, traders, and colonists: historical archaeology in Zimbabwe. *Historical Archaeology* 33(2): 73-89.

Pistorius, J.C.C. & Steyn, M. 1995. Iron working and burial practices among the Kgatla-Kwena of the Mabyanamatshwaana complex. *Southern African Field Archaeology* 4(2): 68-77.

Plug, I. & Roodt, F. 1990. The faunal remains from recent excavations at uMgungundlovu. *South African Archaeological Bulletin* 47: 47-52.

Plug, I. & Sampson, C.G. 1996. European and Bushman impacts on Karoo fauna in the nineteenth century: an archaeological perspective. *South African Archaeological Bulletin* 53: 26-31.

Reid, A. & Lane, P. 2004. African historical archaeologies: an introductory consideration of scope and potential. In: Reid, A.M. & Lane, P.J. (eds) *African Historical Archaeologies*: 1-32. New York: Kluwer Press.

Saitowitz, S. & Sampson, C.G. 1992. Glass trade beads from rock shelters in the Upper Karoo. *South African Archaeological Bulletin* 49: 94-103.

Sampson, C.G., Hart, T., Wallsmith, D.L. & Blagg, J.D. 1989. The ceramic sequence in the Upper Seacow Valley: problems and implications. *South African Archaeological Bulletin* 149: 3-16.

Sampson, C.G., Sampson, B.E. & Neville, D. 1994. An early Dutch settlement pattern on the north-east frontier of the Cape Colony. *Southern African Field Archaeology* 3(2): 74-81.

Sampson, C.G. 1995. Acquisition of European livestock by the Seacow River Bushmen. *Southern African Field Archaeology* 4(1): 30-36.

Schmidt, P.R. 1990. Oral traditions, archaeology and history: a short reflective history. In: Robertshaw, P. (ed.) *A History of African Archaeology*: 252-270. London: James Currey.

Schmidt, P.R. 1995. Using archaeology to remake history in Africa. In: Schmidt, P.R. & Patterson, T.C. (eds) *Making Alternative Histories: The Practice of Archaeology and History in Non-Western Settings*: 119-147. Santa Fe, New Mexico: School of American Research Press.

Schmidt, P.R. 2006. *Historical Archaeology in Africa: Representation, Social Memory, and Oral Traditions*. Lanham, MD: AltaMira.

Schoeman, M.H. 1998a. Excavating Ndzundza Ndebele identity at KwaMaza. *Southern African Field Archaeology* 7(1): 42-52.

Schoeman, M.H. 1998b. Material culture 'under the animal skin': excavations at Esikhunjini, a Mfecane period Ndzundza Ndebele site. *Southern African Field Archaeology* 7(2): 72-81.

Schuyler, R.L. (ed.) 1978. *Historical Archaeology: A guide to Substantive and Theoretical Contributions*. Farmingdale, New York: Baywood Publishing Company.

Sealy, J., Morris, A., Armstrong, R., Markell, A. & Schrire, C. 1993. An historic skeleton from the slave lodge at Vergelegen. *South African Archaeological Society Goodwin Series* 7: 84-91.

Smith, A.B. 1992. *Pastoralism in Africa: Origins and Development Ecology*. London: Hurst & Company.

Smith, A.B. 1993. Different facets of the crystal: early European images of the Khoikhoi at the Cape, South Africa. *South African Archaeological Society Goodwin Series* 7: 8-20.

Stahl, A.B. 1999. The archaeology of global encounters viewed from Banda, Ghana. *African Archaeological Review* 16(1): 5-81.

Stahl, A. 2001. *Making History in Banda: Anthropological Visions of Africa's Past*. Cambridge: Cambridge University Press.

Tarlow, S. 2007. *The Archaeology of Improvement in Britain, 1750-1850*. Cambridge: Cambridge University Press.

Terrell, J. 1998. 30,000 years of culture contact in the south-west Pacific. In: Cusick, J. (ed.) *Studies in Culture Contact: Interaction, Culture Change and Archaeology*: 191-219. Carbondale: Center for Archaeological Investigations. Occasional papers no. 25.

Van der Merwe, N.J., Saitowitz, S.J., Thackeray, J.F., Hall, M. & Poggenpoel, C. 1989. Standardised analyses of glass trade beads from Mgungundlovu and Ondini, nineteenth-century Zulu capitals. *South African Archaeological Bulletin* 46: 98-104.

Van Schalkwyk, J.A. & Smith, B.W. 2004. Insiders and outsiders: sources for reinterpreting a historical event. In: Reid, A.M. & Lane, P.J. (eds) *African Historical Archaeologies*: 325-346. New York: Kluwer Academic/Plenum Publishers.

Vansina, J. 1999. Historians, are archaeologists your siblings? *History in Africa* 22: 369-408.

Voigt, E.A., Plug, I. & Sampson, C.G. 1995. European livestock from rock shelters in the Upper Seacow River Valley. *Southern African Field Archaeology* 4(1): 37-49.

Watson, E.J. & Watson, V. 1990. 'Of commoners and kings': faunal remains from Ondini. *South African Archaeological Bulletin* 151: 33-46.

Welsch, R. & Terrell, J. 1998. Material culture, social fields and social boundaries on the Sepik Coast of New Guinea. In: Stark, M. (ed.) *The Archaeology of Social Boundaries*: 50-77. Washington: Smithsonian Institution Press.

Westbury, W. & Sampson, C.G. 1993. To strike the necessary fire: acquisition of guns by the Seacow Valley Bushmen. *South African Archaeological Bulletin* 50: 26-31.

Whitelaw, G. 1994. Preliminary results of a survey of Bulawayo, Shaka Kasenzangakhona's capital from about 1820 to 1827. *Southern African Field Archaeology* 3(2): 107-109.

Worden, N. (ed.) 2007. *Contingent Lives: Social Identity and Material Culture in the VOC World*. Rondebosch: Historical Studies Department, University of Cape Town.

Wylie, A. 1999. Why should historical archaeologists study Capitalism? In: Leone, M. & Potter, P. (eds) *Historical Archaeologies of Capitalism*: 23-50. New York: Kluwer Academic Press.

Wylie, D. 2006. *Myth of Iron: Shaka in History*. Scottsville: University of KwaZulu-Natal Press.

Yates, R., Manhire, A. & Parkington, J. 1993. Colonial era paintings in the rock art of the south-western Cape: some preliminary observations. *South African Archaeological Society Goodwin Series* 7: 59-70.

3

South Africa in Africa more than five hundred years ago: some questions

Neil Parsons

Introduction

Before the spread of English language and cultural hegemony and resistance to it, there was Afrikaans-Dutch hegemony and resistance to it, and before that there were the post-1500 hegemonies of and resistances to Nguni and Sotho-Tswana. Nomenclature is always a problem. But the 'true' Nguni can be clearly identified with certain clans (including Zulu) among the larger Nguni-speaking group of South-East Bantu speakers. Similarly, there are dominant ancestral lineages among Sotho-Tswana speakers, namely Rolong and Kwena and Kgatla, who can with less certainty be referred as 'true' Tswana. The term 'Tswana' as self-identity appears to date from only c. 1800 (e.g. Barrow 1806) in answer to questions from foreigners in the south. 'Sotho' has been more loosely applied to the whole linguistic group including Tswana, Pedi, and even Khalagari.

The immediate stimulus of this chapter was a visit to the brilliant new museum of the Origins Centre on Wits campus. One of the last displays is an animated image of two maps, which also appear as figures in Tom Huffman's chapter in Himla Soodyall's *The Prehistory of Africa: Tracing the Lineage of Modern Man* (2006: 103 & 107): 'Spread of Eastern Bantu speakers during the Early Iron Age' and 'Late Iron Age movements of Nguni and Sotho-Tswana'.

This chapter is an attempt to get to grips with the prehistory of Nguni and Sotho-Tswana before 1500. It ventures beyond conventional history into heuristic models of the past – models that help us to understand general patterns of development, in order that we may contextualise and further investigate the myriad of details, and then also question the very models themselves. These models are largely drawn from two disciplines, archaeology and historical linguistics – the relationship between which is controversial. The debate over 'talking pots', i.e. whether language groups can be equated with pottery (ceramic) groups, dates back at least to 1966 – when Roland Oliver presented his synthesis of Malcolm Guthrie's Bantu linguistic map with 52 new radiocarbon dates for pottery north of the

Limpopo (Oliver 1966). This problem of 'Bantu expansion' has been a 'major puzzle in the history of Africa' ever since, and has generated much light as well as heat (Bostoen 2007).

Historians have been particularly grateful for the work of David Phillipson (1969 ff) and Tom Huffman (1970 ff). They have seen the spread of carbon-dated pottery groups as clear ceramic trails of migration of Bantu-speaking peoples. Huffman argues that pottery designs express 'group identity because it forms an arbitrary but repeated code of cultural symbols … a single style or large design field that is easily recognised by outsiders'. Designs remain 'a material metaphor' for the women artists who made them, who 'repeat their work' in order to 'please the community' and to 'communicate social messages' through colours and designs (Huffman 2006: 99-100 & 105).

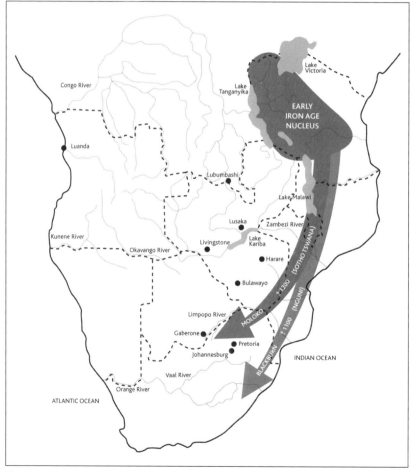

Figure 3.1 Early Iron Age pottery traditions in southern Africa (Eastern Highland, Eastern Coastal & Western Streams after Phillipson & Huffman).

The Phillipson-Huffman models of the Early and Later Iron Age have been by no means universally accepted among archaeologists. Huffman will soon publish a new comprehensive work on the Iron Age in southern Africa. No doubt that will open a new chapter in the story, but it is not the purpose of this paper to engage in the archaeological debate. Instead, the intention is to raise general questions about more than 500 years ago that are relevant to history less than 500 years ago.

Spread of Eastern Bantu speakers during the Early Iron Age

Archaeologists are sceptical about the reconstruction, by historical-comparative linguists and 'linguistic historians', of ancient languages and their spread. But two relatively recent books by Christopher Ehret cannot be ignored, since they are generally accessible to students: *An African Classical Age: Eastern and Southern Africa in World History 1000 BC to AD 400* (1998), and *The Civilizations of Africa: A History to 1800* (2002).

The animated image of the Early Iron Age in the Origins Centre depicts three streams coming from the north. A western stream runs diagonally like a sash out of Angola across the Kalahari to KwaZulu-Natal. An eastern highland stream runs south out of Uganda down Lake Tanganyika and through Eastern Zambia across the Zambezi to the Limpopo. An eastern coastal stream originates in Uganda but runs down the east coast from Kenya to Southern Mozambique and South Africa. To deal with these in reverse order:

Eastern coastal stream

This is based on close similarity between 'Kwale' pottery on the Kenya coast and 'Matola' pottery around Maputo, extending east over the Drakensberg to 'Silverleaves' (250-430 AD) and sticking to the coast to as far south as 'Mzonjani' (420-580 AD) near Durban. Such rapid movement along the coast, to the southern limits around Maputo of winds favouring *lateen* sailing, suggests that the migrants hopped on and off the coast by boat (Mitchell 2002: 264).

Ehret (2002: 31-35) backs Kwale origins around Uganda, which spread to the Kenya coast with his so-called 'Kazkazi' linguistic group, who were responsible for ancestral Swahili culture. But Ehret disputes the idea that Kwale people then spread along the coast as far as Mozambique and Natal. Instead, he has 'Kusi' people from the south end of Lake Tanganyika crossing Malawi into northern Mozambique in the 300-100 BC period. These Kusi, Ehret argues, were the ancestors of the Makhuwa in northern Mozambique, of 'South-east Bantu' in southern Mozambique, and of mysteriously named 'Sala-Shona' who took the Early Iron Age to the Transvaal and KwaZulu-Natal (Ehret 2002: 36 & 227-228).

Bostoen (2007) adds further complexity by arguing from comparative linguistics that pottery was spread south of the Congo Basin from the west into the east independently

43

Lots of factors to explain the
spread of pottery in the east...
(sea travel, herds moving pottery, Asians in the area

from, and before, the spread of Phillipson's 'Chifumbaze' Iron Age ceramics from East Africa. Hunters and herders could spread pot-making equally as well as farmers.

There is also what we may call the Wak-Wak factor: the distinct but unproven possibility that Indonesian proto-Malagasy settled on the northern Mozambique coast – impeding the continuum of Bantu-speaking peoples along the coast. The earliest known artefacts of Malagasy settlers in Madagascar date from only about 650 AD, but pollen evidence of imported plants suggests contact as early as 550 BC. Indonesians in outrigger canoes, rafts, and 'sewn-boats', may have filled the trade gap with Arabia-Persia on the East African coast between the 3rd and 7th centuries AD. Their settlement around the northern Mozambique coast is suggested by the diffusion into Africa of their xylophones, double-valve bellows (suggesting they were smiths attracted by the quality of African iron), rotating bow-drills, sugarcane, Asian species of yam, and pigs – and by the fact that the Malagasy today are predominantly 'Zimba' African (Mozambican) by ancestry though Indonesian by language – (bananas and chickens having arrived from Asia much earlier). However from the 7th century AD the proto-Malagasy came into conflict with Muslim Arab-Swahili traders, who disparaged them as 'Wak-Wak' nonsense-speakers and pagan pig-keepers coming from somewhere near China. That would help explain why they abandoned the African east coast for Madagascar and the Comoros (Domenichini-Ramiaramanana 1992: 333-334; Mitchell 2002: 121; Sinclair 2006: 152-157; Verin 1990: 375-380; Ehret 2002: 188-189).

Eastern highland stream

This stream of the Early Iron Age sweeps from Tanzania through eastern Zambia, over the Zambezi as the 'Gokomere' culture maybe by the 1st century AD, and coming to a halt as the 5th century 'Zhizo' culture around the Limpopo valley. This would correspond with Ehret's Kusi speakers, boosted by iron tools and weapons and radiating out from the south end of Lake Tanganyika after they had adapted their crops to a November–March wet season. By 500 BC the Kusi were spreading to Katanga (southern Congo) as well as to Malawi and Mozambique (Ehret 2002: 211).

Early Iron Age Bantu-speakers around Lake Tanganyika would have encountered both Nilo-Saharans and Twa-Pygmy people (Posnansky 1990a: 300; Ehret 1967, 1968, 1998 & 2002). Twa-Pygmy prehistory has been identified with the woodland savanna 'Tshitolian' and 'Nachikufuan' cultures of southern Congo and northern Zambia dated from 16 000 BC onwards (des Hermens & van Noten 1990: 236). The last phase from about the time of Christ saw the use of pottery and iron tools acquired from neighbouring Bantu-speakers (Sutton 1990b: 315-316; Van Noten 1990: 340-341). Archaeologists have long criticised each other for rigidly classifying sites in Zambia as either Later Stone Age (Twa) or Early

Iron Age (Bantu), rather than seeing subtle interactions – such as hunters beginning to herd sheep or to make pottery (Clark 1970: 37-38; Parkington 1990: 360).

Ben Smith (2006: 87-90) has identified Twa-Pygmies with a 'huge swathe of geometric rock art' through Angola-Zambia-Malawi and northern Mozambique into Southern Congo and western Tanzania up to Lake Victoria. Could the Twa also be the short-statured pre-Bantu 'Mbonelakuti', with iron and cattle, referred to in Eastern African oral traditions (Kusimba & Kusimba 2005)? This begs many questions about Twa-Pygmy interactions with Bantu-speakers (e.g. Miller 1969), and of Later Stone Age and Early Iron Age interconnections, not least an explanation of the Matrilineal Belt across the subcontinent that more or less corresponds with Ben Smith's 'huge swathe'.[1]

Western stream

This is the most problematic of all. The maps displayed at the Origins Centre and published in Soodyall's *Prehistory of Africa* appear to contradict what Phillipson and Huffman published in 1989-1990 and since then. The maps show a great sash of western stream migration striped across Africa from north-western Angola down to KwaZulu-Natal in the south-east. This follows Jim Denbow (1990), tracing western stream culture from 'Benfica' around Luanda down to 'Divuyu' in the Tsodilo Hills west of the Okavango. But Phillipson (1990: 370, 1992: 317) presents the western stream as part of his Eastern Bantu 'Chifumbaze' complex that originated around Uganda. Huffman (1989: 65-70) agrees with this Eastern Bantu assignation. His 'Kalundu' tradition sweeps across Botswana into the 'Happy Rest' culture of the Transvaal by 350 AD and down to the KwaZulu-Natal coast – reaching the limit of summer rainfall for millet cultivation around near East London by AD 800 (Huffman 2002: 10-11, 2006: 102 & 105).[2]

This begs questions about layers of Eastern-Western Bantu interaction and the inadequacy of linguistic classifications in the area in and around Angola (Vansina 1995; Bostoen 2007). There are equally pertinent questions about 'Chifumbaze' interaction with Twa in the woodland to the north and especially with Proto-Khoe or Northern San people in the drier south. Ehret's hypothesis of ancient linguistic transference of Nilo-Saharan words to Khoe, such as –*ku* for sheep, suggests that Khoe-speaking people in the Angola area were already herding sheep and making pottery (either as hunters-with-sheep or as full-blown 'pastoralists') before Early Iron Age arrival.[3] Whether they were already herding cattle is debatable; the Nilo-Saharan *komo* word for cattle could have been imported by Eastern Bantu speakers, but Eastern Bantu speakers in Zambia today use the term *ngombe* rather than *komo* (Phillipson 1990: 371).

Late Iron Age movements of Nguni and Sotho-Tswana

The animated map for this in the Origins Centre shows 'Blackburn' (i.e. proto-Nguni) and 'Moloko' (i.e. proto-Sotho-Tswana) streams, dated c. 1100 and c. 1300 respectively, sweeping out of a Uganda–Tanzania 'Early Iron Age Nucleus' through Mozambique into South Africa. Huffman (2006: 97 & 106-8) believes that the ancestors of the Nguni and the Tswana 'must have lived in East Africa during the Early Iron Age'. Taking his cues from linguists and the anthropologist Hammond-Tooke, Huffman had previously argued:

- Nguni and Tswana languages use an East African suffix *–ini* to indicate the locative (*–eng* in Tswana).
- Nguni, Sotho-Tswana, and Venda have 'Iroquois'-type kinship terminology like Great Lakes or Intra-lacustrine Bantu, while Shona and Tsonga have 'Omaha'-type kinship.

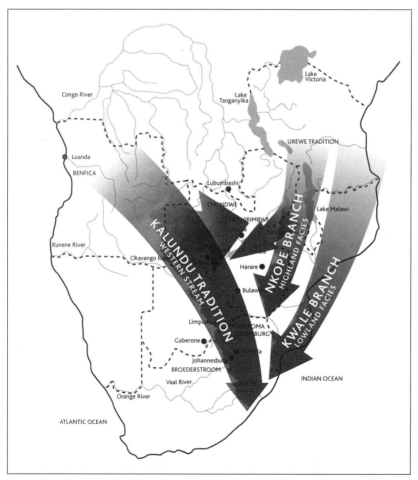

Figure 3.2 Origins of Nguni (Blackburn pottery from c.1100 AD) and Tswana (Moloko pottery from c. 1300) after Thomas Huffman

- Nguni (and neighbouring Southern Sotho-Tswana) practice the *hlonipha* custom of women's avoidance speech in deference to their husband's families; something similar is practised by Intra-lacustrine Bantu, n.b. notably Rwanda.[4]
- Other points of comparison between Nguni (but not Sotho-Tswana) and Intra-lacustrine (Great Lakes) Bantu include metaphors for human bodily fluids and dirt, the nature of 'class' and gender distinctions, predominantly ritual chieftainship pre-Difaqane, beehive-shaped grass-woven houses, and some medical practices.
- Blackburn (Nguni) pottery shows striking similarities to the 'Kalambo' culture on the Tanzania–Zambia border.
- The timing of Nguni and Tswana migrations from East Africa can be explained by climate: during 1000-1300 drought was experienced in East Africa at the same time as southern Africa was having good rains (Huffman 2004: 80-84).

This is not the place to debate whether the sum of these coincidences constitutes a convincing argument. Nor to ask what motives would have impelled people to travel, over so many thousands of kilometres, into lands where people spoke more and more radically different languages. Instead we will apply Occam's Razor, and ask whether we need look quite so far north for proto-Nguni and proto-Sotho-Tswana origins.

The idea that Nguni and Sotho-Tswana must come originally from the Great Lakes of East Africa or even the Nile and Egypt is an old one. Their traditions certainly talk of origins in lands full of reeds and expanses of water (Finlayson 2006: 134). But the traditions could equally well apply to river delta marshlands along the Mozambique coast. Rosalie Finlayson highlights the close relationship of Sotho-Tswana and Nguni languages to the Tshwa-Ronga group of languages of southern Mozambique (Finlayson 2006: 131). Herman Batibo (1996) notes that Nguni and Sotho-Tswana languages share terminology for lakes and the sea, as well as terms for money derived from Arabic or Persian, and suggests an ancestral linguistic relationship with the Makhuwa in northern Mozambique.[5] Ehret argues that his Early Iron Age 'South-east Bantu' (ancestors of Tsonga, Chopi and Gitonga) included the ancestors of the Nguni and Sotho-Tswana who remained in central/southern Mozambique for a thousand years (Ehret 2002: 36 & 227-28).

Here we must disaggregate the terms 'Nguni' and 'Sotho-Tswana' as overlaying 'a number of layers of language and peoples ... most discernible in the coastland, but ... also discernible on the Highveld' (Marks & Atmore 1970: 125). Traditions of origins north of the Limpopo would therefore apply only to the most recent and dominant 'true' Nguni and 'true' Tswana clans.

It has long been recognised from recorded oral traditions that there are at least two early layers of clans or chiefdoms – namely 'Mbo' and 'Lala' – who settled in KwaZulu-Natal some time before the 'pure Nguni' arrived (Marks 1969; Marks & Atmore 1970; Wright & Hamilton 1989). The works of Legassick (1969) and others suggest that a similar conclusion can be drawn with respect to the Sotho-Tswana: the pure or true Tswana clans (Rolong, Kwena and Kgatla) overlay earlier strata of pre-Tswana Sotho clans (Fokeng, Khalagari and proto-Pedi).

Marks and Atmore suggest that Mbo clans were 'Khoisan-Sotho pastoralists and cultivators' who 'came into Natal from the Highveld, avoiding the *tsetse* country to the north'; they are also said to display vestigial links with the Mbo (Ovambo and Ovimbundu) of Angola–Namibia. On the other hand, Lala clans, who were 'skilled workers in iron ore', appear to have come from 'the lower Zambezi area' and can be associated with ancestors of the Tsonga and Shona (Marks & Atmore 1970: 129). But the 19th-century source on which Marks and Atmore rely, A.T. Bryant, also equates the Mbo with people from southern Mozambique speaking 'Tekela' dialects. And it is in the west, not in the east, that today we still find impoverished people called Lala (Balala), described by Breutz (1955/56: 17) as having been 'semi-Bushmen of the Makgalagadi type', near Lehututu in south-west Botswana and probably scattered towards the lower Vaal in South Africa.[6]

Migrations of ancestors of 'true' Nguni and 'true' Tswana out of the Mozambique lowlands into the northern Drakensberg of South Africa (to settle among people *not* speaking a radically different language) could be explained by their displacement during the boom in Indian Ocean gold and ivory trade in the 1100-1300 period. The boom caused Shona-speaking people (specifically Ndau traders) to move down from the Zimbabwe plateau to occupy the coast between the Pungwe and Sabi rivers – the coast known to Arab-Swahili traders as Sofala (*Sufala al-dhahab* or *Sufala al-tibr*, the shoal of the gold sand). Hence what had been a continuum between South-east Bantu speakers and Makhuwa (Makua) speakers on the coast could have been broken and dispersed by Shona immigrants from the interior – and possibly by Nyanja/ Sena/ Zimba coming down the Zambezi to its delta.[7]

Disruption in the coastal zone could also have been caused by a Wak-Wak attack. A new wave of settlers arrived in Madagascar direct from Indonesia around 1100 AD, driven out by instability in the Srivijaya empire of Sumatra (Verin 1990; Hrbek 1992: 13-14; Kropacek 1997: 181; Freeman-Grenville 1962: 15). Another factor could have been tsetse-fly infestation of the coastal zone, opened up by new trade routes and more intensive human settlement. Owners of cattle in the coastal zone would have lusted after the tsetse-free pastures and large Sanga cattle of their relatives already living around the northern Drakensberg.

Origins of Shona

Shona is no more an immutable category than Nguni or Sotho-Tswana is, but has also been compacted from a number of cultural-linguistic layers. Beginning with his 1978 article 'The origins of Leopard's Kopje: an 11th century Difaqane', Huffman has argued that people making 'Kutama' (Leopard's Kopje Phase II) pottery tradition came from the south and occupied former Zhizo culture territory around the Limpopo–Shashe confluence at the end of the 10th century. Kutama people took advantage of Indian Ocean trade revival, after Zhizo people had abandoned the area as a trade emporium – and had reverted to cattle-keeping at Toutswe to the west – because of the downturn in trade on the coast following Wak-Wak raiding c. 950 AD (Huffman 2002, 2005). Huffman sees Great Zimbabwe as the Kutama city that around the 1290s succeeded the earlier Kutama hilltop and valley towns of Mapungubwe at the Limpopo–Shashe confluence (Huffman 1992: 324-26, 2005). However, while acknowledging the Leopard's Kopje-II roots of Great Zimbabwe, albeit enlivened by cultural influences from the north, other archaeologists have cast doubts upon or ignored Huffman's Kutama hypothesis – suggesting that Leopard's Kopje-II was merely a local adaptation of Zhizo, rather than a radical new influx from further south (e.g. van Waarden 1998: 116-17; Pikirayi 2001).[8]

Christopher Ehret has ventured out on an even further limb than Huffman. Ehret lumps all Early Iron Age people south of the Limpopo into what he calls 'Sala-Shona' ('Sala' for those who remained in South Africa while 'Shona' went off to Zimbabwe?). The departure of so many Sala-Shona would have left South Africa open to south-east Bantu immigration from Mozambique. Ehret posits continuity between the ceramic heads of the 'Lydenburg' culture (620-1040 AD in Mpumulanga province) and the later artistic achievements of Mapungubwe and Great Zimbabwe (Ehret 2002: 225-27). This does not take into account the Later Iron Age 'Eiland' ceramic tradition, which developed out of Lydenburg pottery and continued for a thousand years among pre-Tswana Sotho peoples – Khalagari, proto-Pedi, and Fokeng (see van Waarden 1998).

Conclusion

Great sweeping arrows on maps are graphic illustrations of population movement. But the point has often been made that we should be cautious about seeing Bantu expansions as a 'massive exodus from one area to another' of large coherent groups of people, analogous to the rapid migrations of the early 19th-century Difaqane. Instead we should see much slower and progressive *mosaics* of 'immigration, diffusion, invention, and admixture' (Lwango-Lunyiiso & Vansina 1992: 80-81). There are also very strong counter-narratives to seeing Bantu expansion as a single cultural package: any discussion in detail must disaggregate ceramics, pastoral herding and iron technology from language – though each may contain clues about the others, such as the words-and-things approach of language explaining ceramics (Bostoen 2007).

As for this paper, the most obvious conclusion to the above discussion is that the study of Bantu expansion cannot be restricted to Bantu-speaking peoples alone, but must take into account other ethnic-linguistic groupings, as well as questions of independent diffusion and invention of 'progress'. The big picture of the pre-1500 past in South Africa also raises points to consider in the historical reconstruction of the last five hundred years:

- First, the need to recognise the historical importance of non-Bantu groups, notably Northern San, Khoe/ Khoekhoe, and Southern San, as well as Twa further north.
- Second, to plot how and where 'true' Nguni and 'true' Tswana rose to political, cultural and linguistic dominance over previous societies, taking care to distinguish pre-colonial from colonial (and indeed post-colonial) periods.
- Third, the related need to study the traces of people independent or formerly independent from hegemonic groups.
- Fourth, the need for comparative cultural-linguistic studies between pre-1500 and post-1500 societies, e.g. comparison with the archaeological and other historical records of 19th century Kololo conquest of the Luyana in western Zambia resulting in Lozi culture.
- Fifth, the need to map more precisely actual locations identified in oral traditions, etc. in order to produce more detailed and nuanced geographical information on the past.
- Sixth, as has already been recognised in the Five Hundred Years Initiative research project, the need to ignore the constraints on research of present-day political boundaries.
- Seventh, to counter the conventional wisdom of always regarding South African prehistory as well as history as something that begins in the southwestern periphery (the Cape of Good Hope) and then spreads inland.

Notes

1. Genetic evidence shows that different groups of 'Pygmies' in and around the Congo Basin are only extremely remotely related to each other at a time long predating Bantu expansion (Barkham & Soodyall 2006: 141-42) This suggests that the ancient Aka, Twa etc. were ancestral to other Niger-Congo peoples – rather than being their descendants pygmified by forest life, as has sometimes been assumed because today they all speak Bantu languages.
2. The Kalundu tradition embraces at least seven different 'cultures' as distinguished by their pottery – including the 'Baratani' or Lovers' Hill culture in south-east Botswana associated with a Romeo and Juliet love story (Campbell et al 1996).
3. Ehret suggests that Eastern Sudanic (i.e. Eastern Sahelian or Nilotic) people within the Nilo-Saharan language family moved on from Lake Tanganyika to the mid-Zambezi with their sheep and cattle around 300 BC – which is also the earliest possible date for livestock in southern Africa identified by

the pioneer archaeologist Desmond Clark (Ehret 1967, 1968, 1998, 2002: 176; Clark 1970: 31, 1990: 221). Local Khoe hunter-gatherers in the Zambia-Angola-Botswana area must then have adopted livestock herding with alacrity, as livestock and human populations grew and led to southward migrations within the next few centuries. (Cow or sheep milk relieved women from continued lactation, and thus made possible increased childbearing.)

4. Finlayson (1995) traces *hlonipha* among Nguni-speakers to ancient interaction with Khoe herders – though one might argue following Ehret that Khoe herders previously received the custom along with stock herding from contact with Nilo-Saharans. (Interaction with Nilo-Saharan herders might also account for the parallel custom of *ubah*, i.e. 'respect', found among Rwandans.)

5. It used to be commonplace among linguists and anthropologists that Nguni and Sotho-Tswana shared similar origins around the northern Drakensberg escarpment of South Africa. An older generation was even taught that Nguni and Sotho-Tswana were originally one language: Sotho-Tswana having since dropped the initial *n-* from *nkomo* for cow, *nkosi* for chief, and the word Nguni itself becoming 'Koni'. The major linguistic difference between Nguni and Sotho-Tswana was that the Nguni picked up click-consonants after they migrated south to KwaZulu-Natal; they also lost the tradition of respecting clan 'totems' (Ngcongco & Vansina 1997: 231). Marks and Atmore suggest that 'pure Nguni' probably originated with the Koni group of Sotho-Tswana speakers – maybe explaining the continued presence on the highveld of some Nguni-speakers (so-called Transvaal Ndebele) as well as of scattered groups of Koni (Marks & Atmore 1970).

6. Balala as an ethnic term not to be confused with *malata* denoting servants in Setswana, though in this case the social status applied to the ethnicity.

7. See Beach (1980: 424) map 2 of 'very tentative trade routes' before c. 1450 and citing Keith Rennie on Ndau prehistory and the Nyakuimba-Musikanvanhu (Beach 1980: 159-62); also Clement Doke's linguistic sub-zones in Cole (1993) and Cope (1993).

8. I am grateful to an anonymous reader for reminding me to make this point.

References

Barkham, D. & Soodyall, H. 2006. Mitochondrial DNS (mtDNA) and Y Chromosome DNA variation in African populations. In: Soodyall, H. (ed.) *The Prehistory of Africa*: 139-146. Cape Town: Jonathan Ball Publishers.

Barrow, J. 1806. *A Voyage to Cochin China, in the Years 1792 and 1793 … To which is Attached an Account of a Journey, Made in the Years 1801 and 1802, to the Residence of the Chief of the Booshuana Nation, Being the Remotest Part in the Interior of Southern Africa to which Europeans have Hitherto Penetrated.* London: T. Cadell & W. Davies.

Batibo, H. 1996. *The Role of Language in the Discovery of Cultural History: Reconstructing Setswana Speakers' Cultural Past.* Gaborone: University of Botswana, Professorial Inaugural Lecture, March 1996 (mimeo).

Beach, D. 1980. *The Shona & Zimbabwe: An Outline of Shona History.* London: Heinemann Educational.

Bostoen, K. 2007. Pots, words and the Bantu problem: on lexical reconstruction and early African history. *Journal of African History* 48(2): 173-99.

Breutz, P.-L. 1955/56. *The Tribes of Mafeking District.* Pretoria: Department of Native Affairs (Ethnological Publications no.32).

Campbell, A., van Waarden, C. & Holmberg, G. 1996. Variation in the Early Iron Age of south-east Botswana. *Botswana Notes and Records* 18: 1-23.

Clark, J.D. 1970. The spread of food production in sub-Saharan Africa. In: Fage, J.D. & Oliver, R.A. (eds). *Papers in African Prehistory*: 35-42. Cambridge: Cambridge University Press.

Clark, J.D. 1990. The prehistory of southern Africa. In: Ki-Zerbo, J. (ed.) *UNESCO General History of Africa I. Methodology and African Prehistory*: 210-222. Oxford: James Currey.

Cole, D.T. 1993. Doke's classifications of Bantu languages. In: Herbert, R. (ed.) *Foundations in Southern African Linguistics*: 131-47. Johannesburg: Witwatersrand University Press.

Cope, A.T. 1993. A consolidated checklist of the Bantu languages. In: Herbert, R. (ed.) *Foundations in Southern African Linguistics*: 149-72. Johannesburg: Witwatersrand University Press.

Crawhall, N. 2006. Languages, genetics and archaeology: problems and the possibilities of Africa. In: Soodyall, H. (ed.) *The Prehistory of Africa*: 109-24. Cape Town: Jonathan Ball Publishers.

Denbow, J. 1990. Congo to Kalahari: data and hypotheses about the political economy of the Western Stream of the Early Iron Age. *African Archaeological Review* 8: 139-75.

Des Hermens, R. de B. & van Noten, F. 1990. The prehistory of Central Africa. In: Ki-Zerbo, J. (ed.) *UNESCO General History of Africa I. Methodology and African Prehistory*: 223-240. Oxford: James Currey.

Domenichini-Ramiaramanana, B. 1992. Madagascar. In: Hrbek, I. (ed.) *UNESCO General History of Africa III. Africa from the Seventh to the Eleventh Century*: 327-336. London: James Currey.

Ehret, C. 1967. Cattle-keeping and milking in eastern and southern African history. *Journal of African History* 8: 1-17.

Ehret, C. 1968. Sheep and Central Sudanic peoples in southern Africa. *Journal of African History* 9: 213-221.

Ehret, C. 1998: *An African Classical Age: Eastern and Southern Africa in World History 1000 B.C. to A.D. 400*. Oxford: James Currey.

Ehret, C. 2001. Bantu expansions: re-envisioning a central problem of early African history. *International Journal of African Historical Studies* 34: 5-43.

Ehret, C. 2002. *The Civilisations of Africa: A History to 1800*. Charlottesville: University Press of Virginia.

Ehret, C. 2005. Khoisan languages and Late Stone Age archaeology. Unpublished paper presented to 5th Congress of Pan-African Association of Archaeologists, Gaborone, May 2005.

Finlayson, R. 1995. Women's language of respect: *isihlonipho sabafazi*. In: Mesthrie, R. (ed.) *Language and Social History: Studies in South African Sociolinguistics*: 140-153. Cape Town & Johannesburg: David Philip.

Finlayson, R. 2006. Linguistic relationships: how genetic are they? In: Soodyall, H. (ed.) *The Prehistory of Africa*: 125-38. Cape Town: Jonathan Ball Publishers.

Freeman-Grenville, G.P.S. 1962. *The East African Coast: Select Documents from the First to the Early Nineteenth Century*. Oxford: Clarendon Press.

Hammond-Tooke, W.D. 2004. Southern Bantu origins: light from kinship terminology. *Southern African Humanities* 16: 71-78.

Herbert, R. 1995a. Sociolinguistic evidence of Nguni, Sotho, Tsonga and Nguni origins. In: Mesthrie, R. (ed.) *Language and Social History: Studies in South African Sociolinguistics*: 39-50. Cape Town & Johannesburg: David Philip.

Herbert, R. K. 1995b. The sociohistory of clicks in Southern Bantu. In: Mesthrie, R. (ed.) *Language and Social History: Studies in South African Sociolinguistics*: 51-67. Cape Town & Johannesburg: David Philip.

Hrbek, I. 1992. Africa in the context of world history. In: Hrbek, I. (ed.) *UNESCO General History of Africa III. Africa from the Seventh to the Eleventh Century*: 1-15. London: James Currey.

Huffman, T. N. 1970. The Early Iron Age and the spread of the Bantu. *South African Archaeological Bulletin* 25: 3-21.

Huffman, T.N. 1974. The antiquity of lobola. *South African Archaeological Bulletin* 29: 53-79.

Huffman, T.N. 1978. The origins of Leopard's Kopje: an 11th century Difaqane. *Arnoldia* 8(23): 1-23.

Huffman, T.N. 1979. African origins (review of David Phillipson's *The Later Prehistory of Eastern and Southern Africa*. Heinemann, 1977). *South African Journal of Science* 75: 233-37.

Huffman, T.N. 1989. *Iron Age Migrations: The Ceramic Sequence in Southern Zambia: Excavations at Gundu and Ndonde*. Johannesburg: Witwatersrand University Press.

Huffman, T.N. 1992. Southern Africa to the south of the Zambezi. In: Hrbek, I. (ed.) *UNESCO General History of Africa III. Africa from the Seventh to the Eleventh Century*: 318-326. London: James Currey.

Huffman, T.N. 1993. Broederstroom and the central cattle pattern. *South African Journal of Science* 89: 220-226.

Huffman, T.N. 2002. Archaeological background. In: Van Schalwyk, J.A. & Hanisch, E.O.M. (eds) *Sculptured in Clay: Iron Age Figurines from Schroda, Limpopo Province, South Africa*: 9-19. Pretoria: National Cultural History Museum.

Huffman, T.N. 2004. The archaeology of the Nguni past. *Southern African Humanities* 16: 79-111.

Huffman, T.N. 2005. The Mapungubwe cultural landscape. Abstract of paper no.116 & unverified notes by Neil Parsons on oral presentation at 12th Congress of the Pan-African Archaeological Association for Prehistory and Related Studies, Gaborone, 4-6 July.

Huffman, T.N. 2006. Bantu migrations in southern Africa. In: Soodyall, H. (ed.) *The Prehistory of Africa*: 97-108. Cape Town: Jonathan Ball Publishers.

Joy, D., Feng, X., Mu, J., Furuya, T., Chotivanich, K., Krettli, A., Ho, M., Wang, A., White, N., Suh, E., Beerli, P. & Su, X. 2003. Early origin and recent expansion of *Plasmodium falciparum. Science* 300 (5617): 318-21.

Kirby, P. 1968. *The Musical Instruments of the Native Races of South Africa*, 2nd edition. Johannesburg: Witwatersrand University Press.

Knight, A., Underhill, P., Mortensen, H., Zhivotovsky, L., Lin, A., Henn, B., Louis, D., Ruhlen, M. & Mountain, J. 2003. African Y chromosomes and mtDNA divergence provides insight into the history of Click languages. *Current Biology* 13: 464-73.

Kropacek, L. 1992. The development of Swahili civilization. In: Ki-Zerbo, J. & Niane, D.T. (eds) *UNESCO General History of Africa IV. Africa from the Twelfth to the Sixteenth Century*: 181-90. Oxford: James Currey.

Kusimba, C.M. & Kusimba, S. B. 2005. Mosaics and interactions: East Africa, 2000 b.p. to the present. In: Stahl, A. B. (ed.) *African Archaeology: A Critical Introduction*: 392-418. Oxford & Malden, Mass: Blackwell.

Legassick, M.C. 1969. The Sotho-Tswana peoples before 1800. In: Thompson, L.M. (ed.) *African Societies in Southern Africa: Historical Studies*: 86-125. London: Heinemann Educational Books.

Lwango-Lwingo, S. & Vansina, J. 1990. The Bantu-speaking peoples and their expansion. In: Hrbek, I. (ed.) *UNESCO General History of Africa III. Africa from the Seventh to the Eleventh Century*: 75-85. London: James Currey.

Marks, S. 1969. The traditions of the Natal 'Nguni': a second look at the work of A.T. Bryant. In: Thompson, L.M. (ed.) *African Societies in Southern Africa: Historical Studies*: 126-144. London: Heinemann Educational Books.

Marks, S. & Atmore, A. 1970. The problem of the Nguni: an examination of the ethnic and linguistic situation in South Africa before the Mfecane. In: Dalby, D. (ed.) *Language and History in Africa*: 120-32. New York: Africana Publishing Corporation.

Masao, F.T. 1990. The east African coast and the Comoro islands. In: Hrbek, I. (ed.) *UNESCO General History of Africa III. Africa from the Seventh to the Eleventh Century*: 285-296. London: James Currey.

Mason, R. 1987. *Origins of the African People of the Johannesburg Area*. Johannesburg: Skotaville Publishers.

Miller, S.F. 1969. Contacts between the Late Stone Age and the Early Iron Age in southern central Africa. *Azania* 4: 81-90.

Mitchell, P. 2002. *The Archaeology of Southern Africa*. Cambridge: Cambridge University Press.

Ngcongco, L.D. & Vansina, J. 1997. Southern Africa: its people and social structures. In: Ki-Zerbo, J. & Niane, D.T. (eds) *UNESCO General History of Africa IV. Africa from the Twelfth to the Sixteenth Century*: 230-238. Oxford: James Currey.

Oliver, R. A. 1966. The problem of the Bantu expansion. *Journal of African History* 7(3): 361-76.

Parkington, J.E. 1990. Southern Africa: hunters and food-gatherers. In: Mokhtar, G. (ed.) *UNESCO General History of Africa II. Ancient Civilizations of Africa*: 351-361. London: James Currey.

Parkington, J.E. 1993. The neglected alternative: historical narrative rather than cultural labelling. *South African Archaeological Bulletin* 48: 94-97.

Phillipson, D.W. 1969. Early iron-using peoples of southern Africa. In: Thompson, L.M. (ed.) *African Societies in Southern Africa: Historical Studies*: 24-49. London: Heinemann Educational Books.

Phillipson, D.W. 1975. The chronology of the Iron Age in Bantu Africa. *Journal of African History* 16(3): 341-42.

Phillipson, D.W. 1977. *The Later Prehistory of Eastern and Southern Africa*. London: Heinemann.

Phillipson, D.W. 1985. *African Archaeology*. Cambridge: Cambridge University Press.

Phillipson, D.W. 1990. The beginnings of the Iron Age in southern Africa. In: Mokhtar, G. (ed.) *UNESCO General History of Africa II. Ancient Civilizations of Africa*: 262-72. London: James Currey.

Phillipson, D.W. 1992. Central Africa to the north of the Zambezi. In: Hrbek, I. (ed.) *UNESCO General History of Africa III. Africa from the Seventh to the Eleventh Century*: 307-317. London: James Currey.

Pikirayi, I. 2001. *The Zimbabwe Culture: Origins and Decline of Southern Zambezian States*. Walnut Creek, CA: Altamira Press.

Posnansky, M. 1990a. Introduction to the later prehistory of sub-Saharan Africa. In: Mokhtar, G. (ed.) *UNESCO General History of Africa II. Ancient Civilizations of Africa*: 296-305. London: James Currey.

Posnansky, M. 1990b. The societies of Africa south of the Sahara in the Early Iron Age. In: Mokhtar, G. (ed.) *UNESCO General History of Africa II. Ancient Civilizations of Africa*: 383-393. London: James Currey.

Pwiti, G. 2005. Southern Africa and the East African coast. In: Stahl, A.B. (ed.) *African Archaeology: A Critical Introduction*: 378-391. Oxford & Malden, MA: Blackwell.

Sinclair, P. 2006. The cave, the coast and ocean links. In: Blundell, G.(ed.) *Origins: The Story of the Emergence of Humans and Humanity in Africa*: 152-157. Cape Town: Double Storey.

Smith, B. W. 2006. Reading rock art and writing genetic history: regionalism, ethnicity and the rock art of southern Africa. In: Soodyall, H. (ed.) *The Prehistory of Africa*: 76-96. Cape Town: Jonathan Ball Publishers.

Soodyall, H. (ed.) 2006 *The Prehistory of Africa: Tracing the Lineage of Modern Man.* Jeppestown, Johannesburg & Cape Town: Jonathan Ball Publishers.

Sutton, J.E.G. 1990. East Africa before the seventh century. In: Mokhtar, G. (ed.) *UNESCO General History of Africa II. Ancient Civilizations of Africa*: 313-324. London: James Currey.

Tlou, T. & Campbell, A. 1997. *History of Botswana*. Gaborone: Macmillan Botswana.

van Noten, F. 1990. Central Africa. In: Mokhtar, G. (ed.) *UNESCO General History of Africa II. Ancient Civilizations of Africa*: 339-350. London: James Currey.

Vansina, J. 1995. New linguistic evidence and the Bantu expansion. *Journal of African History* 36: 173-195.

van Waarden, C. 1998. The Later Iron Age. In: Lane, P., Reid, A. & Segobye, A. (eds) *Ditswa Mmung: The Archaeology of Botswana*: 115-169. Gaborone: Pula Press: Botswana Society.

Verin, P. 1990. Madagascar. In: Mokhtar, G. (ed.) *UNESCO General History of Africa II. Ancient Civilizations of Africa*: 373-382. London: James Currey.

Wright, J. & Hamilton, C. 1989. Traditions and transformations: the Phongolo-Mzimkhulu region in the late eighteenth and early nineteenth centuries. In: Duminy, A. & Guest, B. (eds) *Natal and Zululand from Earliest Times to 1910: A New History*: 49-82. Pietermaritzburg: University of Natal Press/Shuter & Shooter.

4

Towards an outline of the oral geography, historical identity and political economy of the late precolonial Tswana in the Rustenburg region

Simon Hall, Mark Anderson, Jan Boeyens and Francois Coetzee

Introduction

The purpose of this paper is to offer a broad outline of historical developments in the wider Rustenburg region from about 1700 AD to the late 1820s. While both the oral and the archaeological records are addressed, the emphasis is on the latter because previous reviews by Parsons (1995) and Manson (1995) have already provided an in-depth discussion of the oral material from this period. Our concern is to build upon these insights and explore ideas about their profitable combination with archaeological evidence.

Such a project falls within the ambit of historical archaeology and the methodological and interpretive relationship between material culture and texts. There is a significant literature on how this relationship is meant to work. Most agree that a unidirectional outcome in which one source simply confirms what is evident in the other is a waste of time. In contrast, most would aspire to an aim that profitably combines sources in order to take interpretation into areas that neither source could penetrate in isolation. At the centre of attaining a balance between sources is the issue of evidential scale (see Deetz 1988). Archaeological evidence can only translate into general perspectives on the past and tends to emphasise cultural concerns, while historical interpretation is more detailed and addresses specific context and the actions and agency of named players. In this regard, a key issue is whether the scale of identity glimpsed through the oral records, on the one hand, can be reconciled with the conventional use of ceramic and settlement style as identity, on the other.

This focus on the relationship between archaeology and oral texts is an important project for the 18th and early 19th century. This is because it was a period of significant change within Sotho-Tswana communities, which saw dramatic change in the scale of political, social and economic organisation. Very broadly, early in the 18th century, moderately dispersed communities lived within relatively unconstrained space, while by the early 19th century, chiefdoms were pushing increasingly harder against each other and against the environment in which they were situated. Some chiefdoms decayed both from the external pressure of their neighbours and internal dispute, and lost economic independence, while others mounted aggressive takeovers. Archaeologically, this process is highly visible because of the progressive aggregation of homesteads into large Tswana stone-wall towns, some of which had populations of over 12 000 people (see Pistorius 1992; Hall 1998; Boeyens 2000, 2003). At least two major centres of power were located in the Rustenburg area, namely Marothodi and Molokwane, respectively capitals of prominent Tlokwa and Kwena branches. In the 1820s, further major political change occurred with the onset of the Difaqane and the establishment and expansion of the Ndebele state under Mzilikazi north of the Vaal River, which effectively ended this Tswana period of political centralisation in the Rustenburg area (Rasmussen 1978).

Critical in these events is whether and to what degree the growing encroachment of the colonial world exerted pressure on these societies to change even though this frontier was still physically 'below' the horizon. In asking this question, the 'frontier' should not be conceived of as a simple confrontational line, but a complex and changing zone of interaction. New mercantile and political interests were added to the internal regional networks of African politics, and the question is not to simply disassemble internal and external factors but to engage with the integration of responses. As already indicated, issues of identity are important here, and the extent to which the hardening edges of colonially constructed identities can be reconciled with identity at the archaeological scale is an important concern.

The degree to which external versus internal forces were responsible for the rise and early 19th-century collapse of Tswana chiefdoms in the Rustenburg area is not a new theme and Manson has concluded (1995: 360-1) that

> The heightened violence and upheavals of the 1820s should be seen as an event, albeit profound, in a continuum of change that engulfed chiefdoms on the western highveld. It did not represent a major break from the past heralding the dawn of capitalism into southern Africa ... The stimuli of external pressures and threats, of mercantile capital and of new technology hastened and shaped this transformation, but did not introduce it.

It is in this broad historical outline that the archaeology has an important contribution to make in terms of providing a basic chronological structure, thereby anchoring, confirming, elaborating or pegging back the oral histories and developing an integrated approach to understanding economic and social strategy based upon hypotheses generated by these records. This relationship has barely been explored. However, in order to make the archaeology work within the historical scale will require a large, data-heavy comparative project. Furthermore, and fundamental to this project, is chronological control and the development of both a relative and an absolute chronology that is better than that currently available through radiocarbon dating. As the discussion below highlights, we still have no precision, for example, over when the major towns of the Rustenburg area developed. The allure of combining material and historical evidence for a more sophisticated interpretation of Tswana history will remain just that if we do not attend to much basic archaeological work.

Equally, the historical context provided by the current corpus of oral records for the Rustenburg region is patchy and dependent on a few key texts (see Breutz 1953). These records identify a number of key Sotho-Tswana lineages, that is, ruling dynasties or branches that trace their descent patrilineally to a real or an imagined common ancestor. Lineages, as such, did not form real social or political groups. Political actors were mostly chiefdoms, which were divided into smaller juridical and administrative units such as districts, wards and sub-wards, or homesteads. Membership of these functional political units was made up of many different, and sometimes unrelated, lineage fragments. Nevertheless, most recorded Tswana oral traditions are structured around the genealogies and histories of chiefly lineages, which, evidentially and heuristically, serve as a useful starting point for tracing identities and places in the political landscape. The most visible players in the study area comprise the various Modimosana Kwena lineages, the Fokeng, the Mogopa Kwena, the Po, the Tlokwa, the Tlhako and the Kgafela Kgatla. For the second half of the 18th century the records provide details about the increasingly antagonistic relations between chiefdoms, deadly succession disputes within lineages, the brokering and breaking of political alliance, cattle raiding and, ultimately, regional submission to the new political order introduced by the establishment of Mzilikazi's Ndebele state in the late 1820s. These records are at times relatively precise about the location of the capitals of leading chiefs. The Po settlement of Tobong (Wolhuterskop), for example, is securely identified, as is the early 19th-century Tlokwa capital at Marothodi (Vlakfontein). As the lineage histories recede into the early part of the 18th and 17th centuries, this geographic precision obviously fades, but it is striking how these lineages retain a general geographic position on this landscape.

From an archaeological perspective, the link between a lineage identity and a specific place clearly provides the opportunity to investigate what correlation there is, if any, between the different scales of oral and archaeological evidence. To what extent do the identities depicted in these 'oral geographies' tally with the archaeological data of identity from these places? (See Boeyens 2000 for an extensive discussion of the identity of Kaditshwene.) However naïve such a search may seem, the oral records of specific place and more generally, regional place, provide a basic geographic and broadly historical framework according to which archaeological research can be structured and around which we can develop questions that the archaeology can answer.

The geography of lineages and their relationship to the archaeological record is a theme that runs throughout this paper (Table 4.1). In the first part we revisit the oral records with the aim of 'capturing' the basic geographic essence of 18th- and early 19th-century lineage identities in this region and broadly assess the archaeology in relation to these. The second section is a case study of the Tlokwa lineage early in the 19th century. This considers ways in which the general historical context takes archaeological data on settlement location and commodity production into the domain of changes in regional political power. The exploration of political economy in this section, which is illustrative rather than comprehensive (see Hall et al 2006), is premised on the understanding that economic processes do not take place in isolation but are closely interrelated with social and political processes.

Table 4.1: Draft collation of place names and locations as given in Breutz (1953) and Ellenberger (1939). The focus is from the 18th century and mostly up until the establishment of the Ndebele state in the late 1820s.

1. Except for the farms London 19 KP (Rathateng), Vlakfontein 207 JP (Marothodi) and Rhenosterspruit 908 JQ (Mabele-a-Podi), all farm numbers refer to the old system and have not been converted to the new farm numbers.
2. All dates have been transferred from Breutz (1953) and Ellenberger (1939) without change. For the 17th and much of the 18th century, the chronologies and sequences are speculative. Closer analysis of shared and regional events will no doubt bring the late 18th- and early 19th-century chronologies more into line.

Fokeng			
Chief	*Date [2]*	*Capital*	*Farm/Place [1]*
Sekete III	Early 18th c.		Boschpoort?
Diale	Mid–18th c		Boschpoort?
Ramorwa	Mid–18th c	Phokeng	Phokeng
Sekete IV	Late 18th c.	Phokeng	Phokeng
Katane	Early 19th c.?	Phokeng	Phokeng
Thethe (Mokganwana)	Early 19th c.?	Phokeng	Phokeng
Nameng	1820s	Phokeng	Phokeng
Noge	1820s	Phokeng	Phokeng

Batlokwa-ba-ga-Sedumedi (of Gaborone – Ellenberger 1939)			
Chief	*Date*	*Capital*	*Farm/Place*
Tabane	16th c.?	Thaba Mogale	Magaliesberg
Khoadi	16th c.?	Thaba Mogale	Magaliesberg
Motonosi	Early 18th c.?		Wakkerstroom, Standerton, Harrismith
Tswaane	Early 18th c.?		Harrismith, Tlokwe (Potchefstroom)
Marakadu	Early 18th c.?	Tlokwe	Potchefstroom
Mosima Tsele	Mid-18th c.?	Bote	Houwater, Pilanesberg
Monaheng	Mid-18th c.?	Bote	Houwater, Pilanesberg
Matlhabana	Mid-18th c.?	Itlholanoga, Bopitiko?	Doornhoek 134
Mokgwa	Later 18th c.?	Itlholanoga	Doornhoek 134
Taukobong	1780	Mankwe, Maruping (Pilwe Hill)	Zwaarverdiend 502
Molefe	1810	Kolontwaneng	Silverkrans/Grootfontein 301
Bogatsu	1815–1820?	Marothodi	Bultfontein 712, Vlakfontein 207 JP
Kgosi	1820–1823?	Marothodi	Bultfontein 712, Vlakfontein 207 JP
Leshage	1823–1825?		Ngwato country
Bashe	1825–1835	Letlhakeng or Legageng	Putfontein 559
Bakgatla-ba-ga-Kgafela			
Chief	*Date*	*Capital*	*Farm/Place*
Kgafela	Early 17th c.?	Momusweng (Break with Mosetlha)	Near Makapanstad
Tebele		Ntwane	Near Moretele River
		Momoseu	Near Ntwane
		Tsekane	Leeuwpoort 1356, Southern Waterberg
		Matome	Tussenkomst 188
Masellane		Molokwane	Vliegpoort
Masellane	Early 18th c.	Mabule	On hill on Kruidfontein 649
Kgwefane	Mid-18th c.	Moruleng	Saulspoort
Molefe	Died 1780?	Maramapong	Saulspoort 269
Mmagotso	1780–1790		
Pheto	End 18th c. died c. 1805	Sefikile	Spitzkop 298 (near Northam)
Letsebe	1810	Tlhaka le Moetse	Middelkuil 564
Senwelo	Early 19th c.	Mabule to Tlokwane	Rhenosterkop 1048
Motlotle	1820s	Magakwe or Dithubaruba	Kruidfontein 649 Kruidfontein 649
Pilane		Monamaneng	Kafferskraal 890
Pilane		Bogopana	Witfonteinrand NE of Witfontein 215

Pilane		Mmamodimokwana	Schilpadnest 233
Pilane		Motsitle	(Mabieskraal)
Pilane	After 1837	Mabele-a-Podi/Mmasebudule	?Rhenosterfontein 887, Rhenosterspruit 908 JQ
Kgamanyane		Moruleng	Saulspoort
Kgamanyane	1869	Mochudi	
Bakwena-ba-Modimosana-ba-Mmatau			
Chief	*Date*	*Name*	*Farm/Place*
Mmatau or Tau	1700?	Rathateng	London 19 KP
Sekano	1760–1780	Molokwane	Selonskraal 645, Moedwil 639
Kgaswane	1780–1827	Molokwane	Selonskraal 645, Moedwil 639
Bakwena-ba-Modimosana-ba-Ramanamela			
Chief	*Date*	*Capital*	*Farm/Place*
Ramanamela	Early 18th c.		
Mphele	?		
Mpete	?	Boitsemagano (Mamogowe-Taung)	Brakfontein 898
Powe	1790–1810	Boitsemagano (Mamogowe-Taung)	Brakfontein 898
Bakwena-ba-Modimosana-ba-Maaka			
Chief	*Date*	*Capital*	*Farm/Place*
Khunong (Maaka?)	?		
Makgotse	?		
Maditse	?		
Mojakgomo	?		
Rampe	Early 18th c.?	Still at Rathateng	
Kgosimang	1750–1800	Boitsemagano (Mmamogowe-Taung)	Brakfontein 898
Legwale	1800–1820?	Boitsemagano (Mmamogowe-Taung)	Brakfontein 898
Thebenare Ratsagae	1820–	Boitsemagano (Mmamogowe-Taung)	Brakfontein 898
Bakwena-ba-Modimosana ba Matlhaku			
Chief	*Date*	*Capital*	*Farm/Place*
Morare	Late 16th c.?	Rathateng	London 19 KP
Malegi/Mope	Early 18th c.	Mafatle	Rhenosterfontein 398
Moswane	Mid-18th c.	Molokwane	Selonskraal 645, Moedwil 639
Tswaedi	Mid-18th c.	Molokwane	Selonskraal 645, Moedwil 639
Motlhabane	Late 18th c.	Molokwane	Selonskraal 645, Moedwil 639
Leseyane	Early 19th c.	Molokwane	Selonskraal 645, Moedwil 639

Madintsi	Early 19th c.	Molokwane	Selonskraal 645, Moedwil 639
Bakwena-ba-Mogopa			
Chief	*Date*	*Capital*	*Farm/Place*
Setlhare			
Mogopa	Early 17th c.	Rathateng	London 19 KP
Modise wa Mogopa	Mid-17th c.?	Lokwadi	Zandrivierspoort 747
Modise wa Mogopa	Mid-17th c.?	Phalane mountain	?
Radiphiri?	?	?	?
Sefike	?	?	?
Ditswe Tlowodi	Early 18th c.	Mabjanamatshwana Koppies	North-east of Brits
Mooketsi/More	Mid-18th c.	Mangwatladi/Lengwatladi	West of Pienaars River
More	Late 18th c.	Mabjanamatshwana Koppies	North-east of Brits
More	Early 19th c.?	Gwate (Mamogaleslaagte)	Near hill Thaba ya Morena
Segwati	Early 19th c.	?	?
Bapo-ba-Mogale			
Chief	*Date*	*Capital*	*Farm/Place*
Tshwene	Early 18th c.?	Crocodile (Odi) River	
Mekhise			
Maruatona			
Maimane (regent)	Mid-18th c.	Makolokwe	Wolwekraal 512
Moerane	Late 18th c.		
Moerane	1795–1815	Tobong	Boschfontein 381 (Wolhuterskop – Tlhogokgolo)
Moerane	Died c. 1821		
Semetsa Botloka	Regent 1827–1830		
Moruri	Regent 1827–1830		
Mogale Mogale	From 1837	Mogale's River	Ngakotse tributary of Crocodile River
Batlhako			
Chief	*Date*	*Capital*	*Farm/Place*
?		Mangolwana	Wonderboom (Pretoria)
?		Pharami	Boshoek 268
Leema	Late 17th c.	Toelanie River	near Pella
Seutlwane		Maseletsane	North side of Pilwe Hill
Mabe	Mid-18th c.	Mothoutling	Palmietfontein 567
Motsisi		Legatalle	Ruighoek 426
Molotsi	Died 1820	Legatalle	Ruighoek 426
Mabe	1820	Motsitle	Mabieskraal 620

Bataung-ba-Mobana			
Chief	*Date*	*Capital*	*Farm/Place*
?	1630–1730?	Rakgotletse	Doornkom 896 (SE of Swartruggens)
Modise	Mid-18th c.?	Khibitswane	Boschoek 268 (NE Magaliesberg)
Modise Tsie?	Early 19th c.	Mmamogowe (Boitsemagano)	Brakfontein 898
Maloisane		Mmamogowe (Boitsemagano)	Brakfontein 898
Kgosane	Early 19th c.	Mmamogowe (Boitsemagano)	Brakfontein 898
Sefanyetso	1818–1824	Mmamogowe (Boitsemagano)	Brakfontein 898

The archaeological sequence and issues of origins and identity

The oral traditions and histories for this region clearly depict a geographic patchwork of lineage clusters and a relatively complex and multi-layered sequence in which it is possible to differentiate between older, more established lineages and those that are younger (Plate 1, Table 4.1). Despite the general historic Tswana cultural character of the region, the oral records suggest more diversity in the cultural affiliation and the origins of some of these lineages. The 17th and 18th centuries are clearly also about varying degrees of cultural and social interaction within complex internal frontiers. A primary Tswana identity cannot be assumed. The following section briefly reviews evidence of origins and identity. It is based mainly on a rereading of Breutz (1953) and is guided by Martin Legassick's (1969) synthesis of the Sotho-Tswana literature that, despite the date of publication, has begun to resonate strongly with both the Sotho-Tswana and Nguni archaeological sequences (see Huffman 2002, 2007), which are also discussed below.

We discuss three 'episodes' of identity. These are the dispersal of Kwena lineages into the Rustenburg area dating from the 16th century, the potentially contemporary appearance of Fokeng and Tlokwa lineages, and the consolidation of Po, Tlhako and Kgatla lineages that established or re-established themselves on the northern edge of the Magaliesberg range from around AD 1700. At issue here is whether the archaeological record of the area reflects a deeper and more widespread Nguni substratum that has hitherto been inferred from the oral record. More specifically, the question is raised whether the occurrence of comb-stamped Uitkomst pottery in the region marks the presence and spread of Sotho-ised Nguni.

The Fokeng

We start with the Fokeng. Fokeng origins are ambiguous. Despite records linking the Fokeng to the western Tswana Kwena, Breutz (1953: 20) consistently ascribes 'a very ancient' status to them and maintains that 'their relationship with the other baKwena cannot be proved.'

Legassick (1969: 114), furthermore, suggests that the Fokeng were co-residents with the Kwena and Kgatla and that they were spread over a wide area. Recently, Huffman (2007) has attempted to resolve this ambiguity, as well as the Fokeng's wide distribution, with the suggestion that a Fokeng identity can be linked to the first inland movement of Mbo Nguni out of present-day KwaZulu-Natal between about AD 1450 and 1500. These early Nguni settlers subsequently occupied Type N sites in the northern Free State and Group I sites to the north of the Vaal River (see Maggs 1976; Taylor 1979). According to Huffman (2007), Late Iron Age Ntsuanatsatsi pottery, which is associated with type N stonewalling on the southern Highveld, can be derived from Blackburn, an archaeological expression that is associated with these early Nguni migrants. This is seemingly congruent with oral records that describe Kwena movement south of the Vaal into areas, such as Ntuanatsatsi, already occupied by Fokeng (originally of Nguni descent?).

This is relevant to the Rustenburg area, because it has been suggested that a subsequent Fokeng movement northwards back across the Vaal introduced stonewalling to both western and south-western Tswana (Huffman 2007). According to this new interpretation of the ceramic sequence, the appearance of Uitkomst facies pottery is a result of Fokeng interaction with south-western Sotho-Tswana, represented by Olifantspoort facies pottery, and possibly western Sotho-Tswana, represented by Madikwe facies pottery (Table 4.2). Uitkomst pottery incorporates comb-stamping, a prominent attribute of Ntsuanatsatsi pottery, and it appears to be relatively widespread in the Rustenburg and Zeerust areas (Huffman 2007).

Table 4.2: Combined *Sotho/Tswana* (Moloko) and Nguni (Blackburn) sequence (after Huffman 2004).

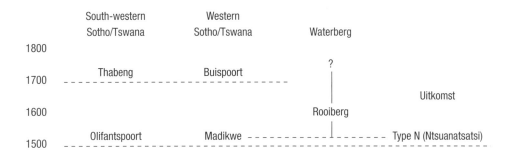

	South-western Sotho/Tswana	Western Sotho/Tswana	Waterberg	
1800				
1700	Thabeng	Buispoort	?	
				Uitkomst
1600			Rooiberg	
1500	Olifantspoort	Madikwe		Type N (Ntsuanatsatsi)

If Uitkomst material does indeed correlate with widespread Nguni-influenced communities in the Rustenburg area, the ethnonym Fokeng is of value only as a general cultural label with little long-term historical specificity. The historic Fokeng may then represent a disjunct fragment of a previously wider identity that, through a process of assimilation, was reduced and geographically compressed by western Tswana communities into their historic distribution. If so, how did a broad cultural label come to stand for a political identity in the more recent oral records? We need more archaeological understanding of this wider distribution and how this might relate to the distribution of historically documented Fokeng on the northern side of the Magaliesberg (Plate 1). More precisely dated archaeological sequences within this area would allow us to assess the relationship between the archaeological identities of primary western Tswana Kwena lineages (Modimosana, Mogopa and Phalane), who became some of the dominant identities in this region, and Uitkomst settlements (Fokeng) (Table 4.2).

It is in this regard that the archaeological sequence in the Marico, further to the west, obliges us to sound a cautionary note. According to Huffman (2002, 2007), Uitkomst pottery occurs stratigraphically under the main stonewalls (and Buispoort pottery) at Mmakgame, the Hurutshe capital immediately predating the historic Kaditshwene. He associates Uitkomst ceramics found at the site with an early radiocarbon date of AD 1645 ± 10 (GrN-5137) that ostensibly confirms the stratigraphic evidence (Huffman 2007). This interpretation is, however, problematic. First, such a stratigraphic sequence is not apparent from Mason's excavations and description of the site (Mason 1986). Second, the so-called early date for the Uitkomst occupation does not exist and is based on a misinterpretation of an already calibrated range of radiocarbon dates for the site (see Vogel 1971: 41). The correct GrN-5137 date, derived from a charcoal sample at a depth of 106–122 mm in Midden 1, is AD 1747 ± 44. Other radiocarbon dates from the same midden are AD 1813 ± 32 (GrN-5339), AD 1734 ± 33 (GrN-5338) and AD 1812 ± 30 (GrN-5307), respectively obtained from charcoal samples retrieved at depths of 75–90 cm, 15–30 cm and 0–15 cm (Mason 1986: 68). Lastly, the main court midden at Kaditshwene, a site that was occupied from about AD 1790 to 1823, has yielded a large component of Uitkomst-like comb-stamped pottery, which is also depicted in sketches by John Campbell (1822), who visited the town in 1820. While the Marico evidence does not resolve the question about the origins of Uitkomst pottery, this style's association with a core western Tswana branch suggests that more research is necessary to clarify its dating and attribution, as well as the historical roots of the Fokeng.

The Modimosana Kwena

The Kwena lineages trace their descent from the senior western Tswana Hurutshe. In Breutz's (1953: 19) record their movement into the Rustenburg area was from the ancestral place of Rathateng, near the junction of the Madikwe and Crocodile (Odi) Rivers, and is part of an initial and complex phase of Tswana fission and dispersal. The initial stages of

Kwena fission are archaeologically equivalent to settlements that predate the use of stone boundary enclosures and which are associated with distinctive Madikwe pottery (Table 2), dating between 1500 and 1700 AD. The historically more resolved Phalane and Modimosana lineages west of present-day Rustenburg, and the Mogopa further to the east across the Crocodile River (Plate 1, Table 4.1), are archaeologically equivalent to a later phase called Buispoort, that is marked by simple rim-nicked and incised pottery and typical scalloped 'Molokwane' type walling (Huffman 2002; see Hall 1998), dating from about 1700 AD. The spread and development of the Madikwe and Buispoort phases are clearly relevant to the interaction with, or replacement of, 'Fokeng'/Uitkomst communities mentioned above.

Molokwane, the large stone-wall town occupied by the Modimosana Mmatau Kwena from their first arrival in the area, as well as settlements on the farm Moedwil (Pistorius 1992, 1997), are potentially important to this question. The Maake section of the Modimosana is linked to another large stone-wall centre on the farm Shylock called Boitsemagano (the Taung name is Mmamogowe) (Table 4.1). These are impressive aggregated towns that reflect significant political power. Pistorius (1997: 120), however, documents considerable change in the Molokwane sequence, and it is not clear whether the final extent of Molokwane represents progressive aggregation through the 18th century, or whether the town grew rapidly over a short period. The latter may well be the case, and the size of the town and the growth of the *kgosing* (the chief's division) may be linked to the political success of Kgaswane, a well-known and powerful chief who ruled between about 1770 and 1828. The oral records for this part of the sequence accord well with the burgeoning growth of Mmatau power and the final physical expression of the Molokwane settlement. The relationship between the oral and archaeological evidence prior to this date is difficult to assess. Clearly there is extensive occupation, redefinition of space and considerable rearrangement of stonewalls at Molokwane. Pistorius (1997), however, ties the arrival of the Mmatau at Molokwane to the 17th century on the basis of radiocarbon dates and, consequently, he suggests that the oral chronology is too shallow. Due to the imprecision of the radiocarbon chronology for this period, such an interpretation must be seen as tentative.

While these earlier, presumably 17th-century, deposits may well relate to an initial Mmatau, or, perhaps more circumspectly, to a general Kwena occupation, the ceramic sequence should provide some control over this. As outlined by Huffman (2002), the rim-nicked and incised Buispoort pottery is associated with western Tswana stone-wall settlements of the Molokwane type from about 1700 AD. The sparsely decorated assemblage from Molokwane is no exception (Pistorius 1984, 1992: 36-7; see also Mason 1986 for the stone-wall site at Olifantspoort). No earlier pottery was found when we sampled the Molokwane pottery collection for geoarchaeological analysis (Rosenstein 2008).

This is important because Buispoort is meant to be derived from Madikwe.

According to the regional sequence, however, if there is indeed a 17th-century occupation at Molokwane, we might also expect to find Olifantspoort or Uitkomst pottery in association with these older deposits. Should such material found be below the final expression of the stone-wall horizon at Molokwane, it may well suggest that the actual Kwena development in the Selons (Ngwaritse) River valley may be an 18th-century event. Additionally, clarity on the local Molokwane sequence may also shed light on the contraction or assimilation of the 'Fokeng'.

It is thus noteworthy that some comb-stamped pottery was uncovered from a household in SEL1, a commoner ward of Molokwane, where it seems to be contemporaneous with the more dominant rim-nicked sample (Pistorius 1984). This case highlights that at politically important towns, such as Molokwane, where issues of identity are firmly locked into the oral records, greater chronological control and precision is needed, coupled to an excavation approach that returns to basic questions around sequence. Comparison with sequences from the Rustenburg and Phokeng area north of the Magaliesberg will potentially provide more clarity on this sequence.

The Tlokwa

Like the origins of the Fokeng, the origins of Tlokwa are also not clear-cut (Plate 1). Oral and archaeological evidence combined casts doubt on a simple Tswana origin. Traditionally, the Tlokwa are linked to the Hurutshe and are said to have separated through fission. Breutz (1953: 22, 200), however, has reservations about this tradition, as well as a Tswana origin. Oral records state that the first Tlokwa chiefs lived at 'Borwa' (in the south) in contrast to the first remembered place, which is Botlokwa, near Polokwane (Breutz 1953: 200). They are also linked to other areas such as Wakkerstroom, Standerton, Harrismith, Thaba Bosiu, Tlokwe (Potchefstroom and Mooi River), and, in the Rustenburg region, with Bote and Itlholanoga in the Pilanesberg, and, progressively through the 18th century, with Mankwe, Pilwe, Kolontwaneng and Marothodi, located mostly between the Pilanesberg in the north and the Elands (Kgetleng) River to the south (Ellenberger 1939; see also Hall et al 2006 and Table 4.1; Plate 1). The doubts about a Tswana origin for the Tlokwa and their widespread distribution are reminiscent to that of the Fokeng, and the possibility that the Tlokwa also have Nguni origins has to be considered.

Archaeological data from Marothodi, an early 19th-century Tlokwa capital near Sun City on the southern edge of the Pilanesberg, is relevant to this issue because elements in the ceramic style separate the Tlokwa at Marothodi from contemporary western Tswana at Molokwane, for example. The prominent decorated attribute on the Marothodi pottery is comb-stamping in rim and neck bands and with comb-stamped arcades on the shoulder. Rim nicking and rim notching are rare. Bands of comb-stamped motifs are separated by red ochre and black graphite bands. This Uitkomst-like pottery contrasts markedly with the Buispoort facies (western Tswana) pottery from the later stone-wall horizons at sites such as Molokwane and Olifantspoort, about 40 km to the south (Plates 1 & 2).

Furthermore, it has been noted that a consistent fabric attribute of Buispoort pottery is the inclusion of large plates of muscovite mica, seemingly added as a temper (Drake Rosenstein 2002). This attribute has been noted at Olifantspoort, Molokwane and Kaditshwene, as well as in Buispoort-like pottery from Mmakgame, which is the 18th-century settlement immediately before Kaditshwene in the Hurutshe sequence. In much of the Buispoort pottery from these sites, as well as in the comb-stamped pottery from Kaditshwene, these inclusions are easily visible to the naked eye and impart a white glittery and slightly greasy sheen to the surface of the pottery. Significantly, comparative geoarchaeological analysis of pottery from earlier Madikwe and Olifantspoort sites shows that this fabric attribute is completely absent in these earlier phases and that the later mica inclusions were a deliberate choice. This technological change runs parallel to a significant reduction through this sequence in the stylistic load carried by the pottery (Hall 1998; Per Fredriksen pers. comm.).

Initially, we viewed changes in the ceramic technology sequence as reflecting the very different scale of ceramic production and use in the later 18th-century town phase. Thus we also explored the thermodynamic and structural properties of the temper. The logic here focused on technological strategies that may have made the large-scale production and use of ceramics more efficient in the later high-density town conditions of the late 18th and early 19th centuries, especially with mounting pressure on the sustainability of basic resources, particularly wood. In addition, the distinctive fabric of Buispoort pottery suggests that it is inseparable from a technology as style issue. One of our assumptions when we started working at the Tlokwa town of Marothodi (Plate 2) was that we would find the same fabric style. This attribute, however, is absent in the Marothodi pottery, as well as Kgafela Kgatla pottery from the Pilanesberg area.

The Po, Tlhako, Mogopa Kwena and Kgatla

In combination, these ceramic stylistic and technological differences between late 18th- and 19th-century settlements could potentially shed light on the possible earlier distinctive origins of western Tswana, as well as the issues raised in connection with an Nguni/Fokeng identity. We can dig back and around these oral sequences in order to assess the wider value of these stylistic and technological attributes and to determine differences in the settlement layouts from which this material comes. The Tlhako, Po, Mogopa and Kgafela Kgatla, for example, would be important archaeological targets in this regard (Plate 1), because the Po and Tlhako have Nguni origins and share the same totem (*tlou* = elephant), the Mogopa records claim western Tswana (Kwena) origins and the derivation of the Kgatla is slightly ambivalent, but they possibly come from western Tswana.

From a secondary point of dispersal near Pretoria, the Po settled the area between the Sterkstroom River in the west and the Crocodile River in the east (Breutz 1953). Named settlements include Makolokwe (mid-17th century) and Tobong (Wolhuterskop – Tlhogokgolo, late 18th and early 19th century) (Table 4.1; Plate 1). The Tlhako are also linked to Pretoria but moved further to the west. Records place them at a number of sites between the Tholwane River, the Matlapengsberg, Mabies Kraal and Pilwe Hill through the 17th century (Breutz 1953: 176, 288) (Plate 1). This distribution is immediately to the west of the Tlokwa, but also partially overlaps with Pilwe Hill, which is also a prominent place in Tlokwa records. There is some archaeological evidence that corroborates the oral records concerning the Nguni origins of the Po (see Huffman 2007), but the provision of a basic and systematic description of pottery and settlement layout throughout the Po sequence is clearly needed. Furthermore, we know of no archaeology that can be linked to the Tlhako in the region, and this clearly presents another opportunity to assess the archaeology in relation to the oral evidence.

The Mogopa records refer to a common origin with the various Modimosana Kwena lineages that hold Rathateng as an ancestral point of dispersal, a link which is reinforced through their sharing of the genesis myth about emergence from the hole at Lowe, near Mochudi in present-day Botswana (Breutz 1953: 83). The Mogopa are linked to the Mabjanamatshwana Koppies and a number of other places during the 18th and early 19th centuries on the eastern side of the Crocodile River (Table 4.1; Plate 1). Again, some of the specific Mogopa places need to be archaeologically tested.

Lastly, we turn our attention to the origins of the Kgafela Kgatla upon which the archaeology can also pass comment (Plate 1). Breutz's records (1953: 247-271) rely heavily on Schapera's (1980) account for the earlier periods of Kgatla history. Kgatla are linked, first, to an origin in the Rustenburg area (Direleng), and then to a process of fission in which the Kgafela and Mosetlha sections were formed. The Pedi, still further to the east, are, in part, an extension of Kgatla fission. A western Tswana affiliation for Kgatla is slightly ambivalent but, according to Huffman (2007), they can be linked to Buispoort, and, furthermore, Pedi pottery is derived from Madikwe. The Kgatla's association with Buispoort pottery is based on the site's possible link with the Mmanaana Kgatla, but it should be noted that even at Buispoort comb-stamped pottery does occur (Van Hoepen & Hoffman 1935).

We also have archaeological observations on Kgafela sites in the Pilanesberg dating from the late 18th and 19th centuries that provide important data points at the younger end of the Kgafela sequence. Mabele-a-Podi, for example, was probably the site where *kgosi* Pilane lived in the mid-19th century. Comb-stamped pottery from associated middens and securely sealed hut floors is similar to the pottery from the slightly earlier 19th-century Tlokwa town of Marothodi. In terms of the ceramic sequence this would place Kgatla within the Fokeng/Uitkomst phase (Table 4.2). The deep sections at Hoekfontein 432 JQ, a Mmakau Kgatla site near Brits, provide an important opportunity to test this assumption and to refine the local ceramic sequence (Küsel & Pelser 2007).

The issue of historical identity is, however, more complex because Kgafela Kgatla oral records recall an earlier occupation of the southern Waterberg before moving south to the Pilanesberg, probably early in the 18th century. These records state that after the initial fission of the Kgafela and Mosetlha, the Kgafela moved north to Tsekane in the southern Waterberg (Breutz 1953: 247), which is close to Leeuwpoort and Rooiberg (Table 4.1). These places are relevant because tin was intensively mined and smelted there from as early as the 15th and 16th centuries (see Friede & Steel 1976; Grant 1990, Grant et al 1994; Hall 1981, 1985; Hall & Grant 1995). Tin, which was also being smelted in the wider Rooiberg region, may have been a resource that attracted competition (Hall & Grant 1995; Huffman 2006). Because we know the regional Rooiberg sequence that is relevant to the time period under discussion relatively well, it is worth considering what general identities are implied.

The Rooiberg tin smelters

In the Rooiberg valley, small 16th- and 17th-century Madikwe homesteads (Hall 1981; Hall et al 2007) are found in exposed valley floor locations immediately on the edges of small drainages. They are associated with both copper and tin smelting. On stylistic and chronological grounds these settlements predate any possible Kgatla presence. Some Madikwe sites, however, are found relatively high up in kloofs where access to water and arable soil may have been an issue. Alternatively, these locations may express anxiety over the arrival of new lineages. These appear in the form of Nguni-speaking people who built distinctive hill-top settlements (Melora walling, Huffman 2007) in the Waterberg from about 1600 AD (Aukema in Huffman 1990). Such hill-top sites include Mabotse, from which one tin ingot probably came (Hall & Grant 1995), and Smelterskop (Hall et al 2007).

Melora-type sites are contemporary with another ceramic phase that appears early in the 17th century (Hall 1985) and is now referred to as Rooiberg (Huffman 2002). According to Huffman (2007), this Uitkomst-like phase spread into the Waterberg from the south out of Fokeng/south-western Tswana interaction, and mixed with Madikwe pottery. Additionally,

Rooiberg walling suggests an organisation that is similar in some respects to Maggs's Type N (Maggs 1976; see Mason 1986: 297). These settlements have usually one central cattle enclosure with smaller enclosures attached to it or linked to smoothly curved, but discontinuous homestead walls. The location of Rooiberg sites is also defensive (Hall 1985, 1998). They are either perched on top of steep-sided hills or, within the Rooiberg Valley, placed on raised ledges in the foothills of surrounding ranges such as the Elandsberg and Rooiberg (Mason 1986; Hall et al 2007).

Dating the local Rooiberg sequence is once again a problem because of the calibration effect. At Smelterskop stratigraphic indications are that an earlier phase of Madikwe smelting underlies Melora walling, with Rooiberg material on top of that. Both Madikwe and Rooiberg people were smelting tin. Melora people may have also been smelting tin but probably not on the hill itself. We know that Nguni migrants were renowned metal workers and that Lete records refer specifically to digging 'for white iron [tin] in the quarries of Ditshiping, which is in the Transvaal, and for black iron at Magopane' (Ellenberger 1937-38: 46). Rooiberg is the only realistic candidate for Ditshiping.

It is possible that the Rooiberg phase smelters also included ancestral Kgatla people. Although circumstantial, it may be instructive to recall where two generations of Mosetlha Kgatla sought refuge during the 19th century. The principle here is that where people moved to, and the locations that they settled, were not random choices but based on prior ancestral connections and an intimate knowledge of these locations, as well as current political relationships. Under Ntshaupe, for example, the Mosetlha Kgatla left Mosetlha just north of Pretoria in the 1820s in order to get away from the growing influence of Mzilikazi and the Ndebele state in the Rustenburg area. He moved north to the Waterberg and onto the north-western edge of the escarpment. Here the group split and Ntshaupe moved east to the Mokopane (Potgietersrus) area where he settled among people of Northern Ndebele descent (Hall 1997). After the power of the Ndebele state had waned, Ntshaupe returned to the ancestral Mosetlha area north of the Magaliesberg. Continuing on this theme, in 1872, during the increasingly oppressive conditions of the ZAR (Transvaal) government based at Pretoria, Chief 'Apie' Makapan, son of Ntshaupe, relocated 5 000 Mosetlha to the southern Waterberg and settled at Mabotse, a steep-sided hill on the farm Buffelshoek (Schoeman 1993; Hall 1997). This settlement stratigraphically overlies a series of earlier 17th-century Rooiberg homesteads as well as a Melora settlement. The 17th-century Rooiberg occupants smelted tin and it is probable that the tin ingot, identified as having been found on Buffelshoek, comes from this settlement. The implication of the Mabotse sequence is that the 19th-century Mosetlha settlement was premised upon a prior knowledge of the hill, which was possibly based upon a direct 17th-century ancestral link. Whatever the case, the

[Handwritten annotation at top: "– movement to new areas, some displays sort of ancestral link, AND a competition for tin making"]

sequence within the Rooiberg Valley potentially indicates competitive relationships over tin exploitation between Tswana (possibly Kgatla lineages) and others with historical roots in the Nguni world. Furthermore, the sequence suggests that competitive exploitation ebbed and flowed in a pulsed manner and was related to markets and political fortunes further afield.

The Kgafela Kgatla left the southern Waterberg because Tsekane was 'unhealthy' (Breutz 1953: 247), and they progressively established themselves from the early 18th century in the Saulspoort region on the north-eastern quarter of the Pilanesberg. Reference to this move is still extant and in some narratives the Tlokwa are also implicated (Grace Masuku, 2004 pers. comm.; Table 4.1). Analysis of some 'copper' earrings from a high-status household in the primary *kgosing* at Marothodi (Tlokwa) proved that they had been made from tin-bronze, suggesting a probable connection to Rooiberg (Hall et al 2006). A combination of this archaeological and historical evidence could indicate that the origins of the Kgafela Kgatla are not obviously from western Tswana. On the other hand, if Uitkomst-like pottery can be securely associated with a core western Tswana lineage such as the Hurutshe, the occurrence of comb-stamped pottery at Kgatla sites need not be ascribed to their sojourn in the Waterberg and interaction with Northern Ndebele speakers.

In summary, the sequence that gives rise to the oral geographies of the later 18th and early 19th centuries is complex. In the early 18th century, another lineage layer is added to this landscape. No mention is made in the oral traditions of people prior to the possible contemporary development of western Sotho-Tswana, south-western Sotho-Tswana, and Nguni-related lineages. It may be significant that the emphasis in the distribution of western Tswana lineages is to the west of the Magaliesberg, while most of the lineages on the northern fringe of the Magaliesberg have Nguni roots. One last, and obvious point about the origins and identity of lineages in the Rustenburg area, is that there is no reason why any one lineage should be classically western Tswana or Nguni. What exactly is the cultural baseline against which the outline of these identities is compared? Viewed in the light of Kopytoff's model of the social and political dynamics of internal African frontiers, the oral and perhaps archaeological ambiguity of 'Fokeng', 'Tlokwa' and perhaps Kgatla is not unexpected. Of particular relevance is the way in which founding charters provide a template for cultural and political variability around a theme, especially where firstcomers and newcomers are concerned (Kopytoff 1987). In this regard, while the oral geographies of these identities in the Rustenburg area provide a structure around which to dig, we need to continually search for subtleties in the archaeology of identity that may reflect the complexity of cultural interactions with more precision than allowed by the oral records.

[Handwritten annotation at bottom: "– Oral history provides a base for further research, – pottery cannot be the only marker – further exploration is needed!"]

The politics of regional production

We now turn to the events of the second half of the 18th and early 19th century. The purpose is to explore some of the oral records and how they may animate the archaeology in relation to the politics of regional production. We focus on two themes. The first reviews relationships between the regional potentials of agricultural production and lineage distribution and conflict. The second is a specific archaeological case study that summarises some of our work at Marothodi, where we are attempting to situate metal production from a relatively shallow synchronic slice of the Tlokwa sequence within the regional politics of the early 19th century (Hall et al 2006).

Agricultural potential and settlement intensification

So far the discussion above suggests that lineage drift from the early 18th century among the Po and the Tlhako was in an east-to-west direction along the northern aspects of the Magaliesberg. The distribution of the Po east of the Fokeng and the Tlhako west of the Tlokwa (Plate 1) indicates that this central region in the Rustenburg was already occupied, and perhaps had been for some time by Fokeng and Tlokwa, and that complex internal frontier processes were at play. The Kwena records suggest that lineage drift was from the lower reaches of the Crocodile River and up into the rumpled landscapes of the Swartruggens region. The independent settlement of Mogopa Kwena lineages, also on the northern aspects of the Magaliesberg between the Po to the west and the Mosetlha Kgatla and Hwaduba to the east and north-east, also suggests processes of accommodation and adjustment. Lastly, the movement of the Kgatla, including perhaps both the Kgafela and the Mosetlha, was from the northern aspects of the Magaliesberg, north towards the southern Waterberg and then southwards to the north-eastern edge of the Pilanesberg sometime early in the 18th century.

Although we are mindful that our relatively small unit of study may falsely exaggerate the pattern of these movements, we suggest that the wider region of the Magaliesberg and the Swartruggens was a highly ranked habitat and, for agriculturists, a desirable area to be established within. The oral records, for example, indicate a convergence and settlement intensification upon the northern aspects of the Magaliesberg in the first half of the 18th century. Archaeological work is required to determine whether the western Tswana emplacement was part of this convergence or whether, as with the Fokeng and Tlokwa, they may have already been on this landscape from earlier in the 17th century. Furthermore, and although it is somewhat mechanistic, some environmental and climatic evidence may also be relevant to this convergence. Palaeoenvironmental evidence suggests that, as part of the Little Ice Age, conditions were significantly cooler and drier in the early 18th century

[handwritten annotation: oral histories/ scientific evidence show climatic conditions played a huge role in the mass movements to Rustenburg]

(Tyson et al 2000). This has been suggested in part, as responsible for the appearance of the Manala and Ndzundza Ndebele lineages in the Pretoria region (Huffman 2004: 95-6). The westward shift from the Pretoria area of the Po and Tlhako may be a continuation of this move.

Deteriorating climatic conditions may also have encouraged the southwards shift of the Kgatla out of the southern Waterberg. Perhaps the reference to the 'unhealthy conditions' encountered at Tsekane is significant here. Furthermore, the records of the Taung of Sefanyetso (Breutz 1953: 160) tell of 'great famine and drought' in the 18th century that prompted a move from south-east of Swartruggens to Khibitswane, which was at the north-eastern end of the Magaliesberg. It may be significant that in the records available for the Fokeng and the Tlokwa, (already resident in the region?), there are no references to climatic stress.

Climatic stress and lineage convergence may mean that the Rustenburg area offered better opportunities for agricultural production than elsewhere in the 18th century, even though populations may have been higher. The agricultural potential of the region clearly was appreciated by 19th-century Boer farmers in the Rustenburg region. A preliminary collation of soil and vegetation in this region (Plate 2) helps make the well-known point, that the high density of archaeological sites in the Magaliesberg and adjacent areas (Mason 1968; Seddon 1968) is a basic reflection of good farming conditions. These conditions lie in a relatively narrow strip of mixed Bushveld varieties that run from east to west along the northern fringe of the Magaliesberg, north-eastwards to the Pilanesberg, and then westwards from Rustenburg, through the Swartruggens and onto the Zeerust region (Mucina & Rutherford 2006). Of importance in this strip, is high ecological diversity within small areas. The soils comprise a mix that includes deep well-drained red loams and dense turf soils, particularly in the Marikana Bushveld and Zeerust Thornveld (Plate 2). These are particularly important for subsistence agriculture because risk can be spread over a variety of soils in anticipation of either drought or too much rainfall. Because of the moisture-retaining qualities of these turf soils, they have the potential to produce a harvest even if rainfall is low and sporadic. *[handwritten annotation: – soil conditions ideal for farming]*

A glimpse of the agricultural potential of the area is provided by Robert Moffat, who, on his way through the Magaliesberg region to Mzilikazi in November 1829, described the area close to Tobong, the deserted town of the Po at Wolhuterskop, as follows (Wallis 1945: 8):

> The country through which we now passed was along a range of hills
> running nearly east-south-east, while the country to the north and east
> became more plain, beautifully studded with small chains of mountains and

conical hills, along the bases of which lay the ruins of innumerable towns, some of amazing extent. The plains and valleys, of the richest soil to a great depth, had once waved with native millet and been covered with pumpkins, water melons, kidney beans and sweet reed, all of which are cultivated through the interior. The ruined towns exhibited signs of immense labour and perseverance, every fence being composed of stones, averaging five or six feet high, raised apparently without either mortar, lime, or hammer. Everything is circular, from the inner fences which surround each house to the walls which sometimes encompass the town.

Elsewhere Moffat remarked that '[e]very species of vegetation was exceedingly luxuriant and immense quantities of native corn grew wild among the ruins of the towns, and which had grown successively from year to year since the destruction of those granaries of the land' (Wallis 1945: 11). It is noteworthy that Moffat did not mention maize. If it was already included in cereal production in the 18th century (see Huffman 2006), an intensifying focus on these turf soils might make even more sense because maize is less resilient than sorghum and millet in terms of its moisture needs. However, no conclusive archaeological evidence has as yet been uncovered in this regard. Contemporary documentary records suggest that maize was not cultivated on any substantial scale by the large western and south-western Tswana chiefdoms, such as the Tlhaping, the Rolong and the Hurutshe, before the upheavals of the Difaqane in the 1820s (see Boeyens 2003 for a discussion of the literature). Early travellers in the Rustenburg region, such as Andrew Smith (1836), claimed that the cultivation of maize was introduced to the Tswana with the invasion of Mzilikazi's Ndebele into the trans-Vaal region.

The norite koppies of the Marikana Bushveld, the hills of the Magaliesberg, the Pilanesberg and the considerable variety of slope and aspect in the Swartruggens Mountain Bushveld provide a rich mix of woody, herbaceous and grass layers. In contrast, north of this strip (Sandy Bushveld and Dwaalboom Thornveld), ecological diversity drops. Dense turf soils, for example, are widespread in the Dwaalboom Thornveld, but plant biomass and plant productivity on these are low (Mucina & Rutherford 2006: 460). To the south, the ecological boundary between the Bushveld and the sour grasslands of the Highveld is particularly sharp (Plate 1). While these grasslands offer seasonal, summer grazing, their potential for crop production is limited.

In summary, the agricultural productivity of this Bushveld strip is entirely congruent with the high archaeological visibility of settlements there through the Late Iron Age. The oral records hint that the area may have come under increasing pressure in the first half of the 18th century. The records from the second half of the 18th century and the early 19th century make this pressure and competition explicit although other factors are also important (Manson 1995, Parsons 1995).

A closer look at the fortunes of some of the Rustenburg chiefdoms during the later 18th and early 19th century draws attention to spiralling conflict, succession disputes, and competition between lineages in which the politics of food security must have been important. The Kwena lineages west of the Magaliesberg, for example, seemed to have wielded regional political power based upon a prime location along the wide drainage of the Selons (Ngwaritse) River Valley and its tributaries (Plate 1). Although crude, Seddon's map (1968: 192) identifies by far the greater number of large, aggregated settlements here, and these include Molokwane and Boitsemagano. These must have depended upon a productive agricultural base and, furthermore, the political power to control it. This power is indeed evident in the longevity of the Mmatau section of the Modimosana Kwena and, in particular, in the chieftaincy of Kgaswane (Breutz 1953; Pistorius 1992) a forceful leader who ruled for a long period in the second half of the 18th century and up until the Difaqane disruptions of the 1820s. As noted above, the success of Kgaswane's rule, which must have included the ability to provide for and, in turn, attract people, must correlate with the process of aggregation that resulted in the final form of Molokwane in the 1820s. This regional presence may also be indicated by the oral records of the Mmatau (McDonald 1940 in Breutz 1953: 110; see also Pistorius 1992: 12), where it is recalled that Kgaswane had seven sub-chiefs under him whose followers were known as the Makgongwana, Ramaditswe's Marope, Masetlha, Maaka, Mobana, Mmanamaana and Manamela. It may also be significant that once established at Molokwane (late 17th or early 18th century?), they did not move, although the settlement underwent considerable transformation. While it may be that some names, such as Molokwane, initially refer more to an area or a number of settlements than one in particular, the fixity of the Mmatau seat of power contrasts with the number of settlement relocations made by other lineages on the northern aspect of the Magaliesberg over the same period (Morton 2003; see Table 4.1). As indicated, the permanence of Molokwane may be attributable to a combination of a prime agricultural position and political power.

Although the Modimosana Kwena succumbed to Mzilikazi and his Ndebele in the 1820s, the oral record does not describe much regional conflict between them and other lineages (Breutz 1953). Prior to the incursions of Pedi raiding in the early 19th century, however, there are references to succession quarrels within the Ramanamela section. In this dispute the Taung from Khibitswane support Powe against his son Tshukudu as well as against the Mmatau, and they are rewarded with a portion of Boitsemagano (the

Taung name is Mmamogowe, Table 4.1). The only other references are to conflict with Sekete of the Fokeng. Indeed, at the end of the 18th century and early in the 19th, it is the Fokeng who are at the centre of numerous conflicts. They are under assault from all sides, a situation exacerbated by their own internal succession disputes. The Fokeng are physically hemmed in by the Kwena to the south, the Tlokwa and Kgatla to the north and the Po to the east. During the contested reigns of Thethe, Nameng and Noge, they are in conflict with the Po over cattle, and several fights are recorded on their borders. The Po relocation to Tobong (Wolhuterskop), late in the 18th century during the reign of the chief Moerane, may be a response to this conflict. The Po, in turn, are in conflict with the Mogopa to the east over land and cattle, while More of the Mogopa is in conflict with Mosetlha Kgatla to the east. Nearer the 1820s, the Mogopa seem to bear the brunt of raiding by Kgatla, Hwaduba, Moletlane, Mako and Seabe, all allies of Pedi expansion from the east. The directionality of this conflict is predominantly in an east/west direction. The agricultural productivity of this strip may therefore have encouraged both political success and the seeds of competitive conflict. As Manson (1995) has suggested, these conflicts relate to struggles over the maintenance of economic independence.

In all of this later 18th- and early 19th-century strife, there seems to be little in the record of alliance and betrayal that encourages the view that conflict was structured around deeper histories of cultural and political affiliation, unlike the possible ancestral links to the Waterberg suggested above for the Kgatla. Though such choices might also reflect long-lived historical connections, there seems to be little pattern in where defeated chiefs, uncles and sons fled when their bids for power failed. Equally, the records do not offer much information on repeated transactions of affiliation between chiefdoms in terms of wife-givers and wife-takers. These issues may become more resolved with closer analysis.

Metal production and political power at Marothodi

There is one alliance, however, that does have a significant historical profile from the later stages of the 18th century. This alliance is between the Tlokwa and the Kgafela Kgatla and it may also be constructed on older ancestral ties. Both of these lineages resided on the northern edge of the Fokeng, and it is against the Fokeng that this alliance was successfully directed. This historical context provides a framework within which to animate and link particular emphases in economic production gleaned from the archaeology to regional political power. Consequently, in the last section of this essay we briefly summarise our work at the early 19th-century Tlokwa capital of Marothodi and suggest some ideas that stem from a mutually reinforcing combination of historical and archaeological evidence (Hall et al 2006).

When the Kgafela Kgatla first established themselves in the areas immediately north and east of the Pilanesberg in the early 18th century they were newcomers on the landscape. The Tlhako were already there as were the Tlokwa on the southern side of the Pilanesberg. As newcomers, the Kgatla initially paid tribute to the Tlhako and initiation schools were only held with Tlhako permission (Breutz 1953: 252). Ultimately, the Kgatla reversed this situation and assumed political control. Up until the early 19th century they had successfully expanded control over territory and incorporated other communities into their political orbit (Manson 1995), but thereafter, political infighting brought on a period of chaos. Before this decline, however, the oral records make it clear that there was a festering conflict between the Tlokwa and the Fokeng sometime between 1780 and 1810 (see Manson 1995). The Elands River is mentioned in these records as a boundary between the Tlokwa and the Fokeng, and Fokeng aggression occurs across it, with specific reference to threats over the destruction of crops. This further emphasises that the events of the later 18th and early 19th centuries are partly based on the politics of food production. Importantly, the records also recall that with the help of Kgatla allies the Tlokwa eventually prevailed and that the Fokeng chief Sekete was killed (Breutz 1953).

The significance of this is that towards the end of this conflict, but most likely after Tlokwa success, the Tlokwa established their capital at Marothodi, perhaps a little before 1810 (Fig. 4.1, Table 4.1). Other records (Ellenberger 1939) indicate that skirmishes continued with the Fokeng during the occupation of Marothodi. Whatever the case, and from what we know of Tlokwa settlements earlier in the regional sequence, the scale of Marothodi is unprecedented. On the basis of its size, Marothodi is a major centre in the region. There is no question that the location of some of the aggregated settlements during this period was based upon defence (Huffman 1986), and this explains the hilltop location of a large town such as Kaditshwene (Boeyens 2000, 2003). However, this principle cannot be generalised. While Marothodi, by virtue of its size, may have been defensive, the actual location is undefendable because it is situated on exposed flats between Pilwe Hill in the east and the Matlapengsberg in the west (Figs 4.1 & 4.2). The historical context suggests that the Tlokwa, along with their Kgatla allies, were politically ascendant after subduing the Fokeng. The confident location of Marothodi out on the flats expresses this. Furthermore, the town is dominated by two large *kgosing* (chiefly divisions) and extremely large cattle enclosures, which also indicate power and wealth (Fig. 4.3). These *kgosing* may mark a turnover in political succession from Bogatsu to his son Kgosi, who ruled up to the establishment of the Ndebele state (Breutz 1953; Ellenberger 1939).

This size and wealth indicated by the extensive cattle enclosures at Marothodi can also be linked to another standout archaeological feature of the town, namely the significant

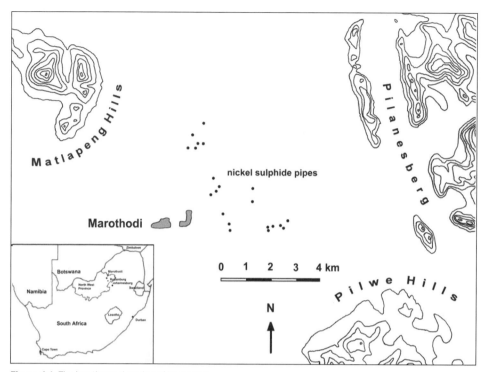

Figure 4.1 The location and setting of Marothodi.

scale of both copper and iron production (Fig. 4.3). Copper production seems to dominate because of the presence of a large number of copper-working areas or annexes that are attached to the back courtyard walls of individual households (Hall et al 2006) (Fig. 4.4). Some homesteads at Marothodi have upward of six of these annexes. The scale of both copper and iron working at Marothodi suggests to us that production was deliberately geared to generating a surplus and that this was so from the inception of the town. Furthermore, the scale of metal production at Marothodi is, as far as we can ascertain, unprecedented in this region. Establishing and affirming its contextual scale is an important future project. Despite the emphasis on iron forges at one Mabjanamatshwana homestead (Pistorius & Steyn 1995), we are not given any indication of the scale or, indeed, the presence of primary smelting activity in and around this complex of settlements. It would also be important to have similar, comparative data from the extensive Mmakau Kgatla complex at Hoekfontein (Küsel & Pelser 2007).

Furthermore, the specific location of Marothodi is also relevant in relation to the copper ore source. This comes from a swarm of nickel-copper sulphide pipes 2 km to the east of the town (Fig. 4.1). While settlement location is always a compromise between various factors, and agricultural potential is obviously an important one, no single area south of

Figure 4.2 View of the second *kgosing* (SU-2) at Marothodi looking west towards the Matlapensberg.

the Pilanesberg confers any particular agricultural advantage (Plate 2). We suggest that high-intensity metal-working at Marothodi was therefore a significant factor in settlement choice and that close proximity to the copper mines perhaps also expresses the regional power and regional advantage to control this resource. This again accords well with the historical context.

Though production and the potential exchange of copper and iron may have been under the control of individual homesteads or even households, the historical context indicates that the Tlokwa chieftaincy had the political power to facilitate this. Iron and copper production that was surplus to local consumption obviously begs the question as to its destination. At this stage we have very little idea, but a combination of historical context and archaeology elsewhere generates several alternatives that can be tested in

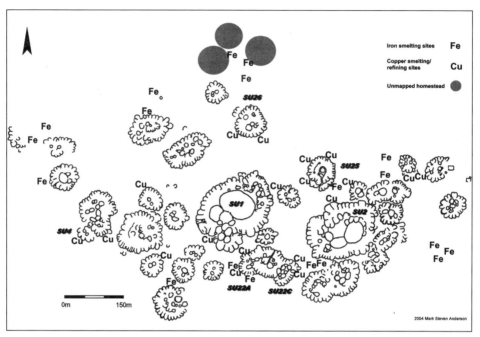

Figure 4.3 Map of the central section of Marothodi.

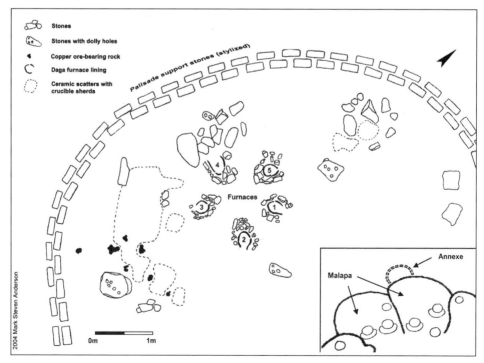

Figure 4.4 Copper crucible furnaces in an enclosure attached to the back courtyard of SU2.

future research. It is fortunate that fingerprinting copper back to Marothodi is imminently feasible given that the nickel content in Marothodi copper is distinctive and high (Hall et al 2006). On the basis of the historical context one might predict that Marothodi copper may have only circulated within the wider Tlokwa, Kgatla and Tlhako world north of the Elands River. Alternatively, distribution could have been much wider. In this regard copper artefacts recovered from Molokwane would be particularly interesting targets for analysis. This is because there is no evidence of any primary metal production from the excavations at Molokwane (Pistorius 1992) and from further extensive survey at this town. This may simply mean that Kgaswane between 1770 and the 1820s, for example, had the power to command metal from within his own political orbit. Alternatively, metal may have been flowing to Molokwane from several sources and Marothodi might be one of those (see also Pistorius & Steyn 1995). It seems that exchange of goods was almost, if not entirely, transacted with 'traditional' commodities. Very few glass trade beads, for example, have been recovered from Marothodi or from other large towns in the Rustenburg region. While these beads clearly place Tswana society within a broad zone of colonial interaction, this presence is only at some distance. Most evidence for trade in this period is regional and within Tswana society. Marothodi, for example, was also a receiver of metal because tin-bronze earrings that have no local trace element fingerprint have been recovered. The earlier discussion of Kgatla historical links with the tin-producing areas of Rooiberg and Leeuwpoort to the north may be relevant here.

We make one last point from the Marothodi case study. While the Marothodi example attempts to interpret distinctive archaeological residues within a regional historical context, we must not lose sight of the way in which metal production, for example, was structured by cultural values, irrespective of changes in the scale of production and the intensity of demands. There is, for example, a sharp contrast between the location of iron- and copper-smelting sites at Marothodi. This can be explained by the gendered nature of iron (male) and copper (female) and by the fact that the structure of metal production is culturally informed by the parallel biological and social careers of men and women. Iron-smelting precincts, for example, are consistently separated from homesteads at Marothodi, albeit sometimes by distances of only 15 to 20 metres. Outer walls enclose and seclude whole smelting precincts while individual iron furnaces within these precincts have a further surrounding wall. This is consistent with the principle that transformations are dangerous and that taboos for such transformations are required for their successful outcome. One such taboo is the seclusion of (and female exclusion from) male-centred transformations, in this case, the site of primary iron smelting (see Ellenberger 1937-8: 44). This absolute principle of spatial removal and seclusion evident in the iron-smelting precincts at

Marothodi contrasts with the location of primary copper-smelting and -working areas. These are directly attached to the back courtyard walls of individual households (Figs 4.3 & 4.4). This is significant because this is domestic space and, more specifically, it is the female-centred work area.

The very explicit spatial separation of iron and copper production at Marothodi is structurally inseparable from the general careers of men and women and, more specifically, finds a direct parallel in the spatial structure of male and female initiation (see Hall et al 2006). Male initiation (*bogwera bo bosweu* – white *bogwera*) was held in a secluded lodge deep in the bush in contrast to female initiation (*bojale*), which was conducted in conjunction with the homestead (see Comaroff 1985: 95 ff; Schapera 1970: 106, 116). Furthermore, the physical and social transformation that is wrought upon boys in the seclusion of the bush and lodge contrasts markedly with the spatial focus of a second stage of male initiation (*bogwera bo bontsho* – black *bogwera*), which was conducted in the great cattle enclosure in the chief's homestead that was adjacent to the court. Once again, there is a structural parallel with iron production because the iron forges are to be found in these central male areas (Pistorius & Steyn 1995), and it is at the forge that the transformed metal completes the process of full 'socialisation' through the shaping of a functioning tool. In contrast, there is only one stage in female initiation, and while there are both primary copper-smelting furnaces and secondary crucible furnaces at Marothodi, they are both located in the same back precincts. A 16th-century Madikwe household also had a copper furnace behind the house (Huffman et al 1996; Hall 2000), and it seems that the values structuring the spatiality of both iron and copper production were long-lived and resilient.

Despite the favourable political circumstances early in the 19th century that put the Tlokwa in a position to control and optimally exploit local ore sources, such opportunities did not override or change the organisation of metal production or limit surplus production at Marothodi, which clearly was structured by the larger cultural system. Interpretation of this production would itself be limited, if in our pursuit of correlations between political and strategic logic and, for example, particular settlement patterns or emphases in commodity production, we lost sight of the cultural logic that structured commodity production.

Conclusion

In summary, we have highlighted some practical issues that we consider important for the future development of these themes. First, while oral and archaeological sequences are obviously chronological, our ability to be more precise is hampered by limitations in both. There are fluctuations in the atmospheric levels of radiocarbon over the last 300 years that reduce the security of dates, and the precision required to really animate the archaeology is lost. Alternative methods such as Optically Stimulated Luminescence (OSL) dating are being explored. Preliminary results generated by Dana Drake Rosenstein (2008), at the control sites of Marothodi, Olifantspoort and Kaditshwene, show some remarkable precision. The method, however, is time-consuming and expensive but her results indicate that OSL is well worth pursuing.

Second, is that the oral records provide a fundamental and important structuring device that, at face value, clearly provide a means of articulating the archaeological and historical scale. The geography of identity and knowing the location of named settlements is a powerful tool for framing and testing more fine-grained archaeological and historical questions. The oral geographies of specific lineages provide a reference around, and through which we can 'dig'. Even if we are sceptical about the veracity of these records in terms of holding identity constant, the archaeology obviously has a controlling role here and contradictions are also potentially powerful as historical statements.

Lastly, digging through sequences of lineage identity provided by oral geographies allows us to compare material signals at several steps in that sequence and, through this comparison, identify scales of change, specific economic emphases, significant changes that may then be compared with regional historical context. Furthermore, the example from Marothodi discussed above, is only one observation through the Tlokwa sequence. To make the Marothodi data really relevant at the historical scale will require that we have equivalent observations from Tlokwa settlements that are both younger and older in the sequence. Once again the oral geographies provide the structure to do this. Identifying sequences that hold the most promise and reward for effort must be a truly collaborative project.

References

Boeyens, J.C.A. 2000. In search of Kaditshwene. *South African Archaeological Bulletin* 55: 3-17.

Boeyens, J.C.A. 2003. The Late Iron Age sequence in the Marico and early Tswana history. *South African Archaeological Bulletin* 58: 63-78.

Breutz, P.L. 1953. *The tribes of the Rustenburg and Pilanesberg Districts*. Department of Native Affairs, Ethnological Publication No. 28.

Campbell, J. 1822. *Travels in South Africa... Being a Narrative of a Second Journey (1820)*. Two vols. London: Westley.

Comaroff, J. 1985. *Body of Power, Spirit of Resistance.*, Chicago: University of Chicago Press.

Deetz, J. 1988. American historical archaeology: methods and results. *Science* 239: 362-367.

Ellenberger, V. 1937-38. History of the Ba-ga-Malete of Ramoutsa (Bechuanaland Protectorate). *Transactions of the Royal Society of South Africa* 25(1): 1-72.

Ellenberger, V. 1939. History of the Batlokwa of Gaberones (Bechuanaland Protectorate). *African Studies* 13(3): 165-198.

Friede, H.M. & Steel, R.H. 1976. Tin mining and smelting in the Transvaal during the Iron Age. *Journal of Southern African Institute for Mining and Metallurgy* 74: 461-470.

Grant, M.R. 1990. A radiocarbon date on a tin artefact from Rooiberg. *Southern African Journal of Science* 86: 63.

Grant, M.R., Huffman, T.N. & Watterson, J.I.W. 1994. The role of copper smelting in the pre-colonial exploitation of the Rooiberg tin field. *South African Journal of Science* 90: 85-90.

Hall, S. 1981. Iron Age sequence and settlement in the Rooiberg, Thabazimbi area. MA thesis. Johannesburg: University of the Witwatersrand.

Hall, S. 1985. Excavations at Rooikrans and Rhenosterkloof, Late Iron Age sites in the Rooiberg area of the Transvaal. *Annals of the Cape Provincial Museums* 1: 131-210.

Hall, S. 1995. Archaeological indicators for stress in the Western Transvaal region between the seventeenth and nineteenth centuries. In: Hamilton, C. (ed.) *The Mfecane Aftermath: Reconstructive Debates in Southern African History:* 307-321. Johannesburg and Pietermaritzburg: Witwatersrand University Press and University of Natal Press.

Hall, S. 1997. Material culture and gender correlations: the view from Mabotse in the later nineteenth century. In: Wadley, L. (ed.) *Our Gendered Past: Archaeological Studies of Gender in Southern Africa*: 209-219. Johannesburg: Witwatersrand University Press.

Hall, S. 1998. A consideration of gender relations in the Late Iron Age 'Sotho' sequence of the Western Highveld, South Africa. In: Kent, S. (ed.) *Gender in African Prehistory*: 235-258. Walnut Creek, London, New Delhi: Altamira Press.

Hall, S. 2000. Forager lithics and Early Moloko homesteads at Madikwe. *Natal Museum Journal of Humanities.* 12: 33-55.

Hall, S. & Grant, M. 1995. Indigenous ceramic production in the context of the colonial frontier in the Transvaal, South Africa. In: Vincenzini, P. (ed.) *Proceedings of the 8th CIMTEC: The Ceramics Cultural Heritage*: 465-473. : Faenza: Techna srl.

Hall, S., Miller, D., Anderson, M. & Boeyens, J. 2006. An exploratory study of copper and iron production at Marothodi, an early 19th century Tswana town, Rustenburg district, South Africa. *Journal of African Archaeology* 4(1): 3-35.

Hall, S., Killick, D., Chirikure, S. & Rosenstein, D.D. 2007. Excavations at Smelterskop: the 2006 and 2007 seasons. Report on file, Department of Archaeology, University of Cape Town.

Huffman, T.N. 1986. Archaeological evidence and conventional explanations of southern Bantu settlement patterns. *Africa* 56(3): 280-298.

Huffman, T.N. 1990. The Waterberg research of Jan Aukema. *South African Archaeological Bulletin* 45-61-70.

Huffman, T.N. 2002. Regionality in the Iron Age: The case of the Sotho-Tswana. *Southern African Humanities* 14: 1-22.

Huffman, T.N. 2004. The archaeology of the Nguni past. *Southern African Humanities* 16: 79-111.

Huffman, T.N. 2006. Maize grindstones, Madikwe pottery and ochre mining in pre-colonial South Africa. *Southern African Humanities* 18: 51-70.

Huffman, T.N. 2007. The last 500 years in the Trans-Vaal. Paper presented at the 500 year initiative conference, University of the Witwatersrand.

Huffman, T.N., Calabrese, J.A., Grant, M.R. & Lathy, G.C.I. 1996. Archaeological survey of Madikwe Game Reserve, North-West Province. Johannesburg, Archaeological Resources Management.

Kopytoff, I. 1987. The internal African frontier: the making of African political culture. In: Kopytoff, I. (ed.) *The African Frontier: the Reproduction of Traditional African Societies*: 3-84. Bloomington: Indiana University Press.

Küsel, U. & Pelser, A. 2007. The reconstruction of the 19th century Tswana settlement site at Mmakau near Brits. Paper presented at the 500 year initiative conference. University of Cape Town.

Legassick, M. 1969. The Sotho-Tswana peoples before 1800. In: Thompson, L. (ed.) *African Societies in Southern Africa*: 86-125. London: Heinemann.

Maggs, T. 1976. *Iron Age Communities of the Southern Highveld*. Pietermaritzburg: Natal Museum.

Manson, A. 1995. Conflict in the Western Highveld/Southern Kalahari, c. 1750-1820. In: Hamilton, C. (ed.)

The Mfecane Aftermath: Reconstructive Debates in Southern African History: 351-361. Johannesburg and Pietermaritzburg: Witwatersrand University Press and University of Natal Press.

Mason, R. 1968. Iron Age settlement in the Transvaal and Natal revealed by aerial photography and excavation. *African Studies* 27: 181-188.

Mason, R. 1986. *Origins of Black People of Johannesburg and the Southern Western Central Transvaal AD 350-1880*. Occasional Paper No. 16. Johannesburg: University of Witwatersrand Press.

Morton, F. 2003. Perpetual motion: resettlement patterns in the western Transvaal and southeastern Botswana since 1750. *Historia* 48(1): 265-282.

Mucina, L. & Rutherford, C. (eds) 2006. The vegetation of South Africa, Lesotho and Swaziland. *Strelitzia* 19. South African National Biodiversity Institute, Pretoria.

Parsons, N. 1995. Prelude to the difaqane in the interior of southern Africa c. 1600-c. 1822. In: Hamilton C. (ed.) *The Mfecane Aftermath: Reconstructive Debates in Southern African History*: 322-349. Johannesburg and Pietermaritzburg: Witwatersrand University Press and University of Natal Press.

Pistorius, J.C.C. 1984. 'n Etno-argeologiese interpretasie van 'n Sotho-Tswana vestigingseenheid op Selonskraal. MA thesis. Pretoria: University of Pretoria.

Pistorius, J.C.C. 1992. *Molokwane, an Iron Age Bakwena Village: Early Tswana Settlement in the Western Transvaal*. Johannesburg: Perskor Printers.

Pistorius, J.C.C. 1997c. Diachronic evidence from the kgosing of Molokwane. *South African Journal of Ethnology* 20(3): 118-132.

Pistorius, J.C.C. & Steyn, M. 1995. Iron working and burial practices amongst the Kgatla-Kwena of the Mabyanamatshwaana complex. *Southern African Field Archaeology* 4: 68-77.

Rasmussen, K. 1978. *Migrant Kingdom: Mzilikazi's Ndebele in South Africa*. London: Rex Collings.

Rosenstein, D. 2008. Sorting out ceramics: correlating change in the technology of ceramic production with the cronology of 18th and early 19th century western BaTswana towns. Unpublished MSc thesis. Cape Town: University of Cape Town.

Schapera, I. 1970. *A handbook of Tswana law and custom*. London: Frank Cass.

Schapera, I. 1980. *A history of the BaKgatla-bagaKgafêla*. Mochudi: Phuthadikobo Museum.

Schoeman, M.H. 1993. A contribution to the ethnohistory of the Mosêthla Kgatla. Unpublished Honours Project. Johannesburg: University of the Witwatersrand.

Seddon, J.D. 1968. An aerial survey of settlement and living patterns in the Transvaal Iron Age: preliminary report. *African Studies* 27(4): 189-194.

Smith A. 1836. Unpublished historical notes on Tswana, Sotho and Matabele Tribes. volume 12. Cape Town: South African Museum Library.

Taylor, M.O.V. 1979. Late Iron Age settlement on the northern edge of the Vredefort Dome. MA thesis. Johannesburg: University of the Witwatersrand.

Tyson, P.D., Lee-Thorp, J., Holmgren, K. & Heiss, G. 2000. The little Ice Age and medieval warming in South Africa. *South African Journal of Science* 96: 121-126.

Van Hoepen, E.C.N. & Hoffman, A.C. 1935. Die oorblyfsels van Buispoort en Braklaagte, noordwes van Zeerust. *Argeologiese Navorsing van die Nasionale Museum, Bloemfontein* 2: 1-24.

Vogel, J.C. 1971. Radiocarbon in nature. *South African Journal of Science* 67(2): 32-42.

Wallis, J.P.R. (ed.) 1945. *The Matabele Journals of Robert Moffat, 1829–1860*. volume. 1. London: Chatto & Windus.

5

Metals beyond frontiers: exploring the production, distribution and use of metals in the Free State grasslands, South Africa

Shadreck Chirikure, Simon Hall and Tim Maggs

Introduction

The grasslands of the Free State area (Fig. 5.1) are part of the southern Highveld of South Africa. This region is mainly composed of an elevated grassy plain which inclines smoothly from an elevation of 1 200 metres in the west to over 1 800 metres along its eastern margin (Wilson & Anhaeusser 1998; Maggs 1976; Mucina & Rutherford 2006). The area is roughly delimited by prominent natural features: the Vaal River on the northern and western frontiers, the Drakensberg escarpment at the eastern boundary, with the Caledon Valley and its confluence with the Orange River forming the southern limit (Maggs 1976, 1980). Historical and archaeological work has revealed that various peoples continuously occupied this area in the last 500 years (Arbousset & Daumas 1852; Breutz 1953; Legassick 1969; Maggs 1976; Huffman 2002). Their activities on the landscape left behind clearly defined settlements and items of material culture which enable the reconstruction of their life ways and time of initial occupation in this area (see Maggs 1976).

So far, the archaeology indicates that the first Iron Age groups settled in this region around the 15th century. Maggs (1976) suggested that these early settlers may have been ancestors of the Sotho-Tswana who radiated from the so-called Bankenveld axis. Recent thinking has, however, added another dimension. Huffman (2007), for instance, has argued for a Nguni identity for the so-called Fokeng peoples. Whatever the case may be, it is clear that this region was an open frontier through which different groups trickled in and out of over time (Maggs 1976; Huffman 2007). This set the stage for the interaction of groups such as the Sotho-Tswana, Nguni, and hunter-gatherers living on the south-western margins.

When compared to the northern Highveld and the KwaZulu-Natal area, the southern Highveld and in particular the grasslands of the Free State were occupied at a fairly late stage by Iron Age farmers (Huffman 2007; Boeyens 2003; Maggs 1976, 1980). The former have long sequences of Iron Age occupation dating back to the first millennium AD

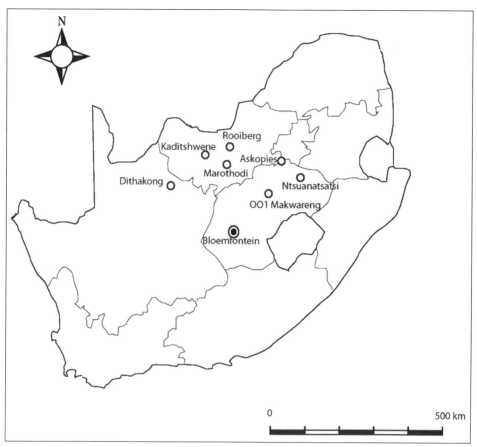

Figure 5.1 Map of South Africa showing the Free State region and some of the sites mentioned in the text.

Figure 5.2 Photograph of ethnographic collection of dung ready for use as fuel in domestic contexts. Courtesy of Tim Maggs.

whereas the initial occupation of the Free State grasslands did not take place until the 15th century (Maggs 1976). This is hardly surprising because the southern Highveld is devoid of the resources which were critical in sustaining a typical Iron Age way of life. However, the increase in human occupation after this period suggests that human beings had developed ways of coping with scarcity and/or austerity. The use of dung as fuel for cooking in the houses (Fig 5.2) presents a telling example of this adaptation to local circumstances.

If the conditions in the Free State grasslands were not ideal for an Iron Age way of life before, how did these societies sustain themselves after? The archaeological and historical evidence for the last 500 years demonstrates that agriculture, trading, herding and hunting were important subsistence and economic pursuits (Maggs 1976; Legassick 1969). The soils, mainly belonging to the Highveld prairie type, were well suited for the purposes of crop agriculture, and these were matched by optimum rainfall (Mucina & Rutherford 2006). This introduces another interesting dimension because, for the soils to be cultivated, metal tools such as iron hoes were essential requirements to the farming communities. Of course, both utilitarian and ornamental metal objects have been archaeologically recovered from the Free State grasslands (Figs 5.3 & 5.4) (Maggs 1976, 1980). Nevertheless, this markedly contrasts with an almost total absence of primary metals production debris in the area. In other parts of southern Africa such as the Bankenveld, Late Iron Age sites are replete with metal smelting debris and finished objects (Hall et al 2006). This invites an audit of the evidence of metalworking and use in our area in order to develop a broad picture.

Archaeology and the evidence of metalworking in the grasslands of the southern Highveld

This section mainly derives from the work carried out by Maggs (1976). It summarises what is known about metalworking from his excavations at sites dotted across the Free State. Quite significantly, Maggs excavated the site of Ntsuanatsatsi (OU 1) (Fig. 5.1) located in the middle of the grassland region. It was occupied by up to 1 000 people during its peak (Maggs 1972, 1976). With this large population, what is the evidence of metalworking and use from this site? According to Maggs (1976), only iron items complete the inventory of metalwork; there are no copper or iron ornamental objects. The most outstanding find was a broad spear which is large in size, when compared to ethnologically documented Sotho spears. If Huffman is correct in his Fokeng Nguni origin hypothesis, then this artefact may have originated from KwaZulu-Natal. Typological and metallurgical studies that can link the object to potential areas of origin, be it KwaZulu-Natal or the Bankenveld Axis, would be needed to further substantiate such a conclusion. Other finds include a small flat-bladed spear and badly corroded iron rods. Additionally and importantly, no remains

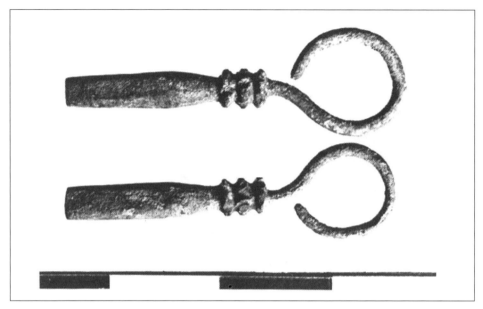

Figure 5.3 Photograph of earrings from OO1 Makwareng site. Courtesy of Tim Maggs.

of ore, slag, furnaces and other primary production remains were found at the site (Maggs 1976: 158).

The multi-component site of OU 2 located on the extreme north-eastern margins of the Free State in Vrede District also produced metal finds (Maggs 1976). This site consists of Type N and V occupations. Iron appears in low frequencies at the Type N section where its use was restricted to utilitarian objects. Only one iron ornament was recovered with no copper items. The limited amount of metal ornaments is also matched by a paucity of other ornamental objects such as glass beads (Maggs 1976: 173). Bone tools appear in fair amounts suggesting a substitution of iron with bone for light duty operations. The Type V section at OU 2 yielded abundant pottery but few items of metalwork. The iron objects consisted of a possible knife blade and a possible tang of a hoe. Again, copper and iron ornamentation seems to be scarce, suggesting austerity and/or scarcity. As with OU 1, no primary production evidence was recovered.

Excavations at the Type V site of OO 1 (Makwareng), located in the Lindley District of the Free State, produced a wide range of metalworking evidence (Maggs 1976). A hoard of iron bangles, hoes, and a sizeable amount of iron bars, possible tangs, adzes, axes, spears and knife blades form part of the assemblage of metal tools recovered. Additional objects include arrow heads, spatulate items, razors, awls, and iron rods sharpened on one end. More interestingly, there is a fair amount of copper working evidence. Wire drawing plates, sandstone crucibles and a casting spill suggest that copper was worked at the site. Copper

Figure 5.4 Photograph of iron hoes from OO1 Makwareng site. Courtesy of Tim Maggs.

ornaments, namely bangles, beads and earrings, complete the list of items retrieved from the excavations. In addition, a few imported metal items such as brass buttons were also found; these may post-date the site. As Maggs (1976) noted, OO 1 falls within the treeless zone where supplies of wood for making charcoal were minimal and yet metal objects were abundant (see Fig. 5.1). In fact almost no charcoal was recovered as dung was the only available fuel. In principle, dung can be used as a fuel in metallurgical operations; archaeologists in Botswana have recovered biomass slag, which, superficially, has close affinities with metallurgical slags (Thy et al 1995; Peter 2001; Jacobson et al 2003; Miller & Killick 2004). This possibility is ruled out, however, on the basis of a lack of smelting evidence in the form of slag and related suites of materials. Also, the dung would have added phosphorus to the smelt, an element which was undesirable because it made metals brittle. Therefore, the big question is where were these metal items coming from? Only provenance studies can throw some light on this issue. The recovery of significant quantities of glass beads shows that this site was well linked with the outside world.

Another site which yielded evidence of metalworking is the site of OND 3, Tihela – which represents the southernmost extent of Type V. Although the excavations were too small, iron and copper objects similar to those recovered from OO 1 were found. These include an iron bead and corroded iron objects. Several small sheets of copper and two short pieces of 4 mm diameter wire make up the list of copper objects. Also, several imported buttons made of copper alloys such as brass were found. The recovered glass beads would place this site in the early 19th century and thus considerably later than OO 1.

Archaeological work carried out at the Type Z site of OXF 1 revealed a ceramic industry remarkably different from that recovered at other sites in the eastern Free State area. The ceramics have more parallels with those recovered at Dithakong and differed in many respects from that recovered from Type V sites (Maggs 1976). However, like most sites excavated in the grasslands, metalwork was present in only modest quantities, consisting of a ring of copper wire. No evidence of slag and other pyrotechnological debris was recovered. This paucity of metal objects was balanced by the abundance of bone tools and implements. This tendency to substitute bone for metal in light duty operations was also attested at the Caledon Valley sites. For instance, site OND 2 only yielded a large assemblage of bone tools with no metal items.

Because the occupants of our communities were farmers, metal objects feature prominently in some grassland communities of the southern Highveld. This is somewhat adversative given the dearth of primary metal production evidence and implicates imports as the source of metal used. Obviously, grasslands are by their nature treeless but what is the availability of other raw materials for metal smelting in our area? This requires a discussion of the geology and vegetation of the grasslands with a view to understanding whether the environment could sustain metal smelting on a significant scale.

Geology, vegetation and the possibility of metal-smelting industries in the Free State grasslands

Geologically speaking, the bulk of the southern Highveld with very little exemption is covered by the sedimentary rocks of the Karoo Super group (Wilson & Anhausser 1998; Mucina & Rutherford 2006). The notable exceptions include the very geologically complex Vredefort Dome in the north and petite outcrops of the Ventersdorp System in the west (Wilson & Anhausser 1998; Maggs 1976). Therefore, what is the known distribution of iron and copper ores in South Africa in general and the Free State grasslands in particular? This is important because local geological conditions may have strongly influenced Iron Age settlement in the past as well as promoting trade and exchange relationships between areas with abundant ore resources and those without (Evers 1974; Hall 1912; Haddon 1908; Junod 1908; Mamadi 1940; Maggs 1976; Huffman 2007; Chirikure 2007).

With a crustal average of nearly five percent by mass, iron is easily one of the most abundant elements in the earth's crust and as such has contributed significantly to human cultural development (Astrup, Hammerbeck & Van den Berg, 1998; Wilson 1998). In South Africa, the examples of the most common iron ores are magnetite (Fe_3O_4), haematite (Fe_2O_3), and goethite (a-$Fe^{3+}O(OH)$). Frequently, quartz, feldspar, calcite, dolomite clays and carbonaceous materials appear as accessory minerals in iron ores (Astrup, Hammerbeck &

Van den Berg 1998). The winning of metallic iron from its ores produces a malleable metal, remarkable for its strong physical properties such as hardness, strength, ductility, and to some extent durability. This, no doubt, is why the metal was highly valued in prehistory (Miller 1995).

Despite the wide distribution of iron ores, the grassland area of the Free State area is devoid of significant iron ore mineralisations (Astrup, Hammerbeck & Van den Berg 1998; Breutz 1950; Geological Survey 1936: 204; Wilson 1998) (see Fig. 5.5). The reasons for this deficiency are largely geological, but because the middle Ecca Beds in Natal and Gauteng possess some lenses of iron ore it would seem that the matching Ecca beds in the Free State may also contain exploitable iron ore. In fact most ore distribution maps are biased in favour of ore bodies exploitable by modern technologies. This bias potentially excludes crops of low grade iron ores which may have been worked in prehistory. For instance, the Phoka of Malawi smelted low grade lateritic ores with up to 35 wt% iron oxide, levels which are completely uneconomical using modern technology (Killick 1990). However, the

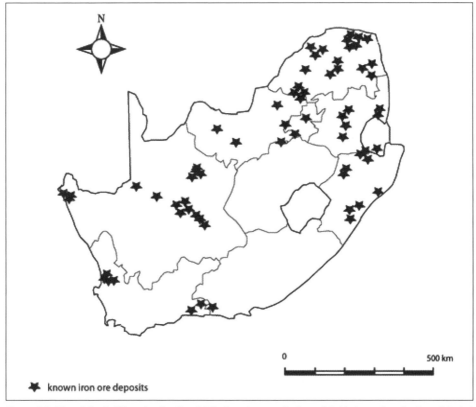

Figure 5.5 Map of South Africa showing the distribution of economically exploitable iron mineralisations. Adapted and modified from the Council for Geosciences. Note the blank patch on the Free State area.

Phoka managed to win metal from these gangue-dominated ores by using huge amounts of charcoal in a two-step extractive process.

When compared to our area, it becomes theoretically possible that iron could have been smelted there even if geologists have recorded no high grade ores. There remains, however, the issue of what fuel was used in the furnaces to facilitate the reduction processes. While the Phoka could depend upon their abundant wood reserves to process low grade ore, the grasslands lack significant tree cover. This environmental situation would have rendered smelting impossible unless the smelters imported the charcoal or used alternative fuel. Perhaps the most important question at this point is how much charcoal was required in indigenous iron smelting industries? This is critical because if the amount is low, then the sparse vegetation prevalent in some grassland areas may have provided the much needed fuel for smelting.

By way of comparison, we turn to studies carried out on charcoal production and iron smelting in other parts of sub-Saharan Africa. Generally, such studies unequivocally demonstrate that indigenous iron smelting was a charcoal intensive process (David et al 1989). Sometimes, iron smelting led to massive deforestation in regions such as Darfur in the Sudan, Mema in Ghana and Buhaya in Tanzania (G. Haaland 1980; R. Haaland 1980; Schmidt 1997). The bottom line here is that prehistoric iron smelting was charcoal intensive. More importantly, this is also linked to the demand for iron in a given society. Thus if the demand was low, then the sparse vegetation occasionally present in some parts may not have been an issue.

The next step therefore is to estimate the amount of iron required to sustain a typical Iron Age community at a site such as Ntsuanatsatsi, believed to have been occupied by 1 000 people (Maggs 1976). To arrive at some figures, we may begin by assuming that each individual used about 1 kilogram of iron per year (Chirikure 2007). Normally, for 1 kilogram of iron to be produced using the bloomery process (assuming that the ore had 80-90% FeO), a kilogram of slag had to form. This waste material was a combination of part of the ferric oxide in the ore and the silicate-dominated gangue materials (Buchwald & Wivel 1998; Chirikure 2006; Degreyse et al 2007). These estimates imply that the 1 000 inhabitants at Ntsuanatsatsi utilised about 1 000 kilograms of iron, which would have resulted in the production of an equivalent amount of slag. Clearly, the charcoal and wood consumption associated with this process were very high if one considers the averages required in bloomery smelting (see David et al 1989).

Of course, these numbers are highly exaggerated but they raise a number of issues when considering the likelihood of metalworking in the study area. Firstly, if the smelting was conducted locally, it would have led to the production of large quantities of slag and other waste materials. Secondly, this smelting would have demanded large quantities of charcoal which the grassland cannot provide or sustain. Thirdly we know that these communities relied on dung as a fuel for domestic use (see Fig. 5.2) (Maggs 1976). At least, this gives us the confidence that the absence of production evidence is real because reasonable quantities of metal smelting remains ought to have been produced. This strongly implicates imports as the major source of iron used in the grasslands.

What then was the situation with copper, another important metal used in the Late Iron Age? Copper possesses a warm colour and rich lustre which has always appealed to mankind (Mason 1982; Wilson 1998), hence its almost exclusive use for ornamentation (Herbert 1984). This is hardly surprising because in iron, the Iron Age farmers had a far more effective metal for tasks such as tilling and clearing the land (Miller 1995).

When compared to iron, copper has a very limited geological distribution (Wilson 1998). Despite this, more than a hundred types of copper ores are known; only carbonate and oxide ores, however, were smelted in the Iron Age (Miller & Sandelowsky 1999). Major and minor copper mineralisations were recorded in almost every province with the exception of the Free State. This is shown by the presence of a blank patch on the mineral resources map of South Africa (see Fig. 5.6) (Wilson 1998). Again, even though these maps are biased towards modern mines, they are reasonable approximations in view of the fact that most modern mines, such as Phalaborwa, were sited on ancient mines. In addition, copper smelting would have exerted its own charcoal demands on the 'treeless' grassland environment. With this absence of local sources of ore and fuel, the metal imports should have satisfied the local demand for copper in our area. Therefore, which regions supplied the copper metal to the Free State? Obtaining the answer to this lies in interdisciplinary work, which is the focus of the next section.

The potential of multi-disciplinary work in provenance studies – some opportunities and constraints

The paucity of critical resources for smelting metals and the absence of waste remains from the production process in the area, strongly suggest an outside source for the metal recovered from the grassland sites. The issue here is how do we infer the movement of metals from primary producing regions to the Free State grasslands? No single discipline can provide answers to this question in isolation; we therefore have to consider strands of evidence from other disciplines.

As a foundation stone, there is a need to construct a regional database of metal artefact typologies using objects archived in South African museums and university collections. The similarities of and differences between artefacts from resource-scarce and resource-

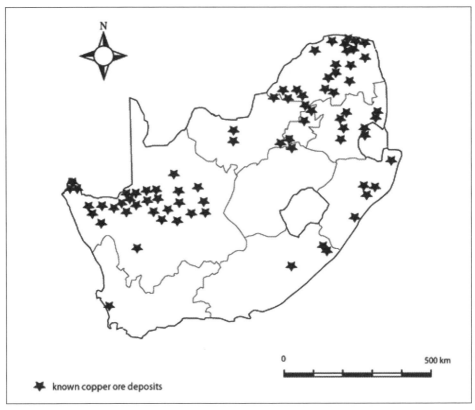

Figure 5.6 Map of South Africa showing the distribution of economically exploitable copper mineralisations. Adapted and modified from the Council for Geosciences. Note the blank patch on the Free State area.

rich areas will provide leads on the potential trade routes in which the metal followed. For example, a type of earring found by Maggs (1976) (Fig. 5.3) in the Free State grasslands has close parallels with that widely used at resource-rich localities such as Marothodi in the Bankenveld (Hall et al 2006). Because the Bankenveld was a mineral-rich area during the Late Iron Age, this may suggest a north-to-south movement of copper items. Caution is, however, required because the full distribution of this artefact category is not known. There is a possibility that the earrings were a common artefact type used by culturally related but not necessarily trading societies during the Late Iron Age. Therefore, there is need to widen the scope by establishing a typological database of metal artefacts recovered at South African Iron Age sites dating to the last 500 years so as to initiate intra- and inter-regional comparisons.

There are some potential difficulties associated with a purely typological approach. For example, likeness does not necessarily indicate exchange of material culture; it can indicate uniform cultural beliefs (Herbert 1984, 1993). Thus similar cultural beliefs often promote typological affinities without necessarily suggesting trade and exchange relationships in metal. These caveats can be redressed through recourse to laboratory archaeometallurgy and analytical chemistry. In this regard, characterisation studies based on physical examination and analytical chemistry are handy in indicating potential geographical sources of raw materials and finished metal objects (Pollard et al 2007; Degreyse et al 2007; Miller et al 2005).

At one level, such characterisation documents the microstructure, chemical composition and fabrication technology employed in making objects while the resultant information facilitates cross-regional comparisons at another level. For instance, if Free State communities merely imported finished objects, then their fabrication techniques may mirror those from areas of origin. Alternatively, if they imported metal ingots and subsequently reworked the metal to suit their own values and tastes, the resulting artefacts may be completely different from those found in the metal's source area. This is consistent with finds of copper-melting crucibles and wire drawing plates recovered from the Free State sites. If these differences can be documented, it will allow us to reach a greater understanding of regional traditions of metal fabrication techniques during the last 500 years and the manifestation of cultural similarities and/or differences across frontiers.

The provenancing of metals is based on the fact that there is a genetic relationship between the chemical fingerprints of ore bodies and the metal extracted from them (Pollard et al 2007). This is because ore bodies possess a unique chemical or isotopic fingerprint which, when correlated with the elemental composition (trace elements) of the metal, can indicate the geological body from which the smelted ores were extracted (Gale & Stos-Gale 1982; Miller et al 2005). In this case, analysing the ore from the source and metal objects from archaeological sites using techniques such as Inductively Coupled Plasma-Mass Spectrometry (ICP-MS) can reveal marked similarities or tight element clustering between the metal and the source. It has, however, been noted that human processing of ores, the reduction technology used and the conditions of operation in the furnaces sometimes result in isotope fractionation which may alter the chemical signatures of the metal (Pollard et al 2007: 192). While this problem affects traditional iron smelting more than it does copper smelting, it has been shown that there are isotopes such as those of lead and strontium which are not affected by anthropogenic processing. As such most provenance studies have attempted to source copper found from archaeological sites across the world using lead and strontium isotopes (Gale & Stos-Gale 1982; Miller et al 2005; Pollard et al 2007).

Potentially, copper objects recovered from the Free State grasslands could be provenanced through lead isotope analyses. This is because the variability of lead isotopes in nature is useful for identifying ore sources; they do not fractionate due to anthropogenic processing (Pollard et al 2007; Miller et al 2005). In southern Africa, Miller et al (2005) sourced the copper ores and artefacts found at the Drierivier site using lead isotope analyses. They concluded that the low lead isotope ratios obtained by ICP-MS matched the copper deposit at Swartmodder more than any other deposit in Namibia. However, we have to be aware of the potential complications inherent in our area. For example, while Miller et al (2005) had access to the ore, slag, and finished metal, we only have finished objects and no ores. Additionally, the recycling of scrap metal and the mixing of metal from multiple sources can alter the isotopic ratios and thus complicate provenance studies. This means that we can only suggest possible, rather than identifying actual, sources. At present such an achievement suffices as our main aim is to develop a broad picture of, and document change in, the circulation of metal during the last 500 years.

Turning to iron, the starting point would be to analyse the microstructure of the objects to reconstruct the extractive technology used. This is achievable through microstructural studies of finished objects (Miller 2001). This is because bloomery iron normally inherits slag inclusions whose chemical composition can be correlated with the slag and that of ores and known geologies. For instance, Miller, Killick and van der Merwe (2001) have suggested that the magnetite ores from Phalaborwa are characterised by high levels of titanium and vanadium which were inherited by the slag and finished objects. According to them, enriched levels of titanium and vanadium can potentially identify artefacts made from the Phalaborwa magnetite. While this suggestion is useful, it is incapacitated by the presence of titaniferous magnetite in virtually all of the former Transvaal from the Pilanesberg to the Murchison Range (Bushveld Complex) (Astrup et al 1998). This means that we have to consider the potential of strontium isotopes in sourcing the iron. New and innovative studies have attempted to source iron from the site of Sagalassos in southwestern Turkey using strontium isotopes with some success (Degreyse et al 2007). As with lead isotope analysis of copper, this method requires a comparative geochemical database. The only complication would be presented by the fact that iron is widely available, which may make it difficult to identify prehistoric sources. Nevertheless, there exist numerous historically documented iron sources such as Thabazimbi and, by making recourse to oral traditions, many of these can be identified and thus contribute towards developing the big picture.

The complexities associated with the chemical sourcing of both copper and iron objects indicates that this method must be augmented with typological and historical evidence. Indeed there is historical evidence of a well developed trade network between some Free State grassland communities and the Iron Age communities of KwaZulu-Natal (Maggs

1976). In particular, oral traditions recount that iron objects from the Zizi of the Tugela basin were brought over the Drakensberg to the Tlokwa and others who in turn traded them to peoples further west (Maggs 1976). Other possible sources would be the geologically complex Vredefort Dome, parts of Mpumalanga, as well as the Bankenveld. In fact there existed a well-developed network between different regions which saw the movement of cattle, glass beads, marine shells and specularite from producers to consumers in different parts of the Highveld (Legassick 1969). This goes on to support the earlier point that object typologies can throw light on potential source areas.

Documentary history may also contain some information on trade in metals. Travellers such as Burchell (1824), Barrow (1806, cited in Maggs 1976), Campbell (1822, cited in Maggs 1976), and Casalis (1861) talk of the existence of trade networks between different groups of people. Scrutinising these early sources can provide potentially useful information on precolonial trade in metals (Friede & Steel 1976; Huffman 2007). Therefore only a combined source approach and a multi-disciplinary framework has the potential to throw some light on how metal was circulated not only in the Free State but also in other regions of southern Africa during the last 500 years.

Conclusion and outlook

This audit has shown that the grassland area of the Free State lacks essential resources for metal smelting, such as suitable ores and trees for charcoal production. In fact so acute was the shortage of wood that dung was used as a fuel for cooking and charcoal is virtually absent from many domestic middens (Maggs 1976). Just as communities substituted stone for wood in construction and dung for charcoal, they also satiated their metal requirements through trade and exchange regimes. Items of material culture such as marine shells, glass beads and earrings similar to those manufactured north of the Vaal in the Bankenveld suggest the existence of multi-directional trade. However, in the absence of a dedicated study to understand the situation in detail, little can be said of the routes which the trade in metals followed. Only a combined archaeometallurgical, historical and isotopic approach may illuminate the situation. More importantly, the Free State grasslands are only a starting point; in future the study will be extended to cover the whole of South Africa. This will enable us to understand the issue of regional interaction and variability more clearly. For instance, we know that the grasslands of Mpumalanga produced copper and iron on a large scale (Hall 1912; Evers 1974, 1975). What therefore distinguishes them from the Free State; is it the environment or the technology used? Also what was the nature of the metals trade in what is now Limpopo and KwaZulu-Natal, regions with historically known specialist metalworkers such as the Lemba and the Nkandla? Only more research can tell.

References

Arbousset, T. & Daumas, F. 1852. *Narrative of an Exploratory Tour to the North-East of the Colony of the Cape of Good Hope.* Translated by J.C. Brown. London: John C. Bishop.

Astrup, J., Hammerbeck, E. C. I. & van den Berg, H. 1998. Iron. In: Wilson, M.G.C. & Anhaeusser, C.R. (eds) *The Mineral Resources of South Africa*: 402-416. Handbook: 16, Pretoria: Council for Geosciences.

Boeyens, J.C.A. 2003. The Late Iron Age sequence in the Marico and early Tswana history. *South African Archaeological Bulletin* 58: 63-78.

Breutz, P.L. 1950. Metallurgy in Africa. *ISCOR News* 15: 771-775.

Breutz, P.L. 1953. The tribes of Rustenburg and Pilansberg districts. *Department of Native Affairs, Ethnologic Publication SA* 28: 7-450.

Breutz, P.L. 1953/4. The tribes of Marico District. *Department of Native Affairs, Ethnologic Publication SA* 30: 1-266.

Buchwald, V.F. & Wivel, H. 1998. Slag analyses as a method for the characterisation and provenancing of ancient iron objects. *Materials Characterization* 40: 73-96.

Burchell, W.J. 1824. *Travels in the Interior of Southern Africa.* London: Longman.

Campbell, J. 1822. *Travels in South Africa: Being a Narrative of a Second Journey, 1820.* London: Longman.

Chirikure, S. 2006. New light on Njanja iron working: towards a systematic encounter between ethnohistory and archaeometallurgy. *South African Archaeological Bulletin* 61: 142–151.

Chirikure, S. 2007. Metals in society: iron production and its position in Iron Age communities of southern Africa. *Journal of Social Archaeology* 7(1): 72-100.

David, N., Heimann, N., Killick, D. & Wayman, M. 1989. Between bloomery and blast furnace: Mafa iron-smelting technology in North Cameroon. *African Archaeological Review* 7: 183-208.

Degreyse, P., Schneider, J., Kellens, N., Waelkens, M. & Muchez, P.H. 2007. Tracing the resources of iron working at ancient Sagalassos (south-west Turkey): a combined lead and strontium study on iron artefacts and ores. *Archaeometry* 49: 75-86.

Evers, T.M. 1974. Iron Age trade in the eastern Transvaal. *South African Archaeological Bulletin* 29: 33-37.

Evers, T.M. 1975. Recent Iron Age research in eastern Transvaal. *South African Archaeological Bulletin* 30: 71-83.

Friede, H.M & Steel, R.H. 1976. Tin mining and smelting in the Transvaal during the Iron Age. *Journal of the South African Institute of Mining and Metallurgy* 76: 461-470.

Gale, N. & Stos-Gale, Z. 1982. Bronze Age copper sources in the Mediterranean: a new approach. *Science* 216: 11-19.

Haaland, G. 1980. Social organisation and ecological pressure in South Darfur. In: Haaland, G. (ed.) *Problems of Savannah Development: The Sudan.* Department of Social Anthropology, African Savannah Studies No. 19. Bergen: Norway ,University of Bergen.

Haaland, R. 1980. Man's role in the changing habitat of Mema during the old Kingdom of Ghana. *Norwegian Archaeological Review* 13: 31-46.

Haddon, A.C. 1908. Copper rod currency from the Transvaal. *Man* 8: 121-122.

Hall, A.L.S. 1912. The geology of the Murchison Range District, Union of South Africa. *Geological Survey Memoir* 6: 166-167.

Hall, S., Miller, D., Anderson, M. & Boeyens, J. 2006. An exploratory study of copper and iron production at Marothodi, an early 19th-century Tswana town, Rustenburg district, South Africa. *Journal of African Archaeology* 4(1): 3-33.

Hanisch, E.O.M. 1974. Copper working in the Messina district. *Journal of the South African Institute of Mining and Metallurgy* 74(6): 250-253.

Herbert, E. 1984. *Red Gold of Africa: Copper in Pre-colonial History and Culture.* Madison: The University of Wisconsin Press.

Herbert, E. 1993. *Iron, Gender and Power: Rituals of Transformation in African Societies.* Indiana: Bloomington.

Huffman, T.N. 2002. Regionality in the Iron Age: the case of the Sotho-Tswana. *Southern African Humanities* 16: 79-111.

Huffman, T.N. 2007. *A Handbook to the Iron Age: The Archaeology of Pre-colonial Societies of Southern Africa*. Pietermaritzburg: University of KwaZulu-Natal Press.

Jacobson, L., Loock, J.C., van der Westhuizen, W.A., Huffman, T.N. & Dreyer, J.J. B. 2003. The occurrence of vitrified dung from the Kamdeboo district, southern Karoo and Dean Staat, Limpopo valley, South Africa. *South African Journal of Science* 99: 26-28.

Junod, H.A. 1908. The Balemba of the Zoutspansberg. *Folk-Lore* 19: 279-280.

Killick, D.J. 1990. Technology in its social setting: bloomery iron working at Kasungu, Malawi, 1860-1940. PhD thesis: Yale University.

Legassick, M. 1969. The Sotho-Tswana before 1800. In: Thompson, L. (ed.) *African Societies in Southern Africa*: 86-125. London: Heinemann.

Maggs, T.M.O'C. 1972. Bilobial dwellings: a persistent feature of southern Tswana settlements. *South African Archaeological Society Goodwin Series* 1: 54-65.

Maggs, T.M.O'C. 1976. *Iron Age Communities of the Southern Highveld*. Pietermaritzburg: Natal Museum (Occasional papers 2).

Maggs, T.M.O'C. 1980. The Iron Age sequence south of the Vaal and Pongola Rivers: some historical implications. *Journal of African History* 21(1): 1-16.

Mamadi, M.F. 1940. The copper miners of Musina. In: van Warmelo, N.J. (ed.) *The Copper Miners of Musina and the Early History of the Zoutpansberg*: 81-83. Pretoria: Government Printer. (South African Department of Native Affairs Ethnological Publication 8).

Mason, R.J. 1982. Prehistoric mining in South Africa and Iron Age copper mines in the Dwarsberg, Transvaal. *Journal of the South African Institute of Mining and Metallurgy* 82(5): 134-144.

Miller, D. 1995. 2000 years of indigenous mining and metallurgy in southern Africa: a review. *South African Journal of Geology* 98: 232-238.

Miller, D. 2001. Metal assemblages from Greefswald Areas K2, Mapungubwe Hill and Mapungubwe South Terrace. *South African Archaeological Bulletin* 56: 83-103.

Miller, D. & Killick, D.J. 2004. The slag identification at southern African archaeological sites. *Journal of African Archaeology* 2: 23-47.

Miller, D. & Sandelowsky, B. 1999. Smelting without ceramics: the Drierivier copper smelting site near Rehoboth, Namibia. *South African Archaeological Bulletin* 54: 28-37.

Miller, D., Young, S.M.M., Green, W.A., van der Merwe, N.J. & Sandelowsky, B. 2005. Sourcing the ore from the Drierivier copper smelting site in central Namibia, using lead isotope fingerprinting. *South African Journal of Science* 101: 344-346.

Miller, D., Killick, D. & van der Merwe, N. 2001. Metalworking in the northern lowveld, South Africa, AD 1000-1890. *Journal of Field Archaeology* 28: 401-417.

Mucina, L., & Rutherford, M.C. (eds) 2006. *Vegetation Map of South Africa, Lesotho and Swaziland*. Pretoria: South African National Biodiversity Institute.

Peter, B. 2001. Vitrified dung in archaeological contexts: an experimental study on the process of its formation in the Mosu and Bobiru areas. *Botswana Journal of African Studies* 15: 125-143.

Pollard, M., Batt, C., Stern, B. & Young, S. 2007. *Analytical Chemistry in Archaeology*. Cambridge: Cambridge University Press.

Schmidt, P.R. 1997. *Iron Technology in East Africa: Symbolism, Science and Archaeology*. Oxford: James Currey.

Thy, P., Segobye, A.K. & Ming, D.W. 1995. Implications of prehistoric glassy biomass slag from east-central Botswana. *Journal of Archaeological Science* 22: 629-637.

Wagner, P.A. 1928. The iron deposits of the Union of South Africa. *Memoirs of the Geological Survey of South Africa* 26.

Wilson, M.G.C. 1998. Copper. In: Wilson, M.G.C. & Anhaeusser, C.R. (eds). *The Mineral Resources of South Africa*: 209-227. Handbook.16. Pretoria: Council for Geoscience.

6

deTuin, a 19th-century mission station in the Northern Cape

Alan G. Morris

Introduction

The excavation of graves from the historic burial ground at deTuin will probably be the last time an archaeological project in South Africa is allowed that specifically excavates human remains for research purposes. Fourteen graves were opened between 1982 and 2002 with the express purpose of identifying who was buried there. The site was known as a temporary station of the Rehoboth people in the 1860s, and the descendant community in Rehoboth, Namibia, was contacted about the project and was kept informed of progress.

The property deTuin is presently a stock farm on the Tuins River (Fig. 6.1) about 50 km west of the town of Kenhardt in the Bushmanland region of the Northern Cape Province (29°22.3'S; 20°41'E). The region as a whole is generally without surface water and all of the farms in the district are supplied with water by borehole. Although the stock on modern deTuin is also watered in this manner, occupation of the site previous to the drilling of boreholes has been possible because of the presence of a permanent brackish spring in the river bed. In particular, deTuin is known as having been the location of a Rhenish mission settlement between the years 1863 and 1868.

The presence of large numbers of graves on deTuin was brought to the attention of Professor A.B. Smith during 1979, and it was decided to investigate the site for possible excavation. The first expedition to deTuin occurred in 1982 under my direction. Three grave sequences were identified, one of these sequences was mapped, and two graves were excavated. The site was again visited in 1994 by Morris when a second grave sequence was mapped and one further grave was opened. A further field season took place in 1995 when four more graves were excavated under the direction of Dr G. Louw. Tanya Peckmann took over the deTuin excavations as part of her PhD project and completed the examination of three graves in 1999 and a final four graves in 2000 (Peckmann 2002). In all, fourteen graves were excavated and these, along with some more general archaeological observations, are the basis for the report which follows.

Despite the basis of the project being physical anthropology, the archaeology of the graves and the settlement site was of great interest and this paper provides a report on the information gleaned from the archaeological and historical context.

The historical context

Of all the mission stations at the Groot Rivier (deTuin, Pella and Warmbad), deTuin was in the 1860s described as the most fertile place 'with more water than other stations' (von Rohden 1888). According to local tradition told to von Rohden (1888), deTuin was a spot where a farmer had formerly started a garden (tuin), but there is no supporting documentation for this assertion. This was a time of considerable political instability and von Rohden writes of the period as a 'time of tribe assembly and dispersal following drought and tribal unrest and a succession of natural disasters'.

The first record of deTuin is by the Rhenish missionary Peter Sterrenberg who in 1863 recorded the presence of 'Bastards, Kafirs, Bushmen and Hottentots' in residence at the site (Marais 1939). On Sterrenberg's recommendations, the Rhenish Mission Society opened a station at deTuin. Sterrenberg was initially in charge, but was replaced by Christian Schroder in 1865, who in turn was replaced by J.C.F. Heidmann in 1866. Heidmann was the last of the missionaries to live at deTuin. He moved with the people of deTuin when they deserted the site in 1868.

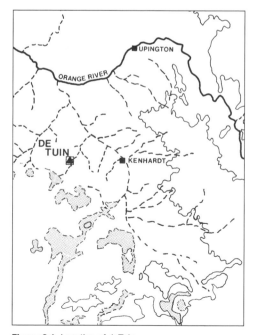

The only description of deTuin in historic times is that contained in von Rohden's report to the Rhenish Mission headquarters in Barmen, Germany (1888). When missionary Sterrenberg began the station in 1863 the community was living in reed huts, but within a year Sterrenberg had built a stone church, school and rectory. In the early years 150 people assembled for prayer in the church and 250 children attended school. Presumably not all of the adults were Christianised, so the 150 members of the church probably represented only a

Figure 6.1 Location of deTuin.

portion of the total adults in the community. There are no estimates of the peak population numbers, but the last missionary at the site, Heidmann, left for Great Namaqualand (Namibia) in 1868 with the majority of the population, about 90 families according to von Rohden. Given a conservative estimate of three children per family, this would give an estimate in the range of 500 to 600 people living at the station at that time. A Total Fertility Rate per woman of 2.1 children is required for parental replacement at low mortality, but this needs to be between 2.5 and 3.3 for replacement at higher mortality levels (Espenshade et al 2003).

No mention is made of a dam (see below) in the von Rohden report but water was a central concern at the station and the available water holes in the river bed did dry out during the prolonged drought in the late 1860s. By the time Heidmann took over in 1866, the continuing existence of the settlement at deTuin had become more tenuous. The drought caused the agricultural harvests to fail for the fifth time in the years leading up to 1869 (Strassberger 1969). Continued harassment of Bastard herds by white farmers, led to the emigration of most of the inhabitants (including Heidmann) to Great Namaqualand. The late 1860s was the time of the Korana Wars and endemic violence in the region forced all mission stations on the Orange River, including deTuin, to be abandoned. Von Rohden (1888) reported that the community at deTuin had been ransacked by 'a wild horde of Korannas' just days before the people departed for the north. By the end of 1868 the entire community at deTuin had moved north under Hermanus van Wyk to eventually settle at Rehoboth, or, in much smaller numbers, dispersed to mission stations closer to the Colony in the south (Vedder 1938). In October 1868, a detachment of 50 mounted Cape Police was stationed at Kenhardt, about 50 kilometres east of deTuin. The deserted settlement was the scene of a battle between Korana and the police on 29 May 1869 when the police tried to drive a large group of armed men back towards the Orange River. The Korana took cover in 'some houses and a stone kraal' at deTuin and after a sharp battle the police were forced to withdraw (Strauss 1979). This is the last mention of deTuin in the 19th-century historical records.

The property of deTuin was not surveyed as a stock farm until the first decade of the 20th century and the family of the current owner has been in possession since 1938.

The archaeological context

The 1982 field season was the first time that any systematic archaeology had been done at deTuin. Although the central focus was on the grave sequence, the whole area was foot surveyed and a number of identifiable features were recorded (Fig. 6.2). The present buildings on the farm consist of two farm houses. DeTuin Noord, on a slight rise on the western bank of the river, was built in 1980/81 very close to the site of the original mission

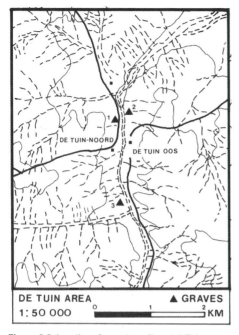

DE TUIN AREA ▲ GRAVES
1 : 50 000   0   1   2 KM

Figure 6.2 Location of cemetery sites at deTuin farmstead.

station. The other house, deTuin Oos, was built just after World War II but is no longer inhabited. Some 40 metres to the east and south-east of deTuin Noord are the ruined foundations of the earliest European structures, probably built around the turn of the 20th century, while about 200 metres further to the south-west are the ruins of an old house which was probably occupied between the wars. All of these structures were built with stone foundations and are still easily visible.

The remains of the original mission station are much less obvious. The highest point of the rise on the west side of the river is about 20 metres south of the present deTuin Noord farmhouse. Present oral tradition suggests that this was the precise location of the stone church built by Sterrenberg. Examination of this location does show a poorly preserved foundation of loose stones. Ceramic pottery fragments were visible on the surface. Several of these were collected but only one fragment was diagnostic. This small fragment is flat (presumably from a plate rather than a cup) and has a green pattern including something that appears to be a plant sprig with several leaves or flowers. Dr Jane Klose of UCT Archaeology kindly examined the diagnostic fragment and identified it as coming from a British green underglaze transfer-printed white earthenware plate (Klose, pers. comm.). The production of red, green and brown transfer-printed wares became common from the 1830s and continued into the late 19th century. Similar pottery has come from the mid-19th century in the Upper Seacow Valley in the Karoo (Moir & Sampson 1993) with a stylised vine motif in grayish-green transfer print. According to Moir & Sampson, this pattern was particularly common in the 1840s and 1850s. Although a single specimen is hardly adequate to confirm that the site of origin was the original location of the Sterrenberg church, the mid-19th century date is consistent with the oral history that this was the location of the original church. Confirmation must await a formal excavation of the site.

In the river bed about 200 metres south of this location is a substantial earthwork structure which is said to have been the remains of the dam made by the 'Basters' in the

1860s. No archaeological confirmation could be made of either the dam or church site from the cursory observations made here.

Although nothing substantial can be said about the historic phase of the archaeological occupation, evidence of Later Stone Age occupation could be seen at various places along the river bed. No large concentrations of artefacts were noted but numbers of Later Stone Age flakes and microlithic tools, ostrich eggshell fragments and beads were recorded as isolated specimens.

During the excavation of Cemetery Site 3 grave sequence (see below) one specific Later Stone Age surface concentration was noted. The location was about 15 metres east of the graves and consisted of a surface scatter of various artefacts covering a circular area of about 10 metres in diameter. Most of the cultural material consisted of undecorated pottery sherds, stone flakes and a few fragments of animal bone, but two pottery lugs were also identified in the scatter. These lugs are very similar to Rudner's Khoekhoe coastal pottery (1968) and much like those seen on the Grootdrink pot collected from further up the Orange River (Rudner 1971). Morris and Beaumont (1991) have suggested that such lugs indicate a link with historic Khoekhoe populations along the Orange River.

Several broken and two complete ostrich eggshell beads were recovered in the grave fill of Cairn 4 in Cemetery Site 3. There is no certainty that the beads are related to the burial itself and they may be inclusions mixed into the grave shaft when it was filled. The beads themselves are large (Fig. 6.3) and are consistent with beads made by late Holocene and historic pastoralists rather than San hunters (Smith et al 1991; Yates 1995), but once again the very small sample prevents a confirmation of this identity.

The cemetery sites

The immediate archaeological attraction of the deTuin site is the presence of three well-marked grave sequences (Fig. 6.2).

Cemetery Site 1 is located about 50 metres west of the Tuins River bed. It is the largest of the grave sequences and consists of 33 graves marked by stone cairns and head and foot stones (Fig. 6.4). The entire site is located within a grove of acacia trees that post-dates the period of interment and many of the graves are badly disturbed by tree growth. Aardvark burrowing activity has also disturbed some of the graves. Although each grave is marked by a cairn, most of the cairns are not visible at surface level, but the graves can be identified by the presence of a head or footstone, or both. A few of the graves demonstrate substantial cairn structures above surface level. The headstone-footstone orientation of each grave is roughly east-west and the graves are located in four indistinct rows running roughly north-south. There are no identifying features to link these graves with the mission period, but local oral tradition identifies the sequence as being older than the beginning of this century. The location of this cemetery is closest to the stated position of the 1860s mission station.

The second of the deTuin grave sequences (Cemetery Site 2), is on the east side of the Tuins River, nearly opposite Cemetery Site 1. The cairns are devoid of plant growth and the stone work is well packed with no displacement of cairn stones. The 13 graves are in two rows; 7 in one row, and 6 in the second. The cairns are placed with the long axis of the grave row roughly in a north-south orientation. Each individual grave is therefore oriented east-west. The cairns are oval in shape and each has an obvious headstone and footstone. The cairns vary in size with the largest being nearly 3 metres from headstone to footstone, while the smallest is only about 1 metre in this dimension. There is no reason to believe that these graves are much older than the turn of the 20th century. They may very well represent the graves of farm labourers who lived on the site in the early years of formal European settlement during the first decade of the 20th century.

The third grave sequence (Cemetery Site 3) is about 1.5 kilometres south of Cemetery Site 1 (Fig. 6.5). The graves were located during the 1982 field season and at that time they were thought to be without head- or footstones and haphazardly placed. Brush clearance during the 1994 season exposed the cairns and showed the graves to be similar to those at Cemetery Site 1. There are 18 graves in this sequence, once again in a roughly east-west orientation and in what appears to be four north-south rows.

Of the three grave sequences, Cemetery Site 2 is the most distinctive in its undisturbed cairns, freedom from plant overgrowth and very well delineated rows. Although the graves were constructed before Mr du Plessis senior's purchase of deTuin in 1938, their obviously recent nature removed them from the focus of archaeological exploration. The remaining two grave sequences, Cemetery Sites 1 and 3, may or may not be associated with the historic mission station, but they clearly pre-date the later, twentieth-century development of the farm.

The graves

Nine graves were excavated from Cemetery Site 1, and a further five graves were excavated at Cemetery Site 3. All the skeletons were of children, ranging in age from newborn to approximately 15 years old. One of the Cemetery Site 1 graves (number 19) contained two individuals, but three graves from the same site had no preserved human remains, giving a final sample of 12 individuals (Tables 6.1 & 6.2). Soil conditions suggest that skeletons had been present, but were not preserved. Cemetery sites can have a wide range of preservation due to local soil conditions, but skeletons of infants are most frequently lost because of their friability. It would not be an unreasonable assumption that these three graves also contained young children.

Table 6.1: Summary of individual graves excavated from Cemetery Site 1.
(adapted from Peckmann, 2002)

Grave Number	Length (m)	Width (m)	Depth (m)	Grave Inclusions	Age at Death
Grave 8 (UCT 335)	1.80	n/data	1.50	White pottery fragment, coffin nails, coffin wood	5 to 6 years
Grave 9	2.66	2.00	1.80	none	?
Grave 10	2.66	2.00	1.80	none	?
Grave 11 (UCT 569)	2.66	2.00	1.50	3 buttons, coffin wood and nails, fragments of ostrich egg shell	13 to 15 years
Grave 12	2.66	2.00	1.80	none	?
Grave 13 (UCT 336)	1.90	n/data	1.50	Fragments of wood	1.5 to 2 years
Grave 14 (UCT 579)	2.66	2.00	1.50	8 coffin nails	3 to 4 years
Grave 19a (UCT 570a)	2.66	2.00	1.45	none	< 1 year
Grave 19b (UCT 570b)				Copper pins, bovid tooth	4 to 5 years
Grave 25 (UCT 571)	2.66	2.50	1.62	none	3 to 6 months
Average grave size	**2.48**	**2.07**	**1.61**		

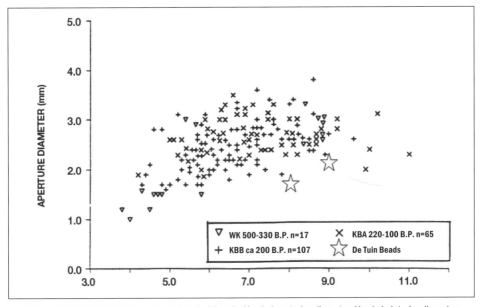

Figure 6.3 Comparison of size of ostrich eggshell beads. X axis is exterior diameter; Y axis is interior diameter. (after Smith et al 1991)

109

Table 6.2: Summary of Individual Graves excavated from Cemetery Site 3.

(adapted from Peckmann 2002)

Grave Number	Length (m)	Width (m)	Depth (m)	Grave Inclusions	Age at Death
Grave 1 (UCT 467)	2.6	0.9	0.95	Coffin nails and straight pins	3 to 4 years
Grave 3 (UCT 468)	2.2	1.5	1.10	none	6 to 7 years
Grave 4 (UCT 469)	2.0	1.8	0.80	none	2 months
Grave 7 (UCT 470)	1.5	0.45	0.70	none	Birth to 2 weeks
Grave 18 (UCT 471)	1.75	0.5	0.80	Coffin wood, nails and straight pins	5 to 6 years
Average grave size	**2.01**	**1.03**	**0.87**		

Not all of the skeletons recovered were complete enough for analysis, but basic long bone lengths could be recorded for some of them (Table 6.3) and the cranial material was examined for signs of porotic hyperostosis (on the vault bones) and cribra orbitalia (on the roof of the orbits) wherever possible (Table 6.4). Long bone length provides some idea of the growth state of the children and the porotic hyperostosis (PH)/cribra orbitalia (CO) provide some information on the health of children up to the time of death. Four of 10 observable crania showed signs of PH or CO, and in each case the lesions were active at death (Peckmann 2002).

All graves in both cemeteries were marked by stone cairns. Many of the cairns had been dispersed by animal burrowing activity but those that were still intact sometimes exceeded two metres in length and width (Tables 6.1 & 6.2). There seems to have been little relationship between the age of the person buried and the size of the cairn. This is quite different from late prehistoric Khoekhoe graves along the Orange River where adults were buried under substantial cairns, but children's cairns were markedly smaller (Morris 1995). The grave shaft is directly below the cairn for most of the graves (Figs 6.6 & 6.7) but the two young infant burials from Cemetery Site 3 (Table 6.2) had a niche off the side of the grave shaft with an additional internal cairn just above the skeleton (Fig. 6.8).

All skeletons were in the extended on back position. Five graves had coffin nails indicating the presence of a formal coffin, while at least two more had wood fragments with no coffin nails, but with shroud pins. Grave 8 in Cemetery Site 1 had coffin screws rather than nails. The practice of joining pieces of wood with screws began in 18th-century Europe, but they only came into common usage in the mid-19th century with the introduction of machinery for mass-producing them (Walker 1999). This suggests that Cemetery Site 1 is unlikely to predate the mission period and certainly could be more recent.

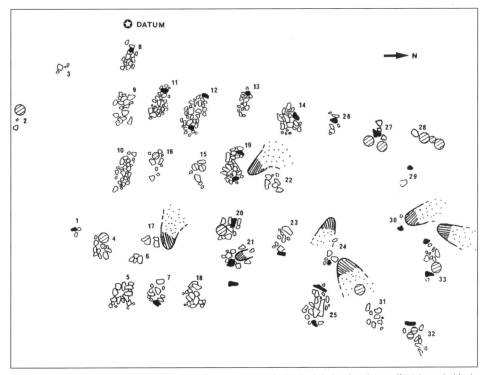

Figure 6.4 deTuin Cemetery Site 1: Large acacia trees marked by hashed circles, headstones/footstones in black, and aardvark burrows marked with stippled openings.

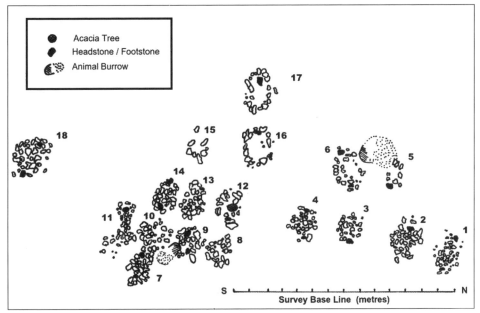

Figure 6.5 deTuin Cemetery Site 3.

Table 6.3: Diaphyseal lengths of long bones (in millimetres, left side)

(some data from Peckmann 2002)

Specimen	Age at Death (years)	Femur	Tibia	Fibula	Humerus	Radius	Ulna
UCT 336	1.5 to 2	160	130	128	122	88	100
UCT 467	3 to 4	194	154	152	142	104	114
UCT 335	5 to 6	236	192	186	164	126	136
UCT 471	5 to 6	228	187	184	163	120	129
UCT 468	6 to 7	218	179	173	156	114	127
UCT 569	13 to 15	452	356	353	274	209	-

Table 6.4: Presence or absence of porotic hyperostosis and cribra orbitalia for skeletons with observable crania.

(some data from Peckmann 2002)

Specimen	Age at Death (years)	Porotic Hyperostosis	Cribra orbitalia
UCT 335	5 to 6 years	slight	slight
UCT 569	13 to 15 years	none	none
UCT 336	1.5 to 2 years	none	none
UCT 579	3 to 4 years	none	none
UCT 570b	4 to 5 years	none	none
UCT 571	3 to 6 months	none	none
UCT 467	3 to 4 years	none	slight
UCT 468	6 to 7 years	severe	slight
UCT 471	5 to 6 years	slight	slight

Grave 13 in Cemetery Site 1 had a stone at the foot and head of the skeleton and traces of wood over the bones. This is evidence of a single plank of wood overlying the skeleton rather than a complete coffin. A similar pattern of burial was witnessed amongst the Christianised Khoekhoe in Namibia by Vedder (1928). 'Before it became the custom to inter in coffins, a grave was dug with its deepest part resembling a coffin. Half-way it broadened out on both sides, on each of which a step was made. The corpse, wrapt in skins or blankets and laid flat on the ground, would then be covered with wooden poles on which the excavated earth was thrown, so as not to be in direct contact with the corpse' (Vedder 1928: 138). Wood fragments from Graves 8 and 13 in Cemetery Site 1 were identified as being from a *Pinus* species (E. February, pers. comm.). Pine trees were grown in the Cape during the 19th century for building material, furniture and for fruit industry boxes and the wood was often reused for coffins in burials (February 1996). Pine trees would not have been present at deTuin, and the evidence of pine wood indicates the importation of the wood as cut planks from the Cape.

The two sites of Cemetery Sites 1 and 3 are not identical in their structure. Both sites have the graves aligned in rows and the orientation of the cairns is roughly east-west. The cairns in Cemetery Site 1 are larger, averaging nearly 2.5 metres in length and over 2 metres in breadth. Cemetery Site 3 cairns are of a similar length, but are narrower on average (Tables 6.1 & 6.2). There is a marked difference between the two sites in terms of burial depth. Cemetery Site 1 burials are universally deep, with the skeletons at least 1.5 metres below the level of the cairn. Cemetery Site 3 graves are much shallower with an average depth of only 0.9 metres. There is no difference in soil between the two sites, both being in loose sand. Late Holocene Khoekhoe graves from along the Orange River were approximately 1 metre in depth in the loose river alluvium (Morris 1995), so the great depth of the Cemetery Site 1 burials is significant.

Discussion

The evidence from the burials of deTuin is similar in many ways to that seen amongst the Griqua. Not only are the burial patterns similar (Morris 1992), but the mortality figures also reflect what we know of Griqua mortality patterns (Peckmann 2002, 2003). Griqua identity rests on cultural affiliation and historic records place the Griqua east of the Kenhardt region (Nurse 1975; Nurse & Jenkins 1975), but the process that resulted in the coalescence of this new grouping of people in the mid-19th century was also operating in Bushmanland and there is no reason to think that the way of life of the people at the historic mission at de Tuin was significantly different from that seen in the Griqua communities further to the east (Morris 1992).

No adults were excavated from the 14 graves. This could be a simple issue of the small sample size, but it does imply a very high rate of childhood mortality. Such high mortality rates are common in pre-industrial populations characterised by high fertility and high mortality. Large numbers of children die before their fifth birthday in these societies. Seventy-two percent of the individuals from the Iron Age site of K2 at Mapungubwe were children (Steyn 1994) and incidences of greater than 50% of children are common in the historic cemeteries in Cape Town (Gregory 1896; Molyneau n.d.). At deTuin, eight of the 12 skeletons (66%) were below five years of age at death. It is almost certain that the historic Griqua groups, who were related culturally to the people of the deTuin mission, had very high fertility rates that would have been coupled with significant childhood mortality (Morris 1997).

The presence of PH and CO in four of ten specimens is strongly suggestive that the population was under some form of stress consistent with the high childhood mortality. These disturbances in the cancellous tissue that produces red blood cells in the cranial bones is typical of iron deficiency anaemia caused by chronic disease (such as inherited blood disorders), intestinal parasites or from low-level poor health in an individual under physiological stress due to malnutrition (Steyn et al 2002; Peckmann 2003). All four individuals with PH and CO had active lesions at death. Peckmann (2003) recorded 66% of the juveniles in her 19th-century Griqua sample showing some sign of PH or CO. She attributed this to the susceptibility to infection of children with low immunity. The value of 40% for affected individuals at deTuin is consistent with the Griqua data.

The long bone lengths of the six measurable individuals (Table 6.3) are not markedly short. Steyn et al (2002) provided data for the early 20th-century Maroelabult site, and all of the deTuin individuals exceed the Maroelabult individuals in long bone lengths for the same age. Peckmann's (2002) Griqua data are more similar to deTuin, but once again the deTuin skeletons exceed the diaphyseal lengths for Griqua, although not by very much. Maroelabult has a particularly heavy disease load as seen from the skeletons (Steyn et al 2002), so the deTuin children are perhaps not as seriously affected. Sixty-four percent of the Maroelabult individuals were under the age of 20 at death.

Can the two cemetery sites be associated with the 19th-century Rhenish Mission at deTuin? Firstly, the style of both cemeteries clearly indicates a strong Christian influence. The graves are neatly ordered in rows and the body posture is invariably extended on back. Nearly every grave has at least a headstone or footstone and frequently both. The burials in Cemetery Site 1 are excessively deep, approaching the ideal 'six foot' depth prescribed for 20th-century Christian graves. There are relatively few grave goods, and those that are present indicate western styles of clothes, coffins and body shrouds. Graves from along the Orange River in the late 18th and early 19th century demonstrate an entirely different pattern with shallower depths, flexed bodies, no grave goods, and cairns without headstones or footstones (Morris 1995). Niche graves, with the body offset from the grave shaft, were also found amongst pastoralists in the region (Morris 1992). Christian evangelisation during the 19th century was marked by an almost immediate shift from flexed to extended burial position (Ashton 1955). Niche graves continued where no coffin was present, but when coffins or wooden grave covers were introduced, the niche graves stopped (Engelbrecht 1936; Ashton 1955; Morris 1992). The evidence of Christian influence is overwhelming and therefore the graves in both cemeteries must represent people who died after the arrival of the first Christian missionary in 1863. But it is possible that the graves could date from after the mission period and could theoretically be graves of farm labourers in the late 19th or early 20th century.

Secondly, the large number of graves does suggest that at least Cemetery Site 1 and Site 3 are not from the post-mission period. In total, the two cemeteries have 51 graves.

The smaller and obviously modern Cemetery Site 2 has only 13 graves. During the 20th century deTuin has been a marginal stock farm and relatively few people have lived on the property. Neither Cemetery Site 1 nor Cemetery Site 3 was in use after the arrival of the current farm owner in 1938, and historical evidence indicates that the farm was deserted for most of the late 19th century. Therefore if the cemeteries represent the normal mortality of the farming community, then it could only be from the period 1900 to about 1935, and it seems unlikely that the population was large enough to generate that number of graves during that period. On the other hand, the relatively short mission period between 1863 and 1868 was marked by a significantly large population at the site of at least 500 people. A ten percent mortality over the period of six years is certainly possible.

However despite the evidence listed above, there is no obvious explanation as to why there would be two cemeteries from the same occupation. Cemetery Site 1 has deeper graves with more burials in coffins, so it is possible that the two cemeteries represent different factions in the community or a change in burial ground with the change over of missionaries.

Possibilities for future research

Sadly, it is not possible to dogmatically state that the two cemeteries at deTuin represent the people of the mission period, although there are good reasons to think that this might be true. There will be no further excavation of

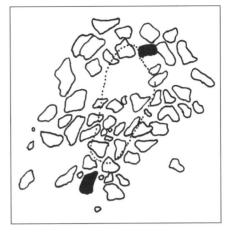

Figure 6.6 Cemetery Site 3: Cairn 13

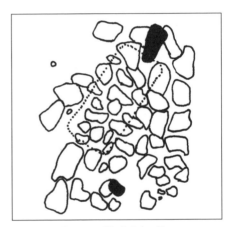

Figure 6.7 Cemetery Site 3: Cairn 18.

Figure 6.8 Cemetery Site 3: Cairn 4.

graves at the site not only because of the change in attitude toward the excavation of graves in South Africa, but also because there is unlikely to be much more to learn from the graves themselves. Work by Peckmann (2002, 2003) has given us clues to the biology of these people and the impact of disease and lifestyle on their health.

The task at deTuin now needs to be taken over by historians and historical archaeologists. Almost nothing is known about the physical structure and settlement pattern of the Bushmanland missions in the 19th century. Historical records from the end of the Korana Wars in 1879 to the division of the land into European stock farms in the early 20th century are virtually unknown. deTuin provides an opportunity to explore an important part of the historical development of modern South Africa and Namibia. Sites such as deTuin can provide us with a wealth of information on the roots of Namibia's 'Baster' communities and also help us to understand the transformation of the KhoeSan people of the northern Cape from independence to dependence as a farm labouring class.

I would strongly suggest the following three thrusts for future research as part of a joint historical/archaeological project:

1. A detailed spatial archaeology of the whole period of settlement at deTuin from the Later Stone Age scatters, through the mission period to the first of the European farms.

2. An historical investigation into the documentary history of the people of the Northern Cape in the last decades of the 19th to the period of European settlement in the early 20th century. This should include the records from the police post opened at Kenhardt in 1869.

3. A joint archaeological and historical investigation of the process of transformation of identities at mission stations especially in view of the shared landscape between the missionised groups and their non-mission neighbours.

Acknowledgements

I thank Mnr H.A. du Plessis for permission to excavate on his property. Graham Louw in 1995 and 1999, and Tanya Peckmann in 2000 took over the field trip supervision for the expeditions in those years. I also thank Elise Fuller for the photographic record in 1994, Royden Yates for the general location maps and the preliminary map of Cemetery Site 1 in 1982, and Vince Phillips and Tanya Peckmann for the final mapping of Cemetery Site 1 in 1999. Over 20 science students participated in the field work over the years and I would like to thank all of them for their enthusiasm and help, particularly Murray Maytom and Janet Putterill who provided the thorough report on UCT 335 and 336 for the first field season in 1982.

Judy Sealy's predilection for collecting decomposing denizens of the highway fringe provided us with a malodorous but constantly interesting trip home to Cape Town after the 1982 expedition. The 1994 and 1995 field trips helped to introduce the 'new' South Africa to Mnr Du Plessis's sons, Riaan and Henry, and we are proud that in some small way we have helped to bring them some understanding of a multi-racial society.

This project was conducted under National Monuments Council Permit numbers 8/94/03/004/51 and 80/99/08/006/51, and funding from the NRF and UCT is gratefully acknowledged.

References

Ashton, H. 1955. *The Basuto*. London: Oxford University Press.

Engelbrecht, J.A. 1936. *The Korana*. Cape Town: Maskew Miller.

Espenshade T.J., Guzman J.C. & Westoff, C.F. 2003. The surprising global variation in replacement fertility. *Population Research and Policy Review* 22: 575-583.

February, E.C. 1996. 'Coffins', wood and the status of the people buried. *Journal of Archaeological Science* 23: 279-282.

Gregory, A.J. 1896. *Report on Suburban Cemeteries*. Cape Town: Government Printers.

Marais, J.S. 1939. *The Cape Coloured People, 1652-1937*. Johannesburg: Witwatersrand University Press.

Moir, R.W. & Sampson, C.G. 1993. European and oriental ceramics from rock shelters in the upper Seacow valley. *Southern African Field Archaeology* 2: 35-43.

Molyneaux, C. n.d. Cemeteries and crematoria committee: tour of inspection by committee on Friday 21st March, 1975. Cape Town.

Morris, A.G. 1992. *The Skeletons of Contact: Protohistoric Burials from the Lower Orange River Valley*. Johannesburg: Witwatersrand University Press.

Morris, A.G. 1995. The Einiqua: an analysis of the Kakamas skeletons. In: Smith, A.B. (ed.) *Einiqualand: Studies of the Orange River Frontier*: 110-164. Cape Town: University of Cape Town Press.

Morris, A.G. 1997. The Griqua and the Khoikhoi: biology, ethnicity and the construction of identity. *Kronos* 24: 106-118.

Morris, D. & Beaumont, P. 1991. !Nawabdanas: Archaeological sites at Renosterkop, Kakamas District, Northern Cape. *South African Archaeological Bulletin* 46: 115-124.

Nurse, G.T. 1975. *The Origins of the Northern Cape Griqua*. Johannesburg, ISMA Paper No. 34.

Nurse, G.T. & Jenkins, T. 1975. The Griqua of Campbell, Cape Province, South Africa. *American Journal of Physical Anthropology* 43: 71-78.

Peckmann, T.R. 2002. Dialogues with the dead: An osteological analysis of the palaeodemography and life history of the 18th and 19th century northern frontier in South Africa. Unpublished PhD Thesis. Cape Town: University of Cape Town.

Peckmann, T.R. 2003. Possible relationship between porotic hyperostosis and smallpox infections in nineteenth-century populations in the northern frontier, South Africa. *World Archaeology* 35(2): 289-305.

Rudner, J. 1968. Strandloper pottery from south and south-west Africa. *Annals of the South African Museum* 49(2): 441-663.

Rudner, J. 1971. Ostrich eggshell flasks and soapstone objects from the Gordonia District, north-western Cape. *South African Archaeological Bulletin* 26: 139-142.

Smith, A.B., Sadr, K., Gribble, J. & Yeats, R. 1991. Excavations in the south-western Cape, South Africa, and the archaeological identity of prehistoric hunter-gatherers within the last 2000 years. *South African Archaeological Bulletin* 46: 71-91.

Steyn, M. 1994. An assessment of the health status and physical characteristics of the prehistoric population from Mapungubwe. Unpublished PhD Thesis. Johannesburg: University of the Witwatersrand.

Steyn, M., Nienaber, W.C. & Meiring, J.H. 2002. An assessment of the health status and physical characteristics of an early 20th-century community at Maroelabult in the North West Province, South Africa. *Homo* 53(2): 131-145.

Strassberger, E. 1969. *The Rhenish Mission Society in South Africa*. Cape Town: Struik.

Strauss, T. 1979. *War along the Orange*. Centre for African Studies, Communications No. 1, University of Cape Town.

Vedder, H. 1928. The Nama. In: Hahn, C.H.L., Vedder, H. & Fourie, L. (eds) *The Native Tribes of South-West Africa*: 109-152. Cape Town: Cape Times Ltd.

Vedder, H. 1938. *South West Africa in Early Times*. Oxford: Oxford University Press.

von Rohden, L. 1888. *Geschichte der Rheinischen Missions-Gessellschaft*. Barman: Wiemann.

Walker, P. 1999. *Woodworking Tools*. Aylesbury: Shire Publications.

Yates, R. 1995. Report on the analysis of ostrich eggshell beads from Geduld. *South African Archaeological Bulletin* 50: 17-20.

7

Reinterpreting the origins of Dzata: archaeology and legends

Edwin Hanisch

Introduction

In tourism brochures, Venda is referred to as the *Land of Legends*. This is very apt, as there are numerous stories, tales, legends and myths about the origins of the *Vhavenda* people, their customs and beliefs, as well as about the land that they inhabit, namely in the north-eastern part of Limpopo Province along the Soutpansberg Mountain Range, northwards into the southern part of Zimbabwe.

It is precisely this plethora of 'legends' that makes research in this area interesting, yet problematic, from the point of view of the archaeologist. The oral history is often contradictory, particularly where political status and intrigue are involved. This became more so with the development of the Thulamela site in the Pafuri area of the northern Kruger National Park, with a conflict of interests between certain Venda and Tsonga clans. With the events leading up to the development and declaration of the Mapungubwe National Park and World Heritage Site, interest amongst local communities increased and claims were made by a variety of different local communities that they were descended from the kings of Mapungubwe.

This has led to new legends being created, where tourists who visit certain Venda villages are told that the people living there are the descendants of tribes that migrated from the north, and who settled at Mapungubwe on their way southwards to the Soutpansberg Mountains (Maphangwa 2003). Some go further to say that they were responsible for the building of the walls at Great Zimbabwe, before moving to Mapungubwe. Again, Mapungubwe was abandoned and these people then settled in the Soutpansberg (S. Moeti 2005 pers. comm.). Further claims were made by a Tsonga clan, who claimed that they had migrated from the Zambezi Valley and settled at Mapungubwe, before moving south-eastwards into Mozambique (Hanisch 2003). It is noteworthy that Prof N.V. Ralushai, who was commissioned to undertake research into the oral history of Mapungubwe, could not find any evidence of legends or knowledge relating to Mapungubwe other than in a song originating amongst the Vhangona (Ralushai 2005). Further research on the Zimbabwean side of the Limpopo River amongst people claiming to be Venda, elicited no knowledge of Mapungubwe other than that of recent origin related to the archaeological work undertaken at various times since the late 1960s (Ralushai 2006 pers. comm.). Ralushai (2005) states further that:

> From the outset, it is important to note that in the present political climate
> (of South Africa), the land claims process tends to distort what people say
> about their relationship with various sites.

Much of the oral history documented in the earlier part of the 20th century and which purported to be the history of the Vhavenda, was actually the history of the Singo rulers, and not that of all the clans that now form an apparently unified group of people. Although it was given that some of the clans had been earlier immigrants, the impact of these on Venda history was considered to be of little importance. In this regard, the late Dr Wilfred Phopi, who had been the ethnographer Dr N.J. van Warmelo's research assistant in Venda for many years in the period between about 1930 to 1950, told me during a visit to the excavations taking place at Dzata in 1989, that he, inadvertently, was part of the reason for the telling of Singo history as though it was the history of the whole Vhavenda nation. In the 1940s, he wrote numerous books on Venda history for use in the local schools. These books were greatly applauded by the local communities because their 'own' history was now available for the Venda children to study. It was only many years later, that Phopi realised that he was telling the history and customs of the ruling Singo clan, and had ignored the histories of the other clans, who were already resident in the Soutpansberg well before the advent of the Singo.

Research in more recent times, by oral historians and archaeologists, has shown that there are alternative histories that can better explain the origins of the Vhavenda, such histories coming mostly from sources not directly related to the ruling families.

In this regard I will present an abridged review of our knowledge about the origins of Dzata, and suggest a different hypothesis more in line with the 'contradictory' archaeological evidence.

Legends on the origins of the Vhavenda

From the above, it can be seen how easily new 'legends' are created and believed by many to be true. Part of the problem of conflicting histories lies in the fact that the Vhavenda are not the homogenous group of migrants that settled south of the Limpopo after 1750 AD, as has been indicated in many of the earlier publications. This latter date relates to the history of the Singo clan, who united the numerous smaller clans with their separate leaders under one centralised authority, based at the town of Dzata in the Nzhelele Valley. According to modern tradition, the leader who achieved this was the legendary Thoho-ya-Ndou (Head of the Elephant), although some earlier versions of the legend suggest that Vele Lambeu, ostensibly the father of Thoho-ya-Ndou,was responsible.

Various early authors have recorded many different versions of what are considered to be the origins of the Venda-speaking peoples. Loubser, in his work on Venda ethnoarchaeology (1991), has given a detailed summary of these publications, and I will therefore not go into specifics, other than to indicate the main schools of thought.

Congo origins

This legend first appears with the advent of the Berlin Missionary Society and its first evangelical outpost in the Tshivhase area in 1872. The Reverend C.L. Beuster, writing in 1879, was the first to link the Vhavenda to the Congo. His evidence was very flimsy, based on unproven similarity in names and language with people in the Congo area (Stayt 1931). This supposition was taught in Beuster's small missionary school as fact, and is still a common belief amongst many people today. Subsequently, this idea was taken up by other authors, notably Grundler and Wessman (Loubser 1991). Available records of the Berlin Missionary Society do not place Beuster as ever having worked in the Congo, although it is clear that the Berlin missionaries were very active along the western coastline of Africa during the 1800s, with penetration into the interior of Africa along the Zaire (Congo) River.

East African origins

A Great Lakes/East African beginning originated with Gottschling in 1905 (Loubser 1991: 151) and was propounded by various authors up until the late 1960s. Ernest Stubbs, a local commissioner writing in 1912, links the role of water in belief systems, which are prevalent under some Venda clans, to legends relating to Lake Fundudzi, which in turn is linked to the East African Great Lakes. Stayt (1931: 12) tells that Chief Senthumule (sic) ' ... is vehement in his assertions that the ancestral home was in the region of Nyasaland (Malawi)... '. More recently, certain local people are trying to prove linguistic similarities between Tshivenda and East African languages. More specifically the suffix *nyika* is given, to show the link between the former German colony, Tanganyika (now Tanzania) and one of the legendary Venda leaders known as Dimbanyika (Lalumbi 2004 pers. comm.; Ramavhoya 2005 pers. comm.). However, it also needs to be indicated that *nyika* occurs in the Shona language, as a reference to land. Furthermore, it must not be forgotten that an early form of Shona was spoken by the early migrants into the Soutpansberg.

Origins from north of the Limpopo

The post-1970 studies in archaeology, history, oral history, linguistics and anthropology clearly show links with Shona-speakers in modern Zimbabwe. The archaeological history demonstrates the cultural, social and political development of a complex society in the Shashe Limpopo Valley and the development of the Mapungubwe kingdom (c. AD 1220 –AD 1280) from which originated the Great Zimbabwe empire. The later fragmentation of this empire at around AD 1450 created groups that moved northwards (Monomotapa), westwards (Khami) and a series of southwards-moving non-unified chieftancies that settled in the Soutpansberg.

Although the evidence for this migration southwards is in many respects fragmentary, it is clear from the nature of many Venda and Shona royal names, place names and traditions that there must be a pre-Singo common origin. Some of this oral history was captured by Stayt (1931) and van Warmelo (1932) as alternatives to the then mainstream theory about the Vhavenda moving as one group into the Soutpansberg. Many oral histories appear to link the Venda quite strongly with the Shona, with van Warmelo's (1932) genealogy of the ruling Singo clan clearly showing that tradition recorded eight generations of chiefs before Chief Makhado, whose reign started in 1864.

Of these, the first three generations are said to have ruled north of Vhembe (the Limpopo River), in what is present-day Zimbabwe. This has been confirmed by Mudau (1940), who at the same time has also collected information to suggest an origin from Matangoni Mountain situated near some large, but unidentified lakes. Nettleton (2006) has stated that the Singo were the last of a long line of Shona invaders into the area south of the Limpopo, suggesting that there had been earlier Shona-speaking migrants well before the advent of the Singo. This links to the descriptions given by Dzivhani (1940) and van Warmelo (1940) of existing clans in the area, and which included Kwevho, Kwinda, Lembethu, Mbedzi, Ndou and Nyai.

The 18th-century dates given to the arrival of a 'unified' group of people into the Soutpansberg, relate to the arrival of the Singo, who, linguistically speaking, were western Karanga, coming from the central-western parts of Zimbabwe. These people are accepted to have been the unifying factor in drawing the earlier clans together to form a centralised political system under the legendary Chief Thoho-ya-Ndou. It is this latter migration that I wish to further discuss, specifically looking at the conflict between archaeological data and oral history and tradition. Growing from this analysis, I suggest a possible alternate history.

The Dzata Heritage Reserve Project

In 1987, the then-President of the apartheid-created Republic of Venda, the late Khosikhulu Patrick Mphephu, ordered that a museum be built at the Dzata Mikondeni archaeological site in the Nzhelele Valley, where the first capital town of a united Venda nation had been built. This museum was intended to open up the Venda culture to other South Africans in an attempt to prove that the Vhavenda were not a secretive, 'backward' nation hiding in the mountains and unwilling to be involved in the ongoing development in South Africa. One section of the museum was intended to be a shrine for what was considered to be the most holy of Venda sacred objects, namely the Ngoma Lungundu Drum. According to legend, this drum had been given by the god, Mwali, to the leader of the southwards migrating Venda (read Singo) to ensure a safe journey to the new lands.

This public disclosure of the sacred drum which, according to tradition, remained hidden in a cave up in the mountains at the village of Tshiendeulu, was to be the ultimate proof that the Vhavenda had now 'opened themselves to the sun', to quote the words of Khosikhulu Mphephu. He unfortunately died before the museum was completed, and none of his advisors or friends knew what he had intended and where the Ngoma Lungundu was actually hidden. It was also indicated clearly that only the reigning king could give permission for the drum to be fetched. The project was undertaken by the Venda Development Corporation (VDC), who employed specialists to complete the building and its design. I will not go into details about all the problems that were encountered, other than to say the VDC withdrew the financial support when it became clear to them that their idea of a museum with its exhibitions could not be completed within the maximum of four years that they normally allowed for the completion of small business projects and the beginning of success and profit-making. Work then stopped on the project.

In 1996, the then Northern Province (now Limpopo) Department of Sport, Art and Culture attempted to resurrect the project and complete the museum. Included in its planning was for proper infrastructure to be created for the viewing of the stonewalls of the old court *(khoro)* and the royal area *(musanda)* with the eventual recreation of this area based on information retrieved from archaeological excavation and oral history combined with the knowledge of traditional building practices related to the royal families. Lack of funding limited this development until 2002-2003.

In view of the fact that this was an archaeological site that would be opened to the public, the regulations as stipulated in the National Heritage Resources Act (No. 25 of 1999) had to be complied with. A Cultural Resources Management Plan had to be compiled, which included a re-evaluation of the existing traditional knowledge about Dzata. It was also necessary to undertake interviews with the local communities to determine to what degree the interpretations of Dzata's history had changed over time.

A steering committee was set up for the project. This steering committee considered it vital that the 26 hectare fenced area around the museum and walled site should be expanded into a larger heritage reserve that could incorporate the full scope of Dzata history as understood by members of the Dzata Steering Committee. This was very specifically the legend relating to the Singo coming from across the Limpopo River with the sacred drum, and settling in the area now known as HaTshiendeulu which lies in a raised valley on top of the central Soutpansberg Mountains, directly north of where Dzata Mikondeni is situated, before moving from the mountains into the Nzhelele Valley.

In view of the fact that I had previously been involved with the 1988 to 1992 planning and research done around the original museum development, I was asked to prepare a Cultural Resources Management Plan for this larger reserve which would include the two ruins associated by tradition with the first settlement of the immigrant Singo at Tshiendeulu[1]. Much information was available from the earlier research process, but more needed to be found for the newly included areas as well as to see how perceptions of history had changed over the intervening 12 years.

A major change noticed was in the availability of information relating to oral history. Informants that had previously freely given information were now saying that they were very much older and had forgotten the details and that I should be talking to the younger members of the community. To see whether the problem was related to something that I did not understand, perhaps regarding local politics, I engaged the services of one of my former postgraduate students in Anthropology, Ms Netshengadzeni Malimavhi. She lived in one of the villages falling under the Mphephu Tribal Authority, and had done her own research on community reactions to persons known to have HIV/AIDS in these local villages. Thus she was known to the various village leaders and communities.

A similar problem arose. People who had freely given information about their own HIV/AIDS-related problems (a very sensitive issue) were suddenly wary and refused to talk. When talking to village leaders, she was told that there was only one old knowledgeable man who could explain all that was needed to know about the Dzata Ruins and Venda history. He turned out to be one of the members of the Dzata Steering Committee, who claimed to have been specifically appointed by the young, recently inaugurated, incumbent of the Mphephu/Ramabulana throne, Khosikhulu Toni Mphephu. Neither I nor Ms Malimavhi could ever get an appointment with this elderly gentleman to discuss Dzata's history, although it was clear from the Steering Committee meetings that he had a very one-sided view of the origins of the Singo and their migration to the Soutpansberg.[2,3]

When moving outside the Nzhelele Valley into the mountains, a very different situation is to be found. Even though several of these villages still fall within the jurisdiction of the Mphephu Tribal Authority, information was freely available, although several informants indicated that they knew more about their own local history than about Dzata. However, it was clear that even this limited knowledge was in many ways similar to that collected in the early and middle parts of the 20th century with some interesting differences, particularly in the oral histories told by members of the Netshiendeulu family which place a new perspective on the history of Dzata Mikondeni.

Locally accepted traditions about the beginning of settlement at Dzata Mikondeni

Broadly speaking, there are two legends about the movement of the Singo into the Nzhelele Valley, namely the entrance into and settlement on top of the Soutpansberg at HaTshiendeulu, with a later movement down into the valley below, where they built the Dzata Mikondeni settlement. The second legend is less accepted locally, and relates that the Singo under the leadership of Dyambeu/Vele Lambeu/Dambanyika settled in the Nzhelele Valley[4]. Both versions, however, have the same ending, that the leader, usually Dambanyika, died up on the mountain when out hunting with his dogs, and was trapped in a cave after a rock fall.

Legend 1 – First Singo settlement at Tshiendeulu

Of the two stonewalled ruins situated at Tshiendeulu, it is accepted that the western ruin is the older of the two, and is not given the same level of importance that is found associated with the eastern ruin. Both figure in the oral traditions but with slight variations in detail. The following is common understanding that underlies the perceived history of the two ruins.

The Singo, under the protection of the magical powers of the Ngoma Lungundu drum migrated from the north-west to settle on top of the Soutpansberg. They built a court and royal area on the lines of a typical Zimbabwe-Khami settlement pattern, using coursing to indicate the royal area (*musanda*). Some informants have claimed that the eastern ruin was where Dambanyika/Dyambeu/Vele Lambeu settled, and that the western ruin was occupied by a senior family member, possibly the chief's sister or *makhadzi* (Lalumbi 2004 pers. comm.). It is said that this chief was inordinately fond of hunting, frequently going out with his dogs to hunt hares and rock rabbits. One of the dogs ran after a rock rabbit into a deep cave, and Dambanyika followed. While inside the cave, a large rock fell across the entrance, entombing him inside.

Legends vary as to the numbers of dogs with Dambanyika, but it is agreed that not all followed their master into the cave. According to one account (Stayt 1931), the dogs remained faithfully outside the cave, until Dambanyika's son, Phophi, came looking for his father and after a long search found the collapsed cave with the dogs guarding it. Phophi is reputed to have been able to talk to his father through the collapsed stone, and was told that Dambanyika was happy to remain where he was. Phophi then returned to the village, and being the eldest son, assumed the mantle of authority. He is said to have left the mountain out of respect to his father, and entered the Nzhelele Valley, where he built Dzata.

There are variations of this legend. One tells that Dambanyika's favourite dog was one of those remaining outside, and when the cave collapsed, the dog (reputedly a female) ran back to the village barking continuously. She attracted the attention of Phophi, who followed the dog back to where his father was imprisoned. Phopi is purported to have entered the village proclaiming his father's death by telling everyone that the Elephant (that is the chief) was dead, but that the head of the elephant (thoho ya ndou) was still alive, thereby declaring himself the next leader under the title of Thoho-ya-Ndou.

Relating to the status of the two ruins, one of the variations explains that Phophi after proclaiming himself to be the chief, could not live in his father's *musanda*, and built a new *musanda* in the eastern part of the village. After living there for many years, Thoho-ya-Ndou vacated the area and went to live in the Nzhelele Valley. It is this perceived association with Thoho-ya-Ndou, that gives the eastern ruin a higher status than the western one.

Legend 2 – First settlement in the Nzhelele Valley

This is simple and straightforward. The migrating Singo entered the Nzhelele Valley and settled at Dzata.

The archaeological data

Dzata Tshiendeulu

Both of the Dzata Tshiendeulu ruins were excavated by Warren Fish, the results of which are recorded in an unpublished Masters thesis.

The western ruin

Fish's excavations concentrated on the western ruin, where numerous features were being exposed by the elements, as well as by a motor track running across part of the site. A large midden in front of the court was dug. Allowing for the variations in the radiocarbon calibration curve, the dates from the various trenches and test pits range between 1435 AD and AD 1650 (Vogel 2000), the latter date coming from a post in layer 1 of trench 8. The majority of the dates, however, range between AD 1435 and AD 1550, with a noticeable gap of eighty years to the two dates of AD 1630 and AD 1650. Pottery recovered was typically that of the Khami period.

The settlement layout shows a court in the front, with a single entrance. When entering, the remains of a single seat in the left-hand wall are visible. The walls are neat, but show no evidence of coursing. This is then the public court. Further to the back, the quality of the stone work improves, and better choice of stone was made to allow the use of coursing in the wall structure. The rear of the ruin is separated by a passage, and the quality of stone work is high, as befitting the status of a royal leader.

The eastern ruin

This ruin is in a better general condition than the western one, although large euphorbia and other tree roots are doing damage to the walls. The coursing is neat, and as in the case of the other ruin, a seat has been built into the wall and is visible on the left-hand side as one enters. A small section of this ruin was opened up by Fish, and a hut floor exposed. Dates from here suggest an age in the mid-1500s, although there is a date from a charcoal sample for AD 1400 from the top layer (Vogel 2000). Again the pottery recovered is Khami.

The impression thus gained is that the western ruin was built before the eastern ruin. This ties in to a certain degree with the one variation of the legend that indicates that Phophi (Thoho-ya-Ndou) moved his residence away from where his father had lived.

Dzata Mikondeni

The accepted legend states that after leaving the Tshiendeulu settlement on the top of the mountain, Thoho-ya-Ndou entered the Nzhelele Valley, where he built his new capital at Dzata. From here he is reputed to have set out to unify all the chiefs under a single centralised authority. Radiocarbon dates for the site vary considerably, with the earliest suggesting a pre-AD 1600 age, ranging through to AD 1810. Loubser (1991) explains that several of the dates are inverted, i.e. older dates in the higher levels with younger dates underneath. It has been suggested that during the cleaning of the assembly area, older charcoal was exposed, swept together and inadvertently deposited on top of the remains from younger fires. The charcoal submitted by Huffman after the 1989 excavations, gave dates that are difficult to place in the radiocarbon calibration curve, but suggest that the abandonment of Dzata was between AD 1750 and AD 1800 (Vogel 2000).

A major factor in determining an age for Dzata lies in the account of Mahumane, a Tsonga man who visited the dark-blue stonewalled capital of the chief Inthowelle at around 1727 to 1728 (Liesegang 1977). The significance in this information is that Dzata Mikondeni is the only known ruin with blue stonewalls. Thus we know that Dzata was definitely occupied in the first part of the 18th century. The radiocarbon dates suggest an occupation that lasted for more than 100 years, ending probably at between 1750 AD and 1760 AD.

The research undertaken by Huffman and Hanisch (1987) on the relationship between known Zimbabwe ruins and Venda history, shows that two phases of development can be identified with Dzata. This is seen in the size of the area covered by original stonewalls, in which a chief's seat could be seen, as well as the remains of a large hut of the size of an audience chamber used by the chief when important visitors came. A second, later audience chamber was constructed when the royal area was enlarged and a new court area built. In addition, the remains of a blocked doorway were found in one of the *musanda* walls,[5] which indicates that there must have been minimally two chiefs who reigned there.

All this information does not fit in with the idea that Dzata Mikondeni was built, occupied and abandoned during the reign of one king, namely Thoho-ya-Ndou. The evidence relating to the period that we associate with the Singo migration into and stay in the Nzhelele Valley, that is from 1700 AD to 1760 AD, suggests that the Singo moved into an area where they knew of an existing town where they then settled. This settlement was enlarged and became the seat of power for an expanding kingdom.

It should be noted that many of the early informants mention Dzata Mikondeni as the first Singo town in the Soutpansberg (Beuster 1879; Gottschling 1905; Wessmann 1908; Stubbs 1912; Harries 1929; Dzivhani 1940; Motenda 1940). It is only later that stories emerged that the Singo briefly settled at Dzata Tshiendeulu (Stayt 1931; Mudau 1940), prior to moving down the mountain to settle in the Nzhelele Valley. Loubser (1991) has suggested that according to some Kwevho and Kwinda informants, Dzata Tshiendeulu was not built by the Singo. Furthermore he states that in his opinion, the most convincing evidence that the Singo never occupied Dzata Tsiendeulu is the fact that their annual *thevula* ceremonies are stricted to Dzata Mikondeni, the implication being that they do not seem to have any concern about Dzata Tshiendeulu in terms of ritual or visitation.

The Singo claims to Dzata Tshiendeulu could be partially the result of the marriage of a Tshiendeulu Kwevho female leader to a Singo headman, but also the fact that the Dzata Tshiendeulu walls are also more impressive than those at Dzata Mikondeni. Considering the fact, as mentioned earlier, that histories are being changed to suit the needs of various rulers, it is possible that the visual contrast might have helped bolster political and prestige claims on the part of the Singo rulers.

Presenting an alternate history of the occupation of the Nzhelele Valley

From the preceding, it is clear that the archaeological evidence is in conflict with the present oral histories, and that the time period in which Dzata Tshiendeulu and Dzata Mikondeni were occupied stretches over a longer time frame than oral tradition would have us believe. It is here that information recovered from the Netshiendeulu family during the research for the Cultural Resources Management Plan can shed some light (Hanisch 2005).

It has been documented in the past that the Netshiendeulu chiefs were part of the Vhatavhatsindi who entered the Soutpansberg long before the Singo arrived. They settled atop the mountains where their descendants still can be found today. The Dzata Tshiendeulu ruin dates fit in with a migration of early settlers from the north, and it would also explain the length of time that this area was occupied. The old *musanda* in the present village is also old, its construction showing elements of coursing, but it is clearly not the original *musanda* dating from the time of entrance of the Vhatavhatsindi into the Soutpansberg. This raises the possibility, as yet unconfirmed, that the two walled sites may relate to the arrival of the Tshiendeulu clan in the area. The antiquity of these ruins clearly predates the known time of arrival of the Singo.

This in turn suggests that the legend stating that Dambanyika entered the Nzhelele Valley and immediately settled at Dzata, may have more than a modicum of truth in it. This would help explain the age discrepancies between the upper and lower sets of ruins. It is also at this stage that the information gleaned from Chief Nkoneni Netshiendeulu and other royal family members during the Dzata Heritage Project comes into its own.

It is said that Chief Mbwaya-penga (Netshiendeulu) was living on top of the mountains, and he was an uncle to Dambanyika/Vele Lambeu. Vele Lambeu visited his uncle and was shown how things are done around the Lwandali (Tshiendeulu) area. Mbwayapenga favoured him, showing him around, telling him to obey and to respect Lwandali mountain, and neither to hunt there nor to visit it without his permission. Vele Lambeu came from the valley, and regularly went into the mountain to hunt. It is agreed that normally a chief would never walk around alone, but because Vele Lambeu was an inveterate hunter, he disliked having people follow him, for fear of disturbing the animals. This explains then, how it would be possible for Vele Lambeu to have been on his own when the cave collapsed on him.

It is thought that the reason for the collapse of the cave had to do with the fact that Vele Lambeu disobeyed his uncle's instructions and was hunting at the mountain without permission. While this is seen as punishment for disobedience, it is possible that while out hunting, Vele Lambeu did enter into a cave which collapsed as a result of an earthquake.

Venda tradition tells that when the earth 'makes noises' it is the great god Mwali showing his displeasure at his people, and the louder the noise, the greater his displeasure which leads to Mwali stamping his feet in anger.

The legends speak of Phophi, the son, becoming chief, and using the name of Thoho-ya-Ndou. The late David Dhavhana (1996 pers. comm.) said that while Thoho-ya-Ndou was a great leader, he was in fact not the legitimate heir to the throne, but a regent appointed because his nephew was too young to reign. During this time, he excelled as a leader. There is no clear evidence that Thoho-ya-Ndou united the different chiefs as has been claimed, this rather being done by Dambanyika shortly after building Dzata. There is no doubt that the early to mid-18th century showed an expansion of the Venda empire, and this could be where people remember him from. Dhavhana also mentioned that when the legitimate heir to the throne was old enough to assume the mantle of power, Thoho-ya-Ndou as regent was not willing to step down. This led to internecine dissatisfaction, and he was forced to flee, leaving Dzata Mikondeni behind. The irate supporters of the new king then are said to have razed Dzata to the ground.

This latter suggestion fits in with the archaeological evidence, where numerous remains of burnt structures can be seen dotted around the landscape. This is further proven by the fact that the audience chamber excavated in 1989 showed that while the structure had been burnt to the ground, the north-westerly quarter had been destroyed shortly after burning as evidenced by the total lack of charcoal posts, consolidated floor and other remains, which were found in the rest of the structure. More importantly, sacred objects, in the form of divining dice, were recovered from the floor of the burnt structure. The four dice were similar in form to those dice excavated elsewhere at Khami Ruins period sites. It is unlikely that such items would have been left behind if the town of Dzata Mikondeni had been voluntarily evacuated.

Conclusion

The discrepancies between oral history and archaeology are never easy to sort out. People are adamant that their knowledge is correct, and forget that stories that were traditionally handed down from grandparents and parents to their offspring around the evening fire, might have changed over time. Certain things will be embellished, while others will quietly be forgotten.

This exercise has been intended to show that more documentation of oral histories and traditions need to be done and cross checked using as wide a range of informants as possible. While the Netshiendeulu version of Singo history may not be entirely correct, it suggests an alternate history that links more closely with what archaeologists have found.

Notes

1 These are known amongst many local persons as Dzata 1, with the lower ruins in the Nzhelele Valley usually referred to as Dzata 2 or Dzata Mikondeni. Fish, in his research on these two ruins, used the name of Mutokolwe, supposedly being the name of the mountain in front of which these structures are situated. These ruins have also been referred to as the Mutokolwe Ruins in the literature (van Heerden 1959; Loubser 1991). Local residents, however, maintain that the only name for these settlements is Dzata 1. Other information suggests that another mountain further away is the actual Mutokolwe. Maps show the these ruins situated on the northern slope of Tshamilora hill. Sometimes the two areas are referred to as the Upper Dzata and the Lower Dzata. For practical purposes, I will refer to the upper ruins as Dzata Tshiendeulu and the lower ruins as Dzata Mikondeni.

2 This has occurred on more than one occasion in other areas, where there appears to be an appointed official, usually a headman, who tells a sanitised version of local history, heavily biased towards creating a favourable impression of the local leader and the community's past and present activities. This seems to be more prevalent in villages that offer cultural activities to tourists than in those that do not.

3 Another issue regarding the reluctance to discuss Dzata openly, is related to tourist guiding, where unofficial and untrained guides to the Dzata Mikondeni site do not want competition to take tourists around and thus lose a potential source of income. Information about Dzata Mikondeni is not given free of charge either, where student researchers have been asked to pay in advance for information relating to the history of the general area (Ramatshimbila 2005 pers. comm.).

4 It is often difficult to know which leader is being referred to, in view of the fact that many royal names are praise names, and more than one name can be used for one royal leader. This custom of giving a chief more than one name, particularly those of ancestors, contributes greatly to genealogical confusion.

5 The practice of blocking a doorway after the death of a chief, relates to the belief that people should never walk in the footsteps of the deceased, and when the successor to the throne continues to use the same *musanda*, a new entrance must be created.

References

Dzivhani, S.M. 1940. The chiefs of Venda. In: Van Warmelo, N.J. (ed.) *The Copper Miners of Musina and the Early History of the Soutpansberg*. Ethnological Publication 8. Pretoria: Government Printer.

Hanisch, E.O.M. 2003. The Manganyi claims: a final report for the Department of Local Government and Housing. Unpublished report. University of Venda, Department of Anthropology.

Hanisch, E.O.M. 2005. A Cultural Resource Management Plan for the Dzata Heritage Reserve. Unpublished report prepared for the Makhado Municipality and the Dzata Steering Committee. University of Venda, Department of Anthropology.

Huffman, T.N. & Hanisch, E.O.M. 1987. Settlement hierarchies in the northern Transvaal: Zimbabwe ruins and Venda history. *African Studies* 46.

Loubser, J.H.N. 1991. The Ethnoarchaeology of Venda-speakers in South Africa. *Navorsinge van die Nasionale Museum Bloemfontein*. 7(8). Bloemfontein: National Museum.

Maphangwa, H. 2003. Tourism in Mukumbani. Unpublished report.

Mudau, E. 1940. Ngoma Lungundu and the early invaders of Venda. In: Van Warmelo, N.J. (ed.) *The Copper Miners of Musina and the Early History of the Soutpansberg*. Ethnological Publication 8. Pretoria: Government Printer.

Nettleton, A.C. 2006. Samson Mudzunga, Dzingoma, and new mythologies. *African Arts* Winter 2006.

Ralushai, V.N. 2005. Oral history of Mapungubwe. Unpublished report.

Stayt, H.A. 1931. *The Bavenda*. London: Oxford University Press.

Stubbs, E. 1912. *The History of the Bavenda*. Grahamstown.

Van Heerden, P.W. 1959. Die bouvalle van Vendaland. *Bantu* 6.

Van Warmelo, N.J. 1932. *Contributions towards Venda History, Religion and Tribal Ritual*. Ethnological Publications 3. Pretoria: Government Printer.

Van Warmelo, N.J. (ed.) 1940. *The Copper Miners of Musina and the Early History of the Soutpansberg.* Ethnological Publications 8. Pretoria: Government Printer.

Vogel, J.C. 2000. Radiocarbon dating of the Iron Age sequence in the Limpopo Valley. In: Leslie, M. & Maggs, T. (eds). *African Renaissance: The Limpopo Valley 1000 Years Ago. The South African Archaeological Society Goodwin Series* 8: 51-57.

SECTION 2

Material Identities

8

Revisiting Bokoni: populating the stone ruins of the Mpumalanga Escarpment

P. Delius and M.H. Schoeman

Introduction

Stonewalled ruins in Mpumalanga materialise the complex dynamics of the area's pre-colonial past. Some of these settlements, such as the Ndzundza and Pedi capitals, continue to resonate in the present and were used as symbols of precolonial independence during the 20th century. Many more have become largely disconnected from memory and tradition. This paper revisits a group of these 'lost sites' and links them with a fragmented history of Bokoni. To do this we establish a dialogue between history and archaeology, that allows us to reflect on the people who lived in Bokoni and their economy.

Archaeological research on the Orighstad–Carolina stonewalled sites

The complex terraced and stonewalled sites between Orighstad and Carolina (Fig. 8.1 & Plate 3) have captivated many generations of South African archaeologists (e.g. Van Hoepen 1939; Mason 1962, 1968; Evers 1973, 1975; Collett 1979, 1982; Maggs 1995; Coetzee 2003; Smith 2006; Maggs this volume). P.W. Laidler, who specialised in precolonial ceramics, was the first archaeologist to visit the sites and collect a ceramic sample. Decoration placement and technique led him to suggest that the pottery associated with the ruins was comparable with pottery of known Zulu origin (Laidler 1932). Laidler did not, however, examine the stonewalled sites in any detail because his passion was pots, not the sites they came from.

Fortunately the sites did not escape the archaeological gaze for long and the Bloemfontein-based archaeologist E.C.N. van Hoepen published a detailed report on these stonewalled sites in 1939. This pioneering study focused on the stonewalled enclosures and terraces on the farms Blouboskraal, Schoongezicht and Boomplaas, and associated engravings on the farms Blouboskraal, Boomplaas and an unnamed adjoining farm (Plate 3). He (Van Hoepen 1939) provided detailed descriptions of the stonewalled enclosures, including their size, architecture and spatial layout. Much of his report focused

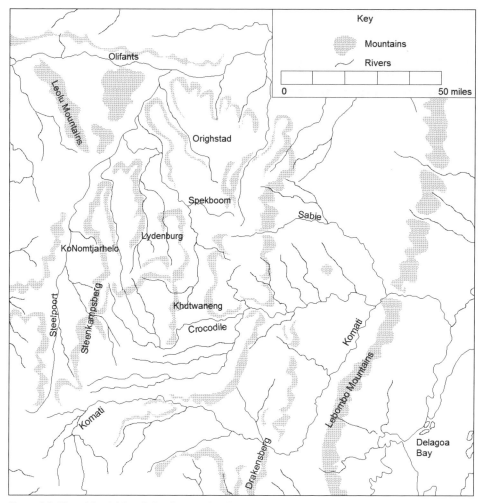

Figure 8.1 Map of the Orighstad–Carolina area in relation to the Indian Ocean coast and other groups (adapted from Aylward 1978).

on the function of features and use of structures. He interpreted the enclosures as African homesteads occupied by polygamous patriarchs, their wives, and children who were the ancestors of the Pedi and Ndzundza people who lived in the areas in the 1930s.

Three decades passed before archaeologists were drawn back to the Lydenburg escarpment sites. The renewed interest was spurred by Revil Mason's 'Iron Age Programme' (Evers 1973). Mason (1962) described the terraced settlements on the escarpment and outlined preliminary excavation results. This brief examination was followed by a preliminary aerial photograph survey, which allowed him to locate 1 792 stonewalled settlements in the drainage basin of the Steelpoort, Sabi, Crocodile and Komati rivers (Fig. 8.1 and Plate 3) (Mason 1968; Evers 1973).

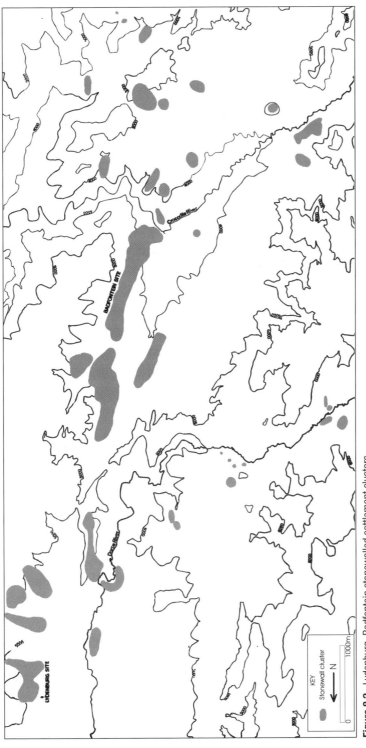

Figure 8.2 Lydenburg–Badfontein stonewalled settlement clusters.

T.M. Evers' contribution to the 'Iron Age Programme' built on Mason's research with an intensive aerial photograph survey of the area between Lydenburg and Machadadorp (Evers 1973, 1975). This study identified 166 stonewalled sites (equivalent to 5 000 settlements, using Mason's definition). Sites tended to cluster on the eastern slopes, but their distribution was uneven and distinct clusters could be observed (Fig. 8.2 & Plate 3). For example, 58 of the 166 identified sites, including both large dispersed – and small settlements on bevels on the valley side, cluster in the Dorpsrivier valley (Marker & Evers 1976).

For Evers (1975), the sites were the remains of homesteads built in fairly uniform patterns. Houses always surrounded a central stonewalled cattle enclosure that had subsidiary enclosures. A smooth ring wall surrounded the whole, separating domestic areas and agricultural terraces. Stonewalled tracks linked the homesteads to one another, and lead from the central enclosures to areas unaltered by construction. These were located downslope from the homesteads and terraces, and were clearly separated from the terraced areas by a higher stonewall at the outer edge of the lowest terrace. This architectural arrangement suggests that the tracks controlled access to the terracing and were built to protect crops from trampling when cattle were moved between the byres and un-terraced downslope grazing areas (Marker & Evers 1976).

Marker and Evers (1976) noted three different types of stonewalled enclosures in the Lydenburg area. The first are simple enclosures, consisting of two concentric circles. These are found in small, isolated settlements. The second are complex in structure with a large central enclosure, generally with two opposed entrances and a number of smaller circles around the perimeter. They are found in large settlements or smaller settlements on the eastern boundaries and middle of valleys. The third consist of an agglomeration of several small circles, and are not associated with terraces. The association of simple enclosures with small settlements and complex enclosures with larger settlements could suggest that the simple enclosures are associated with smaller homesteads and the complex ruins with villages. If this assumption is correct it might indicate a similar cattle ownership pattern to that suggested for Nqabeni. Nqabeni is a stonewalled late farming community site near Babanango in KwaZulu-Natal (Hall & Maggs 1979; Hall 1984). Similar to the Bokoni sites Nqabeni consists of a large central secondary enclosure surrounded by several smaller primary enclosures. This is in contrast with the ethnography, which states that all Zulu homesteads contain a single enclosure. Hall (1984) explains this difference in settlement pattern by arguing that in contrast to the ethnographic model where a single family owned the homestead cattle, several lineage segments sharing a settlement owned the Nqabeni cattle, or that each wife owned her own cattle.

In the late 1970s Dave Collett enrolled for a Masters degree at the University of the Witwatersrand (Wits). His research was designed to complement work done by Mason and Evers and concentrated on the Badfontein valley to the south, an area only briefly examined by Evers (1975) (Plate 3). Here, most settlements were on west-facing slopes, but this was determined by water availability (Collett 1979, 1982). Collett's project focused on the differences between simple and complex ruins noted by Marker and Evers (1976).

In the Badfontein area both simple and complex enclosures occurred within the same settlement. Collett (1979, 1982) concurred with Evers (1975) and Marker and Evers (1976) that the complex stonewalled enclosures were cattle byres, and cattle tracks channelled cattle out of the homesteads and terraces. In addition he found clusters of house remains distributed between complex stonewalled enclosures. This scattered house distribution suggests a different spatial layout to the central cattle pattern found by Evers. In spite of the variation in settlement pattern, Collett (1979, 1982) concluded that the complex enclosures and houses formed homesteads or villages. On the other hand no houses were found at the simple stone ruins, which were randomly located in settlements. Consequently Collett (1979, 1982) interpreted them as small stock kraals. The simple enclosures were associated with agricultural terracing, suggesting that the small stock were allowed to graze between fields.

Collett also corroborated Evers' (1975) arguments about crop production and animal husbandry based on Evers' excavations on a three-square-miles village on the farm Badfontein. Evers (1975) stated that cattle byres, cattle tracks and cattle and sheep/goat bones bore witness to animal keeping, whereas a metal hoe and metal sharpening wear patterns on terrace stones indicated agriculture. Later Klingbeil Nature Reserve excavations also yielded large quantities of grindstones and iron hoes (Marker & Evers 1976). These early assertions about crop production were based on circumstantial evidence, but were shown to be correct when Collett (1979, 1982) found sorghum seeds on *dakha* house floors.

The Wits 'Iron Age Programme' was disbanded after Mason left the university, and systematic research in the Orighstad–Carolina area ended. In the next two decades only a few brief studies were conducted. These include Maggs' (1995) examination of the settlement engravings first noted by Van Hoepen (1939), a UP honours project (G. De Kampe 2006 pers. comm.) and an uncompleted Masters project (S. Tiley 2006 pers. comm.).

In the last few years the archaeological and historical gaze has returned to the area. Coetzee (2003) conducted a heritage survey of the farm Welgedacht and the University of South Africa (UNISA) intends to follow this initial survey with more intensive student research. Two University of Pretoria (UP) honours projects have also examined the stonewalled sites. Coetzee (2005) developed a spatial location GIS model, which suggested the key factor in site selection is proximity to water. This was followed by a smaller scale study by Smith (2006), who tested the nitrogen and phosphorous content, as well as the pH levels, of soil samples from terraces, potential domestic areas and a complex ruin identified by Coetzee (2003). Her results indicated clear spatial differences in the soil chemistry. Smith (2006) argued that the distinct enrichment of the central enclosure soil indicated that it housed cattle, thus supporting the conclusions reached by Evers (1975), Marker and Evers (1976) and Collett (1979, 1982).

A last stand?

Until now all the archaeological research in the area focused on sites located on gentle slopes. These, however, are not the only sites in the area. A local farmer and stonewalled site enthusiast, Eric Johnson, has tapped into local knowledge, including the African names for, and other aspects of the history of, these archaeological sites.

One such remembered place is Marangrang's capital in the Badfontein valley. Marangrang's role in the area's history is discussed more fully in the history section of this paper, so for now we will just note that Marangrang reunited scattered people in the Lydenburg-Badfontein area after the devastation of the Mfecane and built a defensive capital at Khutwaneng.

The Marangrang site expresses the insecurity of the Mfecane and breaks dramatically with the valley settlement pattern. It is located in a kloof, at the end of a valley facing the Crocodile River valley. Two spurs constrict the eastern entrance into the valley. Behind these, terraces and freestanding stonewalled enclosures mark the slopes. These are similar to the sites discussed in the previous section, but this pattern changes as the valley narrows into a kloof. Here densely clustered stonewalled courtyards replace the larger stonewalled enclosures. The kloof seems to contain several hundred courtyards. More courtyards might be located on a buttress half way up the cliff face.

Undoubtedly, the site is geared to defence, and is reminiscent of the contemporary Ndzundza capital KoNomtjarelo.[2] The only visible access is from the valley entrance, since steep cliffs protect both the back and sides of the settlement. Marangrang, however, was defeated while on a raid to the north. This signalled the final end of political and economic independence of the Orighstad–Carolina area. We suggest that this also ended the tradition of building terraced stonewalled sites.

Who lived at these sites?

Van Hoepen (1939) conducted the first detailed examination of the Mpumalanga stonewalled sites, merely a decade after Gertrude Caton-Thompson (1931) published her

Great Zimbabwe findings. Both faced similar challenges: the white South African public did not believe that black Africans were capable of constructing complex stonewalled settlements (see Hall 1994a) and diffusionist models dominated archaeology (Hall 1994a, 1994b; Gardner 1968). In spite of this Van Hoepen (1939) argued that there was no link between the Hamitic people, who were said to have occupied Zimbabwe (Dart 1940), and the Mpumalanga sites. Instead, he suggested that the Mpumalanga sites were built and occupied by the ancestors of the Ndebele and Pedi who were still living in the area.

Van Hoepen's (1939: 61,73) assertion that the sites were built and occupied by black Africans has been corroborated by all subsequent archaeological research.[3] Evers (1973, 1975) narrowed Van Hoepen's broad identification and argued that the sites could be attributed to the Pedi because the settlement layout and ceramics indicated a close cultural affinity with modern Pedi, and in the 18th and 19th centuries a Pedi polity controlled the Lydenburg area. Interestingly, Marker and Evers (1976) noted that the Koni occupied the Lydenburg area, but were led by the Pedi leader Thulare's son (Marker & Evers 1976). However, the historical data, linking the area to the Koni, did not alter Evers' Pedi classification. It is likely that his ceramic-based approach, founded on a link between pots and culture, shaped his reading of the historical evidence (see Hall 1994b for a critical discussion of this approach to ceramics). Collett (1979, 1982), using Evers' ceramics approach, also identified the sites as Pedi.

The Pedi model was dominant amongst archaeologists until Schoeman (1997) argued that this line of reasoning was flawed. She (1997: 33, 205) argued that the sites were Koni because Pedi oral traditions referred to the Kutoane (Badfontein) area as a Koni stronghold, which the Pedi attacked under the leadership of Mampuru. Hunt (1931), however, linked the stronghold – not the valley stonewalled sites – with late-18th century Koni. Schoeman (1997) also did not present any evidence showing that the boundaries of Koni territory corresponded with the area in which these sites occur or that the Koni occupation did not post-date the construction of the stonewalled sites. This paper shows that although Schoeman's argument was less than solid, her identification of the site's occupants was accurate. Her implicit assumption that the Koni were an ethnic group has proved to be wide of the mark. Unfortunately Huffman (2004) accepted Schoeman's (1997) identification uncritically, arguing that these stonewalled sites were the creation of the Koni, who he viewed as a homogenous Nguni cultural group, most likely with Langa origins (Huffman 2004: 98).

We will revisit Schoeman's (1997) identification and Huffman's (2004) subsequent assumptions in the third part of this paper. But we first explore the historical record because a more comprehensive answer to who lived at these sites can be found in the historical and oral accounts about the area. Evers (e.g. 1973; Marker & Evers 1976) was familiar with some of these accounts, but he chose to ignore content that clashed with the ceramic model.

Who lived in Bokoni? – Perspectives from oral sources

This section of the paper explores the answers to the above question that are offered by oral sources. These sources fall into two main categories. The first are traditions collected mainly in the 1860s and 1870s by Berlin missionaries, which include elements of personal testimony gathered from individuals who had lived through the tumultuous transformations in the region since 1800. The second are accounts collected by officials and academics from about 1900 with the inhabitants of the hybrid world of the Ethnology Section of the Department of Native Affairs playing a prominent role. With very limited exceptions, the possibilities offered by contemporary oral sources remain to be explored.

The traditions that have been tapped were mainly collected under conditions that would make most current exponents of the craft of oral history recoil in horror. Informants are often not named, little is known of their life stories, no systematic record was kept of discussions; the information was collected by individuals with exceptionally intrusive personal agendas and usually in a context of deeply asymmetrical power relations. Nonetheless, short of time travel adding a whole new dimension to research, these sources cannot be ignored for they contain embedded fragments of historical narratives and personal experiences that would otherwise be lost to researchers. It is however imperative that they should be handled with critical care and that the most obvious pitfalls should be avoided. One deep donga which we will have to traverse in the journey we plan to take in this paper is the tendency of oral accounts to focus on the powerful – on history's apparent winners – and to downplay the experiences of those individuals and groups whose narratives, however decisive and dramatic in their own times, end in defeat.

One particularly clear example of this tendency in Mpumalanga and one which has important implications for our pursuit of the Koni, is the neglected history of the Ndwandwe. For many years a cosy consensus prevailed that the Ndebele under Mzilikazi had devastated the societies of Mpumalanga and, in particular, that in the 1820s they were instrumental in the destruction of the powerful Pedi Kingdom. While some still hold to this view, closer research and evidence uncovered in the 1970s has suggested that the Ndwandwe played a critical, probably central, role in reshaping power relations in the region. Reinvigorated by a sojourn by the Steelpoort River they returned to challenge Zulu power only to suffer catastrophic defeat in 1826. Some of those fleeing the carnage may have sought sanctuary with the Ndebele and this infusion of population perhaps boosted the power of Mzilikazi's Kingdom. What is certain however, is that the Ndwandwe, once defeated, faded from the record creating a historical vacuum occupied by the expanding reputation of the Ndebele (Delius 1983: 19-24).

It is our contention in this paper that the inhabitants of Bokoni have suffered a rather similar fate. By the time that oral evidence was first gathered in the region the Pedi Kingdom had enjoyed a long, if interrupted, period of political and economic hegemony. It was also the prime focus of an intense, though faltering, missionary effort which ensured that the history of that Kingdom provided the primary focus of historical enquiry. By the 1860s the Swazi Kingdom was the major alternative point of interest while some of the more powerful and recalcitrant local chiefdoms such as the Ndzundza Ndebele, the Pulana and the Kopa were also the objects of some curiosity from missionaries and officials. While much was made of the impact of Mzilikazi's Ndebele, the basic assumption behind most accounts was of history interrupted rather than of a past that had been radically reconfigured. But alerted by the archaeological evidence, a close reading of this material against the grain of Pedi-centrism suggests that a major chapter in the history of the region has been neglected and points to the existence of a political and economic system which certainly rivalled its northern neighbour over several centuries. This social system starts to emerge into clearer focus when we explore questions about identity and to consider the economic and political dynamics of the settlements in the region

The origins of the term Koni are shrouded in controversy and confusion with a range of sources suggesting a bewildering range of options.[4] Two key ideas shape these suggestions. The first and certainly the most widely held view is that the term Koni is the Sotho equivalent of Nguni or Ngoni and was probably the name given by Sotho-speaking communities to Nguni-speaking intruders in a process broadly similar to the development of the term [Transvaal] Ndebele described by Lekgoathi (2003). But this view has been sharply challenged by Makhura (2007: 99) who has argued, partly on the basis of recently recorded traditions, that 'the label Koni has little to do with Nguni. Linguistically Bokone means 'northern region' or northerly direction, while Bakone refers to people of, or from, the north.' He argues as a result that the communities in and around Polokwane, Mokopane and in Mpumalanga, who are today identified as Koni, have migrated into the area from the north. It would be difficult to imagine more diametrically opposed views but the contradiction may not be as profound as it appears at first sight.

The main casualty of this exchange is the idea that all the communities carrying the appellation Koni have an even broadly common origin or that they all have a connection to the stonewalled sites in Mpumalanga. It seems clear from the existing traditions that quite distinct groups of people, who may have followed very different routes into northern Mpumalanga, are involved. It is also likely, as Mönnig (1963) points out, that shifting patterns of status and power led to some groups adopting new elements of identity and that some Roka groups, for example, may have claimed a Koni origin. He also points out that the Koni groups in the region in the 1960s had a bewildering variety of totems and that it is obvious that not all of these have an Nguni origin (Mönnig 1967: 16-17). Whether linguistic, geographic, or assumed, the term Koni is clearly one initially applied by outsiders (as in the case of the Transvaal Ndebele) which may over time have come to have some meaning for the groupings so named. These labels almost certainly would not have conformed to the primary forms of internal identification within these groups which were also probably considerably more diverse and distinct than contemporary onlookers imagined. It is also quite possible that elements of both language and geography were combined in this single term. Berlin Missionary sources in 1860 – heavily influenced by Paris missionaries based in Lesotho – described:

> In the region of Lydenburg are East Betchaunan tribes encountered once more. One names them Bakoni to differentiate them from the Bassuto in the south. The Maperi [BaPedi] under chief Sekwati on the middle of the Olifants River are part of/belong to them [the Bakoni[5]] (Berliner Missions Berichte 1860: 338).

This description, based on a view from the south, sees the Pedi as part of a wider Koni grouping and suggests a geographic dimension to the term. But fragments of tradition collected in one of the key areas of stonewalled settlement instead intimate that the term Koni carries Nguni associations.

In the 1930s the linguist C.W. Prinsloo wrote an MA thesis on *Sekoni* language and focused on what he describes, following Van Warmelo (1935) as the 'Eastern Bakoni' who still resided in the heartland of what he described as 'Bokoni' (the land of the Bakoni) the area between Machadadorp, Lydenburg and Sabie. The men he spoke to all broadly agreed that they were related to the Nguni.

> Some contend that they moved from the North-West of Transvaal with a group of Zulu to the Transvaal Highveld. Here the Koni separated and went to live in Bokoni … The old north-western home is sometimes referred to as … Phateng (at the stick) in the West (Prinsloo 1936: 9).

Others made rather broader claims that the Koni, the Zulu (Swazi) and Mbayi (Pai?) all came from one place. Some old Koni declared they were 'MaPono' (a term referring to Nguni-speakers) and that this was obvious from the fact that they wore the shields of the Pedi in war – a comment which probably owed something to the contemporary perceptions of the Zulu, as well as their location in a context where most of the military threats to the Pedi kingdom emanated from the south. This strong sense of Nguni origins did not, however, prevent these individuals from acknowledging that they shared a great deal in common with their Sotho-Tswana-speaking neighbours. It is also possible that Prinsloo (1936), influenced by the cultural determinism of the times in the work of Van Warmelo and others, searched for a coherence in identity that may well have been missing. Interestingly traditions collected in the 1940s from the Ngomane of Nkapana in the Barberton area recalled that this group had lived in the escarpment area in the 18th century and that at that time 'they were an independent Sotho tribe' but that when they came down the mountain they left the Sotho behind and adopted a Tsonga identity (Myburgh 1949: 105-6)

Research on other communities of this period in the region suggests that while chiefdoms were ruled by dominant lineages they were usually composed of a complex amalgam of groups of diverse origin and disparate cultural forms which were caught up in a constant process of fusion and fission and cultural transformation. There is little reason to believe that the Koni would not have conformed to this wider pattern. But it is also plausible that – as elsewhere on the continent – identity may have been partly conditioned by a particular adaptation to a distinctive environment (Iliffe 1995: 109). As a result those who shared that lifestyle may have been seen as having a common identity irrespective of language, totem or traditions of origin. While the evidence is not available to establish clear conclusions, these suppositions suggest that the exploration of the mode of existence of these communities, which we enter into below, may enhance rather than distract from our understanding of issues of identity.

The history of settlement that Prinsloo was able to construct from his oral sources recalls a large settlement 'Moxômatsi' (Prinsloo 1936: 11) in the district of Belfast to the south of Machadadorp (farm Dalmanutha no. 104) as the first Koni site in the vicinity of Bokoni but this settlement suffered so many attacks by the 'Mapono' (Prinsloo 1936: 11) that they moved to a settlement 'Mohloxo-Pela' (Prinsloo 1936: 11) just east of Machadadorp. While the main village remained in this spot, smaller chiefs began to develop new villages all over the area of which the best known was 'Khutwaneng, Metsi a Thatha' (the shattered water/ water vapour) (Prinsloo 1936: 12).

In the absence of detailed genealogies or lists of circumcision groups it is impossible to establish a clear chronology for this process of settlement but the more detailed oral traditions of neighbouring groups helps to create some kind of time line. There is general agreement that the Maroteng, who eventually established the Pedi Kingdom, settled in

Mpumalanga in approximately 1650. The earliest collected Pedi tradition recalls that as they moved into the area from the south-west, one party crossed the Crocodile River where they encountered Koni groups (Merensky 1862: 328). This suggests that, at the very least, Koni communities had been living in the area since the beginning of the 17th century as there is no suggestion in these or other traditions that the Koni were newcomers to the region.

Maroteng settlement over the next 170 or so years was focused on the area between the south bank of the Steelpoort River and the environs of the Spekboom River which made them close neighbours of Koni groups to the south-west and east. Any conflict which might have arisen from this situation were probably mitigated by a loose hegemony exercised over both groupings by the Mongatane – a Baroka chiefdom which was based in a valley formed by the east flank of the Leolu Mountains to the north of the Steelpoort River.

In approximately 1740, during a period of economic and political growth and towards the end of the long reign of the Pedi chief Moukangwe, the Pedi clashed with one of their Koni neighbours – the Kgomane. The reasons given for this antagonism vary. In one account Mohube, one of Moukangwe's senior sons, who was acting as regent for his increasingly frail father, trespassed on the hunting grounds of the Kgomane who killed him and some of his followers (Hunt 1931: 277; see also Winter 1912: 90). In another account Mohube was killed because his cattle had damaged the crops of the Kgomane (TA SNA 74/1325/07). Both versions suggest that the Maroteng were intent on expanding their areas of control. One source locates this Koni group on the farm Krugerspost which lies north-east of Lydenburg (TA SNA 74/1325/07), but an alternative location has been suggested by the fact that a valley lying in the escarpment that falls away beneath Dullstroom to the Crocodile River is known as gaKomane (E. Johnson 2007 pers. comm.).

Whatever its precise causes or location, this incident sparked clashes which led the Kgomane to appeal to the Mongatane to bring the Maroteng to heel. The fact that they sided with the Kgomane may have been based on the length of their relationship, the relative seniority of that grouping or a fatal miscalculation of relative power. But the outcome of their intervention was clear-cut. The Maroteng challenged their power and initiated a process, that led to the formation of the Pedi Kingdom (Winter 1912: 90-91; Hunt 1931: 278).

During the regency of Mampuru who succeeded the slain Mohube, freed of even notional Mongatane control, the Maroteng renewed their pressure on Koni groups. An expedition was sent:

> against the Bakoni stronghold known as Kutoane (... near Badfontein, south of Lydenburg). This stronghold appeared to the Bapedi to have only

one entrance which was successfully defended by the Bakoni. A Mokoni traitor who had married a Mopedi wife revealed another feasible entrance to Mampuru who ordered his own son Nthobeng to attempt it by night, but he was afraid. Moroamotshe [Mohube's son and the heir apparent] agreed to go with his own koma circumcision school regiment, the Makoa, and with the help of the traitor, climbed into the heart of the stronghold, so that when Mampuru attacked again at dawn the stronghold and its chief Ntsuanyane were soon captured (Hunt 1931: 279-280).

Another, though linked, source amplifies this account telling how

The [Koni] guide brought them behind the stronghold to a big fig tree (Moumo-Ficus elastica?) the branches of which always have strong air-roots and are easily climbed. Then they went up to the top of a big rock with little precipices all around. They thus entered the stronghold without being seen (Winter 1912: 92).

Morwamotše, after a great deal of conflict with his uncle and his cousin, finally became the Pedi King and this account is no doubt intended to demonstrate his superior fitness to rule. But these recurring clashes with clearly formidable Koni groups suggest that they were a major obstacle to the expansion of Pedi power. It may also be that both encounters involved broadly the same groups. As noted above some sources locate the Kgomane close to Badfontein which would make them, at the very least, close neighbours. But if there were different groups of Koni involved to the south-east and to the south-west it would suggest that this contestation was taking place on a fairly broad front of a 100 or so kilometres.

It also appears that Koni groups fell under the sway of the Maroteng from this time. Winter's key informant Ra'lolo recalled that after their clashes with the Maroteng the Kgomane sent a girl to them as a peace offering, and built once more near their old kraal which would suggest the beginnings of a tributary relationship (Winter 1912: 91). While Hunt notes that in the period of Mampuru's regency the Koni became 'incorporated into the Bapedi system, though like all South African tribes in similar case, whether conquered or amalgamated, they continued to retain their clan name and identity' (Hunt 1931: 281). It is probable that this form of rule over time conformed to the wider pattern in the Pedi Kingdom in which subordinate chiefdoms took their chief wives from the Maroteng, recognised overarching ritual and economic rights, and took unresolved disputes to the court system at the Pedi capital. Evidence from the 1860s suggests that particularly powerful chiefdoms exercised regional hegemony within this broader system and this may well have been the case in the 18th century and in relation to Koni groups. Clearly, the fact that the Koni groups feature so centrally in the narrative of the first phases of Maroteng expansion suggests that they were a major force in the region and that they were in command of resources that were fundamental to the growth of the Kingdom.

The importance of these groups and of the area they controlled is also suggested by the critical role they play in struggles for central power in the Pedi Kingdom. When Morwamotše died (1780?) two of his sons Dikotope and Thulare, fought fiercely to succeed him. After a telling attack by Thulare, Dikotope sought refuge with Koni groups at Ohrigstad (Maepa) and formed a military alliance with the Mongatane and Koni against his pugnacious brother. While this episode is reflected in some degree in traditions collected in the 1860s, the renegade Berlin Missionary J.A. Winter provides the fullest account of these events drawn from his key informant Ra'lolo:

> Dikotope wished to go back to their old home at the Mogokgoma-tree lower down the Steelpoort. Tulare said to him: Go on, I shall follow you later.' So Dikotope went, but Tulare remained. One day the cattle-herd[ers] incited by Tulare, drove all the cattle from Dikotope, when they were out grazing, to Tulare. Dikotope was afraid to attack Tulare. The latter formed an *Impi*, and went to kill Dikotope, who fled away with his people to near Ohrigstad. When there, he secretly arranged an expedition against Tulare, joined by the Bakoni and the Ba-Mongatana, who were still sore at having lost their Paramountcy. Tulare heard of this [and struck before the two armies could combine] ... . The ba-Mongatana (with ba-Pasha and Ba-Nkoana) camped on this side [north-east] of the Steelpoort, opposite Tulare on the other side. Early in the morning, when the ba-Mogatana were still smoking dagga, Tulare's men attacked them gaining a splendid victory ... then went back to attack Dikotope's kraal, while the latter was still away forming his Bakoni impi ... . Tulare's forces waited for Dikotope to come. He came but his auxiliaries were still behind. They fought, Tulare again had the victory. Dikotope was killed, as also the Chief of Maepa (the Bakoni), Mo'labini. Now Tulare went home, the real undisputed Paramount Chief of the country. He became the greatest and till today the most renowned Chief of the Bapedi (Winter 1912: 94).[6]

As this source makes clear, during Thulare's reign (1790?-1820?) the Pedi kingdom reached the apogee of its power and prosperity eventually exercising close control over an expanded heartland including the area defined as Bokoni and exercising a looser hegemony over an area described by informants as Lekwebepe – between the Vaal and the Limpopo.

Thulare's death in approximately 1820 ushered in a period of profound political instability as his sons vied for power. Once again Bokoni groups feature prominently in the narrative of strife. Makopole, one of his senior sons though not a designated heir who had distinguished himself through his strength and bravery, left the Pedi capital either as a result of tensions with his father and/or with his brothers and settled amongst the Koni near Lydenburg and built a political base there. Thulare seems to have given his sons special responsibility for different areas of the Kingdom and it may be that Makopole had developed strong bonds with the people of Bokoni over a long period of time. Marriage ties may also have cemented this relationship. What is clear is that Makopole acted increasingly independently and is described as 'chief of the Bakoni' (Hunt 1931: 285).[7]

Any idea that Makopole might have had of a gradual consolidation and expansion of his power were overtaken by a dramatic and destructive turn of events. The death of Thulare unleashed powerful centrifugal forces as his most powerful sons competed intensely for central power and for regional control within the Kingdom. Oral traditions recall one brother succeeding another in bewildering and often treacherous fashion. Attempts by one short-lived incumbent, Phethedi, to conquer Makopole's formidable stronghold failed. But while Makopole was able to fend off attacks from the north, clouds were gathering in the south-east which at first appeared pregnant with possibility, but proved to be the harbingers of an approaching political cyclone.

This period in the history of the region was one filled with menace for those who lived through it but it is also littered with pitfalls for the unwary historian. Two intersecting historical paradigms have shaped this hazardous terrain. The conflicts that follow the death of Thulare are presented in a range of oral traditions as a morality play that demonstrates the hazards of overweening ambition and the erosion of properly constituted authority. Not least of all (although this is never explicitly stated in the traditions but is consistent with core beliefs in the society) because the ancestors who cherished order and co-operation amongst their living kin would been outraged by their unseemly antics and would at the very least have moderated their protection of the community from misfortune. To make this drama effective it is important that the death of Thulare is closely connected to the disasters that follow and this, in our view, leads to a compressed chronology and a related simplification of events. This problem is compounded by the dating of Thulare's death. This is associated in traditions with a solar eclipse (what after all could be a more potent symbol of a disturbance of the proper order?) which can be dated to 1824. The idea that Thulare actually died on the day of the eclipse has been uncritically accepted by a range of historians. We would suggest that while some loose correlation in time undoubtedly exists it could be considerably more elastic than is currently portrayed. This suspicion is deepened by the sense of 'history in fast forward' that dating Thulare's death to 1824 imposes on ensuing events. In reality Thulare's death may have been considerably earlier, perhaps in approximately 1820 or before.

The second source of confusion is colonial historical myopia. The understanding of events in the interior developed by white travellers, missionaries and officials was unsurprisingly shaped by their own particular history. In this particular narrative, for reasons which need not be rehearsed here, the Ndebele, led by Mzilikazi, loomed particularly large as the key conqueror of the area north of the Vaal. When individuals exposed to this narrative encountered African informants who tried to tell them more complicated stories, they often (like most of us when exposed to the unfamiliar) battled to hear what they were being told. Consequently, as noted above, an account emerged which massively inflated the role and impact of the Ndebele.

As we have argued above a clear victim of this historical truncation was one of the most powerful societies in the period and the region – the Ndwandwe – who played a decisive role in the destruction of the power of the Pedi Kingdom. But, as originally formulated by Delius (1983), this version of events runs the risk of replacing one anorexic account with another.

The Mpumalanga lowveld along with the river courses snaking from the highveld down the escarpment and to the coastal plain were important corridors of movement. In the 1810s and 1820s, as the tempo of political change accelerated in the wider region, it seems likely that a multiplicity of groups travelled, raided and even settled for periods of time in Mpumalanga. Aside from the groups lead by Zwide and Mzilikazi, armed men under the authority of Sobhuza, Soshangane, Zwangendaba and Nxaba, to mention only some of the candidates, most likely also left a bloody imprint on the communities in the area (Bonner 1983: 27-28; UA, HC Nachtigal 2: 28-43,138, 350, 381-385, 594; TA SNA 74/ 1325/07; Liesegang 1970: 318-337). Certainly a close reading of the available oral material finds versions of the names of leaders of these groups appearing in accounts of raiders and invaders though often described as subordinates of Mzilikazi. Whether we will ever be able to disentangle the precise sequence of events remains open to question but particular strands are coming into clearer focus. Some of them connect to our core question about Bokoni.

Traditions suggest that Makopole and his Bakoni centred on Ohrigstad clashed with

Sobhuza. Initially they were able to defeat him but subsequently they suffered defeat at his hands. This at first sight appears rather early for such a confrontation to have occurred but the fact that Sobhuza was under considerable pressure from the Ndwandwe in the late 1810s and ultimately retreated north-west to settle among Magoboyi's Sotho on the Komati River well into in Mpumalanga makes such an encounter more plausible. Bonner has described how:

> He regrouped his forces under cover of Magoboyi's authority, and then cut
> loose on his own by attacking neighbouring chiefs. Within the space of a
> year his power had grown to such an extent that he was able to destroy the
> chiefdom of Mkhize ... as the full extent of Sobhuza's ambitions became
> known [Magoboyi] ... seems to have taken the lead in a Sotho backlash ...
> Sobhuza thereupon fell back on the defensive ... (Bonner 1983: 27-8).

While we do not have exact dates for these events they most likely took place before 1819 and possibly before Thulare's death. Makopole probably participated in the successful resistance at this time but it is likely that his defeat at the hands of Sobhuza (or Zwide?) came considerably later.

But probably most important for our account is to contemplate the impact of a pattern of intensive raiding from several quarters from about the mid-1810s on the 'Koni.' Sobhuza may have led the charge but a number of other major players participated, probably most importantly the Ndwandwe who settled on the Steelpoort from the mid-1820s and the Ndebele in the west, probably with mounting effect from about 1826. Added to these already formidable hazards, were the marauding armies of the various pretenders to, and incumbents of, the Pedi throne prior to the Ndwandwe conquest of the Kingdom in 1824/5?. And we shouldn't forget the possibility of raids from groups based in southern Mozambique. The area of Koni settlement would have been right at the centre of this developing military and political vortex. Their settlements with localised cattle herds and probably rich stores of grain situated in relatively accessible river valleys would have been an especially tempting target. Although not without human-made and natural defences, those situated in the southern reaches of Bokoni did not have anything like the same extent of rugged and impenetrable terrain to fall back on, as did the groups located to the north – especially those beyond the Steelpoort River. The consequence for Bokoni communities was profoundly destructive and while it has become commonplace to downplay the impact of this period of raids and migrations on local populations, it is difficult to avoid the conclusion that in this instance and region it was extreme. Prinsloo's informants told him that the Koni were scattered. Some joined the Ndzundza Ndebele, while others, including the Kgwete and Riba groups, settled in the environs of Burgersfort. But the majority took refuge in relatively rugged and inaccessible areas like the Leolu Mountains north of the Steelpoort River and the mountains along the Dwars River (Thaba tša Maphiri) (Prinsloo 1936: 12).

Traditions collected by Nachtigal in the 1860s recalled:

> When Soete was in Pediland with his tribe, the Bapedi could not cultivate any land (out of fear), which led to a serious famine breaking out over them, which dispersed the tribe completely and drove them into the mountains and the woods to feed on roots, wild fruit and game. One part of the tribe yielded to cannibalism (UA, HC Nachtigal 2: 386).

As has been noted above, the area further to the south was even more vulnerable and probably suffered even more comprehensive economic and political dislocation. A mobile hunting and gathering strategy would have provided one means of survival. The reference to cannibalism suggests another – although one that is probably less gruesome than the missionaries imagined and lavishly portrayed. As Delius has argued elsewhere (if, in retrospect, a little glibly) the groups described as cannibals were probably mainly distinguished from others by the fact that 'they secured their subsistence primarily by raiding, and thus were seen as living on their fellows' (Delius 1983: 24).[8] Hunting, gathering and raiding were no doubt points on a continuum of overlapping adaptations to crisis but their centrality in this period bore testament to the disruption of previous forms of production. We know most about the activities of those groupings which leant most heavily towards raiding (the cannibals) because of missionary fascination with their activities. Then, as now, tales of humans feasting on each other sold well and were as a result a boon to the cash-strapped Berlin Missionary Society. The most striking assertion that emerges from these accounts in the context of our pursuit of the people of Bokoni is the comment the 'cannibals were from the tribe of the Bakoni. They were called Makchema ... ' (Wangemann 1876: 98).[9]

This observation, if accurate, would support our contention that the world of the Koni was in considerable disarray. But oral traditions suggest that the remnants of these communities provided the basis for an important attempt at political reconstruction. After the Ndwandwe left the area in 1825 a process of political regrouping began which culminated in the emergence of a new chiefdom led by Marangrang. Merensky penned an account of these events in the 1860s.

The Bakoni settled in the east could once again recover. Two individuals Patane
and Moss emerged as chiefs, in their army was a strong man Morangrang was
his name who, because of his strength and bravery, was held in universal
esteem. One day Patane and Moss set out against the Baroa ... . Both the
chiefs became involved in a quarrel and in the heat of the dispute Patane
stabbed Moss. Then Morangrang sprang up and pushed Patane down. 'Who
shall now be king'? he called to the army. 'You and no other' was the reply
and Morangrang became king of the Bakoni (Merensky 1862: 334).

Winter's informants early in the twentieth century recalled that Marangrang was a
commoner. He was in their account 'No chief, but became a great chief by his valour and
prudence' (Winter 1912: 99).

Merensky provides the most detailed account of Marangrang's rise and fall.

Morangrang now subjected the land of the Bapedi and the Baroa. He
defeated Makhema the cannibals. He also defeated the Bapeli north of the
Lepalule [Olifants River] ... eventually he left the area of Leidenburg and
built his kraal on Moletsi (Dwars River) ... and ruled the land from there
(Merensky 1862: 334).

It seems likely that he occupied Khutwaneng – a settlement that had long been a Koni
stronghold. Accounts collected by Prinsloo suggest that the rule he exercised from there
was far from benevolent:

Here he sentenced many opponents to death and pushed them over the
cliffs. Often he made visitors hold their hands out and then scooped hot fat
into them with a wooden spoon. The resulting bucking provided him with
great entertainment (Prinsloo 1936: 14).

Raiding was also clearly fundamental to his growing wealth and power but his preference
for naked coercion made him vulnerable to those who could combine diplomatic skills
with magical and military power. When Sekwati (who ultimately re-established the Pedi
Kingdom) returned from the north in approximately 1828:

He heard that Morangrang ruled the area and therefore sent him a present
of valuable beads. Morangrang accepted the gift. [However he subsequently

planned another raid across the Olifants against the Bakhalaka (Mphahlele)
chiefdom] The people came in dismay to Sekwati ... he sent a message ... 'Do
not fear, Morangrang no longer has eyes, he is like a bird who has been hit by
a Kiri and wants to die.' Now when the the Bakoni attacked the cattle kraal of
the Bakhalaka they were beaten by the cattle herders and fled. Morangrang
however did not want to yield. It was morning when the people of Matsoban
surrounded him. Until midday he defended himself like a wounded buffalo.
Then eventually his strength left him. He sat down on his shield and called
to his enemies: 'Call your elders that they may kill me, you are children!' ...
'You lie' they replied and killed him. They cut his head off, and carried it
back to the Bakhalaka kraal where it still hangs today. His shield however
was delivered to Sekwati. He did not delay. He hurriedly called his army
together and attacked the kraal of Morangrang on the Moletsi ... and took all
the cattle of Morangrang (Merensky 1862 : 335).[10]

This account's stress on Sekwati's magical power and his indirect role in the defeat of
Marangrang is clearly designed to paper over the rather awkward fact – at least from a
Pedi perspective – that Sekwati did not personally defeat his most powerful immediate
predecessor in the region. Nonetheless, as this and other traditions make clear, Sekwati was
skilfully able to exploit the power vacuum that Marangrang's demise created to entrench
his own power. This process also appears to have involved most of the remnant Koni groups
moving north across the Steelpoort either settling separately or being incorporated into
resurgent Pedi chiefdoms. For the next 40 years this rugged area was to be the new heartland
of the Pedi domain (Merensky 1862; see also Winter 1912; Prinsloo 1936: 13-15).

By the 1830s, beyond the material remains of once flourishing communities, little
was left of the world that Koni communities had made in their heartland. No chiefdoms
existed which were sufficiently powerful to attract detailed comments from the Trekkers
who established their own sparse settlements in these areas from the 1840s. This does not,
of course, mean that the region had been entirely denuded of population. It is clear from
the archival record that many small groups remained *in situ* throughout Mpumalanga
but these were in the main no more than fragments of the chiefdoms that had previously
existed. For example, Prinsloo was told:

When the Zulu danger was forgotten a bit, people especially the Koni of
Maphiri, again slowly moved back to their old residential area. Amongst
others we find them at places such as Xa Sedikane (de Kafferskraal no. 630

dist Lydenburg), Saxa (Rietfontein 129) and Khutwaneng etc. (Prinsloo 1936: 12-13).

When faced with Boer power these households had little option but to accept their authority or to seek sanctuary amidst the more powerful and effectively independent chiefdoms that remained in the region.

But some groups established themselves in regions which fell on the margins of both Pedi and ZAR control and attempted to maintain a degree of autonomy from both sets of rulers. There were moments in the early 1850s when some Koni groups in these border areas took advantage of a period of Boer weakness to make good cattle losses (Delius 1983: 24-29, 37-38, 90-91). In the 1870s, as the ZAR once again appeared fragile, at least in relation to the Pedi Kingdom, a number of groups in the old border areas increasingly openly rejected the authority of the ZAR. Koni groups were very much part of this world and it may well be that elements of Koni identity and history played a part in fuelling this spirit of resistance. Particularly striking in this regard is the story of the Koni group who joined Johannes Dinkwanyane – a pivotal figure in the events that led to the outbreak of war between the Pedi Kingdom and the ZAR in 1876. Merensky reported in 1873:

> There is a Bakoni village at Botschabelo. Their chief, Phassoane was a dear and true man. He was earlier at Ga Ratau [a mission station in the heartland of the Pedi Kingdom] and fifteen of his followers were catechumen. Two years after the establishment of Botschabelo they came here … Some thirty years earlier Phassoane's father lived at Elandsspruit between Lydenburg and Komate. Phassoane had grown up there and now these Bakoni suggested to Dinkoanyane [who planned to leave the mission station] that he should move to their old home. It had many attractions. The land was fertile, there was large quantities of game and caves and kloofs which offered the possibility of defence against anyone, including, if needs be, the Boers (BMB 1875: 138).[11]

Dinkwanyane's attempts to settle at Elandsspruit were thwarted by the Landdros. But the Koni group left Botshabelo with him and stood by him in his deepening confrontation with both Boer and missionary power. Their sense of Koni history may have helped shape this resolve and the decision to establish the formidable stronghold, Mafolofolo, that overlooked the Spekboom River north of Lydenburg. This site within three years witnessed dramatic and tragic confrontations that changed the course of South African history (Delius 1983: 171-212). Nonetheless fifty years later Johannes Dinkwanyane's son Micha ruled over a thriving community on an adjacent farm Boomplaats including *''n groot aantal Koni'* (Prinsloo 1936: 15).

Reading history to understand the archaeology – excavating to understand the history

We next demonstrate that not only the area, but the valley stonewalled sites under examination indeed were Koni as argued by Schoeman (1997) and Huffman (2004), but it is clear from the historical evidence that the people of Bokoni were not a homogenous ethnic group with a uniform identity and history. We start this discussion by focusing on the overlap between the Koni area mentioned in the historic record and the archaeological site distribution.

As discussed earlier, Prinsloo's (1936) reconstruction places Bokoni between the Leolu Mountains, the Spekboom River and the Badfontein valley, including the areas between present day Machadadorp, Lydenburg and Sabi (Plate 4). Other historical sources corroborate Prinsloo's demarcation.

Comparing Prinsloo's Bokoni with the published archaeological maps hints at similarities, but these studies do not provide a detailed regional overview of the distribution of the terraced and stonewalled sites. Mason (1968) mapped all stonewalled sites without differentiating between the different building traditions. His data therefore need to be used with caution, as it also includes unrelated sites such as those of Ndzundza and historic Swazi communities. In contrast to Mason's broad overview, Evers (1973, 1975), Marker and Evers (1976) and Collett (1979, 1982) provided detailed area-specific data for the Lydenburg and Badfontein areas.

A more comprehensive picture emerges from Maggs' research. He (Maggs this volume) has combined earlier aerial survey information with new spatial distribution research. This provides the most accurate information to date on regional site location and distribution. Settlements are located in a north-south belt between Orighstad and Carolina, and tend to cluster along the Komati, Elands-Crocodile, Sabi, Spekboom and Dwars rivers (Plate 4). Clearly there is a correlation between Prinsloo's Bokoni and Maggs' Marateng sites.

The regionally distinct settlement pattern further supports the link between the Koni and these sites. The Lydenburg–Orighstad central enclosures consist of a primary enclosure with several secondary enclosures (see Collett 1979). In contrast the settlement pattern of neighbouring Ndzundza pre-Mfecane sites consist of bi-lobial central enclosures, the pattern is the same for cattle kraals and assembly areas (see Schoeman 1998a, b). Archaeologists have not documented the pre-Mfecane Pedi pattern, but descriptions do not resemble the

Koni pattern. This means that the regionally distinct stonewalled sites occur in Prinsloo's Bokoni only and not in areas associated with the pre-expansion Pedi polity.

In addition to the absence of similar settlement patterns in the Pedi heartland the radiocarbon dates suggest that the Pedi did not build these sites. The Lydenburg sites were dated to the late 17th or early 18th century AD (Marker & Evers 1976). This suggests that at least some sites pre-date Pedi hegemony, signifying that it is unlikely that the Pedi constructed all of the sites. Furthermore, at one site the Marateng ceramics also underlay stonewalls, possibly revealing that this ceramic style pre-dates stonewalling (Collett 1979). Clearly then, the combination of historical and archaeological sources indicate that these stonewalled sites are indeed Koni ruins.

There is one major exception to this pattern: the site cluster along the Komati River does not form part of Prinsloo's Bokoni. Using the oral record to clarify the archaeological chronology helps us to account for this discrepancy. We mentioned earlier that the historical sources recalled that a major Koni centre was located at 'Moxômatsi' (Prinsloo 1936: 11) in the south, from where it moved to 'Mohloxa-Pela' (Prinsloo 1936: 11) due to conflict in the south. Other smaller centres, for example Khutwaneng, were also established at this time (Prinsloo 1936). We know from Pedi traditions that Khutwaneng became a Koni stronghold by the mid-18th century (Hunt 1931: 278-280; Winter 1912: 92). The Khutwaneng site described by Hunt (1931: 278-279) and Winter (1912: 92), however, does not resemble any of the valley sites in the Badfontein area, whereas it is reminiscent of Marangrang's capital. As suggested earlier, Marangrang probably reoccupied an earlier defensive site.

If this deduction is correct, it is possible that the earlier and mid-18th-century violence in the area was persistent enough to result in some defensive site locations. This violence, however, was sporadic rather than endemic if Marker and Evers (1976) are correct that the open valley sites were abandoned during the Mfecane. It is unlikely that the valley sites would have been occupied during a period of constant violence, since they are neither defensive nor easily defendable. Some support for Marker and Evers' (1976) Mfecane abandonment conclusion can be found in Koni sites outside the core area. One of the Koni stonewalled site in the Steenkampsberg, established after the Mfecane, does resemble the Bokoni sites under discussion. This suggests that the settlement layout was still part of the Bokoni architectural tradition in the early 1800s.

That the area experienced violence long before the 19th century is clear from the Roka traditions, they recall being settled in Bokgaga (near modern Leydsdorp) and left there prior to moving south of the Olifants because they feared the 'dogs of the Arabs' (Arab slave traders?) (Mönnig 1963: 170). Pedi traditions also give an account of conditions prior to the arrival of the Maroteng at the Steelpoort/Spekboom River (1650?), which give some sense of what key dynamics at work in the region. The Mongatane who dominated the area when the Maroteng arrived:

> Being Baroka fought with bows and arrows. Before we had come they fought the Mapalakata, the old miners from the east coast, who had very long rifles and killed them all at a place where the Magakala now live (close to the Olifants River) keeping these guns which were always shown at their big festivals and danced around. We believe them to have been Arabs with red fezzes. The Malepa who are still found here with Mohammedan religious laws might have been left by them and intermarried (Winter 1912: 90).

This account is echoed in Hunt's history of the Bapedi:

> Tradition says that either before or soon after the Bapedi came to ... Sekukuniland some people known as Mapalakata made raids into the country. They are said to have been armed with muskets and to have worn long white dresses, so they were probably slave raiders ... . These Mapalakata and their fire-arms seem to have made a great impression on the minds of the Bapedi (Hunt 1931: 276).

Accounts gathered in the 1860s also refer to a later period of what may well have been slave raiding. In addition a period of famine and 'cannibalism' in the 1740s(?) was recalled, this coincided with attacks by the '*Makgalakana a masoana* blacks who had guns who also became known as mapalakate' (UA, HC Nachtigal 2: 605). 'One of their gun locks is in the mission museum' (Wangemann 1876: 97-98). This period of famine suggests that it is possible that changing climatic conditions may also have been a factor.

While guns and raids clearly left a deep and lasting impression it seems probable that they were one dimension of wider connections which linked this region to the coast – probably along routes defined by the major rivers which were also key areas of Koni settlement. The layout of the valley settlements and site locations suggest that the violence did not outweigh the other dimensions.

Oral traditions record at least two violent periods, the first in the seventeenth century and the second later on in the mid-18th century. Violence, however, might have been more intense in the Komati river valley, which not only formed the southern border of Bokoni, but also linked the interior to the coast and thus could have been a slave route. Regular attacks on the area could be the reason why the Komati sites were forgotten, because these might have caused the relocation of Koni centres further north and made the area unsuitable for occupation for many generations. The area thereby faded from memory because it was not worth claiming as it was impossible to live there and it might never have been a major centre, at least not for the surviving powerful Koni lineages.

Who lived in Bokoni? – Perspectives from material culture

The oral and written record allows us glimpses of the people of Bokoni. The historical record, however, is conflicted about the precolonial identity of the people of Bokoni. Furthermore archaeologists and historians disagree – Schoeman (1997) implicitly and Huffman (2004) explicitly viewed the people of Bokoni as an Nguni ethnic group but Makhura (2007) disagreed. A re-examination of the archaeological data might shed some light on this question.

As stated earlier the Bokoni stonewalled sites are regionally distinct. The distinctiveness of the settlement pattern suggests that pre-Mfecane Bokoni people expressed some level of autonomy in their stonewalling. This corroborates the loose control by the Mongatane paramountcy suggested in the oral record.

Economic and political autonomy, however, does not mean that the Koni had a regionally distinct identity. We will explore this below, but do recognise that tracking identity through archaeological material culture is a perilous endeavour. We follow Hall and Mack (1983) and Schoeman (1997) who suggested settlement pattern is about male control and economic boundaries, whereas ceramics inform on marriage and movement across political boundaries.

Collett (1978) named the ceramics he found, Marateng, after a hill in the area. It has been assumed that the name Marateng referred to the Maroteng – the people who established the Pedi royal polity. Clearly this association is flawed because Marateng hill is in Marangrang's core area, and the name Marateng might even refer to Marangrang. Furthermore, based on the limited archaeological research in the area, the Marateng style ceramics found in the Lydenburg and Badfontein archaeological excavations (e.g. Evers 1974, 1975; Collett 1979, 1982) is not only Pedi, but seem to have been used by most of the main groupings. Schoeman has observed Marateng style decoration on sherds from upper Steelpoort river valley sites in the Pedi polity heartland and found similar vessels on Ndzundza sites (Schoeman 1998a, b). Schoeman (1997) argued that the Ndzundza had adopted the regional ceramic style as a result of women's responses to exogamous marriage laws as well as population fluidity in the area. The dynamics of Koni adoption of a regional ceramic style overlap, but also are different. As with the Ndzundza (and the Pedi)

159

the Koni were joined by large numbers of people from other groups, who left when better opportunities arose elsewhere, but like the Pedi they practiced cross cousin marriage, ensuring that women's mobility was more limited. Koni adoption of a regional ceramics style probably then speaks about regional population fluidity, but not internal gendered identities.

In addition to using a regional ceramic style, all the houses found in the Evers and Collett excavations were in the locally dominant rondawel-shape. The houses at the Lydenburg Municipal Grounds (LMG) had stone paved floors and plastered *dakha* fire bowls and verandas. Marateng style pots and grindstones were placed under the eaves (Evers 1975). Klingbeil Nature Reserve research corroborated the LMG data and added another dimension to house construction. The Klingbeil house floors were levelled with gravel on which stones were laid. The floors were then plastered, and a *dakha* veranda and bench built on the side of the house nearest to the kraal. A clay-lined fire bowl was constructed between the bench and the main part of the house (Marker & Evers 1976).

If house form is more than an adaptation to local environmental conditions and is reflective of identity as Schoeman (1997) argued, the Koni had adopted a regional identity, and chose not to express their residential architecture as Nguni, unlike their Ndzundza neighbours who constructed beehive-shaped houses until the Mfecane.[13]

The rondawel houses excavated by Collett and Evers stand in sharp contrast with the beehive shaped houses depicted in the rock art (see Maggs this volume), possibly suggesting that the built houses were different from the idealised imaginings. This contradiction might relate to change through time, but, if contemporaneous, could speak of multiple identities, further suggesting that the identity of the people of Bokoni identity should not be defined solely though contemporary links between material culture and ethnicity.

The historical record about the people of Bokoni support the fluidity and regionalism expressed in ceramics and house form, and regional style is logical if we view identity as shaped by political affiliation rather than ethnic group identification. In this model people who expressed a regional identity in their material culture, could simultaneously express their economic and political independence. In this way the Koni were of an economic unit and of a place, Bokoni, but formed part of a fluid regional population and defined their personal identity accordingly. This identity was not shaped by a primordial ethnicity as missionaries, *volkekunde* and some archaeologists suggested. Instead precolonial Koni identity might relate to other factors, such as intensive agriculture (see Maggs this volume) and control over trade networks.

Site distribution and the economy

The majority of the stonewalled sites discussed in the first part of this paper were not geared for defence; rather they embody earlier and less violent times. Sites are located in river catchments and valleys, with a clear preference for eastern lower valley slopes. Valley floors were avoided and sites cluster between 1 310 and 1 830 m (Evers 1975; Marker & Evers 1976). Proximity to water, however, seems to be the key factor (Coetzee 2005) and Collett (1979) found that the Badfontein sites were located within 3 km of the nearest water sources.

Easy access to water is important for homesteads, but the architecture and articulation of the sites with the landscape suggest that site location was also linked to agro-pastoral concerns. The terrace architecture speaks to the scope of farming. The extent of the terraces suggests production beyond local need, and the extensive cattle control measures indicate large numbers of cattle that could not be herded easily.

A large agricultural surplus would have been important if Marker and Evers' population estimates are correct. They (Marker & Evers 1976) estimated that if occupied concurrently, the Dorpsriver area would have housed an estimated population of between 19 000 and 57 000. They note that this is unlikely for the early occupation, but suggest it is possible that by the end of the period all the sites were occupied, and this corresponds with illustrations in travellers' accounts they consulted. Obviously the Dorpsriver settlements only represent a small portion of the sites in the region, which could mean that the regional population figures were much higher.

It is possible that economic activities were not limited to farming, and that regional trade supplemented scarce local metal resources. Hoernlé (1931) mentions that in the historic period Koni had little access to iron, whereas the Pedi had iron. Evers (1975) and Marker and Evers (1976), however found iron objects in their excavations. This suggests that the iron scarcity did not extend into the precolonial period, and it is possible that the people of Bokoni had access to local iron sources or imported iron. Key iron sources would include the iron deposits between Barberton and the Komati River to the east, the iron ore-bearing hills at KoNomtjarhelo and the mid-Steelpoort valley to the west and the Strydpoortberge to the north (Changuion & Bergh 1999). Amicable relations with neighbours would determine access to these, and the Ndzundza and Pedi might have been key sources of iron.

We do not know the extent of Ndzundza ironworking, but Pedi traditions suggest ironworking goes back to the earliest phase of settlement in the area. While accounts vary there is a very close association between the Maroteng and iron: 'Throughout their history ... there was a small stad of workers in iron living under the close protection of the Bapedi chiefs and no-one was allowed to interfere with them' (Hunt 1931: 276). There are indications that these ironworkers may have had Venda and or Lemba connections. Certainly ironworking appears to have been a core element in Maroteng/Pedi identity and perhaps in the growth of their economic and political power. Early in the 19th century Arbousset commented on the abundance of iron and the high quality of the iron goods produced in the Pedi domain.

But ironworking was far from being a Maroteng monopoly. Nineteenth-century evidence suggests that Baroka groups, originally from north east of the Olifants were 'the iron smelter and smiths in the land', while Phalaborwa remained the centre of a major metal manufacturing and exporting industry (BMB 1863: 6; Delius 1983: 70-71). Nineteenth-century evidence also suggests that the Pedi played a key intermediary role between the metal industries of the lowveld and the societies to the south and west which presumably had developed in previous centuries (Delius 1983: 17, 70-71). It is possible that Arbousset may actually have been referring to areas further to the north when he talked of abundance of iron in the Pedi area. Irrespective of who the sources were, iron was obviously a key trade item and Pedi-controlled trade would have placed the Koni in a precarious position. It might be that the iron on the archaeological sites date from the period when the Baroka were the paramounts, and the scarcity mentioned by Hoernle (1931) related to the period of Pedi control.

In addition to facilitating trade, regional networks could have been important to sustain intensive cattle farming. The Lydenburg–Machadadorp vegetation is predominantly sour grassland. The waterlogged valley bottoms sustain sweet veldt all year round (E. Johnson 2007 pers. comm.), which in part explains site distribution. Most sites were located on the slopes above river valleys, which would have provided ready access to sweet veldt. The available grazing, however, might not have been enough to sustain very large herds and the Koni might have had to practice seasonal cattle transhumance. This would not have been a new practice in southern Africa. Smith (2005) showed that the AD 1000 to AD 1300 K2-Mapungubwe state practiced seasonal cattle transhumance. Transhumance in the context of growing cattle numbers might also have led to increased competition between Pedi and Koni groups for the best winter grazing in bushveld area areas north east of Lydenburg, as is suggested by the traditions discussed earlier.

With an annual rainfall of 660 mm the area is also suitable for agriculture (Collett 1979), but, contrary to our expectations, Mpumalanga river valleys are not suited to crop production. The area has very high magnesium to calcium ratios and because magnesium leaches out of soil easily, the river valleys have very high magnesium levels, which stunt crop development. The hill slopes, where leaching lowered magnesium levels, tend to be more suitable for crop production. It is likely that the Koni farmers noticed the difference between valley and hill slope yields and consequently chose to cultivate the slopes. As the population grew and with this the need for more intensive farming developed, they optimised hill slope crop production through terracing. The combination of better grazing in the valleys and higher crop yields further up-slope might also explain the location of terraces up-slope and grazing in the valleys.

Whilst the settlement architecture speaks of an intensive agro-pastoral economy, the regional site distribution might relate to broader economic and political factors. Sites cluster around the headwaters of the Komati, Crocodile, Sabie and some of the Steelpoort tributary rivers (Plate 5). The Crocodile, Sabie and the Komati rivers flow into the Rio Incomati, which reaches the coast at Ponta Macaneta, on the northern edge of the Bay of Maputo. These rivers formed part of the trade routes from Maputo into the interior (Changuion & Bergh 1999).

We do know that trade from the coast reached the region, for example glass beads were found at the 17th to early 19th-century Ndzundza capital KwaMaza, and there is a good deal of oral evidence of trade in beads with the east coast. It may also be significant that beads and ivory arm bands feature prominently (though not mentioned directly in terms of trade) in traditions dealing with conflicts between the Pedi and the Koni in the 18th century' (Winter 1912: 91; TA SNA 74/ 1325/07; Hogge 1907).[14]

Key items in demand at the coast were ivory and to some extent horns, rhino etc. It is however unlikely that the key areas of Koni settlement were particularly good for elephant hunting which suggests that if their main role in trade may have been as intermediaries rather than primary producers. Control over the trade routes might have been one of the factors motivating Pedi attempts to incorporate Bokoni. The conflict between the Pedi and the Koni, and the Koni defeat might be reflected by the downturn in ivory trade suggested by Hedges for period 1790? to 1715? (Delius 1983: 18).

Trade links with the coast might also have been additional motivating factors for the intensive agriculture and cattle farming that the site architecture articulates. It is possible that the Koni traded cattle and agricultural surplus to the coast. Trade in livestock formed part of the Zimbabwe–Portuguese trade (Ellert 1993) and it is not inconceivable that the Mpumalanga–coastal trade included cattle. Such trade would have had to be seasonal as, in summer, tsetse fly would have made it impossible.[15]

Trade would have been filtered through local structures and politics, and questions about the structure and nature of political power also need to be raised. For some authors the answers to these questions are clear-cut. Prinsloo, for example, asserts that 'A paramount they never knew. Each extended family had a captain' (Prinsloo 1936: 11).

But this conclusion sits uneasily with some of the other evidence, including his own. He also tells us, for example, that while the Koni lived at 'Mohloxo-Pela' (Prinsloo 1936:11) near Machadadorp, 'smaller captains built new villages everywhere. The most famous of these was Khutwaneng, Metsi a Thatha' (Prinsloo 1936: 12). This suggests some form of hierarchy which probably resulted in some form of paramountcy. Certainly by the time the Maroteng arrive in the region, overarching political structures were in place and the Baroka ba Mongatane exercised authority over both the Maroteng and Koni groups.

Pedi traditions suggest that these forms of exaction and control were relatively muted with a strong ritual component but this does not mean that they were insignificant. Once the Maroteng started to extend their control over the region the Koni were brought under rather more systematic forms of centralised political control. But this political order remained highly devolved in much of its operation, with – as noted above – important elements of both regional power and local autonomy. For much of the period 1600-1820 we are therefore probably dealing with a range of forms of political, ritual paramountcy and probably involved dominant lineages expanding their control over diverse populations – a process which in turn brought some economic rewards. It is however by no means clear that one discrete political system incorporated all the groups who might be described as Koni. Indeed, the material on Koni involvement in Pedi succession struggles discussed above suggests that there may have been a number of overlapping and even competing centres of political power in Bokoni. Again the archaeology resonates with this hypothesis. The archaeological surveys have not found any site concentrations that are substantially larger than others, or material culture at any sites that express extreme hierarchy. Rather sites cluster in several locations and this pattern suggests a number of centres.

Conclusion

This paper is the outcome of a shared interest in the history, economy and identity of the inhabitants of Bokoni. Our pursuit of this quarry has resulted in a dialogue between historical and archaeological perspectives and sources which, in our view, suggests some of the rewards which are available from this kind of combination. It is in retrospect quite extraordinary that such well known and relatively accessible bodies of material and analysis have not hitherto cross-fertilised. The first fruits of this engagement connect Orighstad–Carolina stonewalled sites with a dynamic past that does not reduce the Bokoni occupants to a homogenous and static 'volk' and reveal strata of history that are critical to an understanding of the precolonial history of the region.

But even more exciting is the research agenda that this initial encounter suggests. Despite apparently clear identification in oral traditions not one of the Maroteng capital sites in the period 1650?-1825? has been excavated. Archaeological research at these locations could make a vital contribution to exploring questions of Koni and Pedi identity and to understanding the dynamics of conflict and change in the region. Similarly key Bokoni sites – such as those at Khutwaneng and in the Komati River Valley cry out for further work. There are also important bodies of oral material which remain to be fully exploited including histories in Sepedi published since the 1930s and the traditions of the numerous groups in the region who claim some form of Koni identity but whose historical narratives have never been recorded. Research of this kind also has the potential to both benefit from, and contribute to, re-evaluations of the histories of both the Swazi and the Ndwandwe. Perhaps most important of all, in the context of the original conference and this ensuing publication, is that none of this research makes sense or is likely to yield a significant return unless archaeologists and historians work in tandem.

Notes

1. Dialogue between archaeologists and historians has had some success elsewhere, for example see Joubert and van Schalkwyk 1999.
2. Marangrang's capital is not the only defensive settlement in the Badfontein valley; other kloofs house similar sites.
3. Some non-archaeologists, however, do not share this view. Some have put alternative explanations forward. For example, Cyril Hromnick argues that the sites were Indian temples and Richard Wade speculates that the stonewalled sites are the remains of ancient observatories. Both these arguments ignore the archaeological data, such as house floors, which indicate that the sites had residential areas.
4. For one overview see Prinsloo (1936: 3-9).
5. This description predates settlement by Berlin missionaries in the region.
6. See also Merensky (1862: 329), who sees Bakoni involvement but as a result of conquest by Kotope. This seems a little improbable given both the context and the earlier historical interaction. Hunt (1921) produces a narrative very close to Winter's but both used a common informant – Ra'lolo and Hunt was almost certainly aware of the Winter (1912) article although he does not cite it in this context.
7. See also Winter (1912: 98) – he gives the name Tshianyana to the Koni – and Merensky (1862: 332-333).
8. For a fuller, more complex and very interesting discussion of this issue see Kirkaldy (2005: 223-235)
9. Traditions collected later in the 19th century support this observation. See Winter (1912: 99).
10. Hunt (1931: 287) adds the suggestion that a woman sent to Marangrang by Sekwati also contributed to his downfall.
11. See also Delius (1983: 171-172).
12. Radiocarbon Lydenburg AD 1840 ±40 (Pta –1632) from a charred post, calibrated to late 18th or early 19th centuries (Hall & Vogel 1980).
13. This comparison is not without problems; the sites studied by Schoeman (1997) were royal, thus reflecting 'official' identity. Ndzundza commoner sites probably looked different. We do not know whether royals or commoners lived at the Koni sites studied thus far and sites might contain a range of house forms.
14. For a detailed description of types of trade in beads in 19th century see Berlin Missionary Archive, Tagebuch Khalatlolu, 18 September 1861. Salt was also an important trade good.
15. We know from archaeological research that southern African systems of tsetse management did exist.

For example, Manekeni in southern Mozambique, the most recent occupation of which is contemporary with the Koni sites, is situated on the edge of the tsetse belt. Farmers at Manekeni practiced seasonal transhumance and grazed their cattle in the tsetse area in the winter season when tsetse flies are not dangerous (see Garlake 1978).

References

Aylward, A. 1878. *The Transvaal of To-day*. Edinburgh: Blackwood.

Berliner Missions Berichte (BMB) 37 (1860).

Bonner, P. 1983. *Kings, Commoners and Concessionaires.* Johannesburg: Ravan Press.

Caton-Thompson, G. 1931. *The Zimbabwe Culture: Ruins and Reactions*. Oxford: Clarendon Press.

Changuion, L. & Bergh, J.S. 1999. Swart gemeenskappe voor die koms van die blankes. In: Bergh, J.S. (ed.) *Geskiedenisatlas van Suid-Afrika: Die Vier Noordelike Provinsies*: 103-115. Pretoria: Van Schaik.

Coetzee, H.B. 2005. Interpreting distribution patterns of Iron Age sites using landscape archaeology and GIS. Honours project. Pretoria: University of Pretoria.

Coetzee, F.P. 2003. Heritage audit of the farm Welgedacht (137JT), Lydenburg district, Mpumalanga. Unpublished report. Pretoria: UNISA.

Collett, D.P. 1979. The archaeology of the stone-walled settlements in the Eastern Transvaal, South Africa. MSc dissertation. Johannesburg: University of the Witwatersrand.

Collett, D.P. 1982. Excavations of stone-walled ruin types in the Badfontein valley, Eastern Transvaal, South Africa. *The South African Archaeological Bulletin* 37: 34-43.

Dart, R.A. 1940. Recent discoveries bearing on human history in southern Africa. *The Journal of the Royal Anthropological Institute of Great Britain and Ireland* 70(1): 13-27.

Delius, P. 1983. *The Land Belongs to Us: The Pedi Polity, the Boers and the British in the Nineteenth Century Transvaal*. Johannesburg: Ravan Press.

Ellert, H. 1993. *Rivers of Gold*. Gweru: Mambo Press.

Evers, T.M. 1973. Iron Age research in the Eastern Transvaal, South Africa, 1971. *Current Anthropology* 14(4): 487-489.

Evers, T.M. 1975. Recent Iron Age research in the Eastern Transvaal, South Africa. *South African Archaeological Bulletin* 30: 71-83.

Gardner, G. 1968. *Mapungubwe Volume II*. Pretoria: J.L. van Schaik.

Garlake, P.S. 1978. Pastoralism in Zimbabwe. *The Journal of African History* 19(4): 479-493.

Hall, M. 1984a. The burden of tribalism: the social context of southern African Iron Age studies. *American Antiquity* 49(3): 455-467.

Hall, M. 1984b. Pots and politics: ceramic interpretations in southern Africa. *World Archaeology* 15(3): 262-273.

Hall, M. 1984c. The myth of the Zulu homestead: archaeology and ethnography. *Africa: Journal of the International African Institute* 54(1): 65-79.

Hall, M. & Mack, K. 1983. The outline of an eighteenth-century economic system in south-east Africa. *The Annals of the South African Museum* 91:2, 163-194.

Hall, M. & Maggs, T. 1979. Nqabeni, a late Iron Age site in Zululand. *The South African Archaeological Society Goodwin Series* 3: 159-176.

Hall, M. & Vogel, J.C. 1980. Some recent radiocarbon dates from southern Africa. *The Journal of African History* 21(4): 431-455.

Hoernlé, A.W. 1931. A note on bored stones among the Bantu. *Bantu Studies* 5(3):253-255.

Hogge, E.H. 1907. History. Mafefe (Magakala alias Magadimane). Transvaal Archives (TA), Secretary of Native Affairs (SNA), Volume 74/1325/07.

Huffman, T.N. 2004. The archaeology of the Nguni past. *Southern African Humanities* 16: 79-111.

Hunt, D.R. 1931. An account of the Bapedi. *Bantu Studies* V: 291-326.

Iliffe, J. 1995. *Africans: The History of a Continent*. Cambridge: Cambridge University Press.

Joubert, A. & van Schalkwyk, J.A. 1999. War and remembrance: The power of oral poetry and the politics of Hananwa identity. *Journal of Southern African Studies*, 25(1): 29-47.

Kirkaldy, A. 2005. *Capturing the Soul*. Pretoria: Protea Bookhouse.

Laidler, P.W. 1932. The Bantu potting industry and its impact on other native potting industries in South Africa. *South African Journal of Science* 29: 778-791.

Lekgoathi, S.P. 2003. Chiefs, migrants and North Ndebele ethnicity in the context of surrounding homeland politics, 1965-1978. *African Studies* 62(1): 53-77.

Liesegang, G. 1970. Nguni migrations between Delagoa Bay and the Zambezi. *African Historical Studies* 3(2): 318-337.

Maggs, T. 1995. Neglected rock art: The rock engravings of agriculturist communities in South Africa. *South African Archaeological Bulletin* 50: 132-142.

Makhura, T. 2007. The pre-colonial history of Mpumalanga societies. In: Delius, P. (ed.) *Mpumalanga : History and Heritage*: 91-136. Pietermaritzburg: University of KwaZulu-Natal Press.

Marker, M.E. & Evers, T.M. 1976. Iron Age settlement and soil erosion in the Eastern Transvaal. *South African Archaeological Bulletin* 31: 153-165.

Mason, R.J. 1962. *The prehistory of the Transvaal*. Johannesburg: University of Witwatersrand Press.

Mason, R.J. 1968. Transvaal and Natal Iron Age settlement revealed by aerial photography and excavation. *African Studies* 27: 1-14.

Merensky, A. 1862. Beiträge zur Geschichte der Bapeli. *Berliner Mission Berichte*: 327-358.

Mönnig, H.O. 1963. The Baroka Ba Nkwana. *African Studies* 22(4): 170-175.

Mönnig, H.O. 1967. *The Pedi*. Pretoria: Van Schaik.

Myburgh, A.C. 1949. *The Tribes of the Barberton District*. Pretoria: Government Printer.

Prinsloo, C.W. 1936. Klank- en vormleer van BaKoni. MA dissertation. Pretoria: University of Pretoria.

Ramaila, E.M. 1938. *Setlogo Sa Batau*. Pretoria: Craft.

Schoeman, M.H. 1997. The Ndzundza archaeology of the Steelpoort River Valley. Unpublished MA dissertation. Johannesburg: University of the Witwatersrand.

Smith, J.M. 2005. Climate change and agropastoral sustainability in the Shashe/Limpopo River Basin from AD 900. Unpublished PhD Thesis. Johannesburg: University of the Witwatersrand.

Schoeman, M.H. 1998a. Excavating Ndzundza Ndebele identity at KwaMaza. *South African Field Archaeology* 7(1): 42-52.

Schoeman, M.H. 1998b. Material culture 'under the amimal skin': excavations at Esikhunjini, a Mfecane period Ndundza Ndebele site. *Southern African Field Archaeology* 7(2): 72-81.

Smith, C. 2006. Spatial analysis of stonewalled sites on the farm Welgedacht, Mpumalanga. Honours project. Pretoria: University of Pretoria.

Transvaal Archives (TA), Secretary of Native Affairs (SNA) vol. 74/ 1325/07.

Unisa Archives (UA) Hesse Collection (HC) Nachtigal, Tagebuch volumes 1 and 2.

Van Hoepen, E.C.N. 1939. A pre-European Bantu culture in the Lydenburg District. *Argeologiese Navorsing van die Nasionale Museum, Bloemfontein* II(5): 47-74.

Van Warmelo, N.J. 1935. A Preliminary Survey of the Bantu tribes of South Africa. Pretoria: Government Printer.

Wangemann, T. 1876. *Lebensbilder aus Südafrika*. Berlin.

Winter, J.A. 1912. The tradition of Ra'lolo. *South African Journal of Science* 9: 90.

9

The Mpumalanga Escarpment settlements: some answers, many questions

Tim Maggs

Introduction

A dense area of precolonial stone ruins extends in a broad band along the escarpment which separates Lowveld from Highveld in Mpumalanga Province (formerly the eastern Transvaal). Although these ruins have been known archaeologically for many decades they have received relatively little sustained attention. The intention of this paper is therefore to draw attention to the enormous research potential of these settlements, and to propose some as yet untried lines of enquiry that could be followed in future projects. I have adopted this approach because, on the one hand, these settlements arguably provide the most detailed and interesting archaeological footprint of any precolonial farming society in South Africa, and on the other, they have seen surprisingly little serious research. In view of the current renewed interest in the period of the last 500 years, with its multi-disciplinary initiative, now is an appropriate moment for a reassessment.

The paper consists of three components. The first is a summary of the existing published information which provides a broad, though rather shallow, context for these settlements. The second allows me to place on record some bits of previously unpublished work arising out of my own interest in the area over several decades, though never amounting to a full research project. These two provide the 'some answers' of the title. Arising out of them I put forward some ideas towards a different framework of interpretation, which poses possible questions for future research. Hence the answers before the questions, as signalled in the title.

What to call these settlements?

In his thesis, Collett (1982) proposed the name Marateng for the style of pottery associated with these settlements. Marateng is the local name for a mountain in the Badfontein area and is therefore entirely appropriate. I therefore adopted it for my work on the Mpumalanga Escarpment sites, extending its usage to cover not just the ceramics but the whole cultural package including the buildings. Used in this sense, Marateng is already in the literature (e.g. Maggs 1995b; Widgren 2004). However, at the 500 Year Research Group conference in May 2007 I became aware that the almost identical name, Maroteng, applies to the ruling lineage of the Pedi people. The Pedi were located further north but their history was at times interlinked with the people who probably built these settlements (Delius & Schoeman this volume); the potential for confusion in using the name Marateng for the settlements is therefore considerable. Since Peter Delius and Alex Schoeman are researching the history and identity of the builders, we have been discussing the merits and demerits of various possible names for the cultural phenomenon represented by the ruins. Their work has shown that the earliest name yet traced on record for this area is Bokoni (i.e. the land of the BaKoni people). Since the authorship of the ruins is still under investigation, we feel that to use the term BaKoni or Koni (i.e. the name for the people themselves) would prejudge this complex issue. We therefore propose the name Bokoni as the earliest available place name for the area, on the understanding that this does not necessarily imply BaKoni authorship. I will therefore use the term BoKoni in this paper for the Mpumalanga Escarpment settlements and apologise for any confusion arising from my earlier use of the name Marateng. The latter can still be used for the ceramic style, as originally intended by Collett (1982).

Previous research

Earlier work, more fully reviewed by Delius and Schoeman (this volume), particularly that of Evers (1975), Marker & Evers (1976) and Collett (1982), has shown that Marateng fits broadly into the by now well known phenomenon of stone-built settlements of Black, agriculturist communities which flourished in many grassland areas of South Africa within the past 500 years. The homestead layout falls broadly into Huffman's Central Cattle Pattern (Huffman 2004), while the pottery is clearly Moloko, falling within the range of Sotho-Tswana wares. Indeed, Collett (1982) sees the ceramic style as very similar to traditional Pedi pottery. Other aspects of the material culture are typically Late Iron Age, as is the basic economy, with evidence of cattle and small stock as well as the African cultigens *Sorghum* and *Vigna* ('cow peas') (Collett 1982). Evidence of smelting seems quite rare, which is not surprising in a predominantly grassland environment.

The chronology remains imprecise, partly because of the paucity of fieldwork and partly because radiocarbon dating itself becomes of limited value for samples younger than about AD 1600. The few available dates do, however, suggest that the BoKoni sites flourished within the last 400 years (Evers & Vogel 1980).

The distribution of these settlements is relatively easy to establish as they show up well on air photographs, provided they are not blanketed by bush or recent timber plantations. Both Mason (1968) and Evers (1975) used air photographs to plot sites; however the map shown here (Fig. 9.1) seems to be the first attempt to show a complete distribution of this settlement type. The result shows a virtually continuous belt of settlement running from Ohrigstad in the north, through Lydenburg and Machadodorp to Carolina in the south, a distance of 150 km. From this belt several lines of outliers lead off eastwards down the Komati valley and upper tributaries of the Crocodile, but nowhere reach the Lowveld. A cluster to the west in the Steelpoort Valley is shown, but it may not really belong within this settlement type.

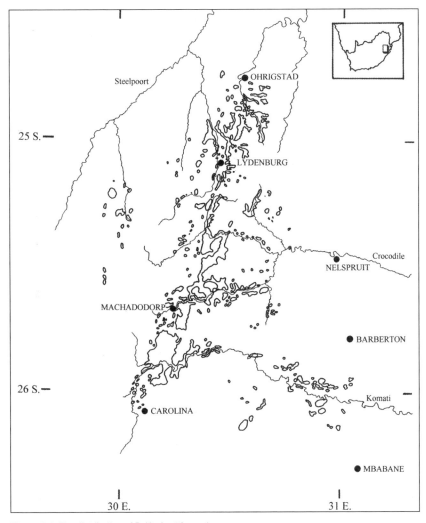

Figure 9.1 The distribution of BoKoni settlements.

Although little has yet been made of the environmental implications of this distribution, there is surely great potential. The escarpment setting is exceptional, for it seems that no other Late Iron Age society was so closely associated with this major South African topographical feature. Settlements cover a considerable range of altitudes, from a little below the crest to some of the deeper incised valleys. Most are in montane grassland, with relatively high rainfall, while the lower outliers extend into savanna. By 1975 Evers had already shown how complex the sites were, with up to 200 homesteads (average 32) in a single built-up area, and how densely settlements clustered in parts of the landscape (Fig. 9.2, from Evers 1975). He tentatively estimated that in an area of the Lydenburg valley

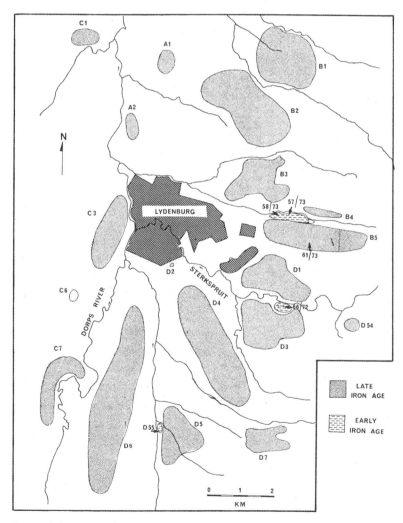

Figure 9.2 An example of the concentrated nature of settlement (from Evers 1975).

somewhat wider than that shown on Figure 9.2, population may have reached as much as between 19 000 and 57 000 at the period of maximum occupation (Marker & Evers 1976). There are numerous other examples of population concentrations of this order among precolonial agriculturist communities in other parts of South Africa, but these were separated from each other by considerable distances. The virtually unbroken belt of 150 km with this degree of population concentration seems to be unique, and therefore requires explanation.

The built settlement pattern

The most striking feature about BoKoni, when compared with all the other known agriculturist societies of the past 500 years in South Africa, is that not only are the homesteads preserved but there are also networks of linking roads and vast areas of agricultural terraces (Fig. 9.3). The road systems are by far the longest and most complex, while the terraces represent, to my knowledge, the only field systems to have survived from precolonial times. We need to consider each of these three built elements in more detail.

Roads are defined by a stonewall on each side. Their function is clearly to connect the homesteads with the open veld, controlling the movement of livestock through the terraced, and therefore cultivated, areas. Roads to individual homesteads are usually quite narrow – often only a metre wide – allowing the passage of only one animal at a time. These

Figure 9.3 One of the large settlements, Rietspruit near Lydenburg.

roads invariably lead to the central enclosure of the homestead. They often join wider communal roads which can be up to 4 km long. It is not yet clear whether the roads were used only in livestock management or whether they also served as a circulation system for pedestrians.

The complex terracing has yet to be studied in any detail, but a few points can be made. Many of the field edges are marked by no more than a single or double row of stones, but there are some cases where substantial walls a metre or more in height have been built and these may even protrude above ground level on the uphill side. Walls roughly follow the natural contours but there are additional stone lines running approximately up-and-down slope, which may define individual plots (Marker & Evers 1976). Fields are narrow, especially on the steeper slopes, and they are quite small. A sample I surveyed averaged around 160 square metres, but there is much variation in both size and shape. This is not surprising since cultivation would have been by hoe.

The terraces and other structures were built on hill slopes where loose stone is naturally available. It therefore seems that stone was carried only short distances to the structures. This brings up the issue of whether the terraced areas represent the total area cultivated. Modern plough cultivation avoids these stony hillsides, concentrating on valley bottom lands with their deeper soils. It seems likely that at least some of these would also have been cultivated. Some evidence concerning this question may be forthcoming from an examination of the outer margins of terraced areas. In some instances there is a substantial

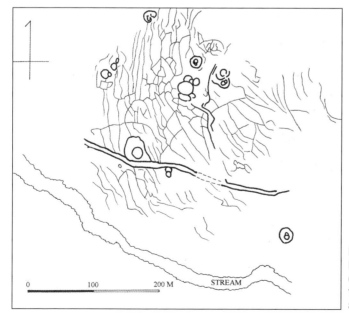

Figure 9.4 A smaller, valley bottom site where the nature of the terracing suggests that terraces were not the only areas that were cultivated.

wall marking the boundary between terracing and open veld (Marker & Evers 1976). As with the roads, these walls were presumably built to keep animals off the fields, therefore these areas of open veld were probably used as grazing land. In other cases there is no such boundary wall and sometimes the edge of the terracing seems to blur into the open veld. Figure 9.4 shows a valley bottom situation where the flatter land is interrupted by a slight stony rise. Here we find a small settlement with the usual range of BoKoni structures, but note how the terracing tends to fade irregularly into the flatter land as if cultivation continued outwards to where the more level ground and lack of stone made terracing redundant.

The homesteads at first glance seem familiar in a Late Iron Age context, with livestock enclosures in the centre, often served by a road. The livestock pens are surrounded by the domestic spaces which are in turn often enclosed by an outer wall. Excavations have shown that houses were built in these domestic areas. Today they are identified by paved and/or daga floors, sometimes with fire-bowl and even trio of fire-stones preserved (Evers 1975; Collett 1982). Nothing remains of the superstructure which means that these houses were built of soft materials. An exception to this are the stone corbelled huts which are occasionally found on this type of settlement (van Hoepen 1939; Myburgh 1956) though they are more common further south on the Highveld where they are associated with a distinctly different type of settlement (e.g. Maggs 1976).

Additional insights into the homesteads are offered to us from the fact that the inhabitants made often quite detailed rock engravings depicting settlement plans. The concentric homestead pattern described above is well emphasised, even though in quite a stylised manner. Figure 9.5 clearly shows two homesteads, each linked to communal roads by a road to the central enclosure, as well as the nesting rings and the houses, represented by dots, in the outer ring.

Figure 9.5 Rock engraving of two homesteads of concentric pattern connected by roads. Dots in the outer rings represent houses. Boomplaas near Lydenburg.

The nature of the houses themselves is less clear and really requires further investigation. Engravings again have something to offer here. The great majority of Iron Age engravings in South Africa represent plan views of structures. The only elevation views of buildings that I know of are from several BoKoni sites and these represent hemispherical houses (Fig. 9.6) (van Hoepen 1939; Maggs 1995a). These apparently show pole and thatch structures similar to traditional Zulu, Swazi and South Sotho 'beehive' houses. However, Alex Schoeman (pers. comm.) has pointed out that the descriptions of the excavated houses may imply cone-on-cylinder structures. Both Evers and Collett excavated paved and/or clay floors, but neither author really addresses the issue of the house form in elevation. The most relevant comment refers to the position of pottery, grindstones and other material around one house 'in positions which suggest that they were kept outside the main body of the dwelling, probably under the eaves' (Marker & Evers 1976: 161). 'Eaves' certainly implies a cone-on-cylinder house form, but no evidence is provided for such a structure. We are told that the walls were built of closely spaced poles, plastered on both sides, while Collett's (1979: 18) two better preserved floors were found under a layer of pole-impressed daga pieces. Since this construction method can apply to both hemispherical and cone-on-cylinder house forms, I consider that there is not enough evidence yet available to determine the shape of the excavated houses. It is possible that both forms were used in BoKoni settlements, and I would contend that at least some would have been hemispherical as reflected in the engravings. Here again is a topic for future research.

Unique features

Most of the range of BoKoni characteristics we have covered so far places us on familiar ground among the many grassland-adapted, stone-building communities of the last 500 years in South Africa. But there are several exceptional features which require closer examination. Here we need to turn to issues concerning regular patterning in the layout

Figure 9.6 Engraving showing a hemispherical house in elevation view. Boomplaas near Lydenburg.

of homesteads. Although I feel there is a long way to go in this field, Evers (Marker & Evers 1976) has put forward a three-part scheme which can be tested in future fieldwork. His simplest pattern comprises two concentric circles; the inner probably being for cattle and the outer domestic, although none have been investigated. The second type repeats the concentric arrangement but now has 'a number of smaller circles around part of, or the whole of' the central circle. The third type is 'an agglomeration of small circles which does not, apparently, conform to the basic pattern of the first two.' This type occurs singly, higher up the valley sides and away from settlements and terracing. My impression is that such complex ruins are relatively rare and might be investigated in terms of being some sort of group livestock posts.

I am particularly interested in Evers' second type, which is characteristic of many of the settlements including the larger ones. I am assuming the first type is likely to have been a humbler version of the second. The few detailed plans published thus far (e.g. Marker & Evers 1976, Fig. 9.4; Collett 1982, Fig. 9.1), as well as many air photos, confirm this layout as the basic pattern of many, if not most, of the larger homesteads.

Figure 9.7 is the sketch plan I made of one of these typical larger homesteads in the central part of the extensive settlement shown in Figure 9.3, which exemplifies this pattern

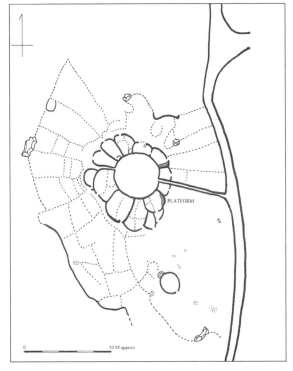

Figure 9.7 Sketch plan of a typical larger homestead.

in some detail. The features I would like to draw attention to are as follows. The first concerns the central enclosure which, being roughly circular, is what I have described as a primary enclosure (Maggs 1976). Note that this has two entrances, the narrow road leading from the wider communal road to the east and, opposite it, another passage leading into the domestic area. But the primary enclosures of precolonial Black farming communities in southern Africa normally have only one entrance. The second oddity concerns the ring of enclosures arranged around the central enclosure, like the petals of a daisy. Note that these abut against the central enclosure, sharing part of its wall, and are therefore what I define as secondary enclosures, and that their entrances face outwards. I know of no other local Iron Age homestead pattern like this. It is, for example, the reverse of the pattern typical of Sotho-Tswana settlements where a ring of primary enclosures, each with a single entrance, open inwards into a central enclosure which is secondary. The central complex of enclosures in these homesteads therefore follows a pattern unique in the South African Iron Age. The pattern, which at first sight looked familiar, turns out to be the opposite of what we would expect from settlements associated with a Sotho culture, as indicated by the Moloko pottery.

Another unusual feature of these BoKoni homesteads is that the domestic areas may be subdivided into compartments by rows of stones. In the case of Figure 9.7 these rows follow a radial pattern, dividing the domestic area into sectors, some with subdivisions. This feature has yet to be studied and explained but, for our purposes, note that most of the radial stone-lines stop short of the central complex of enclosures, leaving a passage between the inner limits of the sectors and the ring of secondary enclosures. Such a passage would serve to protect the domestic compartments and the edible, thatched houses if livestock were penned in the ring of secondary enclosures. Such penning seems the most likely explanation for these enclosures, and it would also explain the need for a second entrance to the central enclosure, which would thereby allow stock to move from the centre via the inner edge of the domestic area into the secondary enclosures. But why go to all this trouble when the stock could simply be penned in the central enclosure?

'Islands of agricultural intensification'

At the 1995 Congress of the Pan African Association for Prehistory, I read a paper entitled 'From Marateng to Marakwet: islands of agricultural intensification in eastern and southern Africa.' The concept was inspired by the work of John Sutton and a variety of other researchers working mainly in eastern Africa; at that time perhaps best encapsulated in the special volume of *Azania* (24 of 1989) titled 'The history of African agricultural technology and field systems'. This volume covered still-flourishing communities, such as the lineage-based irrigation systems of Marakwet in the Kenyan rift valley, as well as extinct cases, known only from their archaeological remains, such as the Engaruka field systems of Tanzania. The last two decades have seen substantial further research on these indigenous African developments, to the point where general features as well as local characteristics are well understood (e.g. Widgren & Sutton 2004). The metaphor 'islands' refers to areas of relatively much more intense agriculture, and higher population, surrounded by 'seas' of more dispersed food production and population.

These highly specialised agricultural regimes of eastern Africa share some of the following features (Widgren & Sutton 2004):

1. Terracing of hillside fields.
2. Specialised manipulation of soil including levelling of plots, mounding and ridging.
3. Irrigation.
4. Stall-feeding of cattle.
5. Manuring of fields.
6. Composting/mulching of fields.
7. Specific crop rotations.
8. Adoption of new crops or crop varieties.

Each 'island' has a particular natural environment which provides advantages over neighbouring areas, particularly with regard to higher rainfall or river flow. However the development of an 'island' is not environmentally determined, since some apparently suitable locales did not see agricultural intensification. The environment allows for possibilities, but it is the social history of each particular area that may lead to the formation of an 'island'. There are no close ethnic or cultural links between 'islands', each being apparently an independent development.

Items 1 to 6 above fall into what has been called 'landesque capital' – activities concerning land and cultivation 'that reach beyond the immediate needs of the coming cropping season' (Blaikie & Brookfield 1987, quoted in Widgren 2004). In the present context, landesque capital consists of the inputs of labour over time to sustain higher agricultural yields. In practice, each of the currently active 'islands' in eastern Africa today has its own 'complex communal rules of land use and labour mobilisation' (Widgren & Sutton 2004).

How does all of this apply to BoKoni? For a start the thousands of hectares of terracing and the hundreds of kilometres of roads represent a massive investment in landesque capital, and are the result of very substantial mobilisation of labour. It is the scale of this investment that sets BoKoni apart from all other precolonial societies in South Africa.

Does this qualify BoKoni as an 'island of agricultural intensification'? To answer this adequately we would need to ask a series of questions, each of which would require substantial further research. The features 1-8 each require a question, and of these we can immediately answer yes only to No.1 – the terracing of hillside fields. As yet we have no information on Nos 2, 6 and 7. As for No. 3 – irrigation – it is clear that most of these terraced hillsides were not irrigated, nor would there be much need in this relatively high rainfall region; however Myburgh (1956) reported signs of what might have been irrigation at one site, and this should be further investigated.

A question that intrigues me is No. 4, the stall feeding of livestock, and linked to it No. 5, the possibility that fields were manured. This brings us back to Figure 9.7 and the reason for the ring of outward opening secondary enclosures – the petals of the daisy. Was this strange arrangement designed for the stall feeding of livestock, perhaps on a seasonal basis? It seems unlikely that such a pattern would have been developed for the daily movement of stock in and out of the homestead. But if parts of the herds were kept in and stall fed over longer periods, this pattern might have made for easier management. Homesteads were relatively dispersed through the terraced areas. This would have facilitated the collection of the unwanted parts of crop plants as fodder, as well as the spreading of manure from stalls onto adjacent fields. Substantial research would be required to address these questions.

And what about No. 8, the possibility of new crops? Large, 'birdbath'-type lower grindstones and two-handed upper grindstones have been recovered from some BoKoni sites. These are normally regarded as being required for the grinding of maize rather than the smaller and softer African cereals. So far sorghum is the only grain recovered from a BoKoni site, but we know that maize was already a staple in precolonial KwaZulu-Natal. Maputo is the probable point of entry of the earliest maize into South Africa; and BoKoni is directly opposite Maputo on the escarpment. Portuguese ships were calling annually at Maputo from at least the 1550s, so there was plenty of time and opportunity for local farmers to adopt maize. Furthermore the higher rainfall, mist belt conditions of the escarpment are not favourable for sorghum, which requires less moisture than maize. Future excavations will need to look into this possibility.

The question of maize therefore remains unanswered, though a positive outcome is likely. In a favourable environment such as this, maize has a much higher yield per hectare than any of the African grains. Its presence as a major crop at BoKoni would greatly help to explain much about the development and expansion of this remarkable society, as well as the exceptional population density, in an environment not otherwise much favoured by agriculturist communities of the past 500 years.

References

Collett, D.P. 1982. Excavations of stone-walled ruins in the Badfontein Valley, eastern Transvaal, South Africa. *South African Archaeological Bulletin* 37: 34-43.

Evers, T.M. 1975. Recent Iron Age research in the eastern Transvaal, South Africa. *South African Archaeological Bulletin* 30: 71-83.

Evers, T.M. & Vogel, J.C. 1980. Radiocarbon dates for Iron Age sites at Lydenburg and White River, eastern Transvaal. *South African Journal of Science* 76: 230-231.

Huffman, T.N. 2004. The archaeology of the Nguni past. *Southern African Humanities* 16: 79-111.

Maggs, T. 1976. *Iron Age Communities of the Southern Highveld*. Pietermaritzburg: Natal Museum.

Maggs, T. 1995a. Neglected rock art: the rock engravings of agriculturist communities in South Africa. *South African Archaeological Bulletin* 50: 132-142.

Maggs, T. 1995b. From Marateng to Marakwet: islands of agricultural intensification in eastern and southern Africa. *Abstracts for 10th Congress of the Pan African Association for Prehistory*. Harare: University of Zimbabwe and National Museums and Monuments of Zimbabwe.

Marker, M.E. & Evers, T.M. 1976. Iron Age settlements and soil erosion in the Eastern Transvaal. *South African Archaeological Bulletin* 31: 152-165.

Mason, R.J. 1968. Transvaal and Natal Iron Age settlement revealed by aerial photography and excavation. *African Studies* 27: 1-14.

Myburgh, A.C. 1956. Die stamme van die Distrik Carolina. *Departement van Naturellesake, Etnologiese Reeks* 34. Pretoria: Government Printer.

van Hoepen, E.C.N. 1939. Pre-European Bantu culture in Lydenburg district. *Argeologiese Navorsinge van die Nasionale Museum Bloemfontein* 2: 59-63.

Widgren, M. 2004. Towards a historical geography of intensive farming in Eastern Africa. In: Widgren, M. & Sutton, J.E.G. (eds) *Islands of Intensive Agriculture in Eastern Africa*: 1-18. British Institute in Eastern Africa & Stockholm University.

Widgren, M. & Sutton, J.E.G. (eds) 2004. *Islands of Intensive Agriculture in Eastern Africa*. British Institute in Eastern Africa & Stockholm University.

10

Post-European contact glass beads from the southern African interior: a tentative look at trade, consumption and identities

Marilee Wood

Introduction

The glass beads that were traded into the interior of southern Africa in the past five hundred years are the most frequently found imported artefacts in archaeological deposits. They have unfortunately been little studied even though they have the potential to help interpret several aspects of archaeological sites where they are present. These include illuminating trade contacts and routes, determining cultural affiliations and refining site chronology. This study includes a brief introduction about using beads in site interpretation and a discussion and interpretation of bead assemblages from four areas in the interior.

Glass bead characteristics

Before discussing the glass beads found in the southern African interior, a few terms used to describe beads should be explained (information from this section was taken from Karklins (1985), and Kidd and Kidd (1970)). Glass beads are first categorised according to their method of manufacture. The methods pertinent to this study include drawing and winding. Drawn beads are made by creating a hollow in a gather (globule) of molten glass either by blowing a bubble into it or perforating it with a tool. (This hollow will remain to form the perforation in the finished bead.) The gather is then drawn or pulled out into a long tube that is next cut into segments the lengths of the desired beads. The resultant segments may then be reheated to round the sharp edges – the length of time this heating process is carried out determines the roundness of each bead. Beads that are not reheated, or are reheated to only a small extent, retain the straight profile of the original tube and are thus called tubes. Beads that are heated until the ends are decidedly rounded but the body retains straight sections are referred to as cylinder,[1] and those reheated to the extent that the entire profile is rounded are known as oblates. Drawn beads may be decorated with stripes or may be composed of more than one layer of glass. Stripes are created by impressing rods of coloured glass on to the exterior of the gather before it is drawn out. Additional layers of glass are made by dipping the gather into molten glass of another colour (or several colours) before being drawn. One additional drawn bead type frequently found in the interior is known as a cornerless hexagon (although they may sometimes be heptagonal or octagonal). These are larger than most other drawn beads and are made by drawing the original tube through a hexagonally-shaped die. The resultant faceted tube is cut into bead lengths and the corners at the end of each angle are ground off using lapidary techniques. Occasionally this type of bead is made from a round tube, in which case all of the facets are formed through grinding.

Wound beads are normally made by heating a thin glass rod over a flame. When the glass is viscid it is wrapped around a metal wire or mandrel. One or two wraps on a thick mandrel will result in an annular (ring-shaped) bead. Spherical (and other shaped) beads are made by winding the desired amount of glass onto a thin mandrel and then shaping the resultant blob by rolling it on a flat or shaped surface or perhaps paddling or moulding it into a more elaborate shape. Once shaped, decoration such as dots or lines of contrasting coloured glass may be added to wound beads. The perforations of wound beads are often slightly tapered and may have residues of chalk, which is used to prevent the bead from adhering to the mandrel. Only one bead in the assemblages under study may have been moulded after winding. It came from Maleoskop and is decorated with seven ridges that run perpendicular to the perforation (see Plate 20). It is a type I have not encountered elsewhere.

Secondary modification refers to the practice of altering beads once they reach their destination. Although this is a common practice in West Africa, it was infrequently done in southern Africa. The only possible instances of secondary modification I have observed involve rounded beads from the interior whose ends have been ground flat – assumedly to make them fit together more tightly when strung (like tubular beads).

Beads as temporal markers

The first production dates of some beads are known, making them useful in determining the earliest possible dates for a given assemblage (but as Kinahan (2000:70) has observed *combinations* of bead types are more reliable as chronological indicators than individual ones). These include:

- Brownish-red (often referred to as Indian red) tubes or cylinders have been made for at least 2 000 years in India (and at times elsewhere) (Francis 2002: 19). They first appeared in South Africa in the last quarter of the 10th century (Wood 2005: 51). European beadmakers copied these beads for use in the African trade. They are usually difficult to date.

- Brownish-red-on-green (referred to as Indian-red-on-green (IROG)) drawn tubes or cylinders are made by adding a thin layer of opaque brownish-red glass to a core of scrap glass that is often some shade of green but can be blackish or even translucent red. These beads were first made in about 1600 in Venice (Francis 1988: 26) and were probably cheaper to manufacture than the solid Indian red ones, which they gradually – but not completely – displaced. Beck stated they were exported to Africa 'by the shipload' in the 18th and 19th centuries. (Beck in Caton-Thompson 1931: 238). IROGs were also made by winding brownish-red glass onto a wound white or yellow core, but they do not occur in the assemblages under study.

- Drawn translucent-red-on-white cylinders and oblates (known as white hearts) were first made in Venice in the mid-1830s (Francis 1988: 26). They arrived in South Africa within a year or two of their introduction (Saitowitz 1990; Wood 1996: 148) and often replaced IROGs within a few decades. They also appeared at about the same time in larger wound forms (sometimes with yellow cores) (Karklins 1985: 81) but this variation has not yet been found in bead assemblages from the interior (although they do appear at Ondini; see Plate 21).

- Cornerless hexagons (they may be heptagonal or octagonal as well), which appear in various shades of cobalt blue, were popular from about 1820 to 1900 (Francis 1994: 66). Van der Sleen (1967: 85) noted that they appeared in southern Africa early in the 19th century and were 'still in use by some tribes in 1910'. Kinahan (2000: 63) records that these beads were popular in Namibia during this same time span. They were mainly made in Bohemia, which had a long tradition of lapidary work – these skills were transferred to glass beads (Francis 1979a:11, 1979b:13, 1998). Venice fabricated them as well (Karklins & Barka 1989: 75; DeCorse et al 2003: 85).

- Annular (or ring-shaped) beads, which were mainly made in Germany, appear in several colours. The light greyish-blue and amber-coloured types date back to the early 19th century. Clear (colourless) examples begin to appear by 1860 and by the end of the century (1880) bright cobalt blue and green ones appear (Francis 1988: 53, 1993: 18). According to van der Sleen (1967) annular beads began to arrive in southern Africa early in the 19th century. Most annular beads found in southern Africa are the cobalt blue variety (pers. obs.).

- Wound opaque turquoise-coloured beads (known as Padre beads in the south-west and Chief beads in the north-west of the USA) were made in China from the early 19th century (Francis 1994: 86, 2002: 170) and were traded into Africa mainly by British and American traders. They were copied by manufacturers in Europe, but the copies do not have the same satiny finish and tend to be more opaque when viewed under magnification (pers. obs.).

- Oyster white (slightly translucent off-white) beads are the only white beads found in southern Africa prior to the 1830s (pers. obs.). From about 1580-1890, Venetians made drawn oyster white beads with clear coats (a thin layer of colourless glass that added shine) (Francis 1992: 19).

- Small drawn opaque pure white as well as pink beads (often termed seed beads) begin to arrive in southern Africa the early 19th century – probably around 1830 (pers. obs.).

The way bead types change through time can be illustrated by comparing assemblages from Dingane's capital, Mgungundlovu (1828-1839), and Cetshwayo's capital Ondini (1872-1879). As Figure 10.1 demonstrates, in the thirty-odd years separating the two capitals, oyster white beads are replaced by pure white ones and red-on-white beads all but replace IROGs.

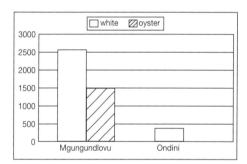 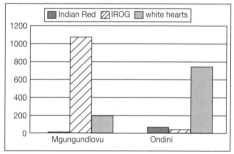

Figure 10.1 Changes in bead types from Mgungundlovu to Ondini (based on data from Saitowitz 1990).

Beads and cultural identity

Because bead preferences vary between different cultural groups, certain bead types can be used to suggest cultural influences. In part these preferences developed based on the bead types that were available and used when trading relations first began. It is likely that most beads reaching the interior prior to 1824 – the date the first British settlement was established at Port Natal (Durban) – came through Delagoa Bay. Although other European powers traded on and off through Delagoa Bay, it is likely that the Portuguese were the first Europeans to establish the trade in glass beads, laying the foundation for bead preferences. This proposition is supported by the observation that a Dutch trading factory, which was established at Delagoa Bay in 1721, failed nine years later partly because the Dutch 'could not supply the local market with the type of beads required' (Newitt 1995: 158). In turn, however, local preferences, which were established centuries before Europeans sailed into the Indian Ocean (Wood 2005), obliged the Portuguese to purchase beads for trade in southern Africa from southeast India (Theal 1898: 303).

Conservative tendencies in certain cultural groups also influenced bead preferences. Both the Pedi and Venda are known for heirlooming beads (Schapera & Goodwin 1946: 144), a practice associated with respect for the past. Beads that were handed down through the generations became highly valued and were thought to have protective and healing powers (DeCorse et al 2003: 82). On a visit to a Venda village in 1948, Barbara Tyrrell (1968: 45) reported that the heirloom beads worn by women represented individual ancestors so were protected and honoured by their owners. If troubles arose the diviner would advise the owner which ancestor was angry and the bead representing that individual would be 'cooled' with suitable incantations and by blowing water on it.

European bead manufacturers copied these older beads and, although the consumers were never fooled by the imitations, they did buy them, thus perpetuating established preferences. An example of this can be seen in the Venda bead collection depicted in Plate 2. Number 19 shows several beads called *Vhulungu ha madi* – they are imitations of older beads of the same name (often called 'beads of the water'). For traders and consumers in conservative areas, it was less risky to deal in known beads, that had established values in the existing network, than trying to introduce new types that might not be accepted.

The way beads were used by various groups influenced choice as well. Cylindrical and oblate beads are well suited for intricate free-standing beadwork, as produced by most Nguni groups (such as Zulu, Xhosa and Ndzundza Ndebele). These rounded beads can also effectively be strung in long strings. Tubular beads, on the other hand, are not well suited to free-standing beadwork but fit together well when strung. Both types are suitable for stitching onto garments. Thus, both tubular and cylindrical/oblate beads are found in assemblages associated with Pedi, Venda and Tswana groups but only cylindrical/oblate beads occur in Zulu and most other Nguni contexts.[2] In sum, rounded beads are not diagnostic – all groups used them – but tubular, as well as annular and hexagonal beads, are seldom found in Zulu assemblages but were favoured by North Sotho, Venda and possibly Tswana groups.

But bead preferences do change. If a bead type is no longer produced it will sooner or later disappear from use and new varieties will be adopted. The pace of this change appears to have been much slower in the interior than closer to the trading ports. Elite control over bead trade and distribution can also be a factor. The early Zulu kings maintained fairly tight control over this trade and attempted to create a pan-Zulu beadwork style as part of their effort to unify the disparate groups that made up the kingdom. Under Mpande's less centralised reign (1840-1872) regional beadwork styles were allowed to develop and the bead trade became so voluminous that beads of many varieties were widely available (Wood 1996: 148-9). Many unfortunate traders, who did not keep up to date with local fashion trends, discovered that they were unable to dispose of their stock. Selecting beads for trade in the more conservative interior would have been less risky.

Available bead resources

Fortunately the Van Riet Lowe Bead Collection, housed in the Archaeology Department at the University of the Witwatersrand, contains collections that describe some of the bead types used by specific groups. The first is a selection of beads collected from Pedi contexts prior to 1941 (Plate 11). It is accompanied by a descriptive list compiled by Van Warmelo who collected the information from 'old women and other reliable informants at Mohlaletse [Sekhukhune's village] and further east'. Names are given for each bead type as well as comments about their age and who used them.

The next is a display of Venda beads that was assembled before 1950 (Plate 12). They were collected by a Major H.A. Pittendrigh from Sibasa and include descriptions and names of the beads plus information on who wore them. The beads were collected from all over 'Vendaland' and information about them was compiled from interviews with chiefs Sibasa, Ramaputa, Makuya, Pafuri, Masia and Rasengane.

There is also a collection of beads (Plate 13) that Van Riet Lowe picked up at Mgungundlovu on a visit there that probably occurred in the 1950s. A large proportion of them are large wound beads illustrating the point that large beads are frequently under-represented in archaeological assemblages because they are easy for passers-by to find and, consequently, may be removed from sites before they can be excavated. Further data about the beads found at Mgungundlovu and Ondini can be found in Saitowitz (1990). I have also examined the beads from these two sites and have photographed many of them (Plates 14 and 15).

It has been observed by several researchers, for example DeCorse et al (2003: 83), that the temporal distributions of many bead varieties are similar in Africa and the Americas, particularly in the 19th century. Therefore, some publications dealing with archaeological glass bead assemblages from that time in other parts of Africa and the West can be used as cross references. Karklins' monograph (1985), which illustrates beads from the 19th-century Levin bead catalogue and the Venetian Bead Book of the same period, is widely used by researchers but it is of somewhat limited value for South African researchers since so few decorated beads are found locally. An article by Ross (1990) describing the beads found at Fort Vancouver, a Hudson's Bay Company post in present-day Washington State that dates from 1829 to 1860, details numerous beads that match those found in South African sites of the same period. Perhaps of special interest are those that deal with southern African glass bead assemblages that date to the last 500 years: Laidler (1934), Karklins and Schrire (1991), Killick (1987), Kinahan (2000), Saitowitz (1990), Saitowitz and Sampson (1992), and Wood (1996). Schofield (1958), it should be noted, contains too many errors to be used without great caution.

Interpreting bead assemblages

To illustrate how this knowledge about beads and bead preferences can best be used to interpret archaeological assemblages, I will discuss several bead assemblages I have analysed. As Figure 10.2 shows, the four sites I will discuss are west and north of Delagoa Bay, the port through which most of these beads probably arrived. After the mid-1820s Port Natal would have been involved as well, especially for beads traded into present-day KwaZulu Natal.

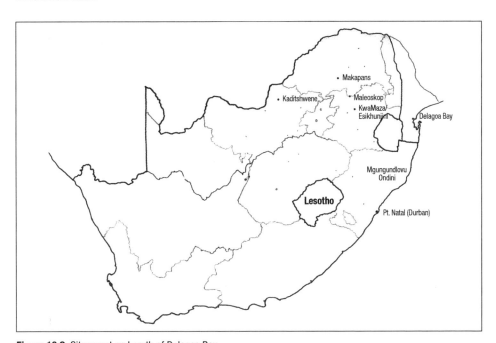

Figure 10.2 Sites west and north of Delagoa Bay.

KwaMaza and Esikhunjini

KwaMaza, in the Steelpoort River Valley, was the Ndzundza Ndebele capital from about 1675 to the 1820s. In her analysis of Ndzundza material culture, Schoeman (1997) found that settlement layout (a male-controlled activity), house form (a joint male-female

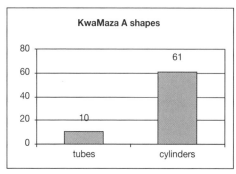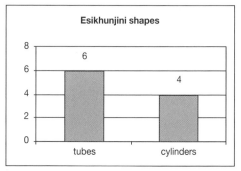

Figure 10.3 Bead shapes – KwaMaza and Esikhunjini.

endeavour) and midden structure (a female activity), followed Nguni principles while ceramic style (female) was Sotho. The 71 beads[3] (Plate 16), which were excavated at elite residences (most came from KwaMaza A), perhaps display Nguni preferences since the majority of them are rounded rather than tubular (see Fig. 10.3), but it is difficult to be certain since we have no Nguni comparative material from this time period. Because the colours and glass quality of both rounded and tubular beads are the same I have combined them in the colour chart (Plate 6). The same has been done below for the Esikhunjini and Kaditshwene assemblages for the same reasons.

KwaMaza was destroyed and abandoned in the 1820s after Mzilikazi invaded the region and the Ndzundza moved to another site, Esikhunjini (mid-1820s to mid-1830s). There the settlement pattern closely resembled that of KwaMaza. Midden structure and ceramics were similar as well but house form showed changes; although the basic beehive structure (male-controlled) remained the same, the thatching and plastering (female domain) took on Sotho characteristics. Schoeman interpreted the continuity of settlement layout, which reflects the public power of men, as expressing the 'perceived political and economic independence of the group, in the context of competition for regional economic and political resources' (1997: 187). But she suggests that the change in house form may have been a response by women to identify more closely with their Pedi neighbours as opposed to the Nguni invaders (Mzilikazi). She also noted it was possible in these times of trouble that more Sotho women were marrying across to the Ndzundza community.

The ten glass beads[4] found at Esikhunjini (Plate 17) all came from the elite residence. Apart from the addition of IROG (Indian-red-on-green) beads, colour preferences have not changed dramatically from KwaMaza (Plate 6), but the apparent continuity is somewhat misleading. The Esikhunjini blue-green beads are a softer shade and more transparent than those at KwaMaza and, as can be seen in Figure 10.3, there has been a shift toward tubular beads that may indicate a move away from Nguni influence toward Pedi preferences.

These observations, however, must be considered very speculative because the samples – particularly at Esikhunjini – are small. It is also possible that the differences between the beads of the two sites are related to time – we do not know at what time the KwaMaza beads were imported and they could conceivably be considerably older than those from Esikhunjini.

Kaditshwene

Kaditshwene, which lies about 25 km north of Zeerust, North West Province, was the Hurutshe (Tswana) capital from about 1790 to 1823. The 131 glass beads from the site (which all came from stratified deposits) are the only Tswana assemblage I have studied so I cannot say if the beads are representative of a larger Tswana aesthetic. When John Campbell visited Kaditshwene in 1820 he was informed by the Hurutshe that they regarded the Cape as the 'bead country', but that they also had contact with Tsonga traders from the east coast (Jan Boeyens pers. comm.). It is probable that if the Kaditshwene beads in this assemblage came from Delagoa Bay via Tsonga traders, they would be similar to those found at KwaMaza or Esikhunjini. On the other hand, if they are distinctly different they would more likely have arrived via trade from the Cape. Figures 10.4 and Plate 18 demonstrate that the Kaditshwene beads are similar to those from Esikhunjini, so are likely to have arrived from the east rather than the south. In addition, because the Kaditshwene beads are more like those from Esikhunjini rather than KwaMaza, it is possible they date to a time closer to the former rather than the latter. However, the possibility exists that the beads found at Esikhunjini were older types that had been heirloomed. One large wound oval-shaped Kaditshwene bead (from KLF 3-1-11 L11) may have arrived from the Cape since it is a type not found in North Sotho contexts.

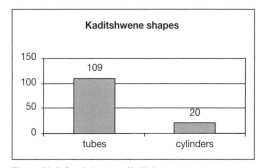

Figure 10.4 Bead shapes – Kaditshwene.

Makapan Historic Cave

The people who took refuge in Makapan Cave in 1854 were principally Kekana Northern Ndebele but include Sotho Tswana sub-chiefs and their followers as well (Amanda Esterhuysen pers. comm.). Many perished in the cave during the siege so strings of beads and a small piece of beadwork on leather have been recovered. Of the beads found at the site, I have examined those collected by Mason in about 1950 (in the Van Riet Lowe collection) and those excavated by Esterhuysen (Plate 19). Of the 523 glass beads[5] found by Esterhuysen the majority are tubular (Fig. 10.5). Because the cylindrical/oblate and tubular beads form two distinct sets, I have separated them for colour analysis. As Plate 8 shows, in the thirty-odd years that separate Makapan from the earlier sites, a wider variety of beads was available. Tubular bead colours bear a relationship to earlier colour preferences but the rounded beads introduce some new colours notably black, pure white and red-on-white. While the preponderance of tubular beads may suggest Sotho influence, the rounded ones may indicate that the trade through Port Natal was reaching the interior.

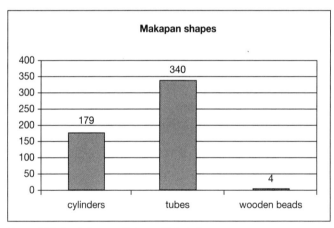

Figure 10.5 Bead shapes – Makapan Historic Cave.

Maleoskop

The final group of beads comes from Maleoskop (Plate 20), a BaKopa (Pedi) community that lived west of Groblersdal, Mpumalanga, from about 1840 up to 1864 when the village was destroyed in a joint Boer/Swazi attack (Boshoff et al 2007; Boshoff & Steyn, in press). The area was also the site of the first Berlin Mission Station north of the Vaal River. Of the 4 389 glass beads[6] I have examined from the site, the vast majority (4 321) came from a rectangular building. The battle raged around this structure and the remains of twelve individuals, who were either taking refuge there or defending it, were found in the excavations. It is likely that many, if not most, of the beads were associated with these people and others involved in the battle.

Table 10.1 shows the division of Maleoskop beads by type. Unlike Makapan, rounded beads make up the vast majority of the assemblage. New colours are evident as well, notably pink in rounded beads and yellow in tubular ones. Interestingly, the colour preferences (Plate 9) evident in Maleoskop's rounded beads appear to be more closely related to those from Ondini (Plate 10 and Plate 21) than to those from the other sites examined so far. This may suggest that trade connections had developed with the Zulu kingdom or via it to Port Natal. Tubular colours are also significantly different than at the other sites. This is probably due to increased trade into the interior as well as the availability of new bead varieties. Some of these new bead types became part of the Pedi canon. As can be seen in Plate 21, the unusual green beads with brownish-red and white stripes as well as the black beads with white stripes are present (in later forms) in the Pedi bead collection at Wits. Cornerless hexagons and annular beads also apparently make their first appearances during this period. It is surprising none of these last two varieties has been found at Makapan. It is possible this is because the site has been visited frequently over the years and the larger, more obvious, beads have been removed. However, it is interesting that the Makapan beads have more in common with those from Kaditshwene and Esikhunjini (Plates 17, 18 and 19) rather than those from Maleoskop, which are temporally closer to Makapan.

Table 10.1: Maleoskop beads by type.

How made and shape	Total
Drawn (cylindrical/oblate)	3 785
Drawn (tubular)	448
Drawn (hexagonal)	97
Wound (annular)	50
Wound (other)	9
Total	**4 389**

Discussion

The assemblages examined here are small time capsules that afford glimpses into which beads were being used at a given place and time. The samples from KwaMaza and Esikhunjini are unfortunately too small to give us more than a hint about the glass beads in circulation and we do not know when in the occupation of KwaMaza (c. 1675-1820s) its beads were deposited. The age of the Esikhunjini beads, however, is well confined within about a ten-year period. The site of Kaditshwene covers a time span of about 30 years and its demise overlaps the beginning of Esikhunjini so it is perhaps not surprising that their bead assemblages are similar. The precision of the date the Makapan beads were deposited is unusual in archaeological assemblages. It enables us to see that, while many of the tubular beads resemble those of the earlier sites, a new range of bead types has been introduced during the thirty-year period separating them. This is probably linked to the development of trade through Port Natal. The large assemblage of beads from Maleoskop also fits into a concise time frame that post-dates the founding of Port Natal. The rather dramatic change in bead preferences found there surely is a direct result of increased trade through that port.

Conclusion

This necessarily brief look at glass beads from the interior illustrates some of the difficulties inherent in such studies as well as suggesting their potential usefulness. Assemblages that are small may give tantalising glimpses into bead types in use but have limited value in reconstructing the bigger picture. The context in which the beads were found must be taken into account and the possibility that some of the beads were heirloomed must be recognised. When bead assemblages from more sites have been excavated, analysed and compared to each other and existing collections, it should be possible to expand and refine the information we can extract from them. Potentially they should be able to provide clues as to who was trading with whom and by what routes, to suggest cultural influences present at a given site and – as arrival dates for various bead types are more securely established – to refine site chronology. If large sites are extensively excavated it may also be possible to explore differential access to beads based on social and/or economic status.

This study is just a beginning and any conclusions drawn from it must be considered tentative since so little work has been done on glass beads found in the interior. This said, it is probable that bead preferences of groups living in the interior were generally more conservative than amongst Nguni living closer to the trading ports. Bead types that were treasured and passed down through the generations by North Sotho and Venda groups underpinned this conservatism. Like other forms of material culture, the beads that a group or individual selected and the way they used them not only reflected but helped form their sense of identity.

Notes

1. This use of the term 'cylinder' is not generally employed (it is often used interchangeably with 'tube') but I find it useful to distinguish beads that are more rounded than tubes yet not as rounded as oblates.
2. Differences in the way beads were used and worn by the various groups can be seen in images in Tyrrell (1968) and the various volumes of *The Bantu Tribes of South Africa: Reproductions of Photographic*

Studies by A.M. Duggan-Cronin. His photos document the period between 1919 and 1939.

3. Only one of these came from the surface – the only white bead with blue stripes – so it is possible this bead is a later intrusion.
4. Two of these beads were found on the surface but are the same types found in the other stratified deposits so should belong to the site.
5. Seventy-eight of these were surface-collected but being in a cave environment all are related to the overall assemblage.
6. Only five beads were recorded as coming from the surface and they are similar to the rest of the finds.

References
Boshoff, W.S., Krüger, D.J. & Krüger, E. 2007. Maleoskop Archaeological Project: third interim report, Gerlachshoop 2005-2006 seasons. Pretoria: UNISA, Department of Old Testament and Ancient Near Eastern Studies.

Boshoff, W.S. & Steyn, M. In press. A war uncovered: human remains from Thabantšho Maleoskop, South Africa. *South African Archaeological Bulletin*.

Caton-Thompson, G. 1931. *The Zimbabwe Culture.* Oxford: Clarendon Press.

DeCorse, C.R., Richard, F.G. & Thiaw, I. 2003. Toward a systematic bead description system: a view from the Lower Falemme, Senegal. *Journal of African Archaeology* 1(1): 77-110.

Francis, P., Jr. 1979a. The Czech bead story. *World of Beads Monograph Series 2.*

Francis, P., Jr. 1979b. The Story of Venetian beads. *World of Beads Monograph Series 1.*

Francis, P., Jr. 1988. *The Glass Trade Beads of Europe.* Lake Placid, NY: The Center for Bead Research.

Francis, P., Jr. 1992. *Twenty Easy Steps to Identifying Most Beads in Most Collections.* Lake Placid, NY: Lapis Route Books.

Francis, P., Jr. 1993. *Advanced Bead Identification.* Lake Placid, NY: The Center for Bead Research.

Francis, P., Jr. 1994. *Beads of the World.* Atglen, PA: Schiffer Publishing, Ltd.

Francis, P., Jr. 1998. The Venetian bead story 1. *The Margaretologist* 11(2): 3-12.

Francis, P., Jr. 2002. *Asia's Maritime Bead Trade: 300 BC to the Present.* Honolulu: University of Hawaii Press.

Karklins, K. 1985. *Glass Beads: The 19th Century Levin Catalogue and Venetian Bead Book and Guide to Description of Glass Beads.* Ottawa: Parks Canada.

Karklins, K. & Barka, N.F. 1989. The beads of St. Eustatius, Netherlands Antilles. *Beads: Journal of the Society of Bead Researchers* 1: 55-80.

Karklins, K. & Schrire, C. 1991. The beads from Oudepost I, a Dutch East India Company outpost, Cape, South Africa. *Beads: Journal of the Society of Bead Researchers* 3: 61-72.

Kidd, K.E. & Kidd, M.A. 1970. A classification system for glass beads for the use of field archaeologists. *Canadian Historic Sites: Occasional Papers in Archaeology and History* 1: 45-89.

Killick, D. 1987. European trade beads in Southern Africa. *The Bead Forum* 10: 3-9.

Kinahan, J. 2000. *Cattle for Beads: The Archaeology of Historical Contact and Trade on the Namib Coast.* Studies in African Archaeology 17. University of Uppsala, Sweden.

Laidler, P.W. 1934. Beads in Africa south of the Zambesi. *Proceedings of the Rhodesia Scientific Association* 34: 1-27.

Newitt, M. 1995. *A History of Mozambique.* Bloomington & Indianapolis: Indiana University Press.

Ross, L.A. 1990. Trade beads from Hudson's Bay company Fort Vancouver (1829-1860), Vancouver, Washington. *Beads: Journal of the Society of Bead Researchers* 2: 29-67.

Saitowitz, S.J. 1990. 19th century glass trade beads from two Zulu royal residences. Unpublished MA thesis. Cape Town: University of Cape Town.

Saitowitz, S.J. & Sampson, C.G. 1992. Glass trade beads from rock shelters in the Upper Karoo. *South African Archaeological Bulletin* 47: 94-103.

Schapera, I. & Goodwin, A.J.H. 1946. Work and wealth. In: Schapera, I. (ed.) *The Bantu Speaking Tribes of*

South Africa: 131-172. Cape Town: Maskew Miller Ltd.

Schoeman, M.H. 1997. The Ndzundza archaeology of the Steelpoort River Valley. Unpublished MA thesis. Johannesburg: University of the Witwatersrand.

Schofield, J. F. 1958. Southern African beads and their relation to the beads of Inyanga. In: Summers, R. (ed.) *Inyanga*: 180-229. Cambridge: Cambridge University Press.

Theal, G.M. 1898. *Records of South-Eastern Africa*. Cape Town: Government of the Cape Colony.

Tyrrell, B. 1968. *Tribal Peoples of Southern Africa*. Cape Town: Gothic Printing Co. Ltd.

Van der Sleen, W.G.N. 1967. *A Handbook on Beads*. York, PA: George Shumway.

Wood, M. 1996. Zulu beadwork. In: Wood, M. (ed.) *Zulu Treasures of Kings and Commoners*: 143-170. Durban: KwaZulu Cultural History Museum & the Local History Museums.

Wood, M. 2005. Glass beads and pre-European trade in the Shashe-Limpopo Region. Unpublished MA thesis. Johannesburg: University of the Witwatersrand.

11

Ceramic alliances: pottery and the history of the Kekana Ndebele in the old Transvaal

A.B. Esterhuysen

Introduction

In South Africa the interpretation of Iron Age ceramics has been strongly influenced by the idea that the producers and users of a pottery style are one and the same, so that style can be used to identify discrete groups of people, or the distribution of a style will mirror the distribution of the group (Huffman 1982, 1983, 2002; Evers 1988: 5). This chapter proposes a different approach to ceramics. Rather than regarding ceramic style as representative of stable cultural behaviour, it treats it as a social object. In other words the meaning and significance of a particular style of pottery will be expressed and negotiated within particular circumstances, and through a number of social encounters and exchanges (cf. Thomas 1991). This chapter lays out the complex social and political processes that defined the 19th-century political landscape, and envisages how diacritical markers, including pottery design, would have formed an integral part of this social discourse. Ceramics from Historic Cave in the Makapans Valley, studied in combination with oral and documentary histories, reveal the nature and extent of the Kekana Ndebele's political network. The context in which a particular style of pottery was found unlocks the possibility that the ceramics represented key marriage alliances forged between the Kekana and at least one section of the Kgatla.

The socio-economic landscape of the 18th and 19th centuries

During the 18th and 19th centuries the socio-economic landscape of the northern region of South Africa was characterised by shifting authority, driven by competition over resources and trade. While chiefdoms in the area had been trading with the Swahili and Portuguese on the east coast for centuries,[1] during the latter part of the 18th century a growth in the demand for ivory in India elicited a corresponding escalation in its exports from Delagoa Bay (Eldredge 1992: 6; Manson 1995: 358). This trade, initially dominated by the English,[2] drove competition and conflict in the region to a new level (Manson 1995:

197

358). To outsiders the established market made this area economically attractive.[3] To the Trekboers and other exiles from the Cape (1820s), the prospect of taking control of the Limpopo ivory trade and setting up profitable trade relations with the Portuguese, held the promise of wealth and independence from British rule (Ferreira 2002: 50).

This trade economy generated a complex web of interactions and exchanges. The balance of political and economic power shifted between chiefdoms, or between settler groups and chiefdoms, producing myriad frontier-like interactions (cf. Legassick 1980). Importantly, while the colonial frontier brought with it notions of superiority (on the part of the coloniser) rooted in 'racial and cultural difference' (Gosden 2004: 5, 22-23), frontier conditions were very much a part of internal African social and political order, and may have been so for millennia (Kopytoff 1989: 10-11). Kopytoff (1989) has described the mechanisms within this social system that triggered the repeated fission, migration and fusion of polities, which led to the frequent formation of new polities on the margins of, or in the spaces between, more established societies (1989: 9). Although Kopytoff did not extend his study to the subcontinent, research in southern Africa (Schapera 1963; Bonner 1983; Delius 1983; Hamilton 1985; Comaroff & Comaroff 1991) also revealed societies that were, on the one hand, highly ordered and, on the other, fluid and negotiable (Comaroff & Comaroff 1991: 139). These studies located the source of this dualism within agnatic politics, which not only defined one's position in society, but also legitimised power, position and material inequality (Schapera 1963: 166; Comaroff & Comaroff 1991: 134). Households were either subordinate or superordinate to one another (Comaroff & Comaroff 1991: 139), but competition and rivalry between equals regularly caused households to split, and if the rivals were royal patrikin, divided the chiefdom.

The structure of this agnatic society made it necessary for men actively to construct social ties and consolidate their position in society, a necessity for chiefs who were required to accumulate a 'fund of power' or to 'accrue social capital' through marital and military alliances, and relationships with chiefs of equal status (Comaroff & Comaroff 1991: 151; see also Kopytoff 1989: 40). As Kopytoff (1989) has explained, a successful social career involved establishing oneself as the head of a large group of people – of wives, children, in-laws, relatives, adherents, dependants and slaves – which unless inherited, involved detaching oneself from an existing group and establishing a new one (Kopytoff 1989: 22; see also Comaroff & Comaroff 1991: 134).

A constant tension thus existed between the 'forces of centralisation' that allowed individuals to establish an economic and political power base, and rival forces competing for that authority (M. Hall 1987: 63). The failure of a chief to perform or fulfil social obligations created the opportunity for individuals with superior political and organisational skills to compete for the power base. Jackson (1983: 84) observed that the rules that governed succession were not sufficient to *ensure* succession; there was always a possibility of a challenge.

> If the rightful heir was man enough to beat down the challenge, he was worthy to succeed. If not, he deserved to succumb to a better man, and the chiefdom gained by the elimination of a weakling or otherwise undesirable person from its apical leadership position (Jackson 1983: 84).

He also stressed that if the members of a chiefdom disagreed with the policies of the chief they could transfer their allegiance to a rival faction, or nominate a new leader and create a new faction group (Jackson 1983: 84).

Once detached, the survival of the splinter group depended on political networking and the leader's ability rapidly to reorganise relationships and to construct new identities to suit the new situation (Kopytoff 1989: 22). Consequently, and significantly, lineages represented a network of political relationships and strategic alliances that were not necessarily based on authentic genealogical (Kopytoff 1989: 41) or biological relationships. Oral accounts were altered to give the new chief legitimacy and the lineage continuity. Hamilton's (1985: 152) analysis of Qwabe oral traditions provides one of the best examples of the creation of 'spurious notions of kinship'. By focusing on the contradictions in the oral traditions and other evidence she reveals how notions of kinship were fabricated early in the 19th century to forge a common identity with the Zulu ruling elite.

Notes and documents compiled by early naturalists, European travellers and missionaries during the 19th century, together with ethnographies of a 20th-century provenance, provide evidence that composite or pluralist societies were indeed the norm. The fracture and movement of groups, the forging of alliances and the harbouring or capturing of foreigners reverberate throughout the oral and documented histories of the northern region (see Van Warmelo 1930; Krige 1937; Ziervogel 1959; Schapera 1963; Jackson 1983; Breutz 1989). Jackson (1983: 127), who has provided one of the more meticulous accounts of the structure of a Ndebele chiefdom, reflected on the 'great variety of clan names and the diversity of their origin' within the Langa chiefdom. Members of the chief's ward were ruled directly by the chief, but other wards were ruled by sub-headmen who were subject to the chief (Jackson 1983: 126). In the case of the Langa chiefdom only two of the four headmen originated from the Langa clan (Jackson 1983). Jackson recorded a total of 128 different clan names within the different wards of the chiefdom (1983: 128). Members of the same clan were scattered amongst the different wards. However, despite sharing common origins, clan members never saw themselves as a unit, and never acted together for ritual or any other purpose (Jackson 1983: 127). Further, Jackson (1983: 127-9) noted that the headmen of the wards were not necessarily related to each other or to the chief, and their ranking was determined by other factors like length of association with the chiefdom and marriage ties with the chief.

The Comaroffs' (1991) study of the Tswana stressed that alliances between chiefdoms of equal rank were essential since they provided the strength to protect and expand economic interests, as well as to prevent the sedition of subordinates from within the alliance partnership (Comaroff & Comaroff 1991: 150). Political networks required continual maintenance and management through, on the one hand, the reaffirmation of political connections and the cementing of new alliances, and on the other, through perpetuating inequality and systematically transforming equal ties into relationships of inequality (Comaroff & Comaroff 1991: 140-150). This was achieved through the careful negotiation and maintenance of relationships through marriage alliances, or through coercion – demanding labour and tribute, raiding for cattle, women and children – and/or completely destroying polities through war (ibid: 140 & 164; see also Parsons 1995: 340).

Marriage alliances reflected the broader political processes, in which wider socio-economic relationships were negotiated and symbolically expressed through the ceremony and union (cf. Thomas 1991: 7). Negotiations around the principal wife were particularly important, as she gave birth to the heir of the chiefdom. She therefore needed to be drawn from a royal line (Mönnig 1967: 256) of appropriate socio-economic standing. To ensure that the next heir was born to a 'properly designated mother', and that suitable socio-economic unions were forged, long and protracted negotiations often occurred between families of high status. Royal families often resorted to infant betrothal to secure such beneficial alliances (Mönnig 1967: 130). Importantly, the broader socio-economic status of both groups was reflected in the transaction – the woman symbolised the socio-economic standing of her own group. The bride price indicated that this status was appreciated and recognised by the 'groom's' family, while the ability of his group to afford the alliance reflected on their own economic standing as equals. A chief thus married for diplomatic reasons (Mönnig 1967: 264) or offered gifts of wives to broker deals.

Multiple unions were, however, one of the major causes of succession disputes amongst descendants in the first or second generation (Schapera 1963: 166). Because the 'principal' wife was not necessarily the 'first' wife, competition for legitimacy between the first-born sons of these wives could occur. The principal wife's failure to produce an heir, could also produce competition between the first born of the first wife and that of a surrogate wife (usually the sister of the principal wife) (see for example Jackson 1983: 37). The practice of levirate, which allowed the uncle or brother to father a child with the principal wife, also created rivalry amongst half-brothers[4] (Schapera 1953: 51; Mönnig 1967: 130, 256-8; Manson 1995: 357). Friction between half-brothers was often exacerbated by their respective maternal kin, who tirelessly promoted the offspring of their own family member over that of another woman's (Schapera 1963: 167). Schapera (1963: 171) explained that a man's non-agnatic maternal kin were his leading partisans, because his maternal relatives stood to benefit materially from his success and wealth. Maternal kin were also the most likely to accompany a man if he seceded or was forced to flee (ibid: 167). If his maternal kin belonged to a 'foreign tribe', which was more often the case amongst the Ndebele who practiced exogamy,[5] he would seek refuge amongst them or solicit military support from them (Schapera 1963: 167). However, having a 'foreign' mother did not necessary confer an advantage during succession disputes. Her foreigner status diminished the aspirant chief's internal support base, and could militate against his succession (ibid: 167). Amongst the Nguni the 'stranger' bride was regarded with suspicion and she was the person most likely to be accused of witchcraft in times of misfortune (Hammond-Tooke 1993: 128, 175).

In summary, ethnographies, oral histories, anthropological and archaeological studies dating to the 19th and 20th centuries provide evidence for intensive mixing of peoples, and numerous and complex processes resulting in the fission, fusion and interaction of different players on the socio-economic landscape. Importantly, these factors highlight that chiefdoms were highly fluid entities and were not lineal in origin. These societies 'were all born not in the beginning but as a part of a continuous and variegated process of interaction and social formation' (Kopytoff 1989: 78). Boundaries (identity or status) were not fixed and the political terrain was defined by a complex web of constructed relationships. Suitable political relationships were constantly negotiated and new histories were obtained, claimed or fashioned accordingly.

Material culture

Importantly, from the perspective of an archaeologist, diacritical markers would have formed a significant part of this social discourse. Visual identifiers would have been employed or made redundant in order to reinforce the illusion of kinship, accentuate an alliance or to emphasise status. For example, in the case of a highly advantageous socio-economic alliance, the chief and elders could have made a strategic decision to foster or display the 'visual identity' of the principal wife. This may have been especially true when exogamy was practiced, as it would have been politic to allow the 'foreigner' bride to express her own identity, and may have alleviated the tensions that existed between the families of the bride and groom (Schapera 1963: 167; see also Preston-Whyte 1974).

On the other hand, when polities became absorbed into more powerful chiefdoms this may have created conditions whereby subordinate groups, and specifically women, were forced to reduce the visibility of their own particular identity. Schoeman (1997) has shown that the Ndzundza of Esikhunjini and UmKlaarmaak (approximately 1820-1860s), who were subordinate to Sekwati's Pedi, made fairly nondescript pottery until the ancillary relationship ended with the death of Sekwati in 1861 (Schoeman 1997: 198). During the 20th century, the Ndzundza developed a highly distinctive visual vocabulary, which extended to their pottery. This expression of 'ethnic' identity emerged from a very specific context in which ordinary people of low status created a distinct identity to survive a harsh and foreign environment (Delius 1989: 248; Hammond-Tooke 2000: 422).

The proclivity of chiefs to establish their position and standing though strategic marriage alliances, and to expand their power base through the incorporation or coercion of other groups, meant that a woman's identity and/or associated status was arguably one of the more mutable aspects of the social universe. Her identity, or the identity of her associated household, could be used, manipulated, or lost depending on socio-economic circumstances. Importantly, this emphasises the need to understand the status of the chiefdom, the role of women in bolstering that status, the relative positions of groups within the chiefdom and external socio-economic pressures in order to comprehend how women, style and decoration, were assimilated, manipulated and used by both men and women of rank.

Case study: the archaeology and history of the Kekana Ndebele

In 1854 Chief Mugombane[6] and the members of his Kekana chiefdom took refuge and were besieged by the Trekboers in what is now known as Historic Cave (Fig. 11.1). It appears that the Kekana spent some time preparing the cave and setting it up as a fortress before attacking and killing between 23 and 28 Trekboers.[7] The murder of Trekker men, women and children in the Makapaanspoort[8] and at Pruissen by the Kekana, and the simultaneous execution of Boer leader Hermanus Potgieter and his party by the Langa Ndebele at Fothane hill[9] signalled the Ndebele's intent to resist the Boers' demands for tribute, labour and land. These actions necessitated and prompted immediate Boer retaliation.

Following the murder of the Trekkers by Mankopane and Mugombane, the Boers sent for reinforcements from Rustenburg and the Soutpansberg. In the time it took for the commandos to arrive, Mugombane and his people had retreated into the Historic Cave and Mankopane had taken refuge in the hills. The Boers discovered the Kekana hideout, and over a period of about a month implemented various strategies to dislodge the Ndebele group. When all their lines of attack failed they placed the Kekana under siege.

By the end of the month the Ndebele resistance dwindled and the Boers entered the cave. The surviving women and children were dispersed among Boers, and their aides.[10] The remarkable preservation of objects within this site constitutes a unique record of the people who occupied the cave. The spatial layout of the cave together with cultural remains echoed the structure and hierarchy of the society trapped within it, the 'royal' core occupied the bottom most protected reaches of the cave, while the subordinate members dominated the slopes and more exposed areas (Esterhuysen 2006). Elements of the material culture,

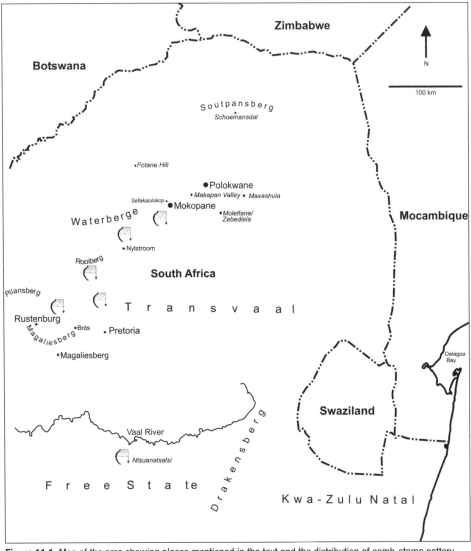

Figure 11.1 Map of the area showing places mentioned in the text and the distribution of comb-stamp pottery.

beaded leather, divining paraphernalia, patterned skirts and cloaks, and decorated ceramics hinted at the broad and varied composition of the polity and by extension at the political networks established by the chiefdom before entering the cave. I pursue this line of thought further through a discussion of the pottery recovered from the site.

Twenty square metres were excavated at the base of the cave, and a further eighteen on the terraced slope (Fig. 11.2). Over 3 800 sherds of pottery were recovered. The undecorated ceramic component (96.6%) comprised a number of black recurved jars and beakers, and large unburnished, recurved and spherical jars. Thirteen pots were refitted from 75 rim and decorated pieces, while 55 individual decorated pieces could not be refitted. The decorated pots and pieces fell broadly into two categories, late Moloko or Letaba/Phalaborwa (Esterhuysen 2006: 38). The most common decoration and decoration techniques included herringbone, single or multiple horizontal lines of punctuates produced by fingernail or stylus (triangular and square), single or multiple incised lines with applied red or black burnish, bangle imprint, cross-hatch between horizontal incised lines, and comb stamping around the neck of the pot with pendant triangles outlined by a single or double row of comb stamping filled alternately with red, buff or black colour (ibid).

The highest percentage of decorated pottery was found in association with the floor at the base of the cave, which multiple lines of evidence suggested was occupied by high status individuals. Ten of the refitted, decorated pots and 39 decorated pieces were retrieved from this living area. Most of the pots were recovered from a raised platform at the back of the floor where they appear to have been stored. The decorated component from the base of the cave comprised a range of styles, some of which were also found in other areas of the cave. However, one particular style or design was unique to this floor. A number of small jars with recurved necks had horizontal or oblique lines of comb-stamping around the neck with pendant triangles outlined by a single or double row of comb-stamping. The triangles were alternately filled with red, buff or black colour (Plate 23). This design was also found at other Ndebele sites in and around the Valley,[11] but was largely absent from the Ledwaba/Maune sites excavated by Loubser (1981 & 1994) and completely absent from ceramic collections excavated from known Ndzundza Ndebele sites (Schoeman 1997).

The earliest incidence of the comb-stamp design, with horizontal lines in the neck, date to the 15th century and come from Ntsuanatsatsi in the north-eastern Free State (Maggs 1976: 140). This site was claimed as an ancestral site by a number of groups, but seemed to be most firmly linked to the BaFokeng and later the BaKoena (ibid: 142, 315). This pottery design then spread across the Vaal into the Balfour, Suikerbosrand, Vredefort and Klipriviersberg areas (Huffman 2002: 14). Mason (1962) initially designated the pottery from these sites 'Uitkomst', after pottery he excavated from the site Uitkomst, which was

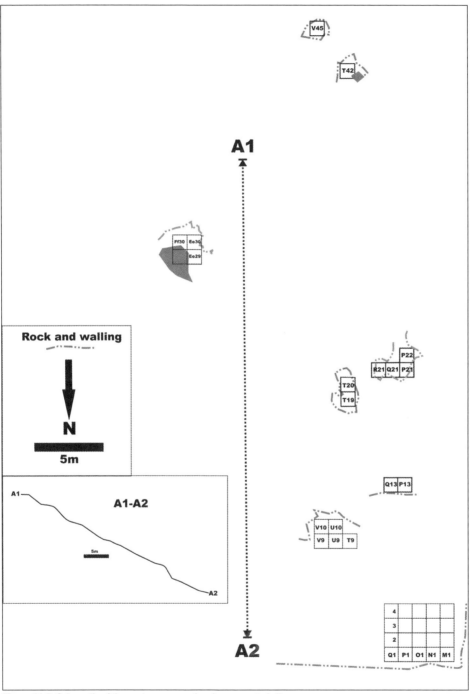

Figure 11.2 Schematic of the eastern cavern showing excavated sites.

comb-stamped and incised with red and black burnish (S. Hall 1981: 15). Later he modified his use of the term, as he felt it did not apply to the Late Iron Age in general (Mason 1986: 739). Instead, he argued that certain features, in particular a horizontal band, with arcade or zig-zag dentates, were limited to an Olifantspoort-Kaditshwene-Klipriviersberg-Sun City group or Kaditshwene Phase pottery[12] which only occurred between 1700-1800 AD (Mason 1986: 743). Ensuing work in the Pretoria-Brits area, Rooiberg, and Waterberg (S. Hall 1981: 83 & 143-5; Huffman 2002: 17) showed that vessels with horizontal and/ or oblique comb-stamping in the neck, comb-stamped chevrons or arcades filled with comb-stamping or red and black colour occurred in these areas from the second half of the seventeenth century. This design field thus extended from south of Johannesburg in a northerly and westerly direction as far as the Waterberg and Mokopane.

The presence of different, but contemporary styles of pottery, stored on a daka floor, occupied by a known group on the occasion of a specific event (Esterhuysen 2006) provided a point from which to begin to think about the social significance of the ceramics. It was immediately clear that ceramic design did not function as an ethnic identifier. If the Kekana Ndebele employed a visual marker to signal their own coherence and therefore difference from others, a phenomenon that you might expect during a period of turmoil, it did not extend to their pottery. Rather, in this case, the ceramics simply seemed to capture and reflect the heterogeneity of the chiefdom. However, the 'elite' nature of the floor unlocked one further possibility, that the disparate designs found in this context were not the result of the subjugation and incorporation of different people, but rather represented key marriage and associated political alliances entered into by the chiefdom. This being the case, then the fact that one of these styles (comb-stamp) had a limited temporal and geographical distribution pointed to the possibility that at least one of the Mugombane's allies were situated to the west and south of the Kekana chiefdom.

In order to verify, understand and move beyond the explanatory limits of the material culture, it was necessary to consult the oral and documentary history of the Kekana Ndebele.

There is some disagreement about the origins of the Kekana branch of the Ndebele (see Fig 11.1 for the location of places mentioned in the text). The Native Affairs Department (1905), Van Warmelo (1930) and Jackson (1983) grouped them with the Southern Transvaal Manala-Ndzundza Ndebele. According to these accounts the Southern Ndebele descended from Chief Musi or Msi, who originated in the Drakensberg or Kwa-Zulu Natal area (Van Warmelo 1930: 10-13). The timing of their movement into the Transvaal is not entirely clear; Van Warmelo (1930) argued that it was Musi who moved and settled north of Pretoria, whereas the information provided by the Native Affairs Department (1905) suggested that the movement only took place after Musi's death. Either way this situated the relocation between 1650 and 1700.

Musi or Msi sired five or six sons, who split up after his death. The Kekana are said to have descended from Matombeni, also known as Kekana, who withdrew to the north and settled at Moletlane (Zebediela) (Van Warmelo 1930: 10-13). Fourie (1922) who provided more or less the same details on the history of the Southern Ndebele did not offer any information about the Matombeni line, and therefore did not necessarily include the Kekana among the Southern Ndebele.

Ziervogel (1959) has presented a different account, contending that the Northern and the Southern Ndebele had very different origins. He maintained that the Muledlana and Lidwaba Ndebele had their origins amongst the Kalanga speakers of Zimbabwe. They then moved south and spent time with the Phalaborwa and the Swazi.[13] Later they moved south-west to the Pretoria area where they came into contact with and became influenced by the Southern Ndebele (ibid: 5 & 181-185). He further claimed that oral traditions preserved by the Ledwaba and Gegana (Kekana), indicated that these two groups shared ancestors until Gegana and Lidwaba, the sons of Madidzi, divided the chiefdom. The Gegana moved to Moletlane (Zebediela) and the Lidwaba to Maxashula (the farm Goedehoop) (ibid: 185). In the 1800s the descendents of Lidwaba moved up onto the Pietersburg (Polokwane) Plateau (Loubser 1981: 10).

At this point the discrepancies in the Kekana family tree come to an end. All versions concurred that three generations after settling at Moletlane, the lineage was again disrupted when on the death of Chumana,[14] his sons Khoopa and Kgaba[15] fought for succession. Kgaba was defeated and settled just outside of Mokopane (ibid: 8). This Kgaba line eventually gave rise to Mugombane. The Khoopa-Kgaba split occurred around the early to mid-1700s, while Mugombane lived from around 1800 to 1855.

The multiple and multiform origin stories are no doubt a by-product of the multiple processes of interaction and social formation, as outlined by Kopytoff (1989). The reasons for these different versions may be better understood through a careful analysis of the internal inconsistencies and contradictions in each of the oral tales (Hamilton 1985). However, for the purpose of this paper, I simply wish to reiterate the composite and fluid nature of the group and to make the point that the group that coalesced as the Kekana under Kgaba, emerged from a mosaic of political and economic relationships that if conflated in time and space could have traversed Zimbabwe, Phalaborwa and the lowveld, Swaziland (proto), Natal, Pretoria and Polokwane. Anyone of these historic relationships may have played an important role in Kgaba's survival and the ongoing success of the chiefdom after he was forced to flee.

The record of events occurring between Kgaba's split and the siege of Mugombane affords an even greater understanding of the larger political landscape and the location of the chiefdom's rivals and allies.

According to the history compiled by the Native Affairs Department, Kgaba[16] and his adherents routed the Bakwena Ba Phalane under chief Ramakok in order to settle in the vicinity of 'Pietpotgietersrust' (Mokopane). However, the histories of the Langa Ndebele[17] and the Phalane (Breutz 1989: 324) suggest that if the Phalane were routed they responded by resettling near Fothane under the protection of the Langa chief Mapela where they once again emerged as a powerful group. After the death of Ramakok his sons disputed the chieftainship, and one of his sons, Mafodi, invoked the aid of Mapela to defeat and expel his brother. Sometime between 1830 and 1840 Mapela attempted to assert his authority over Mafodi, but when Mafodi refused to submit, war broke out[18] (see also Breutz 1989: 324). At this point the Kekana assisted the Langa in defeating the Phalane.

These separate events suggest in the first instance that the Kekana may have subjugated and/or incorporated members of the Phalane, and secondly, that by the 1840s the Langa and Kekana regarded each other as key alliance partners, a strategic relationship that would ultimately prove problematic for the Trekboers.

The same Native Location Commissioner's report[19] recorded that two or three generations subsequent to the Khoopa-Kgaba split, the Kekana were attacked by the combined force of the Ndebele of Zebediele and the BaPedi (Kgatla). Chief Tshumana of the Kekana was killed and the chiefdom retired to Morulaskop near the source of the Nyl River, where they encountered the BaKgatla Ba Mmakau ('Sjambok's tribe'). At this point Mugombane succeeded Tshumana, and after some time returned to Mokopane. Records reveal that the Ndebele chief Zebediela continued to present a problem to the Kekana under Mugombane. Zebediela regularly solicited the Pedi chief Sekwati's aid in subduing and forcing Mugombane to accept his authority, and even a gift of several wives from Mugombane to Sekwati did not stop the attacks (De Waal 1978: 4).

Mugombane's association with the Mmakau features again in both the history of the Mmakau and contemporary Trekboer correspondence. The recorded history of the Mmakau dates back to the second half of the sixteenth century, when the Mmakau, who were settled at Morulaskop (Maharitse), moved south to Hoekfontein (Brits area) (Breutz 1989: 349). Here they were allegedly attacked by Moselekatse between 1826 and 1830, and after their chief was killed they fled back to Morulaskop. It is presumably during this time that the Mmakau encountered the Kekana who fled south after suffering the loss of their chief at the hands of Zebediela. Sjambok[20] took up the chiefship, but when a dispute broke out, the Mmakau chiefdom split and Sjambok returned to Hoekfontein (Breutz 1989: 350).

In 1850 Sjambok took up arms against the Trekboers.[21] After several encounters with the Boers he fled north to Mugombane and joined the growing resistance in the north. The intimacy of this relationship is captured in H.B. Klopper's letter to Pretorius dated 2 March, 1851:

' ... hey [Sjambok] es bey Makapan [Mugombane], hulle vreet uyt een pot. Ook heef ik en kort gehoort dat Makapan and Sambok gereet is met aanstaande lig den menschen aan te val.'[22]

Moselekatse appears to have been the stimulus for a number of the relationships formed between different Kgatla groups and the Ndebele at this time. Chief Nchaupe (BaKgatla Ba Mosetla) and chief Pilane (BaKgatla ba ga Kgafela) both fled northwards following incursions by the *Matabele*.[23] The former retreated to the Kekana and the latter to the Langa. It is possible that the chief called Koupa by the Trekboers and who in 1851 was accused of regularly harbouring Mugombane's spies,[24] was the Mosetla chief Nchaupe.

Mugombane was clearly part of a growing network of resistance in 1851. In addition to the alliances that he entered into with the Langa and the Kgatla chiefs his sphere of influence is said to have extended as far south as the Pienaarsriver (De Waal 1978: 25). Not surprisingly this made his rivals nervous and as a result Zebediela joined forces with the Trekboers to attack Mugombane.[25] From the Boer's oral records and early traveller diaries this attack occurred sometime before the death of Commandant-general Andries Hendrik Potgieter in April of 1852 (Preller 1920-1938: 32-33; Chapman 1971 (1849-1863): 21). Andries Hendrik Potgieter Jr recalled that 'Makapaan' repeatedly attacked hunting and other parties and murdered a group of 'mak Kaffers' under the Potgieters' protection. Potgieter rallied a 'kommande' together and attacked Mugombane. The traveller Chapman[26] (1971: 21), sketched out a slightly different scenario, but recorded the same event. He portrayed the Boers as intent on subjugating the 'natives' and as thereby being argumentative and quick to pick fights, and he depicted Andries Hendrik Potgieter in particular as 'exceedingly cruel in his wars, having been known on some occasions to flog Kaffirs to death'. From this and other contemporary accounts, the core of the conflict between the Boers and Mugombane emerges as the Trekker's demand for tribute, labour, and cattle.[27] Zebediela's motivations may not have been too different.

Discussion

The west-south location of Mugombane's allies hinted at by the material culture is borne out by the oral and written record. Kgaba's movement away from Zebediela after his failure in the fight for succession, and the repeated attacks to which he and his successors were subject by forces to the north- and south-east of Mokopane, made the Kgaba line reliant on socio-economic alliances to the west and south-west of Mokopane. These alliances may have been founded on relationships forged during the ancestral group's journey to and from Pretoria. These early connections, particularly on the maternal line, may have been invoked to support Kgaba and Mugombane after they broke away from their respective chiefdoms. However, it would have been incumbent on Mugombane to constantly maintain these and develop new relationships. The oral and documented histories indicated that he cultivated reciprocal relations with the Langa Ndebele and Kgatla groups, specifically the Mmakau and Mosetla.

The place names recorded in the oral and documentary histories provided the potential to locate the exchange partner/s represented by the comb-stamp pottery. Significantly, comb-stamp has been found at both of the sites occupied by the Mmakau under Sjambok, i.e. Morulakop and Hoekfontein (Pelser 2007 pers. comm.). It is not possible at this point to determine the direction of the exchange, i.e. whether the ceramic type moved with wives given to or received from the Mmakau. The presence of the pottery at both of Sjambok's sites may indicate that comb-stamp was more strongly associated with the Kgatla; this would also make sense if the Mmakau under Sjambok practiced endogamy. Breutz (1989: 350) however, noted that Sjambok arranged his wives according to *Matabele* custom, which may imply a more flexible approach to the custom. Impending results from the excavations at Hoekfontein (Pelser & Kusel 2007), and more intensive excavation around Morulakop my resolve this issue.

Unfortunately, no archaeological studies have been carried out at the Phalane (Kwena), Langa (Ndebele) and the Mosetla (Kgatla) chiefs' capitals, so we have as yet no idea if and how these alliances would manifest materially.

Conclusion

The interpretation of the pottery from Historic Cave was influenced by the apparent fluidity of the 17th- to 19th-century political landscape. The ethnographies, oral histories, anthropological and archaeological studies dating to this period provided evidence for intensive mixing of peoples and associated material culture, and numerous and complex processes resulting in the fission, fusion and interaction of different players on the socio-economic landscape. From this it was argued that spread of a particular design motif also present in the pottery collection recovered from the floor of the elites in Historic Cave, provided a material expression of marriage alliance forged between the Mugombane's ward and groups to the south and west of Mokopane. Through the use of oral and documentary histories these relationships became more defined. Taken together these lines of evidence suggest that that at least some of the senior wives in Mugombane's ward were related to the baKgatla ba Mmakau.

Notes

1. Trade in ivory, hides, and metals may date back to 800 AD. A significant number of glass trade beads were recovered from the site of Schroda, a 9th–century village at the confluence of the Shashe and Limpopo Rivers, Limpopo Province (M. Hall, 1996: 202).
2. Eldredge (1992: 6) notes that the English dominated the trade in Delagoa Bay from the 1750s until possibly as late as the 1780s, and that annual ivory exports may have exceeded 100 000 pounds (45 360 kg) during the 1770s.
3. This may have been exacerbated by an extreme drought that occurred in the area around 1780 (Norström et al 2005: 167).
4. The royal Kekana household is presently challenging the Government's decision to install the son of the principal wife over the child of the late Chief Alfred's first wife. In this case Alfred did not sleep with his principal wife; her son was born of a union with Alfred's uncle or father.
5. Although the tendency is to regard Sotho-Tswana speakers as endogamous and Nguni-speakers as exogamous it should be noted that there are acceptable ways in which these social rules can and will be circumvented to suit the elite (Hamilton 1985: 207ff).
6. Also referred to as Makapan and Mokopane.
7. The number and names of the Trekkers vary between documents (see De Waal 1978: 64-68)
8. Now known as Moorddrift on account of the murders.
9. Subsequently called Moordkoppie.
10. The Portuguese trader Jôao Albasini, who provided the Boers with Tsonga marksmen, took a woman by the name of Aia (De Vaal 1953: 21). Paul Kruger, who would become the ZAR President, allegedly took a woman by the name of Matlhodi Kekana (Paulina). Later, he allegedly allowed her to marry 'kgosi Mokgatle' in exchange for bride wealth (Morton 2005: 203). The Bafokeng Chief occupied a portion of Kruger's farm and provided him with military resources and labour (ibid).
11. Partridge's (1966: 126-127) excavation in Ficus Cave produced a comparable range of comb-stamping and red and black burnish. Similarly, examples of comb-stamping and colour burnish was excavated from the site of Kekane, a site occupied by the Ndebele towards the latter part of the nineteenth century (Moore 1981: 100).
12. Mason identifies his Kaditshwene Phase pottery as Hurutshe. However, this was based on the assumption that he had excavated the Kaditshwene visited by Campbell in the 1800s, which turned out not to be the case.
13. In reality this would have been the predecessor chiefdom to the Swazi.
14. Spelt Tjhumana by Ziervogel (1959).
15. Spelt Kxumbha and Kxhaba by Ziervogel (1959).
16. The Office of the Native Location Commission, Native Affairs Department, Pretoria. No.182/06. History of Chief Valtyn Makapaan and tribe, 30th May 1907: 2.
17. The Office of the Native Location Commission, Native Affairs Department, Pretoria. No. 179/180/06 History of the Bakeberg Masebi, 30th May 1907.
18. The Office of the Native Location Commission, Native Affairs Department, Pretoria. No. 179/180/06 History of the Bakeberg Masebi, 30th May 1907: 3-4.
19. The Office of the Native Location Commission, Native Affairs Department, Pretoria. No.182/06. History of Chief Valtyn Makapaan and tribe, 30th May 1907: 3.
20. Also referred to as Mmamonwana Seamogo Sjambok (Breutz 1989: 350) or Seamoge (Transvaal Native Affairs Department. Short History of the Native Tribes of the Transvaal, Pretoria 1905: 29.)

21. Letter from A.W.J. Pretorius, December 26, 1850, Magaliesberg.
22. Loosely translated - Sjambok is with Mugombane, they eat out of one pot. I have heard that they are planning an attack.
23. Transvaal Native Affairs Department. Short History of the Native Tribes of the Transvaal, Pretoria 1905: 28.
24. S.S.3, R281/51: H.J. van Staden- A.W.J Pretorius, Pienaarsrivier, 7 May 1851. In this correspondence the chief is referred to as Koupa.
25. The Office of the Native Location Commission, Native Affairs Department, Pretoria. No.182/06. History of Chief Valtyn Makapaan and tribe, 30th May 1907: 4.
26. Chapman travelled through the interior of South Africa from Natal to Walvis Bay between 1849-1863.
27. Khosilintse informed Moffat (November 1854) that it was on account of the Boers raiding for children and cattle that the Kekana killed nine Boers in 1854 (Moffat 1976: 378). Complaints about local resistance and resultant loss of labour are common in Boer correspondence written between 1850 and 1853 (see De Waal 1978: 52-55).

References

Bonner, P. 1983. *Kings, Commoners and Concessionaires: The Evolution and Dissolution of the Nineteenth-century Swazi State.* African Studies Series 31. Cambridge: Cambridge University Press.

Breutz, P.L. 1989. *A History of the BaTswana and Origin of Bophuthatswana: A Handbook of a Survey of the Tribes of the BaTswana, S-Ndebele, Qwaqwa and Botswana.* Ramsgate: Dr P.L. Breutz.

Chapman, J. 1971. *Travels in the Interior of South Africa 1949-1863. Hunting and Trading Journeys from Natal to Walvis Bay & Visits to Lake Ngami & Victoria Falls.* Cape Town: A.A. Balkema.

Comaroff, J. & Comaroff J. 1991. *Of Revelation and Revolution. Christianity, Colonialism and Consciousness in South Africa.* Volume 1. Chicago: University Press.

Delius, P. 1983. *The Land Belongs to Us.* Berkeley: University of California Press.

Delius, P. 1989. The Ndzundza Ndebele. Indenture and the making of ethnic identity. In: Bonner, P., Hofmeyr, I., James, D. & Lodge T. (eds) *Holding their Ground.* Johannesburg: Witwatersrand University Press.

De Vaal, J.B. 1953. Die rol van João Albasini in die geskiedenis van die Transvaal. *Agrief-jaarboek vir Suid-Afrikaanse Geskiedenis* 16(1). Elsierivier: Nasionale Handelsdrukkery vir die Staatsdrukker.

De Waal, J.J. 1978. Die verhouding tussen die blankes en die hoofmanne Mokopane en Mankopane in die omgewing van Potgietersrus (1836-1869). Unpublished Masters thesis.

Eldredge, E. 1992. Source of Conflict in southern Africa, c. 1800-1830: the 'Mfecane' reconsidered. *Journal of African History,* 33: 1-35.

Esterhuysen, A.B. 2006. Let the ancestors speak: an archaeological excavation and re-evaluation of events prior and pertaining to the 1854 siege of Mugombane, Limpopo Province, South Africa. Unpublished PhD thesis. Johannesburg: University of the Witwatersrand.

Evers, T.M. 1988. The recognition of groups in the Iron Age of Southern Africa. Unpublished PhD thesis, Johannesburg: University of the Witwatersrand.

Ferreira, O.J.O. 2002. *Montanha in Zoutpansberg: 'n Portugese Handelsending van Inhambane se Besoek aan Schoemansdal, 1855-1856.* Pretoria: Protea Boekhuis.

Fourie, H.C.M. 1922. *Amandebele van Fene Mahlangu.* Utrecht: La Riviere en Voorhoeve.

Gosden, C. 2004. *Archaeology and Colonialism: Cultural Contact from 5000 BC to the Present.* Cambridge: Cambridge University Press.

Gosselain, O.P. 1999. In pots we trust: the processing of clay and symbols in sub-Saharan Africa. *Journal of Material Culture* 4(2): 205-230.

Hall, M. 1987. *The Changing Past: Farmers, Kings & Traders in Southern Africa, 200-1860.* London: James Currey.

Hall, M. 1996. *Archaeology Africa.* Cape Town: David Philip.

Hall, S. 1981. Iron Age sequence and settlement in the Rooiberg, Thabazimbi Area. Unpublished MA dissertation. Johannesburg: University of the Witwatersrand.

Hall, S. 1998. A consideration of gender relations in the Late Iron Age 'Sotho' Sequence of the Western Highveld, South Africa. In: Kent S. (ed.) *Gender in African Prehistory*. London: AltaMira Press.

Hamilton, C. 1985. Ideology, oral traditions and the struggle for power in the early Zulu Kingdom. Unpublished MA dissertation. Johannesburg: University of the Witwatersrand.

Hammond-Tooke, D. 1993. *The Roots of Black South Africa*. Johannesburg: Jonathan Ball Publishers.

Huffman, T.N. 1982. Archaeology and ethnohistory of the African Iron Age. *Annual Review of Anthropology* 11: 133-50.

Huffman, T.N. 1983. Hypothesis evaluation: a reply to Hall. *The South African Archaeological Bulletin* 38: 57-61.

Huffman, T.N. 1986a. Cognitive studies of the Iron Age in southern Africa. *World Archaeology* 18(1): 84-95.

Huffman, T.N. 1986b. Archaeological evidence and conventional explanation of southern Bantu settlement patterns. *Africa* 56(3): 280-298.

Huffman, T.N. 1988. Boschoek and the Central Cattle Pattern. In: Evers, T.M., Huffman, T.N. & Wadley L. (eds) *Guide to Archaeological Sites in the Transvaal*. Prepared for the Southern African Association of Archaeologists Excursion, Department of Archaeology, University of the Witwatersrand.

Huffman, T.N. 2001. The Central Cattle Pattern and interpreting the past. *Southern African Humanities* 13: 19-35.

Huffman, T. N. 2002. Regionality in the Iron Age: the case of the Sotho-Tswana. *Southern African Humanities* 14: 1-22.

Jackson, A.O. 1983. The Ndebele of Langa. *Department of Co-operation and Development, Ethnological Publication* No. 54. Pretoria: Government Printer.

Kopytoff, I. 1989. The internal African frontier: the making of African political culture. In: Kopytoff, I. (ed.) *The African Frontier: The Reproduction of Traditional African Societies*. Indiana: University Press.

Krige, J.D. 1937. Traditional origins and tribal relationships of the Sotho of the Northern Transvaal. *Bantu Studies* 11: 321-356.

Küsel, U. & Pelser, P. 2007. The reconstruction of the 19th century Tswana settlement at Mmakau. Unpublished paper presented at the Five Hundred Year Initiative Conference. 26-27 May 2007.

Legassick, M. 1980. The frontier tradition in South African history. In: Marks, S. & Atmore, A. (eds) *Economy and Society in Pre-Industrial South Africa*. London: Longman.

Lekgoathi, S.P. 2004. The Native Affairs Department, anthropology, the making and bifurcation of the 'Transvaal Ndebele,' 1905-1945. Paper presented at the History Research Seminar Series, University of the Witwatersrand.

Loubser, J.H.N. 1981. Ndebele archaeology of the Pietersburg area. Unpublished MA dissertation. Johannesburg: University of the Witwatersrand.

Loubser, J.H.N. 1994. Ndebele archaeology of the Pietersburg Area. *Navorsinge van die Nasionale Museum Bloemfontein* 10(2): 64-147.

Maggs, T. M.O'C. 1976. *Iron Age Communities of the Southern Highveld*. Pietermaritzburg: Natal Museum.

Manson, A. 1995. Conflict in the Western Highveld/Southern Kalahari c. 1750-1820. In: Hamilton, C. (ed.) *The Mfecane Aftermath*. Johannesburg: Witwatersrand University Press.

Mason, R.J. 1962. *Prehistory of the Transvaal*. Johannesburg.

Mason, R.J. 1986. *Origins of Black People of Johannesburg and the Southern Western Central Transvaal AD 350-1880*. Johannesburg: University of the Witwatersrand, Archaeological Research Unit.

Mönnig, H.O. 1967. *The Pedi*. Pretoria: J.L. Van Schaik.

Moore, M.P.J. 1981. The Iron Age of the Makapan Valley Area, Central Transvaal. Unpublished MA dissertation. Johannesburg: University of the Witwatersrand.

Morton, F. 2005. Female *Inboekelinge* in the South African Republic, 1850-1880. *Slavery and Abolition* 26(2): 199-215.

Native Affairs Department. 1905. *History of the Native Tribes of the Transvaal*. Pretoria.

Norström, E., Holmgren, K. & Mörth C-M. 2005. Rainfall-driven variations in δ^{13}C composition and woody anatomy of *Breonadia salicina* trees from South Africa between AD 1375 and 1995. *South African Journal of Science* 101: 162-168.

Ohinata, F. 2002. The beginning of 'Tsonga' archaeology: excavations at Simunye, north-eastern Swaziland. *Southern African Humanities* 14: 23-50.

Parsons, N. 1995. Prelude to Difaqane in the interior of southern Africa c.1600-c.1822. In: Hamilton, C. (ed.) *The Mfecane Aftermath*. Johannesburg: Witwatersrand University Press.

Penn, N. 2005. *The Forgotten Frontier*. Cape Town: Double Storey Books

Pistorius, J.C. 1992. *Molokwane, an Iron Age Bakwena Village*. Johannesburg: Perskor Printers.

Preller, G.S. (ed.) 1920-1938. Voortrekkermense. Volumes I-IV. Cape Town: Nasionale Pers Beperk.

Preston-Whyte, E. 1974. Kinship and marriage. In: Hammond-Tooke, W.D. (ed.) *The Bantu-speaking People of Southern Africa*. London: Routledge & Kegan Paul.

Schapera, I. 1974. *David Livingstone, South African Papers 1849-1853*. Van Riebeeck Society second series No. 5. Cape Town: National Book Printers.

Schapera, I. 1953. *The Tswana*. Ethnographic survey of Africa. Southern Africa part III. London: International African Institute.

Schapera, I. 1963. Kinship and politics in Tswana History. *The Journal of the Royal Anthropological Institute of Great Britain and Ireland* 94(2): 159-173.

Schoeman, M.H. 1997. The Ndzundza archaeology of the Steelpoort River Valley. Unpublished MA dissertation. Johannesburg: University of the Witwatersrand.

Thomas, N. 1991. *Entangled Objects: Exchange, Material Culture and Colonialism in the Pacific*. Cambridge, MA: Harvard University Press.

Van Warmelo, N.J. 1930. Transvaal Ndebele Texts. *Department of Native Affairs Ethnological Publications volume 1*. Pretoria: Government Printer.

Ziervogel, D. 1959. *A Grammar of Northern Transvaal Ndebele*. Pretoria: J.L. Van Schaik.

SECTION 3

'Troubled Times': Warfare, State Formation and Migration in the Interior

12

Rediscovering the Ndwandwe kingdom

John Wright

Introduction

The history of the Ndwandwe kingdom is one of the great casualties of the particular circumstances in which southern Africa's precolonial pasts were narrated and written from the late 1820s onward. The break-up of the Ndwandwe kingdom under Sikhunyana kaZwide after its defeat by the Zulu under Shaka kaSenzangakhona in 1826 destroyed its ruling elite and ruptured the processes in which memories of the kingdom's past were being transmitted orally by intellectuals linked to that elite. To be sure, groups of Ndwandwe lived on in the polities which consolidated in the 1820s and 1830s as the Zulu, Swazi and Ndebele kingdoms, but under conditions in which public narrations of their histories, like those of other subordinate groups, tended to be suppressed in favour of tellings of the histories of the respective ruling groups. As Socwatsha kaPhaphu (1921: 10), one of James Stuart's informants put it,

> In the Zulu kingdom, people did not discuss matters of former times to avoid
> being put to death ... . For a person who spoke about these things would be
> killed. It would be said, 'Where did you get this from? You will spoil the land
> with this talking.'[1]

Another group of Ndwandwe, which had broken away from Zwide's rule in about 1820 under the leadership of Soshangane kaZikode, went on to establish what became the Gaza kingdom in southern and central Mozambique. In this case, Gerhard Liesegang tells us (1981: 181-182, 202), memories of its past became fragmented after the defeat of the Gaza by the Portuguese in 1895 and the deliberate breaking-up of its ruling elite by the new colonial overlords. The overall effect was that by the beginning of the 20th century, at the latest, 'officially' sustained tellings of the history of the old Ndwandwe kingdom had effectively come to an end.

For their part, the white writers who arrived in the Zulu kingdom in the 1820s and 1830s left records which fed into an entire colonial mythology about Shaka and his times but made only the barest mention of the Ndwandwe. Literate observers never reached the kingdom of Zwide and Sikhunyana; one of the consequences was that very little evidence was recorded in writing which could serve as a counter to the notion, which was becoming widely established among white people and black people alike in southern Africa by the 1840s, that Shaka and his Zulu armies had been the prime aggressors in a chain reaction of wars and migrations which had disrupted life across the eastern half of the sub-continent in the 1820s and 1830s. As is well known, the historical circumstances in which this notion developed and spread have been the subject of critical and often acrimonious debates since the late 1980s. While no one denies that the period of the 1820s and 1830s was one of political and social upheaval among black societies on an apparently unprecedented scale, few historians would now argue that the phenomenon can be attributed mainly to the aggressions of the Zulu.

Recent research (Hamilton 1998; Wright 2006; Wylie 2000; 2006) from a number of different perspectives has indicated that the whole idea of 'the wars of Shaka' (or the 'Mfecane' or 'Difaqane' as they have been labelled in the literature since the late 1960s) as it originally emerged was based less on 'fact' than on the kind of evidence which could be turned to the ideological needs of new political groupings that were coming into being in southern Africa from the early nineteenth century onward. On the one hand were the often parvenu ruling groups which had come to power in the new black states that had emerged in eastern southern Africa from the 1820s onward. For many of them, the notion of 'the wars of Shaka' fed comfortably into 'official' explanations of how the new societies had come into being and of how their ruling groups had come to hold power.[2] On the other hand were the new European and European-descended settler communities that were taking root in the same region in the same period. For them, the notion of 'the wars of Shaka' provided an essential backdrop to the European 'civilising mission' which they liked to see themselves as engaged in and which justified their presence as intruders in southern Africa.

The development of these new perspectives has been accompanied by the growth of a concern on the part of a number of historians, including myself (Wright in press), to seek to move beyond the Zulu-centric approaches that have dominated the writing of precolonial history for so long. In this paper I continue with this project by seeking to focus attention on the historiography and history of the Ndwandwe kingdom more comprehensively than has previously been done. The paper is divided into two sections. In the first, I sketch out the ways in which the history of the Ndwandwe kingdom has been treated in the literature since the 1820s, when literate commentators first became aware of the kingdom's existence. I also touch – very briefly, because of the lack of evidence – on the question of how this history has been treated by oral historians in black societies. In the second section, drawing on a combination of primary and secondary sources, I go on to outline how a connected narrative of the history of the Ndwandwe kingdom might be put together from a 'post-Zulu' perspective.

Treating the Ndwandwe past from the 1820s to the present

Zwide and the Ndwandwe kingdom were occasionally mentioned in settler historical writings from the early 1820s onward, but always very briefly and in passing and usually as role-players in the rise and expansion of Shaka's Zulu kingdom.[3] Mostly the references were made, often confusingly, to one or other of three particular episodes: the wars fought in the late 1810s between Zwide and Dingiswayo kaJobe, king of the Mthethwa and patron of Shaka; the wars fought c. 1819-c. 1820 between Zwide and Shaka, wars which were portrayed as having ended in the defeat of the Ndwandwe by the Zulu; and the battle fought in 1826 between the Zulu and a revived Ndwandwe polity under Sikhunyana kaZwide, an event which ended in the defeat and final break-up of the Ndwandwe. Occasional references were also made to the role played by the Ndwandwe in the early 1820s in driving away the people under the leadership of Mzilikazi kaMashobane who went on to form the core group of the Ndebele kingdom, though more and more, as the century progressed, this expulsion was attributed to the Zulu under Shaka (Arbousset 1968: 185; Thomas 1970: 156-158).

These episodes of Ndwandwe history were heavily downplayed by Theophilus Shepstone (1875), Secretary for Native Affairs in Natal, in an influential article on what he saw as the military and political revolution which had taken place in the Zululand-Natal region with the rise first of Dingiswayo and then of Shaka. Shepstone's main aim was to put forward the idea that these changes had been occasioned by Dingiswayo's observations of 'civilised' European military organisation in the course of a journey which he was supposed to have made to the Cape Colony during a period of exile in his youth. The article served to cement into place the notion that the context for the rise of Shaka and the Zulu kingdom was to be found in the expansion of the Mthethwa kingdom under Dingiswayo and ultimately in the European civilising mission. Its focus on the role of Dingiswayo was reinforced by another influential account written long before by H.F. Fynn (1965a: 60-71) and published in the same collection as a reprint of Shepstone's article. J.Y. Gibson (1903) followed suit in the first book-length account of Zulu history, *The Story of the Zulus*, as did all subsequent writers until the 1970s, with the Ndwandwe serving as bit players in the central drama acted out by the Mthethwa and the Zulu.

In the first two decades of the twentieth century, Natal colonial official and historian James Stuart recorded statements on Ndwandwe history from some forty of the nearly 200 informants whom he interviewed (Webb & Wright 1976-2001). A full analysis of these statements would need to take into account the politics of relationships between the Zulu and Ndwandwe ruling houses in the years of political instability that followed the British victory in the invasion of the Zulu kingdom in 1879. In the early 1880s the British attempted to set up an autonomous Ndwandwe polity under a grandson of Zwide as one of several chiefdoms which were intended to serve as counterweights to the influence of the Zulu royal house under Cetshwayo and then of his son Dinuzulu (Guy 1979: 73-76; 160, 161, 183, 193, 194; Laband 1995: 337, 351, 412). This particular line of action on the part of the colonial overlords soon gave way to different policies, but it would have contributed to the deep hostility between the Zulu royal house and rival elements that marked 'Zulu' politics well into the 20th century. The statements on Ndwandwe history made by Stuart's informants need to be seen against this background. Many of them were no more than brief snippets; of the rest, most focused on the wars between Zwide and Shaka. Some constitute valuable sources of evidence recorded nowhere else, but they are noticeably much thinner on detail than most of the statements which Stuart recorded on the history of Shaka's kingdom. How far this difference was a product of Stuart's own line of questioning and how far of a relative lack of knowledge of Ndwandwe history on the part of his informants is difficult to say. Of the hundred or so historical testimonies which Stuart (1923, 1924a, 1924b, 1925, 1926) published in his five Zulu-language readers, only four (including a nineteen-line set of Zwide's praises) touch on Ndwandwe history, compared with several dozen on Shaka and the early Zulu kingdom.[4]

The main contemporary significance of Stuart's pieces on Ndwandwe history was that they fed into Alfred Bryant's (1929) major compilation, *Olden Times in Zululand and Natal*. Bryant still saw the history of the Ndwandwe kingdom very much as an adjunct to that of the early Zulu kingdom, but he was the first writer to try to put together a more or less continuous narrative of Ndwandwe history (even if his account is to be found scattered through several widely separated chapters) from the time of the kingdom's origins in the late eighteenth century until its final break-up in 1826 (Bryant 1929: 158-175, 193-195, 204-216, 316-318, 586-594). Besides describing the wars of c. 1819-c. 1820 and 1826 between the Ndwandwe and the Zulu, he gave attention to the origins of the Ndwandwe chiefdom, its migration from southern Mozambique to northern Zululand, its political expansion under Zwide, and the Ndwandwe diaspora after the break-up of Zwide's kingdom in c. 1820. It is only on the last of these topics that he cited his sources in any detail; for the rest, he drew from the scraps of information recorded by earlier authors and from such oral histories as he had been able to collect himself. His account remained the standard published source of reference on the history of the Ndwandwe until it was overtaken by the work of academic researchers in the 1970s.

By the 1920s a few black writers were beginning to publish compilations of African custom and history, together with fictionalised accounts of the past, in which brief mention of the Ndwandwe was made (Molema 1963: 80-81; Fuze 1979: 14, 23, 47-50; Dhlomo 1937: 54-56, 58). They drew heavily on previously published works by white authors and added nothing by way of new perspectives or information to the stereotyped literary picture of Ndwandwe history. The lineage of works by white and black writers bearing on the history of the Ndebele kingdom which began to appear in the 1920s added a few new scraps of evidence about relations between Zwide's Ndwandwe and Mzilikazi's Khumalo in the late 1810s and early 1820s ('Mziki 1926: 26-27; Mhlagazanhlansi 1944: 7; Posselt 1978: 162). By the 1950s even these were falling away in the face of the powerful stereotype that Mzilikazi had originally been driven away by Shaka (Hughes 1956).

It was not until after World War II that the Ndwandwe once again featured to any marked extent in a printed work. This time it was not in a conventional history but in E.A. Ritter's (1955) fictional biography, *Shaka Zulu*, published in Britain for a popular readership. As Dan Wylie (2000: 217-237) has demonstrated in a critical analysis of the book, Ritter drew heavily on Bryant's *Olden Times* in establishing the basic narrative, and then used his imagination to flesh out in great detail what he saw as particularly dramatic events. Among these were the wars between the Zulu and the Ndwandwe, which Ritter – and the publisher's editor – built up into a story which has fuelled the fantasies of Western readers about Shaka's warrior nation for half a century. As Wylie (2000: 229) puts it:

> The central clashes between the Zulu and Ndwandwe polities, ending with
> the flight of Zwide and the general disintegration of the Ndwandwe, [have]
> become the cynosure of Shaka's military courage and tactical genius, and
> [are] regarded as a hinge event in the rise of Zulu power.

Ritter gives credit to the Ndwandwe as courageous fighters, but overall they emerge from his account as the anti-heroes and the Zulu as the heroes. This attitude coloured the treatment of Ndwandwe history in subsequent popular accounts of Zulu history, including Donald Morris's (1966: 53-55) widely read *The Washing of the Spears* and Brian Roberts's *The Zulu Kings* (1974: 48-53).

In the era of African decolonisation in the 1960s, when Western academic historians were for the first time turning their attention to the history of African societies, treatment of Ndwandwe history began to be partly detached from treatment of Zulu history. In his influential *The Zulu Aftermath: A Nineteenth-Century Revolution in Bantu Africa*, John Omer-Cooper (1966: 29) had the Ndwandwe as forming one of three large autonomous power blocs which emerged in the Zululand-Natal region at the end of the 18th century (the others were formed by the Ngwane of Sobhuza and the Mthethwa of Dingiswayo). He went as far as describing the defeat of Sobhuza's people by the Ndwandwe and their subsequent flight from southern to central Swaziland as marking 'the true beginning of the Mfecane' (Omer-Cooper 1966: 29), but soon veered back towards orthodoxy. The relevant chapter of his book is, after all, entitled 'The Zulu kingdom'; in it, Omer-Cooper (1966: 32-33) gives a standard account of the Ndwandwe-Mthethwa-Zulu wars, now fleshed out with references to Ritter's 'dramatic account' of a battle between the Ndwandwe and the Zulu. Ndwandwe history is thus still an adjunct to Zulu history.

Not until the 1970s, and the development of the precolonial history of southern Africa as a field of concentrated academic research, did Ndwandwe history become a clearly distinct topic in its own right. The first academic historians to turn their attention to the Ndwandwe were David Hedges (1978) and Philip Bonner (1983), the former in an unpublished study entitled 'Trade and politics in southern Mozambique and Zululand in the eighteenth and early nineteenth centuries', and the latter in a published history of the precolonial Swazi kingdom. Hedges (1978: 156-165) used unpublished Portuguese sources, as well as testimonies in the James Stuart Collection, to produce an account which placed the rise and expansion of the Ndwandwe kingdom in the context of moves towards greater political centralisation throughout the region from Delagoa Bay to the Thukela river. In this account, the Ndwandwe played a key role in conflicts over control of a rising trade conducted by European, Indian and American merchants and whalers who visited Delagoa Bay to exchange cloth, beads and brass for ivory and cattle. For his part, Bonner (1983: 23-24) used evidence drawn from the Stuart Collection, together with oral testimonies which he collected from a number of Swazi informants, to provide a searching account of the origins, expansion, and rivalries of the Swazi and Ndwandwe polities. His analysis led him to reach the radical conclusion, which Omer-Cooper had previously pointed to but whose significance he had not fully appreciated, to the effect that it was likely that Zwide, not Dingiswayo, was 'the real prototype of Shaka', and that the aggressions of the Ndwandwe, not the Zulu, were 'the catalyst of the shattering events of the Mfecane' (Bonner 1983: 23-24).

The studies produced by Hedges and Bonner laid the basis for other academic historians to take up research into the political history of the Tongaland–Swaziland–Zululand region in the late 18th and early 19th centuries in ways that moved far beyond the Zulu-centric stereotypes that had long predominated among academic and non-academic writers. Using detailed analysis of testimonies in the Stuart Collection, Carolyn Hamilton (1985) provided, among other things, a nuanced examination of the expansion of the Mthethwa and Qwabe chiefdoms. In my own PhD thesis (Wright 1989: 180-193), I drew on these earlier studies, particularly Hamilton's, to put forward a chronology of the early stages of Zulu expansion, and to argue that the virtually universal idea that Zwide's kingdom had broken up as a consequence of defeat at the hands of the Zulu needed thorough reassessment.

Despite the novelties of the perspectives which they took and of the arguments which they developed, all the researchers mentioned here to a greater or lesser degree, still held the long-established assumption that the most powerful and important of the states of eastern southern Africa by c. 1820 was that of the Zulu. It took the well-known 'Mfecane' debates of the late 1980s and 1990s, conducted against the background of political changes in South Africa which saw the end of white domination and the beginnings of democratically elected government, to jolt historians into 'post-colonial' and 'post-Zulu' reflections on the history of the era. Although they often disagreed fiercely on other issues, by the later 1990s most historians working in the field had explicitly or implicitly accepted that the role of the Zulu needed to be decentred and alternative accounts developed. The originator of the debates, Julian Cobbing (1988, 1992), argued that the main impetus behind the political transformations which, to the accompaniment of a sharp rise in political violence, took place in the Delagoa Bay hinterland from the late 1810s onward was a rapid increase in slave trading and raiding in the region. He saw states such as those of the Ndwandwe and the Zulu as originally defensive formations which themselves took to slaving (Cobbing 1988: 507; 1992: 6-7). Some commentators disagreed strongly that slaving had been a major factor in the politics of the Delagoa Bay hinterland before the early 1820s (Eldredge 1994, 1995); others were prepared to accept that, despite the lack of confirming evidence, it may well have played some role (Wright 1989: 193-207; Etherington 2001; Wylie 2006), though none took their arguments as far as Cobbing did and none presented the Ndwandwe or the Zulu as having been 'slaving states'.

In his often original, if sometimes quirky, rethinking of southern African history in the first half of the 19th century, Norman Etherington (2001: 79-84, 122-123) sees the Ndwandwe as one of the most important polities of a number that were jostling for power in the region east of the Drakensberg in the early decades of the century. But his treatment of their history is not helped by his speculation, which hardens into an assumption, that Zwide was seeking to reconstitute a kingdom of 'abaMbo' peoples that had supposedly existed in the seventeenth and early eighteenth centuries. His argument is based on an uncritical reading of Bryant's treatment of evidence on the abaMbo, and takes no account of alternative discussions of 'abaMbo' as an identity marker which Carolyn Hamilton and I have put forward (Hamilton 1985: 269-70, 474-477; Wright 1989: 310-319; Wright & Hamilton 1996: 24-31).

In a chapter in the *Cambridge History of South Africa*, I have sought, among other things, to recast the history of the period in a way which puts forward the Ndwandwe rather than the Mthethwa as the major actor in the politics of the region east of the Drakensberg until the break-up of Zwide's kingdom in c. 1820, and as a major actor in the eastern highveld and adjoining lowveld thereafter until Shaka's victory over Sikhunyana in 1826. I also argue that the flight of Soshangane, Zwangendaba and Nxaba from the lower Mkhuze–Mfolozi region in c. 1820-21, a flight which forms an integral part of the 'Zulu aftermath' in conventional accounts, was in fact more likely to have been a flight from Zwide (Wright in press).

The foregoing examination focuses on the treatment which has been accorded to Ndwandwe history in the published literature. It says very little about how Ndwandwe oral pasts have been constructed over the years, and continue to be constructed today, whether by Ndwandwe people themselves, or by Zulu, Swazi and others. This is for the simple reason that there is virtually no readily accessible evidence on the subject. An important exception is to be found in the records of the Swaziland Oral History Project, now housed at the University of the Witwatersrand. The records include a body of tape-recordings, some made as far back as the 1960s, gathered together in the late 1980s and early 1990s, together with transcriptions and translations from the original siSwati into English, that bears on the history of the Ndwandwe in the early nineteenth century. A thorough analysis needs to be made – and published – of how Ndwandwe history is portrayed in this archive, and of the political contexts in which this history, together with the archive itself, was produced.[5] By the same token, there is scope for extensive fieldwork to be done into the question of how Ndwandwe history is being orally portrayed today in KwaZulu-Natal in this period of post-colonial government and declining Zulu nationalism.

Towards a narrative of the history of the Ndwandwe kingdom

The evidence on the origins, migration and expansion of the Ndwandwe chiefdom has been reviewed in detail by Hedges (1978: 155-165) and Bonner (1983: 9-26); what follows is drawn from their analyses. In the first half of the 18th century the *abakwaNdwandwe*, the people of Ndwandwe, lived somewhere to the south of Delagoa Bay. By at least the middle of the century they had moved southward and established themselves in the amaGudu-Nongoma region between the middle Phongolo and the Black Mfolozi. There is no record of why they moved but it is possible that they did so to avoid falling under the sway of the Tembe kingdom. Under the rule of Mangobe, Hedges (1978: 119-126) tells us, the Tembe were actively expanding southward from the southern shores of Delagoa Bay from about the 1720s. By the middle of the century they were the dominant power in the region south of the bay between the Lubombo mountains and the Indian Ocean. Hedges does not indicate why they might have been expanding at this time; possibly the reason had to do with competition for what remained of a trade in ivory to Portuguese merchants at Delagoa Bay, a trade which was falling off through the first half of the 18th century (Hedges 1978: 119-23).

There is no record of what groups the Ndwandwe came into contact with during their migration or of what groups they subjugated or ousted in order to establish themselves in the Phongolo–Black Mfolozi region. But, as a migrant and therefore unusually predatory polity, moving through and settling in what must have been a hostile political environment, the Ndwandwe chiefdom would have had to use an unusual degree of force against other chiefdoms in order to survive. Its leaders would have had to tighten control over their own adherents – or would have seized opportunities to do so – to a degree beyond what was usual in more sedentary, less predatory chiefdoms. It way well have been one of the earliest chiefdoms to give its *amabutho*, or age-grades of young men, a more military inflection in the service of the chief (Wright 1978). In the event, the Ndwandwe leaders chose to end their migration when they felt they were safely beyond the reach of the Tembe kingdom. They established their domination over what was good cattle country, with access to spring and summer grazing on high-lying ridges to the west and to winter grazing in lower-lying savanna areas to the east (Hedges 1978: 159).

From soon after their arrival, the Ndwandwe faced renewed pressures from the expansion of other chiefdoms on their borders. To the north-east, a section of the Tembe under Mabhudu, a son of Mangobe, was expanding south-eastwards across the Maputo-Phongolo river by the 1750s. After the death of Mangobe in the late 1750s or early 1760s, Mabhudu in effect was able to establish himself as an autonomous chief and build up a relatively powerful chiefdom in the region between the Maputo-Phongolo and the sea. It is very likely that one of the factors underlying the growth of his power was the rapid expansion of a trade in ivory to British and Indian merchants who were visiting Delagoa Bay in increasing numbers in the 1760s and 1770s. One of the important trade routes that developed in these years extended southwards from the bay to Mabhudu territory and beyond (Hedges 1978: 127-129, 135-140).

To the north, the Ndwandwe were faced with the growth of the Dlamini chiefdom. The Dlamini were the rulers of another group which, probably a little after the Ndwandwe, had migrated southwards from the Delagoa Bay region. Faced by the Ndwandwe chiefdom to the south, they had come to a halt in the region to the east of the Lubombo hills in the basins of the Lusutfu (uSuthu) and Ngwavuma rivers. Sometime in the 1760s or 1770s, under pressure from the expanding Mabhudu kingdom to the north-east, they had gradually shifted westward over the Lubombo into what is now southern Swaziland. To begin with, the Dlamini seem to have been tributary to the Ndwandwe ruling house, and their chiefly houses had intermarried for several generations. But over time the Dlamini rulers were able to establish virtual autonomy from the Ndwandwe, and perhaps even to challenge the authority exercised by the Ndwandwe south of the Phongolo (Bonner 1983: 9-12, 24-26).

To the south-east the Ndwandwe faced a major challenge in the same period from the expansion of the Nyambose chiefdom in the region south of the lower White Mfolozi river. Under Khayi and then his son Jobe, the Nyambose chiefly house extended its authority over neighbouring chiefdoms and sought, with some success, to augment the power which its chiefs were able to exercise over their adherents in what came to be called the Mthethwa kingdom. The territories into which they expanded comprised good elephant country, and it seems probable that one of the major factors driving Nyambose expansion at this time was the desire to expand a trade in ivory to the Mabhudu kingdom to the north. By the early years of the 19th century, at the latest, the Nyambose leaders had established good trading relations with the Mabhudu, an alliance which threatened to shut out the Ndwandwe from much of the trade with Delagoa Bay (Hedges 1978: 180-183; Hamilton 1985: 110-119). It also posed a direct threat to the Ndwandwe ruling house's hold over the eastern margins of its sphere of influence, an area through which the trade route ran between the Mabhudu and Mthethwa kingdoms. In this area, at the southern end of the Lubombo range, lived an offshoot of the Ndwandwe which in the late 18th century seems to have been under the rule of Zikode. To the south of it, extending as far as the Mfolozi, were the Msane, the Jele or Ncwangeni, and the Nzimela, all of whom were apparently related to the Ndwandwe (Bryant 1929: 276-277, 447-448; Hedges 1978: 161-163). The Ndwandwe main house under Langa, and then his son Zwide, claimed authority over all these groups, but in practice they acted with a good deal of autonomy. Their location on the main trade route between the Mabhudu and Mthethwa chiefdoms gave them a certain strategic advantage which they used to play off the Ndwandwe and Mthethwa ruling houses against each other (Hedges 1978: 164-165).

In the 1790s and early 1800s the political temperature in the territories to the south of Delagoa Bay was gradually rising. The ivory trade at the bay was declining as European and Indian traders shifted their main operations northward, and as wars between the European powers disrupted commerce on the high seas. Chiefdoms involved in the trade sought to hold on to as much of it as they could in order to continue bringing in the prestige imports of cloth, beads and brass which had become important sources of patronage for ruling houses (Hedges 1978: 145-147). At the same time, a demand for cattle at the bay was rising to meet the need for provisions of American and British whalers who, from the late 1780s onward, were making the bay a centre of their operations. The region round the bay was poor cattle country because of the presence of tsetse fly; middleman suppliers at the bay, such as the Tembe and Madolo polities, were soon importing cattle from chiefdoms further and further afield to the south and west in what are now the Zululand and Swaziland regions. Among the suppliers was the Mthethwa kingdom; another was very probably the Ndwandwe kingdom, though there is no direct evidence on this. Cattle were pivotal to the social and political functioning of all the polities of eastern southern Africa; as chiefs traded off parts of their herds in order to acquire prestige imports, so the incentives would have increased for them to extract more cattle by way of tribute from their own adherents, and to raid cattle from weaker neighbouring chiefdoms (Hedges 1978: 147-152, 198-199).

Another factor which very probably made itself increasingly felt among the chiefdoms of the Delagoa Bay hinterland after about 1810 was a trade in slaves at the bay to European and Brazilian slavers. Julian Cobbing (1988: 503-7; 1992) has argued that by the early 1820s the level of the trade had reached such a pitch as to disrupt social and political life across much of the eastern side of the subcontinent. The evidence which he puts forward does not support this position, but *pace* what some of Cobbing's critics have argued (Eldredge 1995: 126-139), it seems likely that a low-level but rising trade in slaves at Delagoa Bay was in fact taking place before 1820. It is well accepted that at this time Brazilian slave-traders were buying larger and larger numbers of slaves from Portuguese-controlled ports in south-eastern Africa, and that French smugglers were seeking new sources of labour in the same region for the French colony on Reunion island and the British colony on Mauritius. The main supplying ports were Quelimane and Mozambique, well to the north of Delagoa Bay, but it is difficult to believe that some slaving did not take place at Delagoa Bay as well. Certainly a trade in slaves was well established there by the early 1820s; on the face of it, there is no reason to think that it did not begin some time earlier (Wright 1989: 196-203). Cobbing (1988: 1992: 5-7) cites evidence that the Ndwandwe kingdom, among others, sold war captives to traders at the bay. It is quite possible that this took place from time to time, but the evidence that he goes on to cite to the effect that the Ndwandwe kingdom was a slaving state does not, in my view, bear out his argument.

Whatever the precise dimensions and impact of the Delagoa Bay slave trade, there can be little doubt that the Portuguese presence at the bay was an important factor in the politics of the hinterland. The Portuguese had set up their first permanent trading station at the bay in 1782, had been driven out by the French in 1796, and had returned in 1799. This time they set up a small garrison to safeguard their trading operations against other European powers and the chiefdoms at the bay (Hedges 1978: 130, 145-146). They may not have had the power to bring any of these chiefdoms directly under their authority, but they frequently sought to intervene in local politics to their own advantage by playing one chiefdom off against another (Wright 1989: 203-204). How the consequent tensions and disputes among these chiefdoms affected polities further afield, such as that of the Ndwandwe, is not on record, but it is more than likely that they served to sharpen already rising conflicts.

By the 1810s, if not before, the Ndwandwe ruling house, now under Zwide, was coming to feel that its ability to maintain not merely its sphere of influence but the integrity of the kingdom itself was under threat. Inside the core region of the kingdom, one of its responses was to seek to tighten its hold over men of fighting age through the system of enrolling them into state-controlled *amabutho*. It is likely that at this stage the Ndwandwe were becoming better organised for warfare than were any of their neighbours. This was partly because of the particular circumstances in which the Ndwandwe kingdom had come into being in the mid- and later 18th century, and partly because of the rivalries which were developing in the early 19th century between it and its expansionist neighbours.

Beyond his kingdom's borders, Zwide turned his forces with unusually destructive violence on a number of neighbouring chiefdoms, aiming, it seems, not simply to seize their cattle and to establish them as tributaries, but to destroy their ruling houses and to thoroughly subjugate them. Most notable were the attacks on the Dlamini polity under Sobhuza which was expanding on the northern margins of the Ndwandwe kingdom. Bonner (1983: 27-28) talks of four successive attacks made by the Ndwandwe on the Dlamini, with Sobhuza being forced to flee from the Shiselweni area in southern Swaziland further and further to the north-west as far as the Dlomodlomo mountains some 150 km away. In the course of his flight he had to abandon many of his adherents, and was saved only by Zwide's becoming involved in wars on his other borders.

Chief among the kingdoms which rivalled that of the Ndwandwe was the Mthethwa state under Dingiswayo kaJobe, who had been ruling probably since the 1790s. Hamilton (1985: 123-130) distinguishes three major phases of Mthethwa expansion under Dingiswayo. First was a period of strategic consolidation of the sphere of influence which the Mthethwa had been establishing north of the Mfolozi river in the south-eastern marches of the Ndwandwe kingdom. Second was a period in which Dingiswayo moved to extend his control over the coastal plain from the Mfolozi southwards, a region of relatively high rainfall, good agricultural land and varied grazing. This brought him into confrontation with the large

Qwabe chiefdom south of the Mhlathuze, but in the event he was able to overawe it relatively easily. In a third phase, the Mthethwa expanded from the lowlands westward into the interior between the White Mfolozi and the Mhlathuze. This move, I argue, was made at least in part to pre-empt the possible expansion into it of the Ndwandwe from the north (Wright 1989: 162-163). After forcing the chiefdoms of the region to submit to his authority, Dingiswayo redirected the main thrust of Mthethwa expansion northwards across the middle White Mfolozi into the south-western and western marches of the Ndwandwe kingdom. He also sought to establish friendly relations with the large Hlubi chiefdom further to the west (Wright 1989: 163, 177-178).

Mthethwa control of the region south of the White Mfolozi and of the main trade routes to the north posed a growing threat to the security of the Ndwandwe kingdom. It is hardly surprising that Zwide's reaction was a violent one. The precise sequence of events is not clear, but in the first instance he apparently set out to destroy the sphere of influence which Dingiswayo had recently established on his south-western and western borders. In an attack against two Khumalo chiefdoms under Donda and Mashobane respectively, he killed the chiefs and brought their people under his domination. The neighbouring Ntshali under Mlotha suffered a similar fate. Then, in a fierce attack reminiscent of their campaigns against the Dlamini, the Ndwandwe fell on the amaNgwane under Matiwane in the region of what is now Vryheid, seized their cattle, and drove the chief and many of his adherents out of their territory (Bryant 1929: 162, 163, 172-173, 421; Wright 1989: 178-179).

Zwide was also concerned to bring more firmly under his authority the eastern borderlands of his kingdom, where the writ of the Ndwandwe chiefs had always been weak. At some stage he attacked Zwangendaba, chief of the Jele section of the Ncwangeni. The limitations of Ndwandwe power in this region are shown up in a story that Zwide was captured by the Jele and held for a while before being released (Bryant 1929: 162; Hedges 1978: 164). At a later stage Zwide turned his attention to his south-eastern border where a section of the Nxumalo Ndwandwe under Malusi lived. The latter had married a sister of Dingiswayo and Zwide seems to have regarded his allegiance as suspect, so had him killed (Bryant 1929: 163-164; Hedges 1978: 193). This move was instrumental in provoking Dingiswayo into launching a major attack on his rival in the late 1810s. As is well known, the outcome was that the Mthethwa chief was captured and put to death, and his forces defeated and driven back in disorder. The weakly integrated kingdom which he had formed was left leaderless and rapidly fell apart into its constituent chiefdoms. Quite suddenly, the Ndwandwe were left as the strongest power east of the Drakensberg.

Zwide's next step was to try to extend his control over the territories south of the White Mfolozi which had previously been dominated by the Mthethwa. The main obstacle he faced was the rapidly rising Zulu chiefdom under Shaka to the south of the middle White Mfolozi. This previously insignificant chiefdom had been brought under the overlordship of Dingiswayo during the reign of Shaka's father Senzangakhona. As a young man, Shaka himself had served in Dingiswayo's forces, where his abilities as a fighter and leader had brought him to the notice of the Mthethwa king. On the death of Senzangakhona, Dingiswayo had assisted Shaka to seize the Zulu chiefship and, with the aim of stabilising the western borderlands of the expanding Mthethwa kingdom, had encouraged him to strengthen his chiefdom through a campaign of internal political and military reforms and of aggressive expansion against his more immediate neighbours (Hamilton 1985: 132-136, 335ff).

In the period c. 1819-1820 Zwide launched two and possibly three attacks against the Zulu chiefdom with the aim of destroying it as a rival centre of power. As indicated in the discussion of Ritter in the first section of this chapter a certain mythology has accrued round these campaigns in the literature and it is difficult to get a clear picture of them from the available evidence. But it seems that under Shaka's astute leadership, the Zulu were able to avoid destruction by hiding or destroying their stocks of grain and retreating with their cattle to the south, either to the broken and forested Nkandla region or beyond the Thukela to the heights of what is now the Kranskop area. The Ndwandwe are said to have retreated in the first instance without having come up against the Zulu, thus affording Shaka a breathing space (Jantshi kaNongila 1903: 184-185; Mmemi kaNguluzana 1904: 270-271; Dinya kaZokozwayo 1905: 102-103; Baleni kaSilwana 1914: 16-17; Bryant 1929: 173-175, 193-195). He used it to bring together an alliance of southern chiefdoms whose leaders preferred, or were cajoled or forced, to subordinate themselves in varying degrees to the Zulu rather than to the Ndwandwe. The key event in this process was the sudden attack Shaka made on the large Qwabe chiefdom, whose ruling house had been weakened by internal conflict. He killed the chief, Phakathwayo kaKhondlo, who was hostile to the Zulu, and assisted Nqetho, a member of the Qwabe chiefly house who supported Shaka, to accede to the chiefship (Hamilton 1985: 172-175).

Soon afterwards Zwide made another attack on the Zulu, but the forces of the alliance under Shaka proved strong enough to halt the Ndwandwe in what recorded accounts describe as a fierce battle on the Mhlathuze river.[6] The common – Zuluist – view is that the fight ended in a resounding defeat for the Ndwandwe, and that the various sections of the kingdom then went into flight to escape from Shaka, with the main house under Zwide fleeing northwards across the Phongolo, and the sections under Soshangane of the Nxumalo, Zwangendaba of the Ncwangeni-Jele, and Nxaba of the Msane making off in separate groups towards Delagoa Bay. A different reading of the available evidence suggests, however, that the Ndwandwe forces, though badly mauled and forced to retreat, were not destroyed and that in his move northward Zwide retained a considerable following.

Ndwandwe versions of these events, as recorded in the archive of the Swaziland Oral History Project, give a picture of the causes of the Ndwandwe diaspora which, as one might expect, differs significantly from the received Zuluist version (Mkhatshwa 1982a: 7-15, 1982b: 17-28; Nxumalo 1983: 7-9). They tend to downplay, or even omit altogether, mention of confrontation with the Zulu, and to highlight traditions that the break-up of the Ndwandwe kingdom was due mainly to internal political tensions. This is consonant with the evidence cited above that the Ndwandwe rulers had never fully succeeded in bringing their eastern marchlords under their authority. The latter were apparently prepared to support Zwide in the initial stages of his confrontation with the Zulu, when it appeared that the Ndwandwe were likely to be the victors, but the check to Zwide's power at the battle of the Mhlathuze gave them the opportunity, which they had probably long wanted, to throw off their allegiance and to move away, not necessarily all at the same time, to regions where they could set themselves up as independent rulers. In the same period, numbers of the Khumalo who had been subjugated by Zwide made off to the north-west under the leadership of Mzilikazi, son of their former chief Mashobane. They too are usually seen in the literature as having been 'driven out' by Shaka (Bryant 1929: 420-423; Omer-Cooper 1966: 129-131); more likely is that they chose to move away to assert their independence from both the Ndwandwe and the Zulu.

The subsequent careers of Soshangane, Zwangendaba and Nxaba are well enough known and will not be dealt with here. The concern of this paper is with the career of the main house under Zwide, which, because of the paucity of evidence, has never been given adequate treatment in the literature. What we have instead is a number of 'outside' comments made by historians of the Zulu, Swazi, and Pedi kingdoms (Bryant 1929: 209-212; Bonner 1983: 28-29, 237-238; Delius 1983: 22-23). This has left the history of the Ndwandwe after c. 1820 in a curious world of shadows. The polity that reconsolidated under Zwide and his son Sikhunyana evidently grew into a powerful one, as it suddenly appears on stage again in a major confrontation with the Zulu in 1826, but there are virtually no sources on its history in the first half of the 1820s. The most the historian can do is speculate on the basis of a few snippets of evidence.

In his summation of the evidence available to him in the 1920s, Bryant (1929: 209-212) had Zwide migrating north-west across the Phongolo through the eastern parts of what is now Mpumalanga province to the Nkomati river. Here, after defeating the Pedi under Thulare (Thulwana), he proceeded to settle and rebuild his kingdom. Other sources (Rasmussen 1978: 35-40) assert that the Pedi were defeated not by the Ndwandwe but by the Khumalo/Ndebele of Mzilikazi, but in an authoritative review of the evidence in his history of the Pedi kingdom, Delius (1983: 19-25) supports the idea that it was the Ndwandwe who were responsible.[8] One of Bonner's (1983: 29) informants has Zwide first moving northward into southern Swaziland and meeting fierce resistance from the Mamba people; after this he changed direction to the north-west and settled near the Nkomati. By contrast, Cobbing (1982: 6), followed by Etherington (2001: 122-123), holds that the Ndwandwe remained very much *in situ* in their territories near the Phongolo river, where, in the 1820s, they became a major slaving state. The evidence makes clear, however, that after its confrontation with the Zulu, the Ndwandwe ruling house abandoned its heartland in the amaGudu-Nongoma area, and that this area, and other strategic parts of former Ndwandwe territory were colonised early in Shaka's reign by sections of the Zulu royal house (Hamilton 1985: 219, 221-222, 364-367). The most likely scenario is that Zwide first moved north across the Phongolo to try to seize Swazi cattle, then turned away to the north-west to put some distance between himself and the Zulu on the one hand and the unstable area round Delagoa Bay on the other. He settled in the upper Nkomati region, and proceeded to reconsolidate his kingdom.

The territory which the Ndwandwe came to dominate extended from the Olifants river in the north to the Phongolo river in the south. They raided the Pedi, the Dlamini and other polities that had accumulated significant holdings of cattle. Within a short space of time the Ndwandwe had become a major predatory state, one which, according to a British trader who operated in the Zulu kingdom, was regarded with some fear by Shaka (Isaacs 1970: 71). No doubt the compliment was returned by Zwide, who seems to have avoided making attacks on his upstart rival; at least there is no evidence in the records which suggests that he did.

Somewhere to the south-west of the Ndwandwe, near the upper Vaal river, a similar kind of polity was emerging under Mzilikazi of the Khumalo (Cobbing 1976: 15ff; Rasmussen 1978: 27ff). This polity, the nucleus of what later came to be the Ndebele kingdom, is usually portrayed as having rapidly established its dominance over the Sotho-speaking peoples of the region north of the Vaal; I would argue that it did not emerge as a major actor in the area until after the collapse of the Ndwandwe kingdom in 1826.

Zwide died in late 1824 or early 1825. Shortly before or after this event, a dispute seems to have arisen over the succession to the kingship between his sons Sikhunyana and Somaphunga. The upshot was that after Zwide's death, Sikhunyana was able to make himself king, while Somaphunga broke away with a number of adherents and went off to give his allegiance to Shaka (Wright 1989: 338-344). There is some hint in the sources that at about this time Sikhunyana shifted the Ndwandwe kingdom's political centre of gravity from the Nkomati southward (Ngidi kaMcikaziswa 1904: 70; Ngidi kaMcikaziswa 1905: 79; Ndunu kaManqina 1910: 4), a move which seems to have been seen by Shaka as a threat to his hold over the north-western borderlands of his new kingdom. The dispute within the Ndwandwe royal house encouraged him to strike a blow that would eliminate the most formidable rival power that he faced. He was further encouraged to act by the presence at Port Natal in the southern part of his dominions of a number of British traders and their retinues of black adherents equipped with firearms. In mid-1826 Shaka summoned the traders to support him in an expedition against the Ndwandwe, and in August or September of that year he accompanied his army in an invasion of Ndwandwe territory from the south-east (Wright 1989: 338-44; Wylie 2006: 372-383).

Leaving their crops standing, and driving their livestock, the inhabitants of the region fled before him. From the north, Sikhunyana and his forces advanced to the izinDololwane hills north of the upper Phongolo, and here the two armies met in a fierce battle. The Ndwandwe forces were defeated and numbers of women and children were massacred. The victorious Zulu then proceeded to round up the cattle of the Ndwandwe and – so determined was Shaka to annihilate their polity – to destroy all their homesteads and fields of grain (Fynn 1965b: 86-90; Maclean 1992: 67-69). Some of the surviving Ndwandwe warriors are said to have been incorporated into Shaka's own army (Maclean 1992: 68). Sikhunyana himself managed to escape, but the sources are not clear on what his subsequent fate was. Without leaders to cohere round, and with their cattle in the hands of the victors, the Ndwandwe broke up. Large numbers submitted to Shaka and were permitted to resettle in the former Ndwandwe territories south of the Phongolo, but now under the rule of senior members of the Zulu royal house (Ndukwana kaMbengwana 1902: 358; Maphuthwana kaDidiza 1921: 230). Others went off to make their submission to Sobhuza of the Dlamini, to Soshangane of the Nxumalo, and to Mzilikazi of the Ndebele (Bryant 1929: 425, 593-594; Fynn 1965a: 68).

The disintegration of the Ndwandwe kingdom had a politically highly significant 'aftermath'.[9] It allowed Shaka to establish unchallenged domination of the former Ndwandwe territories north of the Black Mfolozi. It encouraged opposition to Shaka to emerge more strongly, if still secretly, in the ranks of the Zulu royal house, a movement which culminated in his assassination at the hands of his brothers in September 1828. It opened the way for the re-establishment of the Dlamini kingdom as a major power north of the Phongolo and of the Maroteng (Pedi) kingdom in the middle Olifants region, and for the emergence of the Ndebele kingdom on the northern highveld. In retrospect it can be seen as an event that was crucial in shaping the politics of eastern southern Africa in the 19th century.

In post-colonial South Africa, the history of the Ndwandwe kingdom needs to be given much more systematic attention than was the case in the era of colonialism and its accompanying 'Zulucentricity'. Three avenues of further research suggest themselves. First, as indicated above, there is scope for investigation into how Ndwandwe and other people today, especially in KwaZulu-Natal, remember the history of the Ndwandwe kingdom, even if, given the current politics of Zulu 'royalism', the topic is likely to be a highly sensitive one. Second, research into the records left by the colonial bureaucracies that were set up in Zululand from the 1880s onward – records that are now housed in archives repositories in Pietermaritzburg, Durban and Ulundi – would in all likelihood help to shed more light on the history of Zwide's kingdom. And third, field research by historians and archaeologists to find specific sites mentioned in the documentary records could fruitfully be done in at least three different regions. One is the amaGudu-Nongoma area, where the broad locations of half a dozen Ndwandwe royal homesteads are given by Bryant (1929: 164, 208) and by Stuart's informant Luzipho kaNomageje (1904: 354). This research would need to take account of fieldwork, so far unpublished, done by Ronette Engela (pers. comm. 2007). Another region is the heartland of the new Ndwandwe kingdom as established by Zwide in c. 1820 in the upper Nkomati valley. Without giving his sources, Bryant (1929: 212) identifies several farms in what is now the Carolina–Barberton area as the location of Zwide's settlement. Luzipho (1904: 355) gives the place of Zwide's death as near kwaMtholo, which Bryant (1929: 212) identifies as a hill near the Nkomati. A third is the izinDololwane area north of the upper Phongolo river that seems to have been settled by Zwide's son and successor, Sikhunyana, in 1825-6, and which was the site of the final defeat of the Ndwandwe by the Zulu in 1826.

Research along the lines suggested could not be expected to produce spectacular results, but would certainly help establish a clearer picture of the place of the Ndwandwe kingdom in the history of the KwaZulu-Natal–Swaziland–southern Mozambique–eastern Mpumalanga region in the late 18th and early 19th centuries.

Notes

1   Translated here from the Zulu original.
2   This argument is developed at greater length in Wright (2006-2007).
3   The earliest reference to the Ndwandwe that I have so far come across is to Chief 'Zeite' (Zwide) as mentioned in a document written by Captain William Owen in May 1823 some months after he had arrived at Delagoa Bay and published in Theal (1898: 470). Chief 'Esconyana' (Sikhunyana) is mentioned in J.S. King's account of the British trading settlement at Port Natal which was published in Cape Town in the issues of the *South African Commercial Advertiser* of 11 July 1826 and 18 July 1826 and reprinted in Thompson (1968: 249). The earliest mention of Zwide ('Ozueeda') in Cape documents is in a letter from Henry Somerset to Major-General Bourke of 29 August 1828, published in Leverton (1989: 91). Zwide had by this time been dead some years.

4   For the record, the four are as follows: I. 'Indhlu ka Ntombazi wa oLanga' [The house of Ntombazi wa oLanga], in Stuart (1923:46), (testimony given by Socwatsha kaPhaphu on 3.10.1921, original notes in Stuart Collection, File 58, nbk. 22, pp. 1-2); II. 'Imp' enkulu e ya-liwa uTshaka no Zwide eMhlatuze' [The great battle which was fought by Shaka and Zwide at the Mhlathuze], in Stuart (1924a: 7-11), (testimony given mostly by Socwatsha kaPhaphu on 3.10.1921, original notes in Stuart Collection, File 58, nbk. 22, pp. 2-9); III. 'uDingiswayo ka Jobe (inkosi ya kwa Mtetwa)' [Dingiswayo kaJobe (king of the Mthethwa)], parts I-III, in Stuart (1924b: 14-42), (testimony given by Matshwili kaMngoye, November 1903 (original notes missing from Stuart collection); IV. 'Izibongo zi ka Zwide ka Langa' [The praises of Zwide kaLanga], in Stuart (1925: 58-9), (name of informant and location of original testimony not yet found).

5   Work towards eventual publication of a selection of testimonies recorded by the Project is proceeding (Hamilton 2007).

6   For example Omer-Cooper (1966: 33, 57, 64), who draws on Bryant (1929: 206-7), who draws on Stuart (1924a: 7-11), whose account was drawn mostly from testimony given to him by Socwatsha kaPhaphu on 3.10.1921 (see note 4 above).

7   Even Bryant (1929: 209) indicates this. Socwatsha (Stuart 1924a: 11) states that Zwide was able to make his escape with a number of his cattle, and that though the Zulu forces burnt Zwide's homestead they were unable fully to press home their victory at the Mhlathuze (original account in Stuart Collection, File 58, nbk. 22, pp. 7-9, dated 3.10.1921). Ndlovu kaThimuni (1919: 230) told Stuart that Zwide still commanded large forces when he took to flight.

8   See also Ndukwana (1900: 278-9).

9   Wright (in press). I have given the relevant section of the chapter the heading 'The Ndwandwe aftermath'.

References

Arbousset, T. 1968 [1846]. *Narrative of an Exploratory Tour to the North-East of the Cape of Good Hope.* Cape Town: Struik [1st edn. Cape Town: A.S. Robertson, Saul Solomon].

Baleni kaSilwana. 1914. Testimony. 10 May. In: Webb, C. de B. & Wright J.B. (eds) 1976-2001. volume 1. 1976.

Bird, J. (ed.) 1965 [1888]. *The Annals of Natal,* volume 1. Cape Town: Struik [1st edn. Pietermaritzburg: P. Davis and Sons].

Bonner, P. 1983. *Kings, Commoners and Concessionaires: The Evolution and Dissolution of the Nineteenth-Century Swazi State.* Cambridge: Cambridge University Press.

Bryant, A.T. 1929. *Olden Times in Zululand and Natal.* London: Longmans, Green.

Cobbing, J. 1976. The Ndebele under the Khumalos. Unpublished PhD thesis. Lancaster: University of Lancaster.

Cobbing, J. 1988. The Mfecane as alibi: thoughts on Dithakong and Mbolompo. *Journal of African History* 29: 487-519.

Cobbing, J. 1992. Grasping the nettle: the slave trade and the early Zulu. In: Edgecombe, D.R., Laband, J.P.C. & Thompson, P.S. (eds) *The Debate on Zulu Origins: A Selection of Papers on the Zulu Kingdom and Early Colonial Natal.* Pietermaritzburg: Department of Historical Studies, University of Natal.

Delius, P. 1983. *The Land Belongs to Us: The Pedi Polity, the Boers and the British in the Nineteenth-Century Transvaal.* Johannesburg: Ravan Press.

Dhlomo, R.R.R. 1937. *UShaka.* Pietermaritzburg: Shuter and Shooter.

Dinya kaZokozwayo. 1905. Testimony. 2 March. In: Webb, C. de B. & Wright J.B. (eds) 1976-2001.volume 1. 1976.

Eldredge, E. 1994. Delagoa Bay and the hinterland in the early nineteenth century: politics, trade, slaves, and slave-raiding. In: Eldredge, E. & Morton, F. (eds) *Slavery in South Africa: Captive Labor on the Dutch Frontier.* Boulder: Westview Press and Pietermaritzburg: University of Natal Press.

Eldredge, E. 1995. Sources of conflict in southern Africa c.1800-1830: the *'mfecane'* reconsidered. In: Hamilton, C. (ed.) *The Mfecane Aftermath: Reconstructive Debates in Southern African History.* Johannesburg: Witwatersrand University Press and Pietermaritzburg: University of Natal Press.

Etherington, N. 2001. *The Great Treks: The Transformation of Southern Africa, 1815-1854.* Harlow: Longman.

Fuze, M. 1979 [1922]. *The Black People and Whence They Came.* Lugg. H.C. (transl.) Cope, A.T. (ed.) Pietermaritzburg: University of Natal Press. [Translation of *Abantu Abamnyama Lapa Bavela Ngakona.* Pietermaritzburg: private publication.]

Fynn, H.F. 1965a [1888]. History of Godongwana (Dingiswayo) and (in part) of Chaka. In: Bird, J. (ed.). *The Annals of Natal*, volume 1: 60-71. Cape Town: Struik [1st ed. Pietermaritzburg: P. Davis and Sons].

Fynn, H.F. 1965b. [1888] Campaign against Sikonyana, king of the Endwandwe. In: Bird, J. (ed.). *The Annals of Natal*, volume 1: 86-90. Cape Town: Struik [1st edn. Pietermaritzburg: P. Davis and Sons].

Gibson, J.Y. 1903. *The Story of the Zulus.* Pietermaritzburg: P. Davis and Sons.

Guy, J. 1979. *The Destruction of the Zulu Kingdom.* London: Longman.

Hamilton, C. 1985. Ideology, oral traditions and the struggle for power in the early Zulu kingdom. Unpublished MA thesis. Johannesburg: University of the Witwatersrand.

Hamilton, C. 1998. *Terrific Majesty: the Powers of Shaka Zulu and the Limits of Historical Invention.* Cape Town: David Philip.

Hamilton, C. 2007. Personal communication. 18 October.

Hedges, D. 1978. Trade and politics in southern Mozambique and Zululand in the eighteenth and early nineteenth centuries. Unpublished PhD thesis. London: London University.

Hughes, A.J.B. 1956. *Kin, Caste and Nation among the Rhodesian Ndebele.* Manchester: Manchester University Press.

Isaacs, N. 1970 [1836]. *Travels and Adventures in Eastern Africa.* In: Herman, L. and Kirby, P.R. (eds) Cape Town: Struik [1st edn. London: 1836].

Jantshi kaNongila. 1903. Testimony. 11 and 12 February. *See* Webb, C. de B. and J.B. Wright (eds) 1976-2001. volume 1. 1976.

Laband, J. 1995. *Rope of Sand: The Rise and Fall of the Zulu Kingdom.* Johannesburg: Jonathan Ball.

Leverton, B.J.T. (ed.) 1989. *Records of Natal, Volume Two, September 1828 – July 1835.* Pretoria: Government Printer.

Liesegang, G. 1981. Notes on the internal structure of the Gaza kingdom of southern Mozambique 1840-1895. In: Peires, J.B. (ed.) *Before and after Shaka: Papers in Nguni History.* Grahamstown: Institute of Social and Economic Research, Rhodes University.

Luzipho kaNomageje. 1904. Testimony. 2 November. In: Webb, C. de B. & Wright, J.B. (eds) 1976-2001. volume 1. 1976.

Maclean, C. 1992. *The Natal Papers of 'John Ross.'* In: Gray, S. (ed.) Pietermaritzburg: University of Natal Press.

Maphuthwana kaDidiza. 1921. Testimony. 5 June. In: Webb, C. de B. & Wright J.B. (eds) 1976-2001. volume 2. 1979.

Mhlagazanhlansi. 1944. *My Friend Kumalo.* Bulawayo: [publisher not given].

Mkhatshwa, B. 1982. Transcript of interview conducted by D. Dlamini for Swaziland Broadcasting Services. 1 July. In: Swaziland Oral History Project archives (University of the Witwatersrand), notebook 1, pp. 7-15, notebook 2, pp. 17-28.

Mmemi kaNguluzana. 1904. Testimony. 25 October. In: Webb, C. de B. & Wright, J.B. (eds) 1976-2001. volume 3. 1982.

Molema, S.M. 1963 [1920]. *The Bantu Past and Present.* Cape Town: C. Struik [1st edn. Edinburgh: W. Green].

Morris, D. 1966. *The Washing of the Spears.* London: Jonathan Cape.

'Mziki [Campbell, A.A.], 1926. *'Mlimo: the Rise and Fall of the Matabele.* Pietermaritzburg: Natal Witness.

Ndlovu kaThimuni. 1919. Testimony. 2 September. In: Webb, C. de B. & Wright, J.B. (eds) 1976-2001. volume 4. 1986.

Ndukwana kaMbengwana. 1900. Testimony. 17 September. In: Webb, C. de B. & Wright, J.B. (eds) 1976-2001. volume 4. 1986.

Ndukwana kaMbengwana. 1902. Testimony, 28 October. In: Webb, C. de B. & Wright, J.B. (eds) 1976-2001. volume 4. 1986.

Ndunu kaManqina. 1910. Testimony. 24 April. In: Webb, C. de B. & Wright, J.B. (eds) 1976-2001. volume 5. 2001.

Ngidi kaMcikaziswa. 1904. Testimony. 19 November. In: Webb, C. de B. & Wright, J.B. (eds) 1976-2001. volume 5. 2001.

Ngidi kaMcikaziswa. 1905. Testimony. 22 October. In: Webb, C. de B. & Wright, J.B. (eds) 1976-2001. volume 5. 2001.

Nxumalo, J. & Nxumalo, B. 1983. Transcript of interview conducted by D. Dlamini for Swaziland Broadcasting Services. 3 June. Transcription and translation by K. Simelane. In: Swaziland Oral History Project archives (University of the Wiwatersrand), Ndwandwe History, box 1, notebook 1: 7-9.

Omer-Cooper, J. 1966. *The Zulu Aftermath: A Nineteenth Century Revolution in Bantu Africa*. London: Longmans.

Posselt, F.W.T. 1978. *Fact and Fiction: A Short Account of the Natives of Southern Rhodesia*. Bulawayo: Books of Rhodesia.

Rasmussen, R.K. 1978. *Migrant Kingdom: Mzilikazi's Ndebele in South Africa*. Cape Town: David Philip.

Ritter, E.A. 1955. *Shaka Zulu*. London: Longmans Green.

Roberts, B. 1974. *The Zulu Kings*. London: Hamish Hamilton.

Shepstone, T. 1875. The early history of the Zulu-Kafir race of south-eastern Africa. *Journal of the Society of Arts*. 29 January. Reprint in Bird (ed.) 1965. pp. 155-166.

Socwatsha kaPhaphu. 1921. Testimony. 3 October. In: James Stuart Collection, Killie Campbell Africana Library, Durban. File 58, nbk. 22.

Stuart, J. 1923. *uTulasizwe*. London: Longmans, Green.

Stuart, J. 1924a. *uHlangakula*. London: Longmans, Green.

Stuart, J. 1924b. *uBaxoxele*. London: Longmans, Green.

Stuart, J. 1925. *uKulumetule*. London: Longmans, Green.

Stuart, J. 1926. *uVusezakiti*. London: Longmans, Green.

Theal, G.M. (ed.) 1898. *Records of South-Eastern Africa*, volume 2. London: Govt. of Cape Colony.

Thomas, T.M. 1970 [1873]. *Eleven Years in Central South Africa*. Bulawayo: Books of Rhodesia [1st edn. London: John Snow].

Thompson, G. 1968 [1827]. *Travels and Adventures in Southern Africa* volume 2. Forbes, V. (ed.) Cape Town: Van Riebeeck Society [1st edn. London: Henry Colburn].

Webb, C. de B. & Wright J.B. (eds) 1976-2001. *The James Stuart Archive of Recorded Oral Evidence Relating to the History of the Zulu and Neighbouring Peoples*. 5 volumes. Pietermaritzburg: University of Natal Press.

Wright, J. 1978. Pre-Shakan age-group formation among the northern Nguni. *Natalia* 8:23-29.

Wright, J. 1989. The dynamics of power and conflict in the Thukela-Mzimkhulu region in the late 18th and early 19th centuries: a critical reconstruction. Unpublished PhD thesis. Johannesburg: University of the Witwatersrand.

Wright, J. 2006a. Reconstituting Shaka Zulu for the twenty-first century. *Southern African Humanities* 18: 139-153.

Wright, J. 2006-2007. Beyond the 'Zulu aftermath': migrations, identities, histories. *Journal of Natal and Zulu History*.

Wright, J. In press. Turbulent times: political and social transformations in the north and east. In: Ross R., Hamilton, C. & Mbenga B. (eds) *The Cambridge History of South Africa*, volume 1.

Wright, J. & Hamilton, C. 1996. Ethnicity and political change before 1840. In: Morrell, R. (ed.) *Political Economy and Identities in KwaZulu-Natal: Historical and Social Perspectives*: Durban: Indicator Press.

Wylie, D. 2000. *Savage Delight: White Myths of Shaka*. Pietermaritzburg: University of Natal Press.

Wylie, D. 2006. *Myth of Iron: Shaka in History*. Pietermaritzburg: University of KwaZulu-Natal Press.

13

Swazi oral tradition and Northern Nguni historical archaeology

Philip Bonner

Introduction

The Swazi Kingdom has been depicted in studies by Kuper, myself and others as something 'sui generis' (Marwick 1940; Kuper 1947; Matsebula 1972; Bonner 1983). Starting life as some kind of cross-breed between a refugee and a conquest state, it fused a disparate set of chiefdoms, cultures, languages and even economic practices into a single syncretic unit, albeit divided into three distinct strata each enjoying differential status and access to resources. Interpreted in this manner, the late 18th century/early 19th-century Swazi Kingdom stands apart from, or in between, the much more centralised and homogenous Zulu Kingdom or state to the south, and the highly variegated Sotho chiefdoms or paramountcies further west, which have been conventionally viewed as more loosely organised but culturally cognate. Certainly, as I understood it thirty years ago, it commanded attention because of its unusual ancestry, which gave it its singular atypical hybrid character and, potentially, its own ambiguous historical vocation.

Surprisingly little concerted or sustained attention has been paid to the precolonial African histories of the 18th and early 19th centuries in South Africa since the early 1980s, and even less to a systematic effort to compare and to calibrate them. Hamilton (1985) and Wright (1989) have made two of the few major contributions in this regard, showing, among other things, the comparative heterogeneity of the Zulu Kingdom/state, and its internal structuring into distinct strata, moulded along analagous (but more disguised) lines to those employed by the Swazi. A handful of other studies have examined the internal structures and dynamics of African polities elsewhere (Makhura 1993; Lekgoathi 2004). Aside from them, the precolonial African history of this area has been most extensively and illuminatingly explored by archaeologists (see for example Loubser 1981, 1988; Pistorious 1992; Schoeman 1997; Hall 1998; Boeyens 2003). Despite some important shafts of insight that they have thrown on this subject, however, these still remain all too few, as other epochs have by and large attracted more attention. These absences are unfortunate since a closer study of the history of the last 400 to 500 years may well hold the key to understanding and reinterpreting many current South African identities.

Despite the sparseness of the recent literature, a certain drift of reinterpretation can already be discerned. One is a growing recognition of the intense fluidity, mobility and interconnectedness of African societies, of the multiplicity of southern Africa's internal frontiers, and of the consequent hybridity or mixedness of its indigenous cultures over this period. Whereas an earlier generation of students of precolonial South Africa tended to telescope this flux, energy and political and cultural creativity into the late 18th and early 19th centuries, it now seems reasonable to hypothesise that this can be pushed back by at least a

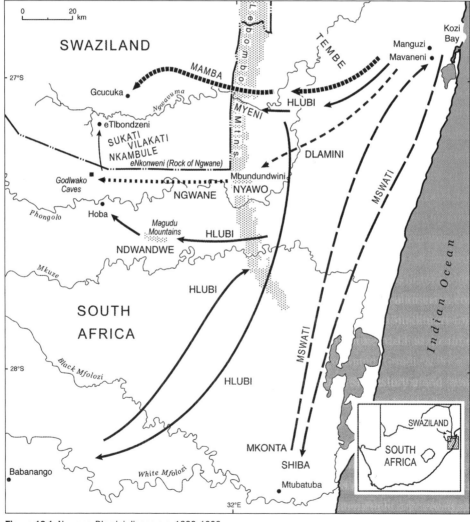

Figure 13.1 Ngwane-Dlamini diaspora c. 1680–1800.

further 200 years, and that renewed attention of both a focused and a comparative kind could now profitably be applied. Viewed against these other data and in comparative perspective, the Swazi state of the late 19th/early 20th century, no longer stands out as so distinctive and singular, but rather as representative, at least to some extent, of processes being reproduced over much of the subcontinent and at considerably earlier times. Indeed, the revisiting of the Swazi case, including a close historical/archaeological investigation of some of its key sites, could not only illuminate the early – and, more importantly, the prehistory of state formation in this broad east coast area, but also shed light on the nature, implications and fluxes of cultural hybridity and identity formation across a much broader geographical frame.

Two features of the potentially available data for the area of modern Swaziland – and an extensive swathe of country to the east, south and west – which make it stand out as a candidate for closer scrutiny are, firstly, the dearth of any archaeological studies of this part of the world in the period under consideration, and secondly, the exceptional richness of its oral historical traditions. This means that the latter can play an unusually important role in directing archaeological enquiry, both in the sense of guiding it towards the most significant sites and suggesting a set of questions or intellectual agenda for such investigations to pursue. What also appears to distinguish the area further – at least for Swaziland proper – is that these mainly unpublished collections of traditions continue to be relayed by word of mouth and to survive. This is significant because it allows us to explore current oral traditions, which have not entered into a public or documentary record, either because they have been too localised, or because they have lain partly dormant or latent and unrecognised by all but a local few – or because of a combination of both.

Archaeology and oral testimony

As Warren Perry (1996) notes, almost all archaeological research conducted in Swaziland has been concerned with the Stone Age. Some post-15th century Iron Age sites have been identified in the course of this research but none had – at the time of the writing of his thesis – been systematically surveyed or excavated (Goudie & Price-Williams 1983).

Perry's thesis sets out to correct this imbalance. In the end, however, it makes only a limited contribution to extending our empirical understanding of the later Iron Age in Swaziland, engaging rather in an extended contestation with what he terms 'the settler model' of pre- and post-Mfecane/Difaqane historical interpretation, and relying too uncritically on the work of Julian Cobbing. With regard to the smaller canvas of Swaziland itself, the results are somewhat thin and disappointing. The hoped-for insights of aerial photography scarcely materialised; excavation only proceeded at five sites, and then mostly by surface survey accompanied by a few one metre square and one half metre deep excavations. This process generated a small and preliminary body of data, which yielded few conclusions, and none to the questions which will be raised in this paper (despite eTibondzeni having been one of the sites examined) (Perry 1996: 122-157). Several of Perry's questions and approaches, it should be recognised, are innovative and potentially illuminating. Unfortunately, as he himself notes, research limitations prevented these from being adequately pursued (Perry 1996: 157).

Only one other Iron Age archaeological study of Swaziland has since been conducted, which was undertaken by Ohinata (2002). Here a systematic excavation was conducted at Simunye in the lowveld of northern Swaziland. This has strong potential interest for the issues raised in the 'northern' component of this paper, exploring as it does a Tsonga site which yielded dates of AD 1688-1730; 1811 (1899, 1918) 1939. What the relatively rich artefactual remains recovered from this site offer are a base point for comparison over the role of trade, and for cultural assimilation in this melting pot of a region. This unquestionably represents a promising beginning to the historical archaeology of this area, but one which needs systematic extension.

By contrast, some of the richest oral histories of any part of South Africa document Swaziland and its environs. This currently vibrant corpus of oral traditions remains uncontaminated and unconstrained by publication and invites further exploration/ exhumation. Here the very exercise of archaeological investigation may well stimulate the recollection and transmission of previously half-buried or at least largely localised and barely known traditions, so that archaeology could advance research into oral history, at the same time as oral history can help guide archaeological research. This marriage or harnessing together of the disciplines in the same locus of investigation thus offers the possibility of exciting, productive and possibly path-breaking research.

A further important methodological opening is also presented by combining oral history and archaeology in the area of Swaziland and its environs. Two of the areas/case studies selected for discussion in this paper are the site or the locus of partly silenced and partly suppressed oral histories; the first area, eTibondzeni in the south of modern Swaziland, is the site of the royal homestead of Hlubi, who was absorbed or conquered, by his Dlamini nephew Ngwane (i.e. the then 'Swazi' king) in the late 18th century (see below). This tradition was either deliberately or accidentally marginalised in published Swazi history, and only came to light during Carolyn Hamilton's enquiries into Swazi oral traditions in the early-mid-1980s. Its undoubted authenticity in this case makes it apparent that a very real possibility exists that other oral traditions remain latent, socially embedded but not publicly exposed, in other parts of South Africa and that fresh historical/archaeological enquiries may reactivate them and stimulate their transmission. The second site-case study examined-exhumed in this paper is that of Moyeni's branch of the Magagula in north central Swaziland. Here, Magagula oral traditions were collected and published by myself in the 1970s and early 1980s, so a degree of 'contamination' undoubtedly has occurred.[1] Subsequently, further collections of oral traditions undertaken for post-graduate studies by Thabani Twala, have revealed fresh and crucially significant traditions, which have further potential to guide archaeological enquiry, and to set a somewhat different intellectual agenda. These surfaced partly because they were tapped into by Thabani Twala – that is to say he made what has become an all too rare excursion into the local area to collect them – but partly because of changed political circumstances in modern Swaziland, which have prompted the Magagula to make new claims to an autonomous status as chiefs or kings in today's Swazi political order (Twala 2000: 11-24). These bear all the signs of having been latent or confined in Magagula society rather than being recently invented to meet the requirements of the time. Again, the combination of previously collected traditions; newly gathered traditions; and archaeological enquiry, offers us challenging possibilities that advance our understanding of the last several hundred years.

Such an investigation, and such an approach may well have much wider application than within the borders of Swaziland itself. All over South Africa 'new' oral traditions are now surfacing, mainly in the context of land claims litigation. The most important question that arises in this regard, for both oral historians and archaeologists, is how much have they been fabricated, and if so, out of what? One striking example of the restimulation of oral histories in this context is that of the Ngomane of Hoyi, situated just to the north of modern Swaziland. This group, apparently originally related to the Magagula, claimed once to have held sway over much of the southern section of the Kruger Park, over which they have recently tabled a land claim. A close examination of past and present oral traditions of the Ngomane combined with archaeological investigations, for which the two previous case studies mentioned could be used as a control, promise to open up new methodological perspectives in a combined oral history/archaeology which might be of value country-wide, as well as serving the more limited purpose of illuminating the pre-history and early history of what used to be called state formation in this area, and hence on the tortured issue of the construction of present identities.

The discussion that follows falls into two parts. The first considers the oral history and potential archaeological sites in the early Swazi (or more accurately Ngwane) Kingdom, and hence the pre- and early history of state formation in this area. The second examines the oral history and potential sites of antecedent chiefdoms to the Swazi in central, north and further to the north and west of present Swaziland, with a view to apprehending other, equally deep, vectors of flux and political and identity formation in the region.

Early Ngwane traditions

Thirty plus years ago, when I was carrying out my research on the 19th-century Swazi state, my fellow graduate student, David Hedges, was undertaking a similar exercise for the 18th century and even before in the broad northern Nguni area (Swaziland mainly excluded). Hedges (1978) traced the processes of social reconstruction in the area back to at least the 16th century. Substantial chiefdoms, he showed, existed in northern Zululand and southern Mozambique from the mid-16th century on. Impetus for political transformation was drawn from regional ecological complementarities between, for example, the wetter coast and the dryer uplands which promoted inter-regional trade and the demands of larger-scale processes of production like hunting and burning which required the co-ordination of larger bodies of manpower than the pre-existing lineages could provide. Both of these activities, he contended, elevated dominant lineages into positions of authority in more broadly based political structures. Superimposed on these endogenous forces, was the ivory and cattle trade to Delagoa Bay which boomed to new heights from 1750 on. Between them, these factors (to which, in my own work, I added drought) gave rise to the late 18th-century northern Nguni states (Hedges 1978; Bonner 1983).

Hedges built his argument mainly on Portuguese sources and the then unpublished Stuart papers. Swazi oral traditions collected at more or less the same time by myself in southern Swaziland and by Carolyn Hamilton in the 1980s, greatly amplify, refine and in some senses alter the outline that Hedges sketched out. The material collected by Hamilton, in particular, and her role in the transcription, translation and editing of these, provides a large part of the material on which this paper is based. She could be (but may not want to be) considered as its absent author or ghost writer. What these traditions reveal is a much broader swirl of movement in this area reaching back much further in time than Hedges could document and than I could imagine. The story, as disclosed by these traditions, starts north of Delagoa Bay sometime in the 17th century. Thereafter, the oral traditions of several Swazi sub-groups offer suggestive leads to the prehistory of state formation (or political aggregation) in this area. Oral testimony furnished by Simbimba Ndlela, for example, suggests that an early chief of the Dlamini (subsequently the royal Swazi lineage), named Mswati, had ventured as far south as the region of Mtubatuba in today's northern KwaZulu-Natal. A rough reckoning by generations (back from Dlamini, alias Sidwabasiluthuli, who ruled at around 1750) suggests that Mswati held power in the late 1600s. The recollection of Mtubatuba persists largely because survivors of the Mkhonta and Shiba lineages lived at this point in the area of Mtubatuba, the Shiba furnishing Mswati's son Ludvonga with his chief wife and co-wife.[2] According to the account provided by Simbimba Ndlela, which is the richest and fullest that describes these events, Mswati learnt that the then ruling Zulu

King was about to attack him and force him to reveal the secrets of the annual *incwala* (first fruits) ceremony. The attribution of the identity of Zulu to this king is anachronistic as the event long pre-dates the Zulu rise to power in the region, while the name later given in the testimony to this figure (or, by one reading, the person who warned Mswati) Langa Mkatshwa, strongly suggests that it was the father or grandfather of Shaka Zulu's great rival Zwide who was contemplating (or providing advance warning of) the deed.

GENEALOGY I

EARLY NGWANE/SWAZI ROYAL GENEALOGY

Mswati

(c. 1670)

Ludvonga

Hlubi	Dambuza	Mamba
(married to	(alias Dlamini	
Lomakhetfo)	alias Sidwabasiluthuli	
	married to LaYaka, alias	
Ndlela	LaMuguni)	

Ngwane

Ndvungunye

Sobhuza

(alias Sumholo)

(died 1838)

Upon receiving this news, Mswati decamped to the former abode of the Ngwane people in the coastal area further north. Skirting the Lebombo he proceeded to Mavaneni, in the area of Ngogweni at Mangwanazi close to Kosi Bay.[3] Here Ludvonga succeeded Mswati. Ludvonga then sired Hlubi, Dambuza (later named Dlamini) and Mamba. A split or succession dispute followed (highly embellished in the oral traditions) at which point Hlubi and Mamba departed travelling along and across the Lebombo mountains through the Ngwavuma gorge. Hlubi, who appears to have been still young, grew up at Vuma in the present Myeni territory (named Ndabeni/Mangwazane) where Hlubi's son and heir Ndlela[4] was born. The name of one of Ludvonga's wives Lomakhetfo who was the mother of Hlubi, is remembered in both the Shiba and Ndlela traditions (though with one disagreement) adding some sense of veracity to the account.[5] Hlubi some time thereafter retraced his grandfather Mswati's footsteps back south, reaching as far as the Mkhuze river (the Shiba testimony records/claims that the Ngwane ruled between Mavaneni and Mkhuze). Shiba traditions also offer some confirmation to this movement, asserting that the Shiba were now compelled to *khonta* (render submission) to Hlubi.[6] One Mkhonta tradition records their chief encountering Dingiswayo and Yaka (of the Ndwandwe), which appears to have induced them to wish to return to their own homeland of Manyiseni in the vicinity of Delagoa Bay. As they returned, however, they too collided and fought with Hlubi (who 'was then quarrelling over the kingship with the people of Ngwane').[7] According to Sam Mkhonta, 'We met Hlubi at Babanango. They were heading towards the Thukela.' With his forces now apparently augmented by new Shiba and other adherents, Hlubi was about to meet his match. In a bloody fight on the Mkhuze River with 'the Zulu' (presumably the Ndwandwe) recorded in Hlubi's praises as 'He who stained the Mkhuze red with blood', Hlubi was vanquished and together with the Shiba fled west to Magudu hill, a site at this time apparently not being occupied by the more formidable Ndwandwe, the centre of their kingdom having drifted further south.[8] How long Hlubi stayed at Magudu Hill is unclear, but at some time in this period he is supposed to have rescued his brother Dlamini who had continued to rule over the Ngwane near Kosi Bay, after the latter had been driven south to 'Ntungwa' (i.e. towards later Zululand) by another (possibly Tsonga) group from Manguza in Southern Mozambique. This mission Hlubi carried out with the aid of Mamba (his and Dlamini's third half-brother) who had been long settled at Gcucuka in Southern Swaziland (where there were caves). Together they brought Dlamini back to Mbundundwini, on the west side of the Lebombo mountains where the Nyawo chiefdom was later based. There Dlamini remained, until he died, interestingly, of smallpox.[9] From Magudu, Hlubi subsequently headed north to Hoba, on the south side of the Phongola River, and then by subterfuge to eTibondzeni, which lay on the north side of the river, where they subdued and incorporated the Sotho chiefdoms of Nkambule, Sukati and Vilakazi (the latter Nguni?).[10]

This chronicle of Hlubi is unknown in the published Swazi archive (apart from a School Primer based on oral traditions compiled by Carolyn Hamilton (1990: 60-62)), yet he and his group were clearly of pivotal influence in this period, and a key actor in what may be termed the prehistory of state formation in this area. The traditions which testify to his odyssey and activities also clarify a number of obscure and fragmented allusions elsewhere in the oral record which also attest to their antiquity – notably James Stuart's cryptic question to himself (in turn to be addressed to one of his interviewees): 'Ndlela (i.e. Hlubi's son) built at Mahamba – not known if Ndlela's existence caused Dlamini to live on or near Lebombo.'[11]

Dlamini, who remained on the Lebombo until his death, had taken as his chief wife, a daughter of the Ndwandwe King Yaka (alias Langa). The son and heir born to this marriage was Ngwane. After Dlamini's death Ngwane and the bulk of his people (including the Mkhonta) descended the Lebombo. Some disagreement exists in the literature as to where Ngwane subsequently settled. One group of sources suggest he moved west along the northern banks of the Phongola River before pushing out feelers south of the river to the area of Magudu (Bonner 1983: 12), but a spread of oral traditions, previously largely unknown (at least to a wider public), until the Swaziland Oral History Project started to collect them in the early 1980s, attest in a fairly conclusive fashion that he now crossed the Phongola River and settled, like Hlubi before him, at Magudu. Phuhlaphi Ndzibandze, for example, records that Ngwane crossed the Phongola River to Magudu which area he found 'densely populated', so he moved north to build at Nkokweni, a mountain near the rock of Ngwane just north of the Pongola River.[12] There is some indication that his move back across the Phongola was precipitated by an attack by the Ndwandwe, and that he may briefly have retreated to the Lebombo, before settling at Nkokweni.[13]

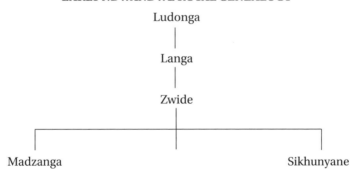

GENEALOGY II
EARLY NDWANDWE ROYAL GENEALOGY

Ludonga

Langa

Zwide

Madzanga   Sikhunyane

Three details, encapsulated in two oral traditions relating to this time, may well be significant. Firstly Ngwane left behind his mother, LaMnguni, on the Lebombo.[14] Secondly, as the Mkhonta recount, 'When we crossed with Ngwane all the ambabuthfo zund'ad' (an Ntungwa/Zulu linguistical trait). Thirdly 'when we first came here everybody would hide in the mountain'.[15] Two deafening silences in the oral record also insistently demand our attention. Neither the Ndlela nor Mamba traditions provide any detail about how they were conquered or absorbed by Ngwane. All we can see or infer is that Ngwane, in ways which remained unclear, absorbed all these heterogeneous pre-state nuclei, constructing in the process the core of the Ngwane Swazi kingdom/state.

What clues and research agenda may all this suggest for the historical archaeologist? Firstly, these oral testimonies, despite their silences and occlusions, provide us with a much deeper and more detailed prehistory of state formation (or the later phases of political aggregation) than were previously known to or registered by archaeologists and historians. Secondly, the traditions pinpoint a number of key sites of settlement (e.g. eTibondzeni). If dug, the evidence of material culture, size, layout and so on could add immeasurably to outline information furnished by the as yet unpublished traditions. Thirdly the testimonies, along with documentary evidence previously cited, suggest the strong possibility that competition for trade underlay these cycles of conflict, one epicentre of which was the elusive Mavaneni. Presumably archaeological investigation of the area inland of Kosi Bay would offer the opportunity of unlocking some of these secrets. Finally, the oral traditions suggest high degrees of heterogeneity among the proto-Swazi group, as they incorporated groups of diverse types, and also offer suggestions of a possible chronology/sequence of such mixing. What they fail to tell us, however, is anything about the character and dynamics of the cultural/political mixing that occurred. Their main value in this context is that they precisely pinpoint *where* it happened. What they promise therefore, is to offer guidance as to where to direct archaeological investigations. In turn the archaeological evidence would probably suggest ways of interrogating the oral record further, or even further questions to address to its surviving repositories.

The oral record and the scope for historical archaeology further north

A second zone of political aggregation and territorial conflict was the area in the north, as well as to the north and west, of today's Swaziland. Here a cluster of genealogically related chiefdoms held sway comprising the various offshoots of the Magagula and Ngomane. Up to the irruption of the Ngwane (later known as the Swazi) under Sobhuza I (or Somhlolo) in central-north Swaziland (north of the Lusuthfo River) in c. 1820, the Magagula had been the dominant political force in this area (Bonner 1983: 30-31). One of the larger and perhaps the most powerful of these Magagula groups, so its oral traditions tell us, had begun an eastward movement from the highveld from a point of origin known as Tshemilembule (later a police station on the Breyton railway bus road, probably a little south and east of Carolina), three to four generations earlier [80-90 years?] which would place this movement around 1740. (The basis of this computation is obviously critical).[16]

Departing under the leadership of Nyandza they seem to have moved fairly directly and

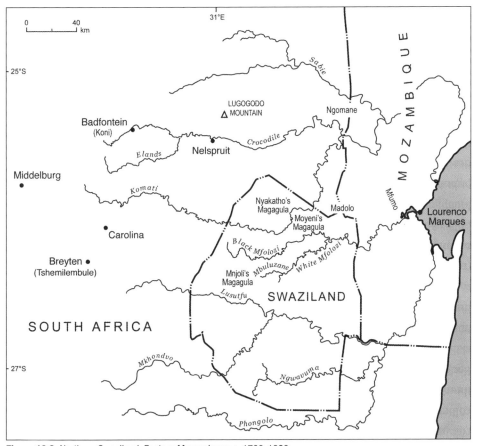

Figure 13.2 Northern Swaziland, Eastern Mpumalanga c. 1700-1820.

swiftly into today's northern Swaziland in the vicinity of the Komati River, possibly hinting at a course of movement east down the Komati River. The senior section (the Nyakatho) then split under Magodongo (or after his death), out of which emerged the newly dominant section led by Moyeni, who settled in the eBulandzeni area.[17] A third sub-section of the Magagula who faced Sobhuza's Ngwane as they colonised central Swaziland, was that led by Mnjoli, who was based on the Mdzimba mountains at a village known as LaNcabane.[18] Mnjoli and Moyeni are said in the traditions to be half-brothers, but the genealogies of the two sections do not appear to bear this out.[19] Mnjoli's section nevertheless seems likewise to have originated in the highveld of the old Transvaal, and 'came down to this place from the Sotho in the West'. The chronology of this move, moreover, almost exactly parallels that of the Nyakatho section, having begun under Zubuku, three generations before Mnjoli (who is described as being old and rheumatic at the time of Sobhuza's arrival in the Mdzimba mountains of central Swaziland).[20]

GENEALOGY III

MAGAGULA

CHIEFLY/ROYAL GENEALOGY

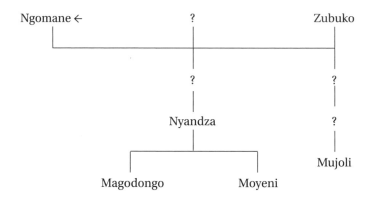

A similar point, and possibly even trigger of movement in the second quarter of the 18th century to that of the other branch just discussed could thus be suggested. Finally, the Ngomane chiefdoms lying presently to the north of today's Swaziland are also claimed to be of the same stock to the Magagula – by both main branches of the Magagula.[21] In the Magagula traditions the division is said to have occurred a generation before Sobhuza's conquest of the Magagula.[22] This calculation is dubious. Ngomane genealogies published in the 1920s and 1950s suggest a lengthy, independent, or at least separate history of the Ngomane, who nevertheless appear related in some way to the Magagula (Myburgh 1949).[23]

The three Ngomane chiefdoms today are minuscule and, in numerical terms, insignificant (Myburgh 1949). It is all too easy for them to be bypassed by the historian and written off. Yet in the pre-Sobhuza, and as some would have it – in the pre-Difaqane period, they were a significant and powerful force on the landscape. Like Magagula, the Ngomane claim a westward point of origin. Describing themselves as vaSika (from the Tsonga verb *sika*, to descend) they claim to have come down from the mountains leaving the Sotho behind (Myburgh 1949: 106). Their peregrinations through this period are confusing. An early place of residence was Mugogodo Mountain, near White River. Later the chiefdom moved to the Middelburg district in possibly the mid-18th century (Myburgh 1949). One problem rendering the deciphering of the sequence and direction of their movements difficult, is conflicting genealogies.

GENEALOGY IV
NGOMANE CHIEFLY GENEALOGY

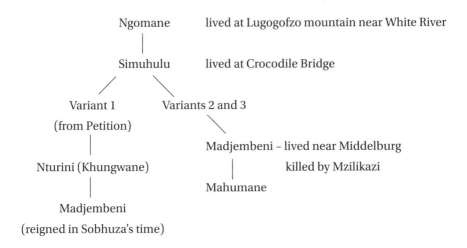

Ngomane   lived at Lugogofzo mountain near White River

Simuhulu   lived at Crocodile Bridge

Variant 1   Variants 2 and 3
(from Petition)

Madjembeni – lived near Middelburg

Nturini (Khungwane)   killed by Mzilikazi

Mahumane

Madjembeni
(reigned in Sobhuza's time)

What is evident when comparing the various versions of these is that a major disruption occurred in the reign of Madjembeni at which point several of the Ngomane subgroups appear to have split away. According to A.C. Myburgh's interviewees, Madjembeni lived in the Middelburg district and the chiefdom consisted of vaMbayi. According to the same tradition Mzilikazi, fleeing west, attacked them, killing Madjembeni and caused the Ngomane to take refuge near Nelspruit (Myburgh 1949: 106-108 and esp. 117-119, 125-7). A familiar feature of accounts of disruptive invasions in the oral histories of several groups in this area is to blame Mzilikazi, when in fact any alien group could have been responsible (see Delius (1983: 19-24) regarding Zwide and the Pedi). It seems perfectly credible therefore that the flight of the Ngomane from the highveld could have occurred considerably earlier than the Difaqane, and that it could conceivably have been triggered by the clash between the Pedi and the neighbouring Koni group, the Kgomane, then apparently living in the Lydenburg, Badfontein area which they date to about 1740-50 (Delius & Schoeman, this volume).

All this is highly speculative and tenuous. The linking of the Kgomane to the Ngomane is even more so. Ultimately all they have in common is a similar name. What may be better founded, however, is that much of the various Koni groups' power and prosperity in the 18th century was connected to control over the trade routes into the interior, and the escarpment, following the Sabie, Crocodile, Elands and Komati valleys. All of the Magagula/Ngomane groups originated/sojourned in this area. Conflict in each case drove them east, apparently down the river valleys, until they eventually came to rest in the middleveld/

lowveld. Ngomane traditions of the late 18th century seem to indicate a large-scale, powerful, probably trading polity sitting astride the Komati/Crocodile valleys. Ngomane land claims in the 1960s, for example, embraced the Kruger National Park Reserve from the Komati to the Sabie, and took in a large swathe of Portuguese territory (Myburgh 1949: 105). All of the river valleys they and the Magagula controlled extended west to the escarpment, to the Koni, the Pedi and other trading polities. Magagula traditions moreover recall the early 19th century Magagula king, Mnjoli, hunting buffalo and elephants with muskets in their favoured hunting grounds around Mliba hill. When dying, elephants were made to fall towards the west to denote the point of origin of the Magagula.[24] The Moyeni branch, moreover, appear to have had an intimate link to the chiefdoms adjacent to the Portuguese fort at Lourenço Marques. Traditions from the Moyeni section recall Moyeni being smuggled away as a young boy after his father had died because some councillors feared the regent Ngwanga would kill him. According to this tradition the young boy now took refuge among 'The Sotho'.[25] Later, so the Mnjoli section's tradition records, when besieged by Sobhuza I's Ngwane, he descended the mountain and found the army asleep. He then jumped over the warriors to escape to Mfuna. Mfuna was the Tsonga trading chiefdom closest to the Portuguese port of Lourenço Marques.[26] The Moyeni section's traditions recall a similar escape, Moyeni evading the Swazi armies and 'burrowing under the grass until he rose at Madolo – hence his praises "Sigelodla singa Maguphane"'.[27] Madolo was another chiefdom immediately adjacent to Lourenço Marques. Both chiefdoms oscillated between semi-client status and conflict with the Portuguese, usually over questions of trade (Hedges 1978). An additional important detail contained in the Mnjoli section's tradition is that Moyeni escaped to his children in Mfumo, whom he had sired while in exile, although in this instance the circumstances of the exile were different (he had fled a Zulu attack which both sub-sections record as preceding the invasion of Sobhuza I).[28]

One final fragment of oral information collected by the missionary Nachtigal in the late 19th century from 'an old follower of Saptoba' (Sobhuza) provides more evidence of tight trading linkages to the west. According to this, Moyeni fought with Sobhuza after refusing to surrender a refugee son of Zwide (the old Ndwandwe king) following the defeat of Sikhunyane Ndwandwe (Zwide's heir) by Shaka (i.e. about 1826) and had only been able to compel him to do so after he had secured the help of Portuguese riflemen from Delagoa Bay (see Genealogy II).[29]

The foregoing provisional analysis of the oral data offers both a framework question/hypothesis for historical archaeological investigation, as well as pointing to potential sites and locations. The hypothesis is that trading relations of considerable scale and intensity extended along river valleys westwards from Lourenço Marques to the interior, and that these may have generated middle ranking chiefdoms which served both as an initial brake on, and then a building block of the later Ngwane phase of state formation. The sites through which this hypothesis can be explored, are multiple. Moyeni's capital and site of burial (Mawulwane) are known,[30] as is the site of Mnjoli's capital LaNcabane.[31] Even the search for Tshemilembule might be worthwhile. Likewise several early Ngomane sites are identified in the oral traditions (Myburgh 1949). Of more general significance, the Ngomane assert that in the late 18th century they 'gradually became Shangaan' (Myburgh 1949: 108). Similarly, the Magagula were incorporated within the Swazi kingdom in two phases, first under Sobhuza and second under Mswati II. The first, so the traditions indicate, was partial and incomplete; the second more comprehensive. It was now, the traditions record, that Moyeni's Magagula abandoned their dialect of Sesotho and began to speak Seswati. Could these examples not also offer further possible insights on hybridity and a calibration of assimilation, which might be compared to other partly analogous situations? At the very least the archaeology would significantly augment and problematise the oral traditions generating fresh hypotheses and conclusions.

Conclusion

A huge stretch of territory extending from the Pongola River to Kosi Bay, in the east, the Crocodile River in the north and Breyten–Middleburg area in the west appears, from the available published and often unpublished oral traditions, to be the site of intensive trade, frequent movement, constant mixing and of embryonic state formation from at least 1700 on. These oral traditions identify sites, rulers, and the identities of key historical groups at the time. The traditions raise a variety of questions which they themselves cannot answer. Archaeological investigations, when guided and informed by the traditions, may well be able to provide at least some of the answers to the questions the traditions raise. Unhappily, at present, almost no archaeology of this kind has been undertaken. Archaeological investigations may also help render active latent, localised oral traditions, of the sort that seem to be presently activated by land claims across much of South Africa. Further, the combination of neglected oral traditions together with archaeological enquiries in the three or four broad zones/epochs discussed in this paper could conceivably offer a kind of control for combined historical/archaeological studies which might be conducted elsewhere.

Notes

1 In 1999 I was requested by my Honours student Thabani Twala to accompany him to the Magagula chiefly homestead in north-western Swaziland. He was collecting oral testimonies there, and the young chief had insisted on seeing me before Thabani could be allowed to proceed any further. I agreed,

and subsequently attended a meeting with the chief and his assembled elders at the foot of Moyenis mountain. The chief introduced us to his councillors, including Mankwempe Magagula, who he noted, I had interviewed over 30 years before. He then drew out a copy of my book *Kings, Commoners and Concessionaires*, fixed upon one passage where I had written that Sobhuza had ultimately conquered Moyeni, that Moyeni had fled, and had subsequently returned khonta (tender allegiance) to Sobhuza. He then turned to the end note which provided the source of the information, which was none other than the unfortunate Mankwempe Magagula whom he had reintroduced me to earlier. He then turned to the somewhat embarrassed Mankwempe, and asserted 'He wants to retract his statement.'

2 O.T. Sam Mkhonta, interviewed by Carolyn Hamilton and Henry Hlahlamelo Dlamini, Swaziland; O.T. Simbimba Ndlela, 4 September 1983, interviewed by Prince Mahlaba Dlamini, Isaac Dlamini, Maboya Fakudze, Embo State House, Swaziland, 1982; Simbimba Ndlela interviewed by Carolyn Hamilton and Henry `Hlahlamelo' Dlamini, eTibondzeni, 27 July 1983; O.T. Msila Shiba, Jabulani Dlamini.
3 See also O.T. Maboya Fakudze interviewed by P. Bonner and Prince Magangeni Dlamini 23 May - 10 June 1970, Lobamba, Swaziland.
4 O.T. Phuhlaphi Nzibande interviewed by Carolyn Hamilton and Henry Dlamini, Swaziland 1983.
5 O.T. Msila Shiba.
6 O.T. Msila Shiba.
7 O.T. Sam Mkhonta.
8 O.T. Msila Shiba.
9 O.T. Phuhlaphi Nzibandze, James Matsebula interviewed at Lobamba royal homestead 1967.
10 O.T Simbimba Ndlela.
11 J. Stuart Papers: testimony John Gama, 18 December 1898.
12 O.T. Phuhlaphi Ndzibanze; *see* O.T. Mandlambovu Fakudze; Mgodwa Masange; Mbali Hlophe, Jabulani Dlamini, Sam Mkhontu and Tigodvo Hlophe.
13 O.T. Phuhlaphi Sibandze.
14 O.T. J. Matsebula
15 O.T. Sam Mkhonta.
16 O.T. Mankwempe Magagula, Mevane Magagula, Mcedzane Magagula, Mmemo Masilela, 21 June 1970, Mandlangampisi, Swaziland.
17 Ibid; O.T. Mbhuduya Magagula, Ganda Magagula, Singugu Magagula, Mavelebaleni Ginindza, 20 December 1971, Dvokolwako, Swaziland.
18 O.T. Mlhuduya Magagula.
19 Ibid; O.T. Mankwempe Magagula, interview Magida Magagula, 11 June 1970, Nkambeni, Swaziland. O.T. Phica Magugula, 19 April 1970, Kutsimuleni, Swaziland.
20 O.T. Mbhuduya Magagula.
21 ibid; O.T. Makwempe Magagula; O.T. Magida Magagula.
22 O.T. Mbhuduya Magagula; O.T. Makwempe Magagula.
23 *See* Myburgh 1949 pp. 105-9, for the Ngomane of Nkapana (Hoyi), pp. 117-119 for the Ngomane of Npapana (Siboshwa) and pp. 125-127 for the Ngomane of Nkapana (Lugedlane).
24 O.T. Mbhuduya Magagula.
25 O.T. Madwenpe Magagula.
26 O.T. Mbhuduya Magagula.
27 O.T. Mankwempe Magagula.
28 O.T. Mbhuduya Magagula.
29 University of South Africa Library, Pretoria, Nachtigal A., 'Das Tagebuch des Missionarn' typescript, 4 volumes, Volume 3, p. 382.
30 O.T. Mankwempe Magagula.
31 O.T. Mbhuduya Magagula.

References

Boeyens, J.C.A. 2003. The Later Iron Age sequence in the Marico and early Tswana history. *The South African Archaeological Bulletin* 58: 63-78.

Bonner, P. 1983. *Kings, Commoners and Concessionaires: The Evolution and Dissolution of the Nineteenth-Century Swazi State*. Cambridge: Cambridge University Press.

Delius, P. 1983. *The Land Belongs to Us*. Johannesburg: Ravan.

Goudie, A.S. & Price-Williams, C. 1983. *The Atlas of Swaziland*. Lobamba: The Swaziland National Trust Commission.

Hall, S. 1998. A consideration of gender relations in the Late Iron Age 'Sotho' sequence of the Western Highveld, South Africa. In: Kent, S. (ed.) *Gender in African Pre-History*: 235-260. London: Rowman/Altamira Press.

Hamilton, C.A. 1985. Ideology, oral traditions and the struggle for power in the early Zulu Kingdom. Unpublished MA dissertation. Johannesburg: University of the Witwatersrand.

Hamilton, C. (ed.). 1990. *In Pursuit of Swaziland's Pre-colonial Past: Eulandza Umlandvo*. Manzini, Swaziland: Macmillan Boleswa.

Hedges, D.W. 1978. Trade and politics in southern Mozambique and Zululand in the eighteenth and early nineteenth centuries. Unpublished PhD Thesis. London: University of London.

Kuper, H. 1947. *An African Aristocracy: Rank Among the Swazi*. London: Oxford University Press.

Lekgoathi, S.P. 2004. The Native Affairs Department, Anthropology and the the making and bifurcation of the Transvaal Ndebele. Unpublished paper.

Loubser, J.H.N. 1981. Ndebele archaeology of the Pietersburg area. Unpublished MA dissertation. Johannesburg: University of the Witwatersrand.

Loubser, J.H.N. 1988. Archaeological contributions to Venda ethno-history, Unpublished PhD dissertation. Johannesburg: University of the Witwatersrand.

Makhura, T.J. 1993. The Bagananwa polity in the North Western Transvaal and the SAR c. 1836-1896. Unpublished MA dissertation. South Africa: University of Bophuthatswana.

Marwick, B.A. 1940. *The Swazi*. London: Cambridge Univesity Press.

Matsebula, J.S.M. 1972. *A History of Swaziland*. Cape Town: Longman.

Myburgh, A.C. 1949. *The Tribes of the Barberton District*. Union of South Africa, Department of Native Affairs, Ethnological Publications No. 25, Pretoria.

Ohinata, F. 2002. The beginning of 'Tsonga' archaeology: excavations at Simunye, north-eastern Swaziland. *South African Humanities* 14.

Perry, W.R. 1996. Archaeology of the Mfecane/Difaqane: transformations in post fifteenth century Southern Africa. Unpublished PhD dissertation, City University, New York.

Pistorius, J.C. 1992. *Molokwane, An Iron Age Bakwena Village*. Johannesburg: Perskor Printers.

Schoeman, M.M. 1997. The Ndzundza archaeology of the Steelpoort River Valley. Unpublished MA dissertation, University of the Witwatersrand, Johannesburg.

Twala, T. 2000. The politics of placing in historical and contemporary Swaziland: the Magagula case. Unpublished Honours dissertation. Johannesburg: University of the Witwatersrand.

Wright, J.B. 1989. The dynamics of power and conflict in the Thukela-Mzimkhulu region in the late 18th and early 19th centuries: a critical reconstruction. Unpublished PhD dissertation. Johannesburg: University of the Witwatersrand.

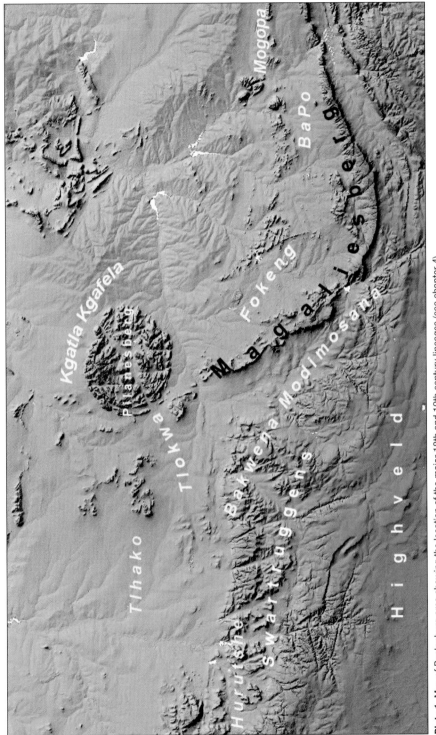

Plate 1 Map of Rustenburg area showing the location of the major 18th and 19th century lineages (see chapter 4).

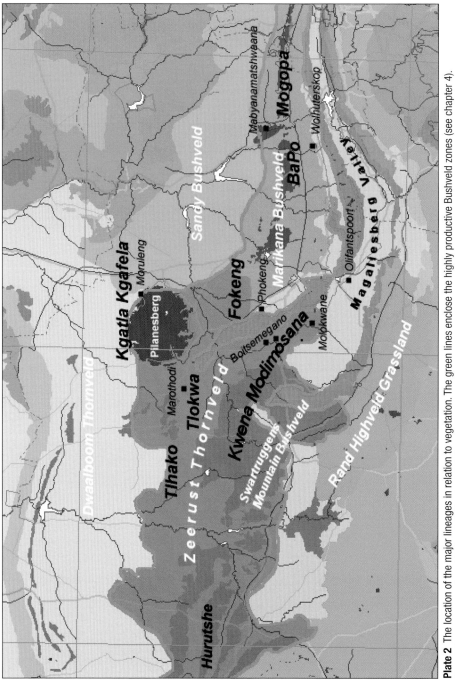

Plate 2 The location of the major lineages in relation to vegetation. The green lines enclose the highly productive Bushveld zones (see chapter 4). (Vegetation base map from Mucina & Rutherford 2006)

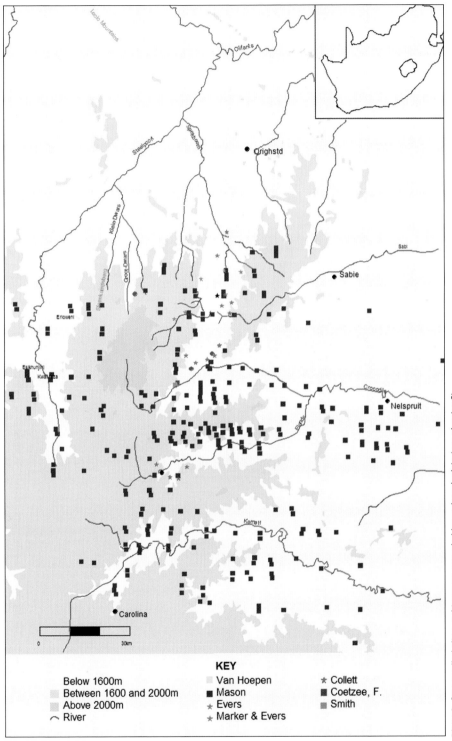

Plate 3 Stonewalled sites and terraces recorded by archaeologists (see chapter 8).

KEY

Below 1600m	Van Hoepen	★ Collett
Between 1600 and 2000m	■ Mason	■ Coetzee, F.
Above 2000m	★ Evers	■ Smith
∼ River	★ Marker & Evers	

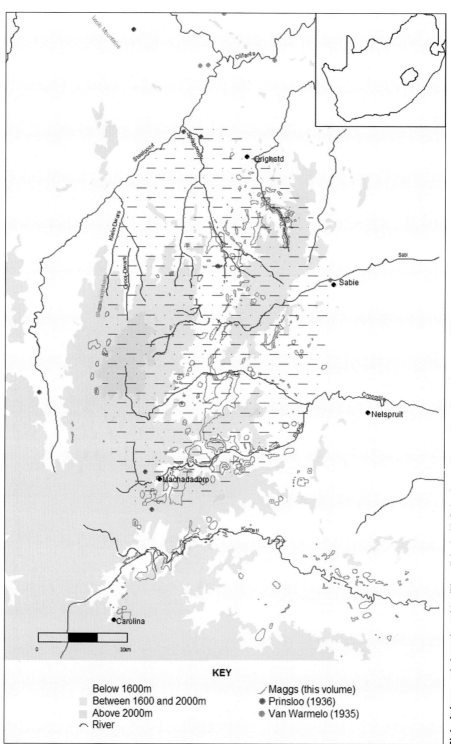

KEY

Below 1600m
Between 1600 and 2000m
Above 2000m
∼ River

╱ Maggs (this volume)
● Prinsloo (1936)
● Van Warmelo (1935)

Plate 4 Areas and places in oral traditions linked with Bokoni superimposed on Maggs (see page 171).

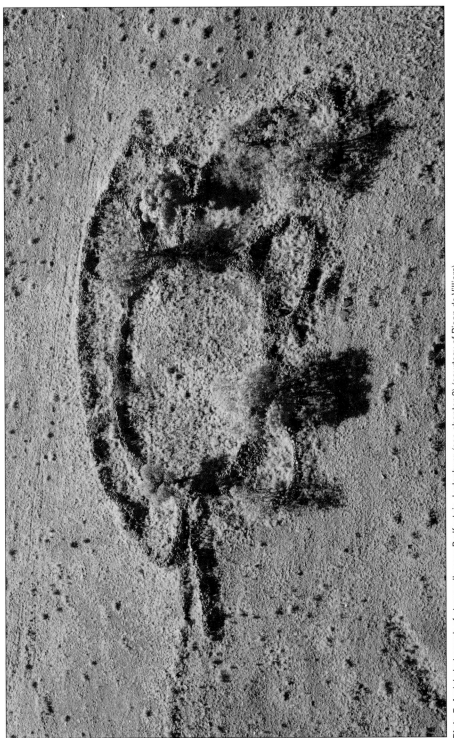

Plate 5 Aerial photograph of stonewalls near Badfontein, Lydenburg (see chapter 8) (courtesy of Riaan de Villiers).

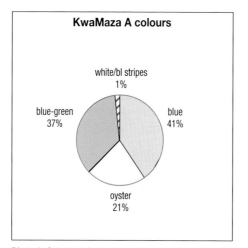

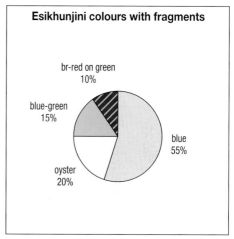

Plate 6 Colour preferences – KwaMaza (n=71) and Esikhunjini (n=10) (see chapter 10).

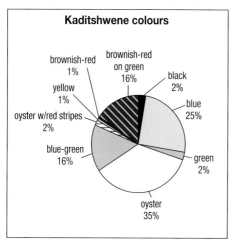

Plate 7 Colour preferences – Kaditshwene (n=129).

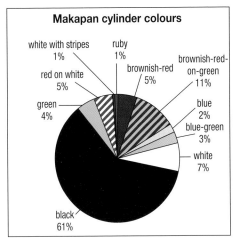

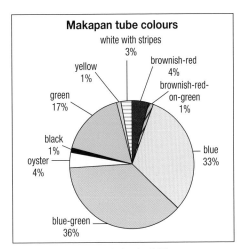

Plate 8 Colour preferences – Makapan Historic Cave cylinder/oblate (n=179) and tubular (n=340).

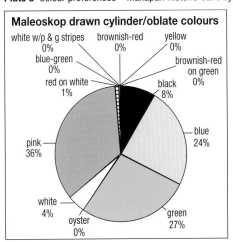

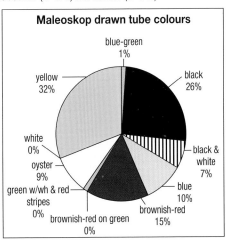

Plate 9 Colour preferences – Maleoskop cylinder/oblate (n=3785) and tubular (n=448).

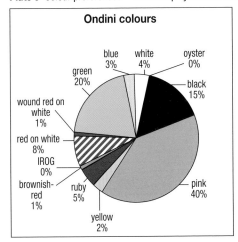

Plate 10 Colour preferences – Ondini (n=8923)

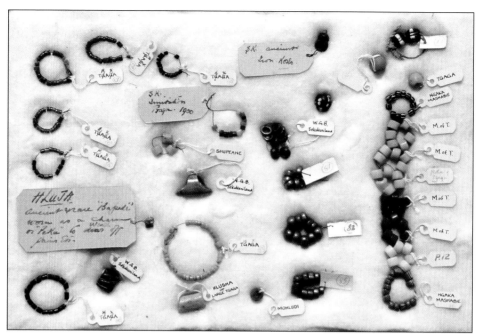

Plate 11 Pedi beads, Van Riet Lowe collection, University of the Witwatersrand (see chapter 10).

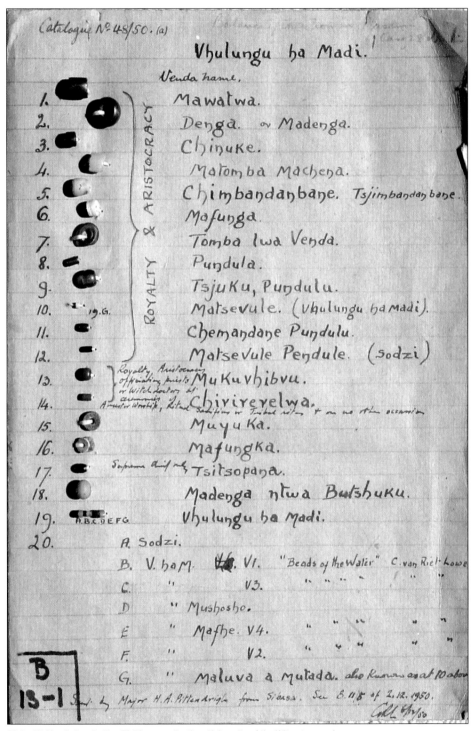

Plate 12 Venda beads, Van Riet Lowe collection, University of the Witwatersrand.

Plate 13 Mgungundlovu beads, Van Riet Lowe collection, University of the Witwatersrand.

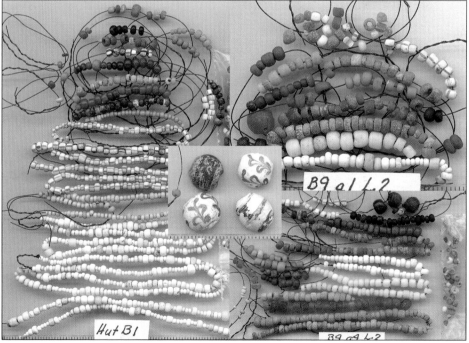

Plate 14 Mgungundlovu beads.

Plate 15 Mgungundlovu beads, Van Riet Lowe collection, University of the Witwatersrand.

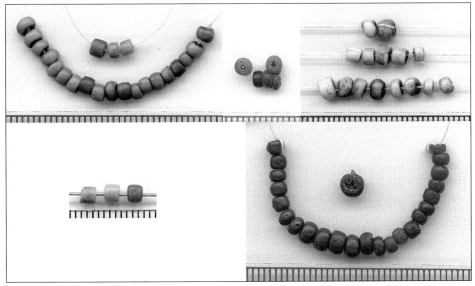

Plate 16 KwaMaza beads (brownish-red beads at lower right are actually blue-green like the others – they changed colour when burned in a fire).

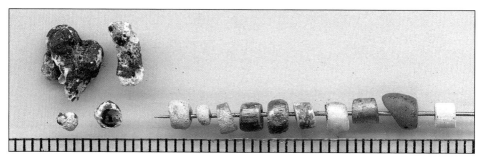

Plate 17 Esikhunjini beads.

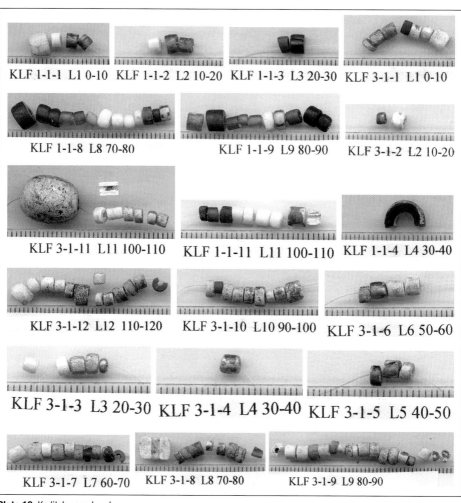

KLF 1-1-1 L1 0-10   KLF 1-1-2 L2 10-20   KLF 1-1-3 L3 20-30   KLF 3-1-1 L1 0-10

KLF 1-1-8 L8 70-80   KLF 1-1-9 L9 80-90   KLF 3-1-2 L2 10-20

KLF 3-1-11 L11 100-110   KLF 1-1-11 L11 100-110   KLF 1-1-4 L4 30-40

KLF 3-1-12 L12 110-120   KLF 3-1-10 L10 90-100   KLF 3-1-6 L6 50-60

KLF 3-1-3 L3 20-30   KLF 3-1-4 L4 30-40   KLF 3-1-5 L5 40-50

KLF 3-1-7 L7 60-70   KLF 3-1-8 L8 70-80   KLF 3-1-9 L9 80-90

Plate 18 Kaditshwene beads.

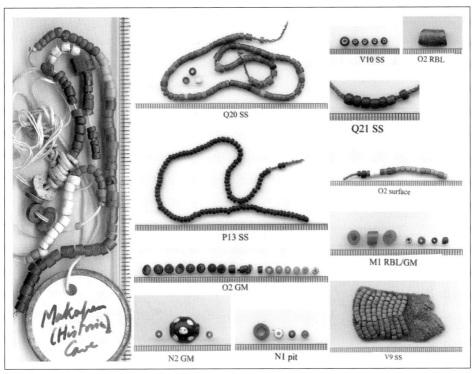

Plate 19 Makapan Historic Cave beads.

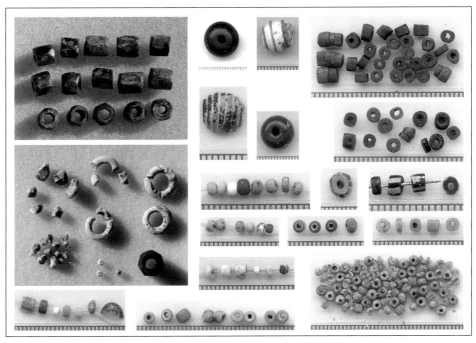

Plate 20 Maleoskop beads.

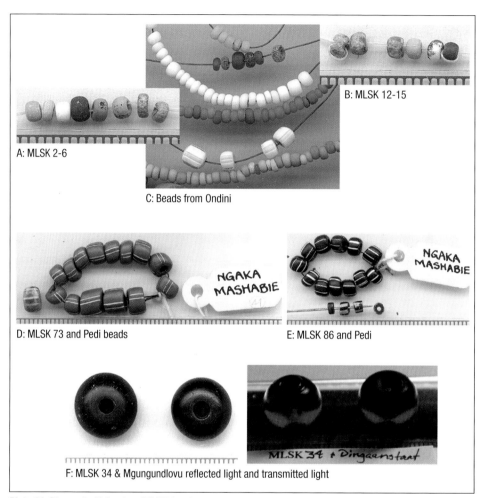

A: MLSK 2-6

B: MLSK 12-15

C: Beads from Ondini

D: MLSK 73 and Pedi beads

E: MLSK 86 and Pedi

F: MLSK 34 & Mgungundlovu reflected light and transmitted light

Plate 21 Diagnostic Maleoskop (MLSK) beads.

Plate 22 The Makapans Valley.

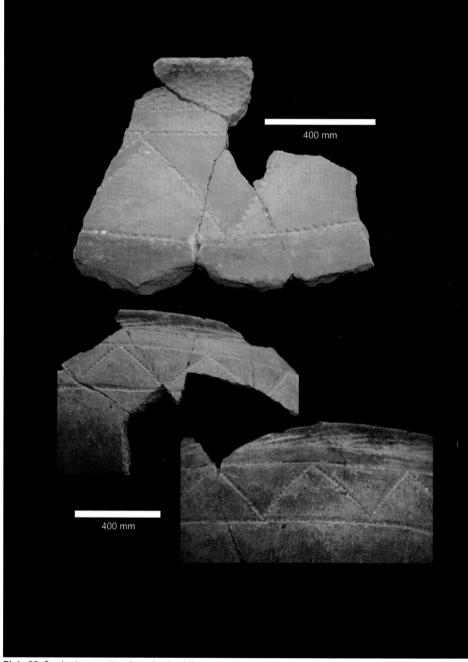

Plate 23 Comb-stamp pottery (see chapter 11).

14

Mfecane mutation in Central Africa: a comparison of the Makololo and the Ngoni in Zambia, 1830s-1898

Ackson M. Kanduza

Introduction

The Ngoni in Zambia and Malawi would agree with J.D. Omer-Cooper's (1995) assertion that 'the Mfecane survives its critics' in that the Mfecane still looms large in their own history. Omer–Cooper responded to revisionist views and accepted some major refinement of what caused, and how the main actors contributed to, a major historical process called the Mfecane in south-eastern Africa at the beginning of the 19th century. In Zambia, the Ngoni of Chipata are the only ethnic group whose recent origin is traced from the south of the country. They settled in what became the Chipata district in about 1870 where they usurped Chewa sovereignty. There are ten Ngoni Chiefs but two of them, namely Mishoro and Mshawa, are not of the Jere clan. Two additional Ngoni Chiefs, traditionally administered from Feni (the Ngoni headquarters in Chipata), are in the Mchinji district in Malawi (Lukhero 1985). Some of the justifications for settling there were the lush pastures and mountains that provided military defence. The topography was also a nostalgic reminder of Swaziland and Zululand. They share this history and celebrate it annually on the last Saturday of February together with Mbelwa's Ngoni who are in northern Malawi. These Ngoni groups were originally one of several refugee groups driven from their homeland by the Mfecane.

Another such group settled in the Western and Southern Provinces of Zambia. The Makololo, with their headquarters at Linyati in northern Botswana, asserted political and military power in western and southern Zambia in about 1838 and became a colonial power in Bulozi (Lozi country in the Zambezi flood plain and its eastern plateau). They extended power over the Masubiy Toka and Leya in the Livingstone area. The Lozi overthrew their colonisers in 1864 but have retained, to this day, southern Sesotho as their main language. The Lozi derive part of their identity from their Luba–Lunda origin (Gluckman 1951; Mainga 1973). They spoke Luyana before Kololo colonisation (Lubinda 1994). In contrast,

257

the Ngoni of Chipata in Eastern Province of Zambia claim to speak Chingoni; a language which bears extremely limited resemblance to Sizulu or Siswati (Soko 1994; Miti 1996, 2006) despite oral and cultural evidence that their origins lie in Swaziland or Zululand. In the context of the 19th-century history of eastern-central Africa, the Makololo and Ngoni should be regarded as refugees – they had been violently displaced and made homeless for varying but long periods of time. They settled in what became Zambia when they were assured of protection and security in contrast to early 19th-century disturbances in south-eastern Africa.

Over approximately the last two hundred years, observers from diverse intellectual backgrounds have shown that the Mfecane can be regarded as a regional historical process because it created refugee groups who wandered over the subcontinent. From the 1930s to the 1960s, about a century after the Makololo and Ngoni left south-eastern Africa, anthropologists used oral history and oral traditions to link the Ngoni in Zambia, Tanzania and Malawi to the Zulu, Swazi, Ndwandwe, Maseko and Mthethwa in Swaziland and South Africa. Ngoni ceremonies, dances and songs share an affiliation with those of the Swazi and the Zulu in KwaZulu-Natal in South Africa. Historian Leroy Vail (1983) considered Ngoni migration into Central Africa as a precolonial foundation of the southern African regional economy. Strong linguistic links between Silozi in Western Zambia and Southern Sotho (in Lesotho) are further testimony to Vail's assertion. It is thus necessary that new studies of the Mfecane should extend beyond the borders of South Africa. Renewed studies such as those by John Wright on the Ndwandwe and Philip Bonner on the Swazi (in this volume), to whom the Zambian Ngoni are historically connected, justify fresh studies of Ngoni groups in Malawi, Tanzania and Zambia.

This discussion is a preliminary attempt to re-examine the Mfecane in the diaspora as a contribution to the historiography of the Nguni people in Southern Africa. The debates on the Mfecane in South Africa do not sufficiently recognise the significance of the Mfecane beyond the Zambezi and this paper attempts to bring that awareness to the historiography. This discussion attempts to explain factors and circumstances which shaped cultural change among the Makololo and Ngoni during migration and final settlement in Zambia, while acknowledging that culture is a hybrid phenomenon that is always in a state of transition. Cultural practices that are observed publicly and regularly such as dance or rituals of death, succession or marriage are also subject to change and adaptation. These may be reflected in popular oral history (Le Beau & Gordon 2000).

The discussion is organised around four major themes. First, it examines the changing composition of the Kololo and Ngoni as they migrated and settled in what came to be known as Zambia in the 20th century. Second, it discusses how the distance covered during migration affected political, military and cultural institutions and practices. Third, the paper considers the nature of final settlement in terms of how the Makololo and Ngoni adapted to their new homes. Fourth, the discussion focuses on language change and acquisition among the Kololo and Ngoni when they reached and settled in Zambia. In this discussion of the Mfecane refugees in Zambia, oral sources are important because they have served as a foundation for all written accounts since the 1830s and they continue to inform current historical interpretations. Oral sources informed early written accounts of missionaries and adventurers (Read 1937; Mainga 1973; Ambrose 2002), while anthropologists from the 1940s also heavily relied on Ngoni oral informants (Barnes 1951; Gluckman 1951; Read 1970). These sources still inform historical summaries in contemporary encyclopedia entries and advertisements for cultural tourism attractions (Wikipedia 2007; Livingstone Tourism 2007; Zambia African Safari 2007). Linguists continue to rely on oral sources in their studies of language policies and development in southern Africa (Lubinda 1994; Miti 1996). Cultural ceremonies, dances and songs among the Ngoni and the Lozi use oral information, create new perceptions of history and pass on popular versions of the history of the Makololo and the Ngoni since the nineteenth century (oral discussion with Dr John M. Lubinda, Gaborone, 30 June 2007).

Composition of the refugee groups

Of the two groups, the Makololo were the first to settle down in Zambia in 1838. These Makololo were part of the Mafokeng people of north-eastern Lesotho. Sebetwane, who succeeded his father, Patsa aka Mare, left Lesotho following a defeat by the Batlokwa in 1823. The Ngoni under Zwangendaba, part of the Ndwandwe under Zwide, also left south-eastern Africa in 1823 after Shaka defeated Zwide and crossed the Zambezi into Zambia in November 1835. The Makololo and the Ngoni raided and assimilated new people as they migrated northwards. In doing so the new Makololo and new Ngoni reshaped their individual, cultural, identity and political histories. The Ngoni took a longer time than the Makololo in migration and came into contact with many different groups of people before settling down in Chipata in about 1870 (Lancaster 1937; Smith 1956; Ambrose 2002).

Makololo

The Makololo easily absorbed Sotho–Tswana speaking people as they migrated northwards on the plateau of South Africa and into Botswana. Thus, the Makololo remained a relatively uniform group in terms of language and cultural practices throughout the course of their migration. Sikololo was infiltrated with Setswana; but it converted a Luyana language (in Bulozi) from the Lunda Kingdom before the 16th century into a dialect of Southern Sesotho.

These factors added to circumstances which maintained group solidarity and cultural continuity. The Makololo were a southern Sotho group under the leadership of Sebetwane but became diversified with people who spoke languages closely related to Southern Sesotho as the Makololo migrated northwards (Elderkin no date; Smith 1996). Sebetwane, who, according to Livingstone and the oral traditions, was a popular and efficient leader (Livingstone 1858; Ellenberger 1912), died at Linyati in northern Botswana in 1851 and was succeeded by his son, Sekeletu. The death of Sekeletu in 1863 was one of the major factors which led to the Lozi rulers regaining political power in 1864 (Mainga 1973).

Cultural and language uniformity helped to ensure effective leadership and political stability as the Kololo moved northwards and when they settled in Zambia. There was also a relatively high degree of uniformity which helped the Kololo to maintain their institutions and be in a position to impose their political system on the Toka and Leya in the Livingstone area and the Luyana in the Zambezi flood plains. They did not assimilate many locals when they settled in Zambia.

The refugees were mainly comprised of old men, women, boys and girls. In 1853 David Livingstone estimated that there were only about 500 adult Makololo men. He also stated that there was a higher mortality among Makololo men compared to their women, which probably implies that Makololo women outnumbered their male counterparts. The high mortality among Makololo men was due, in part, to malaria and because men were in regular military service while women engaged in domestic work, where there was better protection from malaria-carrying mosquitoes. Regular deployment in raids and military defence duties and frequent bouts of malaria impacted heavily on the physical energy and health of the Makololo men. These refugees had characteristics which ensured group solidarity and reproduction.

Ngoni

Zwangendaba's Ngoni were not as lucky as the Makololo. In northern Nguniland in south-eastern Africa, Zwangendaba and his group were part of the Ndwandwe confederacy. The Ndwandwe had defeated the Mthetwa under Dingiswayo. Shaka defeated Zwide, leader of the Ndwandwe. They split and one of the breakaway groups was led by Zwangendaba (Barnes 1951). One version of oral tradition among the Chipata Ngoni treats Zwangendaba as one of the commanders of Shaka. Zwangendaba is reported to have failed in one of Shaka's assignments and thus chose to flee rather than face the wrath of Shaka. Indeed in many songs and oral praises, the Ngoni in Chipata group Shaka, Zwide and Dingiswayo together. As Zwangendaba moved northwards through Swaziland and southern Mozambique, he absorbed some Swazi such as the Maseko, Thawete and Lukhele clans. Zwangendaba also picked up some Nguni from Soshangane who had settled in southern Mozambique after leaving Natal. Zwangendaba passed through Zimbabwe, the southern part of Eastern Zambia, Malawi, north-western Tanzania and the northern part of Zambia before reaching Chipata in about 1870 (Langworthy 1972). On crossing the Limpopo, the Ngoni of Zwangendaba encountered people who were vastly different from themselves in terms of political, cultural and military practices. Compared to the Makololo, Zwangendaba's Ngoni passed through many new and hostile environments and thus expended more resources and energy than the Makololo. The concept of an origin in Zulu–Swaziland remains in the popular consciousness of the Ngoni in eastern Zambia. For example, a prominent Zambian politician in the 1970s and 1980s, Siteke Mwale, recalled that his grandfather had named him after his home place in Swaziland which is now known as Siteki Town (pers. comm.).

Group fluidity

The composition of the Kololo and the Ngoni was not static. In addition to the natural growth of the population, both the Kololo and Ngoni incorporated many foreigners who were captured in raids. Some of these foreigners joined the Makololo and the Ngoni for protection (Barnes 1951; Gluckman 1951; Langworth 1972). The Ngoni migrated long distances and thus came into contact with many different groups, with whom they interacted in a variety of ways and from whom they married many women and recruited young people for military service. In fact, by the time the Ngoni settled in Chipata in the early 1870s, they were a mosaic. It is a history of strength and creative adaptation to study how the Ngoni assimilated new people, changed in many ways and were still able to sustain their Nguni identity. The Makololo, in contrast, were less diverse because of the shorter distance that they covered before finally settling down in an area shared by Botswana, Namibia and Zambia. With the exception of Khoisan country in eastern Namibia and western Botswana, the Makololo migrated through groups of people with whom they shared many cultural and linguistic characteristics.

Between the 1850s and 1860s, both the Makololo and Ngoni of Chipata experienced a significant decline in population. Under Sekeletu, the Makololo did not mount successful raids to augment their numbers. In the approximately 26 years that they spent in Zambia as overlords, the Makololo did not marry or capture many women from the Lozi and Toka Leya in Livingstone, which could have helped the population to grow. The Makololo women outnumbered foreign wives at the time of the Lozi overthrow. Also, as noted above, Makololo women may well have outnumbered Makololo men in the 1850s because many Makololo men died from malaria and poorly executed wars. Despite regaining their political power in 1864, Livingstone (1858: 92) wrote that 'those people who when I was at Linyati were treated as dogs have, as it were, in one day changed positions with their tyrannical and cruel masters and the wives and children of their former oppressors have in turn become their slaves'. At least two issues should be underlined from Livingstone's observation. First, xenophobia in southern Africa has long historical roots as a strategy of disarming and dominating strangers and people of different identities. Second, both the Makololo and Ngoni had an exaggerated sense of their military power but realised that their reproduction depended on marriage, and social intercourse with the people they found in central Africa.

The decline in the population of the Ngoni was largely because of a split into at least three groups following the death of Zwangendaba in 1848 near Lake Tanganyika. During their long migration, these Ngoni groups kept a few aristocratic Ngoni women but the majority of women who married into the group came from central Africa, and would have included women who were either Bemba, Namwanga, Lungu, Nsenga or Chewa. The final Ngoni settlement was among the Chewa.

Between the mid-1850s and about 1870, the Ngoni lost part of their population following a series of military encounters with the Bemba, although ultimately the Bemba failed to use guns acquired from slave traders effectively against a group with superior military skills. Few pure Ngoni women remained by the time the Chipata Nguni settled in Zambia in the early 1870s after having been migrants for about fifty years. A dialect of Sizulu called Singoni is spoken in a few villages of Mbelwa's Ngoni (northern Malawi), which implies a significant presence of Zulu or Swazi women in that group. This was not the case among the Ngoni in Chipata and Mchinji. Atkins wrote that the Ngoni of Chipata and Mchinji 'spoke nothing but Nyanja, with an isolated word here and there, to betray an older tradition, (1953: 35). More recent research of Lazarus Miti has shown that the Ngoni in Chipata and Mchinji District of Malawi speak Cinsenga (Hodgson 1933; Atkins 1953). Thus, the Chipata Ngoni had difficulties in keeping their language and some cultural practices. For example, those cultural practices relating to girls or marriage were difficult in the light of ever declining number of women who were intimately in touch with real Nguni or Ndwandwe or Swazi and Zulu cultural values. These values were further eroded by the relatively low cost of marrying foreign Nsenga and Chewa women (because chickens or goats were used as *lobolo* instead of cattle).

Distance
The distances the Makololo and Ngoni covered between south-eastern Africa and their final destinations in Zambia influenced political and cultural change and enriched their

heroic history. To a large degree, the heterogeneity among the Ngoni when compared to the homogeneity of the Makololo, was a result of the large number of different people they interacted with from the time they left south-eastern Africa in the 1820s. According to oral sources, following a series of military encounters in the Malawi–Tanzania–Zambia triangle and the death of Zwangendaba in 1848, the Ngoni of Chipata decided to return to Zululand. In Zambia alone, for example, they met the Bemba, Bisa, Kunda, Nsenga, Senga, and Tumbuka. The Makololo covered a much shorter distance than the Ngoni and thus were not as exposed to different populations. The Mfecane thus bequeathed to Zambia an extraordinary social and political culture. The Ngoni and Bemba fought several wars over a 15-year period (Langworthy 1972). The Ngoni eventually withdrew and settled in the Nsenga and Chewa areas in 1870. Because of this, a collective joking relationship evolved between the Bemba and the Ngoni. The cousinship now exists between all who trace their origin from the Eastern Province and those from the Northern and Luapula Provinces (Langworthy 1972). The Ngoni fought the Bemba, and one of their most prized captives was a princess whose son became a Bemba *Chitimukulu* (king) in the 1960s. The women acquired in this way were a major force in transmission of cultural elements such as language, food preparation and marital practices. Young men were also captured, but they were under the direct and collective control of the Ngoni men, and therefore had to adopt Ngoni military, political and cultural values. The foreign women who were brought into Ngoni society served as a sustained external influence while the men were transformed into Ngoni through military service.

The longer distance that the Ngoni covered in their migration transformed their culture more than was the case with the Makololo. There were a few things the Ngoni held dear and which they considered critical to their Ngoni identities. Cattle remained central to their economy. In fact, the lush pastures of Chipata encouraged a pastoral economy and food production was learnt from the Chewa. Cattle were also a major rationale for occasional raids on their neighbours. Cattle were also essential in conducting Ngoni marriage. As in Zululand, cattle helped the Ngoni to socialise their children. Girls knew that a transfer of cattle for their marriage conferred prestige on them and their families. A strong and ubiquitous attitude was that '*mwana wacanakazi ofunika kuti akule bwino cifukwa oyenela kuzyuzya khola la awisi*' (a girl should be chaste because she is expected to fill her father's kraal). Boys learned various rites of passage into adulthood because they were herd boys and had to be ready for military mobilisation at any time. The Ngoni could not leave the Chipata area because it was ideal for their pastoral economy which was the foundation of Ungoni (Ngoniness) (Kanduza 1992). This was despite a high human mortality in Chipata. Many tropical places with lush pastures support populations of mosquitoes which carry a malaria vector. The headquarters of the Ngoni King is at Feni, which means 'a place of death', because of the many people who died from malaria in the early days of settlement. In fact, between 1898 and 1914 the Ngoni tried to move their royal palace to a healthier place at Mchinji (Fort Manning) in Malawi but the British colonial administration overruled the decision (Barnes 1954; Omer-Cooper 1969; Illife 1979).

Settlement

The Ngoni settled at Chipata, a fortress or a place of protection. Accordingly, the natural defences provided by the mountains and passes, combined with the lush pastures attracted the Ngoni. The place was also well watered. The Ngoni followed the structure in Zululand for their villages in Zambia. Briefly, the centre of a village was the cattle kraal. Houses were arranged according to seniority. Young men occupied *malaweni* (boys' dormitories) which were situated so as to make it easy to mobilise them whenever the village needed defence. The men were in age regiments. For military purposes, all regiments were controlled by the King, *Nkosi ya makosi*. The King also fed the regiments throughout the migration and they could be called for military duties at any time. Mobilisation of the Kingdom among the Chipata Ngoni was relatively easy because all of the chiefs, except two, were brothers. The foreign ones, however, became Ngoni through cultural assimilation which the Zwangendaba group must have perfected during their 50-year migration. The Ngoni occupied only a small area of what became Chipata District, implying that they were numerically a small group. Barnes (1951) showed, and Illiffe (1979) suggested, a similar view about the Ngoni in Tanzania, that the military destruction of the Chipata Ngoni may have been exaggerated because they did not displace many of the people they found. Moreover, archaeologists have found many diverse varieties of pottery among the Ngoni who adopted styles from the many peoples they met (Collet 1985).

The Makololo established their capital at Linyati, leaving the traditional Lozi headquarters at Lealui and Limulunga relatively autonomous, although weakened by royal conflicts for succession. However, the Makololo raided their neighbourhood frequently. They overstretched themselves to such an extent that, in a short period of 26 years, Makololo rule came to an end. In spite of this, they left two architectural legacies that are today apparent in Lozi settlements: grass fencing around groups of houses or the village; and the thatching of grass houses. As a result Lozi settlements look different from those of other Zambian groups who migrated from the Luba-Lunda Kingdom at about the same time the Lozi did. The grass fence was both a security and health barrier. It was a health barrier in that it helped to leave the area inside the fence free from mosquitoes, through the frequent use of kraal (cattle) manure, which served as a repellant. Second, the Lozi are well-known for their thatching skills, which are generally uncommon among people from the Luba-Lunda kingdom. The colonial administration recognised this thatching skill and made good use of it as many Lozi thatchers were deployed to different parts of the country (oral interview with Lubinda, 21 May, 2007, MMumba, 23 May, 2007, Gaborone). Clearly, migration of and settlement by the Mfecane refugees in what became Zambia brought about at least some lasting positive legacies. The revisionist historiography of the Mfecane in South Africa tends to emphasise violent destruction as being the major result. In this way, the present discussion has value in its attempt to contribute a broader and a more balanced understanding of the Mfecane in southern Africa.

Cultural practices

This discussion recognises new social, cultural and political values which the Mfecane refugees introduced into predominantly matrilineal societies, which did not have centralised political institutions. The precolonial origin of southern African globalisation or regional integration has been transmitted to the present in complex historical processes (Vail 1983). It is not clear from oral and missionary sources whether or not the Makololo practised circumcision when they ruled over the Lozi, Toka and Leya in Zambia. Circumcision is not a social or cultural practice found among the Lozi, Toka and Leya in Zambia yet the Makololo are known to have practised it in their original homeland. Circumcision, which the Makalolo practised, is found among the Luvale, who are north of Bulozi. The Luvale did not adopt circumcision from the Makololo. In fact, cultural practices among the Lozi resemble those found among most Zambian groups which originated from the Luba–Lunda Kingdom. Two major ceremonies in Bulozi appear not to have been affected by Kololo rule or presence. Some time in February or March, when the floods of Zambezi plain reach a peak, the Lozi observe the Kuobomboka ceremony. The Lozi King, Litunga (keeper of the earth), moves from Lealui in the plain to Limulunga on the eastern plateau. It is a major ceremony on which the Makololo do not seem to have left any imprint. Some time in July the Litunga returns to the flood plain and this ceremony is called Kufuluhera (Mainga 1973).

The Makololo probably did not affect these ceremonies because their seat of power was in the south. The Lozi leaders who overthrew Makololo domination were in the northern part at Lukulu and Kalabo. By keeping their capital at Linyati in the south, the Makololo left the main centres of Lozi power at Lealui, Limulunga and further north at Kalabo relatively intact. The Makololo thus failed to capture and control all the factions in the conflict for political power in Bulozi. The period of Makololo political hegemony in south-western Zambia, from 1838 to 1864, was too short for profound cultural changes to take root. The decline in the Makololo population, especially among men, was a major limiting factor in entrenching their cultural practices. Recapture of Lozi political power was bloody as many Makololo men were slaughtered. The inheritance of Makololo women and the introduction of written Sesotho from about 1883 by the Paris Evangelical missionaries based at Morija in Lesotho are the most important factors in the loss of Siluyana.

The Ngoni preserved their *Incwala (NKhwala)* ceremony. In his discussion of marriage among the Zambian Ngoni, John A. Barnes (1951), an anthropologist, recognised that insufficient information made it difficult for him to have a well informed discussion. He overcame this problem by relying on anthropological accounts of the Ngoni in Malawi and the work of Hilda Kuper on the Swazi. This is a useful strategy for any historical study of the Zambian Ngoni because of their close ties with the Ngoni in Malawi and the Swazi. The Swazi continued to practise their Incwala during the colonial period. Read stated that the Mbelwa Ngoni in Malawi abandoned the *Incwala* ceremony before they settled down in their new home (1937). A plausible explanation is that after the death of Zwangendaba, the Ngoni in Malawi and Tanzania could not celebrate *Incwala* because they had no rightful heir to Zwangendaba. They also feared attacks from the Zambian Ngoni who had the rightful heir to Zwangendaba.

According to Luckhero (1985) who shared a *Laweni* (they were in the same age regiment) with Mpezeni III and who worked with Barnes as a research assistant in the 1940s and 1950s, the Ngoni of Zambia only abandoned their *Incwala* ceremony after suffering a military defeat at the hands of the British South African army in 1898. The colonial administration banned *Incwala* ceremonies due to the fear that the Ngoni would rise in rebellion or attack their Chewa or Kunda neighbours for cattle and food. Then, this first fruit and annual purification ceremony was held at about the time that *maswela*, a kind of a pumpkin, was harvested, generally in December or January. This was usually a period of food shortage during the 'hunger months', especially in years following poor harvests, and raids for food were both a consequence of scarcity and an assertion of political hegemony. In south-eastern Africa, the search for and control over economic resources was at the centre of many of the Mfecane conflicts and the Zambian Ngoni carried this tradition forward in their oral, popular and ceremonial history. The ceremony and the raids were also a way of enforcing the political hegemony the Ngoni had established over the Chewa, Kunda and Tumbuka. This domination was partly facilitated by deep divisions among the Chewa in whose country the Ngoni finally settled.

This also has implications for modern-day politics. Intense tribal and political rivalry in Zambia between 1968 and 1973, led the government to object to efforts to revive the *Incwala* in the early 1970s. After persisting and a careful consultation of the Ngoni, and finding some

Incwala songs at a Chimuti village in Chief Mshawa (one of the two non-Jere chiefdoms), the Ngoni succeeded in convincing the Zambian Government to start the *Incwala* on the last Saturday in February annually (personal testimony). It is significant that Mbelwa's Ngoni in Malawi attend the *Incwala* in Chipata. This is in recognition that Mpezeni was the rightful heir to Zwangendaba. Today, the *Incwala* is an occasion for celebrating Ngoni history. Male participants wear military attire and carry traditional weapons. Age sets have disappeared but elders from chiefdoms are recognised as cultural leaders. Postcolonial freedom is also an occasion to assert sectional identity and group political influence in a country with diverse nationalities. Consequently, national political leaders support or identify with the *Incwala* in order to win Ngoni votes in Chipata District or wherever there are concentrations of Ngoni groups in urban areas (Lukhero 1985; Soko 1994). Like in many traditional ceremonies and other forms of dancing and singing, ordinary people also utilise the *Incwala* as an occasion to speak about national politics. The Ngoni also use the *Incwala* to celebrate their history and their heroic migration from Zululand and have integrated south-eastern African Ngoni history. They praise Shaka, Zwide and Dingiswayo as if they legitimately succeeded each other in one polity. The Ngoni in Zambia therefore today present a unified history of the Mfecane. Zwangendaba is regarded as the father of the present Ngoni in their new home. They sing for the resurrection of Zwangendaba so that he will take them back to Swaziland: 'Come let us go to Swaziland where people die fat.' They remind their audience, 'Do you hear? The Ngoni come from the south-east' (Soko 1994: 17).

Thus, the *Incwala* is an historical text and is constantly reinterpreted according to the consciousness of every participating generation and circumstances of the time. These generations are either groups of scholars such as the Mfecane revisionists or ordinary people who make popular history through song, dance and oral narratives. The songs acknowledge the leadership of Zwangendaba since leaving south-east Africa. Each Ngoni group, either from Malawi or Zambia, recognises its own heroes and how they contributed to the survival of the Ngoni. People from each chiefdom introduce songs about what they contributed to the Ngoni polity. Thus, the occasion of the *Incwala* marks a review of the position of the Ngoni in the wider national political network and remains a unifying force of the Ngoni despite isolated texts of rebellion or alternative histories.

The *Incwala* is an occasion for homecoming and a journey into the history of the Ngoni. In urban areas there are organised Ngoni dance groups (personal testimony, Poole 1949). They practise and arrange to travel to Mutenguleni where the ceremony takes place annually. These groups organise transport for all those who want to take part in the ceremony and to renew ties with their homes. The groups introduce new symbols, particularly in their dress as it is not all who wear skins as special attire for the ceremony. Compared to the way the Swazi perform their *Incwala*, the ceremony at Mutenguleni reflects the cultural adaptation and dynamism of a refugee community keen to proclaim the creation of a new home. There are many who have been born in urban areas and travel to Chipata because of the *Incwala*. Many parents use the occasion to introduce their children to Ngoni history and culture and psychological satisfaction is immense. This is also done among the Lozi where the occasion of the Kuomboka is, for some, an opportunity to immerse their children in Lozi culture. The *Incwala* is an assertion of identity and a recognition of wider links which the Ngoni have evolved over time.

Language is one way in which this history can be seen and reconstructed. First, there are a few songs which are sung in a mixture of Sizulu and Siswati (Read 1937; Soko 1994). A study of names yields useful information on language and cultural change and also enriches the Mfecane historiography. For example, Tawate among the Ngoni in south-western Tanzania is related to Thawete among Chipata Ngoni and Tsabedze in Swaziland and Zululand (interview with Felix Tawete, 19 May 2007, Gabarone). Second, there are expressions that are verbally difficult to identify. Third, songs are sung in what is actually a dialect of Chinsenga widely spoken among the Nsenga people. The Ngoni married many wives from this group, who later influenced language development among the Ngoni. Often, pronunciation is sufficient to distinguish Ngoni from Nsenga, but it is nonetheless often difficult to separate what is claimed to be Ngoni from Nsenga. For example, the Ngoni in Chipata sometimes use the Nsenga words, *mkwasu* or *mkwawo* for sister/brother or comrade, while on other occasions, *mnakethu/mfowethu* (personal testimony) words that reveal their cultural ties with Swazi- and Zululand are used. The earlier pair of words shows how contemporary history has been shaped by the Ngoni's arrival in a new home and their taking of Nsenga wives. There tends to be clear differences between Chichewa and Chingoni. Yet the Ngoni settlement in Chipata has been surrounded by the Chewa from the time the Ngoni ended their migration. In effect, the Ngoni occupied what was Chewa country when they settled in Chipata in the late 1860s. Language is not a key feature in identifying the Ngoni in Chipata where their claims of a distinct language can be dismissed after critical examination. Yet, it would be misleading to deny what the Ngoni claim to be their separate language as an aspect of their history, identity and consciousness.

Chingoni represents a fascinating and complex history of migration, assimilation and cultural change. After encountering the Bemba in the mid-1850s, the Ngoni migrated southwards and crossed the Luangwa River into a plateau of what is the Eastern Province of Zambia. They passed through Bisa and Kunda country. They also met the Nsenga Ambo in the Luangwa valley. The Ambo are part of the large Nsenga group on the southern part of the plateau and they extend into north-western Mozambique. There was intense interaction between the Ngoni and the Nsenga from the early 1860s before the Ngoni eventually integrated with the Chewa and settled in Chipata district. The Nsenga and Kunda speak closely related languages and Chingoni is a variation of Chinsenga. Curiously, Chibemba influence on Chingoni is largely untraceable. The Ngoni married many Nsenga and Kunda women. There are no indications as to how much Sizulu or Siswati the Ngoni still spoke when they settled in Chipata district. Since it was about 50 years between their departure from south-eastern Africa and their arrival in Chipata, they must have retained their original Nguni language(s) as a military and ritual necessity. However, they did not have many Nguni women except a few loyal ones. The long history of Ngoni migration resulted in considerable assimilation and cultural change. The Ngoni assimilated as much as they were incorporated by the people among whom they settled.

The main area of this cultural exchange is reflected linguistically. While the Ngoni displaced some Chewa in Chipata district and were virtually surrounded by the Chewa, the language they speak is closer to Chinsenga than to Chichewa. This meant the presence of more Nsenga than Chewa women among the Ngoni. Women play an important role in transforming and transmitting language from one generation to another. There was also a stereotype among the Ngoni which affected the rate at which they married Chewa women and also intermingled with the Chewa in general. The Ngoni feared witchcraft among the Chewa more than they thought it existed among the Nsenga (Barnes 1951: 37). With the passage of time, however, geographical proximity between the Ngoni and Chewa presented chances of the Ngoni increasing the number of Chewa women they married. The Ngoni also mounted several raids on the Chewa and the booty from the defeated Chewa included women.

Linguists studying language development and diffusion have suggested assimilation as one way in which people adopt new languages. In a study of the language situation in postcolonial Botswana, for example, Nyati-Ramahobo (2006), discussed how language rights affect language development in a society. These studies also deal with the relationships between democracy and language development. Nyati-Ramahobo explained that these rights exist on a continuum ranging between assimilation and maintenance. There are regulations and practices which encourage assimilation or expressly prohibit use of some languages. In the case of Botswana, at independence in 1966, the constitution recognised both English and Setswana as official languages. This virtually prohibited, without any explicit statement, about 25 other local languages from regular use in the public arena and for official business. In 1998 Setswana was also recognised for use in parliament and with this change, Botswana modified an assimilation-prohibition model with a model that tolerated only one indigenous language. In Zambia, language development and policies since 1964 have been affected by a fear of tribalism and the perceived need to promote national unity in a country with at least 73 African languages.

Studies of current or recent influences in language development have some useful insights in understanding our study or discussion. At this stage, only some tentative ideas will be noted. First, in the case of the Makololo, their political power helped Sikololo to develop as a lingua franca in Bulozi. However, it is important to recognise that internal divisions in Lozi society helped to establish Makololo political power and, consequently, Sikololo as a highly visible language. There was a significant degree to which the indigenous language of the Lozi was creolised. Sikololo continued to grow because, for about 20 years after the fall of Makololo power, the use of Sikololo was encouraged as missionaries of the Paris Evangelical Mission based in Lesotho used the language in church, schools and published books in Sikololo. British colonialism also encouraged Sikololo. In contrast, the Ngoni in Chipata did not have any of the European colonial forces which helped the development of Sikololo.

For the Chipata Ngoni, their language did not become part of the dominant language clusters which emerged in Zambia. In fact Sizulu disappeared completely, possibly as a result of the long migration that the Ngoni undertook. It should be noted, however, that among Mbelwa's Ngoni who are culturally part of the Chipata Ngoni, Sizulu is not dead but is best described as being in the intensive care unit. Whereas Makololo women played a critical role in developing and maintaining Sikololo, the small number of Swazi or Zulu women among the Ngoni was a serious cause for the death of Sizulu. In trying to replace these women, the Ngoni married women from their hosts and thus Ngoni men were accomplices in the death of their language or were fathers of their new language. Their Sizulu was assimilated and eventually surrendered to death. For the Ngoni, their claim to have a language called Chingoni is a way of marking their distinct cultural identity, expressed through language, popular history and traditional ceremonies. In fact much of Ngoni history and the contribution of the Ngoni to Zambian history during the last 190 years can be best understood in the context of the history of the Mfecane. In the context of present national states and boundaries in southern Africa, the Mfecane was a transnational historical process. The Mfecane forced migration which also transported diverse cultural and political values into Zambia.

Conclusion

Two military events are markers of the periodisation in this discussion. In about 1823, the Makololo and Ngoni left south-eastern Africa following their military defeats. In 1898, the

Ngoni suffered a military defeat at the hands of the British South Africa Company and at about the same time British colonisation of Bulozi and the whole of Zambia was completed. In focusing on selected aspects of Makololo and Ngoni history between the 1830s when they reached Zambia and 1890s, a sense of chronology has been sustained throughout the discussion by noting changes and agents of change among the Makololo and Ngoni while in Zambia. Chronology is shorthand for processes of change and initiators of change. The discussion has also acknowledged that history is a changing text among academics and ordinary people who write or create their history through ceremonies, songs and popular consciousness. In that broad direction, the discussion has pointed to the value of broadening studies of the Mfecane beyond South Africa.

Women have emerged in this discussion as key actors in broadening Mfecane history and keeping the balance between continuity and change. For the Makololo in south-western Zambia, the prevalence of a large number of Sikololo-speaking women was a key factor in transforming Siluyana into a dialect of Southern Sesotho. The death of Sizulu or Siswati among the Ngoni in eastern Zambia could be explained, to a large extent, by the almost virtual absence of Ndwandwe, Zulu or Swazi women. It is only in popular consciousness that the Ngoni in eastern Zambia claim they have a distinct language. Research by anthropologists from the 1930s to the 1960s, and, more recently, by linguists has shed much light on factors that affected language and cultural change among the Mfecane refugees in Zambia. Historical research, such as that suggested in this discussion presents a holistic account of what changes took place and how the transformation was sustained. In this way, one value of this work is presenting a long history of transnational change in southern Africa.

References

Ambrose, D. 2002. *Lesotho Annotated Bibliography*. Roma: Institute of Education, National University of Lesotho.

Atkins, G. 1950-1953. The Nyanja-speaking population of Nyasaland and Northern Rhodesia. *African Studies* 9-12: 35-39.

Barnes, J.A. 1951a. *Marriage in a Changing Society: A Study in Structural Change among the Fort Jameson Ngoni*. London: Oxford University Press.

Barnes, J.A. 1951b. The Ngoni of Fort Jameson. In: Colson, E. & Gluckman, M. (eds) *Seven Tribes of Central Africa*: 194-252. London: Oxford University Press.

Barnes, J.A. 1951. The perception of history in a plural society: a study of an Ngoni group in Northern Rhodesia. *Human Relations* 4: 295-303.

Barnes, J.A. 1954. *Politics in a Changing Society: Political History of the Fort Jameson Ngoni*. London: Oxford University Press.

Elderkin, E.D. n.d. Silozi in Namibia. Unpublished mimeograph.

Ellenberger, D.F. 1912. *History of the Basotho, Ancient and Modern*. London: Carton Publishing Co. Ltd.

Gluckman, M. 1951. The Barotse in north-western Rhodesia. In: Colson, E. & Gluckman, M. (eds) *Seven*

271

Tribes of Central Africa: 194-252. London: Oxford University Press.

Hodgseon, A.G.O. 1933. Notes on the Achewa and Angoni of the Dowa District of Nyasaland Protectorate. *Journal of the Royal African Institute* LXIII: 123-164.

Illiffe, J. 1979. *A Modern History of Tanganyika*. Cambridge: Cambridge University Press.

Kanduza, A.M. 1992. Peasant politics in Chipata. In: Kanduza, A.M. (ed.) *Socio-economic Change in Eastern Zambia*. Lusaka: Historical Association of Zambia.

Langworthy, H. 1972. *Zambia Before 1890: Aspects of Precolonial History*. London: Longman.

Lancaster, D.G. 1937. Tentative chronology of the Ngoni: genealogy of the chiefs and notes. *Journal of the Royal African Institute* LXVII: 77-90.

Le Beau, D. & Gordon, R.J. (eds) 2000. *Challenges for Anthropology in African Renaissance: A Southern African Contribution*. Windhoek: University of Namibia.

Livingstone, D. 1858. *Dr. Livingstone's Cambridge Lectures*. Cambridge: Deighton Bell and Co.

Livingstone Tourism. 2007. http://www.livingstonetourism.com/pages/history.htm

Lubinda, J.M. 1994. Patterns of lexical cross-language adoption and influence: from southern Sotho to Silozi. Unpublished conference paper, 1st World Congress on African Linguistics, University of Swaziland, Kwaluseni, 18-22 July 1994.

Luckhero, B.M. 1985. *Ngoni Ncwala Ceremony*. Lusaka: Kenneth Kaunda Foundation.

Mainga, M. 1973. *Bulozi under Luyana Kings*. London: Longman.

Miti, L.M. 1996. Subgrouping Ngoni varieties within Nguni: a lexicostatistical approach. *South African Journal of African Languages* 16(3): 83-93.

Miti, L.M. 2001. *A Linguistic Analysis of Cinsenga: A Bantu Language Spoken in Zambia and Malawi*. Cape Town: CASAS.

Miti, L.M. 2006. *Comparative Bantu Phonology and Morphology: A Study of the Sound Systems and Word Structure of the Indigenous Languages of Southern Africa*. Cape Town: CASAS.

Moreau, R.E. 1944. Joking relationships in Tanganyika. *Africa* XIV (7): 386-400.

Nyati-Ramahobo, L. 2000. The language situation in Botswana. *Current Issues in Languange Planning* 1: 243-268.

Omer-Cooper, J.D. 1995. The Mfecane survives its critics. In: Hamilton, C. (ed.) *The Mfecane Aftermath: Reconstructive Debates in Southern African History*: 277-300. Johannesburg: Witwatersrand University Press.

Omer-Cooper, J.D. 1969. Aspects of political change in the nineteenth century. In: Thompson, L. (ed.) *African Societies in southern Africa*: 207-229. London: Heinemann.

Poole, E.H.L. 1949. *Native Tribes of the Eastern Province of Northern Rhodesia: Notes on their Migration and History*. Rhodesia: Government Printer.

Read, M. 1937. Songs of the Ngoni People. *Bantu Studies* XL: 1-35.

Read, M. 1956. *The Ngoni of Nyasaland*. London: Frank Cassiman and Co.

Smith, E.W. 1956. Sebetwane and the Makololo. *African Studies* 15: 49-74.

Soko, B.J. 1994. *Zwangendaba ou L'epopee Ngoni: Etude Ethnolinguistique des Lounges Ngoni dans le Contexte Malawie*. Zomba: University of Malawi.

Vail, L. 1983. The political economy of east-central Africa. In: Birmingham, D. & Martin, P.M. (eds) *History of Central Africa* 2: 200-237. London: Longman.

Wikipedia. 2007. http://en.wikipedia.org/wiki/Lozi people.History and culture

Winterbottom, J.M. 1937. A note on the Ngoni paramountcy. *Man* 58: 126-127.

Zambia African Safari. 2007. http://www.zambia-the-african.safari.com/ngoni-people.htm

List of Contributors

Historical archaeologies of southern Africa: precedents and prospects

Joanna Behrens
Department of Anthropology and Archaeology
University of South Africa
Pretoria 0003

Natalie Swanepoel
Department of Anthropology and Archaeology
University of South Africa
Pretoria 0003

South Africa in Africa more than five hundred years ago: some questions

Neil Parsons
University of Botswana
Gaborone

Towards an outline of the oral geography, historical identity and political economy of the Late Precolonial Tswana in the Rustenburg region

Simon Hall (main author)
Department of Archaeology
University of Cape Town
Rondebosch 7701

Mark Anderson
Department of Archaeology
University of Cape Town
Rondebosch 7701

Jan Boeyens
Department of Anthropology and Archaeology
University of South Africa
Pretoria 0003

Francois Coetzee
Department of Anthropology and Archaeology
University of South Africa
Pretoria 0003

Metals beyond frontiers: exploring the production, distribution and use of metals in the Free State grasslands, South Africa
Shadreck Chirikure (main author)
Department of Archaeology
University of Cape Town
Rondebosch 7701

Simon Hall
Department of Archaeology
University of Cape Town
Rondebosch 7701

Tim Maggs
Department of Archaeology
University of Cape Town
Rondebosch 7701

De Tuin, a 19th-century mission station in the Northern Cape
Alan G. Morris
Department of Human Biology
University of Cape Town
Observatory 7925

Reinterpreting the origins of Dzata: archaeology and legends
Edwin Hanisch
Department of Anthropology and Archaeology
University of Venda
Thouyandou 0950

Revisiting Bokoni: populating the stone ruins of the Mpumalanga Escarpment
P. Delius
Department of History
University of the Witwatersrand
Johannesburg 2001

M.H. Schoeman
Department of Anthropology and Archaeology
University of Pretoria
Pretoria 0001

274

The Mpumalanga Escarpment settlements: some answers, many questions
Tim Maggs
Department of Archaeology
University of Cape Town
Rondebosch 7701

Post-European contact glass beads from the southern African interior: a tentative look at trade, consumption and identities
Marilee Wood
Department of Archaeology
University of the Witwatersrand
Johannesburg 2001

Ceramic alliances: pottery and the history of the Kekana Ndebele in the old Transvaal
A.B. Esterhuysen
Department of Archaeology
University of the Witwatersrand
Johannesburg 2001

Rediscovering the Ndwandwe Kingdom
John Wright
School of Anthropology; Gender and Historical Studies
University of KwaZulu-Natal
Pietermaritzburg 3201
and
Rock Art Institute
University of the Witwatersrand
Johannesburg 2001

Swazi oral tradition and Northern Nguni historical archaeology
Philip Bonner
Department of History
University of the Witwatersrand
Johannesburg 2001

Mfecane mutation in Central Africa: A comparison of the Makololo and the Ngoni in Zambia, 1830s-1898
Ackson M. Kanduza
Department of History
University of Botswana
Gaborone

Index

Compiled by Marthina Mössmer